D1601123

# JUSTICE FOR CHILDREN

# JUSTICE FOR CHILDREN

## The Right to Counsel and the Juvenile Courts

Barry C. Feld

HV
9104
.F44
1993
West

NORTHEASTERN UNIVERSITY PRESS   Boston

Northeastern University Press

Copyright 1993 by Barry C. Feld

All rights reserved. Except for the quotation of short passages for the
purposes of criticism and review, no part of this book may be repro-
duced in any form or by any means, electronic or mechanical, including
photocopying, recording, or any information storage and retrieval system now known or to be invented, without written permission of the
publisher.

**Library of Congress Cataloging-in-Publication Data**

Feld, Barry C.
    Justice for children : the right to counsel and the juvenile court
  / Barry C. Feld.
            p.  cm.
    Includes bibliographical references and index.
    ISBN 1-55553-157-1
    1. Juvenile justice, Administration of—United States.
    2. Juvenile courts—United States. I. Title.
    HV9104.F44   1993         92-38429
    364.3'6'0973—dc20


Designed by Karen Sullivan

This book was composed in Sabon by Coghill Composition Company
in Richmond, Virginia. It was printed and bound by Thomson-Shore,
Inc., in Dexter, Michigan. This paper is Glatfelter, an acid-free sheet.


MANUFACTURED IN THE UNITED STATES OF AMERICA

97  96  95  94  93  5  4  3  2  1

For Ari and Julia

# CONTENTS

# TABLES

# ACKNOWLEDGMENTS

The data used in this study are housed in and made available by the National Juvenile Court Data Archive which is maintained by the National Center for Juvenile Justice (NCJJ) in Pittsburgh, Pennsylvania, and supported by the Office of Juvenile Justice and Delinquency Prevention (OJJDP), U.S. Department of Justice. The data that are analyzed and reported in Chapter Three were collected originally by the California Bureau of Criminal Justice Statistics and Special Services, the Minnesota Supreme Court Judicial Information System, the Nebraska Commission on Law Enforcement and Criminal Justice, the New York Office of Court Administration, the North Dakota Office of State Court Administration, and the Pennsylvania Juvenile Court Judges' Commission. The Minnesota Supreme Court's Judicial Information System collected the original data analyzed and reported in Chapters Four, Five, Six, and Seven.

The Minnesota State Bar Foundation, the University of Minnesota Law Alumni Association, and the Center for the Study of Youth Policy, University of Michigan, provided partial funding for preliminary statistical analyses of the Minnesota data. The National Juvenile Court Data Archive's Visiting Scholar Program, which was supported by OJJDP, enabled me to complete the multistate and Minnesota statistical analyses. I received exceptional support and assistance in assembling, organizing, and interpreting the data from Dr. Howard Snyder, NCJJ Director of Systems Research, Ms. Ellen Nimick, NCJJ Senior Research Assistant, and Mr. Terry Finnegan, NCJJ Computer Programmer.

A number of colleagues generously provided constructive critiques of earlier drafts of this manuscript as it first appeared in several articles: Steve Coleman, Gary Crippen, Dan Farber, Floyd Feeney, Richard Frase, Don C. Gibbons, Martin Guggenheim, Candace Kruttschnitt, Anne Rankin Mahoney, Ellen H. Nimick, H. Ted Rubin, Robert Scott, W. Vaughan Stapleton, and Michael Tonry. Although I attempted to address many of their concerns, I absolve them of responsibility for any failure on my part to follow their advice. Dean Robert Stein has been extraordinarily generous in his support and encouragement throughout my career. Neither the respective state agencies which collected the data, the National Center for Juvenile Justice, nor the Office of Juvenile Justice and Delinquency Prevention bear any responsibility for the analyses, interpretations, or conclusions presented herein.

In a number of chapters, I have used (with considerable alterations and additions) portions of articles of mine that have been published elsewhere. I am grateful to the following journals who have kindly allowed me to use those articles:

In Chapter Three, "*In re Gault* Revisited: A Cross-State Comparison of the Right to Counsel in Juvenile Court," *Crime and Delinquency* 34 (October 1988): 393–424.

In Chapters Four and Five, "The Right to Counsel in Juvenile Court: An Empirical Study of When Lawyers Appear and the Difference They Make," *Journal of Criminal Law and Criminology* 79 (Winter 1989): 1185–1346.

In Chapters Six and Seven, "Justice By Geography: Urban, Suburban, and Rural Variations in Juvenile Justice Administration," *Journal of Criminal Law and Criminology* 82 (Spring 1991): 156–210.

In addition, I must also thank the authors and copyright holders of the following works, who permitted the inclusion of excerpts in this book:

North Carolina Law Review Association for Janet E. Ainsworth's "Re-Imagining Childhood and Reconstructing the Legal Order: The Case for Abolishing the Juvenile Court," *North Carolina Law Review* 69, 1083–1133. Copyright 1991. Reprinted by permission of the North Carolina Law Review Association.

New York University Press for M. A. Bortner's *Inside a Juvenile Court: The Tarnished Ideal of Juvenile Justice.* Copyright 1982 by New York University. Reprinted by permission.

*Criminal Law Bulletin* for David Duffee and Larry Siegel's "The Organization Man: Legal Counsel in the Juvenile Court," *Criminal Law Bulletin* 7, 544–553, 1971. Copyright 1971 by Warren Gorham

Lamont, Inc. All rights reserved. Reprinted by permission of *Criminal Law Bulletin.*

Macmillan Publishing Company for David Matza's *Delinquency and Drift.* Copyright 1964 by John Wiley & Sons. Reprinted by permission of Macmillan Publishing Company.

The University of North Carolina Press for John C. Henretta, Charles E. Frazier, and Donna M. Bishop's "The Effects of Prior Case Outcomes on Juvenile Justice Decision-Making," *Social Forces* 65(2), 554–562. Copyright 1986 by The University of North Carolina Press.

Little, Brown and Company for David J. Rothman's *Conscience and Convenience: The Asylum and Its Alternatives in Progressive America.* Copyright 1980 by David J. Rothman. Reprinted by permission of Little, Brown and Company.

New York State Bar Association, Committee on Juvenile Justice and Child Welfare for Jane Knitzer and Merril Sobie's *Law Guardians in New York State: A Study of the Legal Representation of Children.* Copyright 1988. Reprinted by permission.

*Wisconsin Law Review* for Joel F. Handler's "The Juvenile Court and the Adversary System: Problems of Function and Form," *Wisconsin Law Review.* Copyright 1965. Reprinted by permission.

The Regents of the University of California for John Sutton's *Stubborn Children: Controlling Delinquency in the United States, 1640–1981.* Copyright 1988 by The Regents of the University of California.

*Journal of Criminal Justice* for John H. Laub's "Patterns of Offending in Urban and Rural Areas," *Journal of Criminal Justice* 11. Copyright 1983 by Pergamon Press Ltd. Reprinted by permission.

Farrar, Straus & Giroux, Inc., for Robert H. Wiebe's *The Search for Order 1877–1920.* Copyright 1967 by Robert H. Wiebe. Reprinted by permission of Hill and Wang, a division of Farrar, Straus & Giroux, Inc.

Rand Corporation for Peter Greenwood, A. Lipson, A. Abrahamse, and Frank Zimring's *Youth Crime and Juvenile Justice in California: A Report to the Legislature* (R-3016-CSA). Copyright 1983. Reprinted by permission of Rand Corporation.

Patricia Feld is the most important person in the world to me. Her love, support, and encouragement have sustained me throughout our life together. I hope that this book, and the years of research that preceded it, are worth the extra burdens she graciously accepted. I have dedicated this book to our children, Ari Daniel and Julia Elise, whose growth and development are a source of inspiration. I hope that a society that purports to care about children will provide justice for their generation.

# JUSTICE FOR CHILDREN

# INTRODUCTION

The United States Supreme Court's decision *In re Gault* (387 U.S. 1 [1967]) transformed the juvenile court into a very different institution than that envisioned by its Progressive creators. The Progressives envisioned a procedurally informal social welfare agency situated in a court-like setting making individualized, offender-oriented dispositions. The Supreme Court's various due process decisions engrafted procedural formality onto the juvenile court's traditional, individualized-treatment sentencing schema. Judicial and legislative efforts to harmonize the juvenile court with *Gault*'s constitutional mandate have modified the purposes, processes, and operations of the juvenile justice system. Increasingly, as the contemporary juvenile court departs from its original model, it converges procedurally and substantively with adult criminal courts.

Central to the "criminalized" juvenile court is the presence and role of defense counsel. *Gault* held that juvenile offenders were constitutionally entitled to the assistance of counsel in juvenile delinquency proceedings because "a proceeding where the issue is whether the child will be found to be 'delinquent' and subjected to the loss of his liberty for years is comparable in seriousness to a felony prosecution" (387 U.S. at 36). *Gault* also decided that juveniles were entitled to the privilege against self-incrimination and the right to confront and cross-examine their accusers at a hearing. Without the assistance of counsel, these other rights could be lost as well. "[T]he juvenile needs the assistance of counsel to cope with problems of law, to make skilled inquiry into the facts, [and] to insist upon regularity of the proceedings. . . . The child 'requires the guiding hand of counsel at every step in the proceedings against him' " (*Gault*, 387 U.S. at 36). *Gault* reflected the Warren Court's commitment to personal rights and individual autonomy, and the Court's belief that counsel was the essential prerequisite to the implementation of all other procedural safeguards. In subsequent decisions, the Supreme Court has reiterated the crucial role of counsel in the juvenile justice process. In *Fare v. Michael C.*, for example, the Court noted that "the lawyer occupies a critical position in our legal system . . . . Whether it is a minor or an adult who stands accused, the lawyer is the one person to whom society as a whole looks as the protector of the legal rights of that person in his dealings with the police and the courts" (442 U.S. 707, 719 [1979]).

More than two decades after the *Gault* decision, the promise of counsel remains unrealized for many juveniles. Although there is a scarcity of data, surveys of representation by counsel in several jurisdictions suggest that lawyers actually appear much less frequently than the law on the book might lead one to expect. In many states, including Minnesota, less than half of the juveniles adjudicated delinquent receive the assistance of counsel to which they are constitutionally entitled (Feld 1988a, 1989, 1991). The most comprehensive study available reports that in three of the six states surveyed, nearly half or more of juveniles were unrepresented (Feld 1988a).

The following chapters analyze juvenile justice administration by focusing on variations in rates of representation and the impact of counsel in juvenile delinquency and status proceedings. These analyses provide the first systematic, statewide examinations of the circumstances under which lawyers are appointed to represent juveniles, the case characteristics associated with rates of representation, the effects of representation on case processing and dispositions, and the influence of social structural characteristics on juvenile justice administration. A primary focus of this study is to examine the relationship between procedural formality, as evidenced by lawyers, and juvenile justice administration. Part of the analyses treat the availability and role of counsel as a dependent variable using case characteristics, court-processing factors, and social structural features as independent variables affecting rates of representation. Other parts treat the presence of counsel as an independent variable, assessing lawyers' impact on juvenile court case processing and dispositions. These analyses of the role of counsel and procedural formality in contemporary juvenile courts attempt to answer the interrelated questions, when are lawyers appointed to represent juveniles, why are they appointed, and what difference does it make whether or not a youth is represented? One important feature that emerges is an apparent relationship between increased procedural formality and the severity of sanctions in juvenile justice administration.

## ORGANIZATION OF THIS BOOK

Chapter One begins by examining the origins of the juvenile court. Ideological changes in the cultural conception of children and in strategies of social control during the nineteenth century led to the creation of the juvenile court, a "non-legal" social welfare agency in which attorneys seldom appeared. The Supreme Court's *Gault* decision in 1967, which granted, among other procedural rights, the right to counsel, began the process of transforming the juvenile court from a welfare institution into a legal one (Feld 1984, 1988b). It appears, however, that despite *Gault*'s promise of counsel, the actual delivery of legal services lags behind the theoretical availability of counsel in many jurisdictions. Chapter One analyzes the legal doctrines that allow so many youths to appear without the assistance of counsel and some collateral legal issues that arise when unrepresented juvenile defendants are convicted and sentenced. It also introduces the idea that within a state there is not *a* juvenile court but rather varieties of juvenile justice. Despite laws and rules of statewide applicability, juvenile courts vary considerably, and a court's social structural context affects juvenile justice administration.

Chapter Two describes the data and methodology used in the ensuing chapters. It describes the sources of the data and the data coding protocols used to facilitate interstate and intrastate comparative analyses. It describes the analytic strategies used to answer the questions of when do lawyers appear in juvenile court and what difference does their presence make.

Chapter Three provides a comparative assessment of the implementation of *Gault* in six states: California, Minnesota, Nebraska, North Dakota, New York, and Pennsylvania. These states were selected simply because they were the only ones that collected information on representation in juvenile courts. Two important points emerge from this interstate comparison. First, rates of representation vary considerably among the states; in the three large, urban industrial states attorneys appear about twice as often as they do in the three more rural, midwestern states. Second, after controlling for variables such as the seriousness of the offense, prior record, or pretrial detention status, the presence of an attorney appears to be an aggravating factor in the sentencing of young offenders, regardless of the overall rates of representation.

Chapters Four and Five provide an in-depth analysis of the determinants and effects of representation in one state, Minnesota. The variability of juvenile courts is analyzed by comparing juvenile justice administration in counties in which lawyers are routinely present, sometimes present, and seldom present. While certain factors, such as pretrial detention, the seriousness of the present offense or prior record, affected overall rates of representation, the differential presence of counsel was associated with differences in pretrial detention, sentencing, and case-processing practices.

Chapters Six and Seven build on the findings that juvenile courts vary considerably and that the presence of an attorney is associated with differences in juvenile justice administration. Using the presence of an attorney as an indicator of a formal, due-process orientation, Chapter Six attempts to account for variations in rates of representation. Although all the juvenile courts operated under the same statutes and rules of state-wide applicability, certain social structural variables appear to affect courts' procedural and substantive policies. A court's urban, suburban, or rural social context strongly influences the ways in which cases are selected, heard, and disposed. Chapter Seven examines the influences of race and gender on juvenile justice administration in different structural contexts. It reports that the "individualized justice" of juvenile courts places female and minority youths at a disadvantage.

Chapter Eight examines some of the policy implications raised by finding varieties of juvenile courts, "justice by geography," and a relationship between procedural formality and sentencing severity in juvenile justice administration. The substantive and procedural convergence between juvenile and criminal courts eliminates virtually all of the differences in strategies of social control between youths and adults. Recent changes in the juridical conception of young offenders have accompanied the juvenile court's transformation from an informal, rehabilitative agency into a scaled-down criminal court. Chapter Nine concludes by questioning whether there is any reason to retain a separate juvenile court whose only distinction is its persisting procedural deficiencies. It examines three possible alternatives to the contemporary juvenile court, which punishes in the name of treatment while denying to juveniles the elementary procedural safeguards insisted upon for adults.

# chapter one

# JUVENILE COURTS, THE RIGHT TO COUNSEL, AND PROCEDURAL FORMALITY

Ideological changes in the cultural conception of children and in strategies of social control during the nineteenth century led to the creation of the juvenile court. At the dawn of the twentieth century, Progressive reformers applied the new theories of social control to the new ideas about childhood and created a social welfare alternative to criminal courts to treat criminal and noncriminal misconduct by youth.

The United States Supreme Court's decision *In re Gault* (387 U.S. 1 [1967]), however, began transforming the juvenile court into a very different institution than the Progressives contemplated. Unlike the Progressive vision of an informal clinic acting in a child's "best interests," *Gault* engrafted formal trial procedures and emphasized the judicial rather than welfare role of juvenile courts (Feld 1984). In the past two decades, legislative, judicial, and administrative responses to *Gault* have modified the court's jurisdiction, purpose, and procedures (Feld 1987, 1988b, 1991). As a result, juvenile courts increasingly converge procedurally and substantively with adult criminal courts (Feld 1984, 1988b). While the juvenile court has been transformed from an informal, rehabilitative agency into a scaled-down criminal court in some states or parts of states, in too many instances its procedural deficiencies persist despite constitutional and legislative restructuring. This chapter examines the creation and procedural modification of the juvenile court over the past century.

## INTRODUCTION

Between 1870 and World War I, railroads changed the United States from an agrarian to an industrial society by fostering economic growth, changing the processes of manufacturing, and ushering in a period of rapid social and economic modernization (Hays 1957; Hofstadter 1955; Kolko 1963; Wiebe 1967). Traditional social patterns were subject to new challenges as immigrants, primarily from southern and eastern Europe, and rural Americans flooded into the burgeoning cities to take advantage of new economic opportunities. The "new" immigrants differed in language, religion, political heritage, and culture from the dominant Anglo-Protestant Americans who had preceded them (Hofstadter 1955; Higham 1988). They predominantly were peasants; their cultural and linguistic differences from the dominant culture, coupled with their numbers, hindered their assimilation. Overburdened by population increases, cities proved unable to provide even basic needs (Trattner 1984). Crowded ethnic enclaves, urban ghettos, poverty, disorder, crime, and inadequate social services were untoward features of modern urban industrial life.

## PROGRESSIVES AND THE CHILD

Changes in family structure and function accompanied these social structural developments. These included a reduction in the average number of children per family and their spacing, a shift of economic functions from the family to other work environments, and a modernizing and privatizing of family life that substantially modified the roles of women and children (Kett 1977; Demos and Boocock 1978; Degler 1980; Lasch 1977; Wells 1979). The latter development was especially noticeable in the upper and middle classes, which had begun to view children as corruptible innocents whose upbringing required special attention, solicitude, and instruction (Aries 1962; Gillis 1974; Kett 1977; DeMause 1974). "By the turn of the century, the attributes of childhood were being applied to teenagers, who only a generation earlier would not have been distinguished from older adults. Since as children they were assumed to be vulnerable, malleable, and in need of adult guidance, training, and control before they could graduate to full personhood, adolescents now became targets of paternal adult attention" (Ainsworth 1991:1095). Wishy (1968:94–114) traces the emergence of the new ideas of childhood and child rearing through children's books and child-rearing manuals for parents from 1860 to 1900. Degler (1980:86–110) relates changes in child-rearing methods and women's social roles during the nineteenth century to new perceptions of children as innocent, fragile, and dependent.

The social construction of childhood as a recognizable developmental stage is a relatively recent phenomenon (Ainsworth 1991). Prior to the past two or three centuries, there was neither a fully separate social status based on youthfulness nor a corresponding age or legal segregation. Young people were perceived as miniature adults or inadequate versions of their parents who did not require any special protection or discrete legal status (Aries 1962). Even in the early nineteenth century the newer views of children as socially distinct from adults were only beginning to alter child-rearing practices. The trend of age differentiation was accentuated as commercial and industrial developments enabled young people to achieve economic independence (Marks 1975). By the end of the nineteenth century, however, the preparation of children for adult roles and their autonomous departures from home became much more restrictive (Kett 1977). As a result, women, especially in the middle and upper classes, assumed a greater role in supervising the child's moral and social development (Platt 1977; Wishy 1968).

The social and economic changes associated with modernization and industrialization sparked the Progressive movement. Progressivism encompassed a host of ideologies and addressed issues ranging from economic regulation to criminal justice, and social and political reform. Progressive reformers passed antitrust legislation (Bringhurst 1979), compulsory school attendance laws (Cremin 1961), railroad regulations (Kolko 1965), criminal justice reforms (Rothman 1980), child welfare laws (Tiffin 1982), child labor laws (Trattner 1965), urban welfare reform (Trattner 1984), business regulations (Wiebe 1962), and "good government" civil service reforms (Hays 1957).

One unifying theme of the Progressive movement was that professionals and experts could develop rational and scientific solutions to social problems that would be administered by the state (Sutton 1988). Hays (1957) and Wiebe (1967) attribute the Progressives' reliance on state agencies to the newly emerging middle class of college-educated technocrats, corporate managers, and professionals who viewed the decline of the older order as an opportunity to realize their own potentials through the development of rational, scientific, and managerial solutions to a host of social problems.

Progressive reliance on the state reflected a fundamental belief that state action could be benevolent, that government could rectify social problems, and that Progressive values could be inculcated in others (Allen 1964, 1981). Progressives felt no reservations when they attempted to "Americanize" the immigrants and poor through a variety of agencies of assimilation and acculturation to become sober, virtuous, middle-class Americans (Rothman 1980; Platt 1977).

The Progressives' trust of state power coupled with the changing cultural conception of children and child rearing led them into the realm of "child-saving" through child labor laws, child welfare laws, compulsory school attendance laws, and the juvenile court system. Many Progressive legislative programs shared a unifying child-centered theme. "The child was the carrier of tomorrow's hope whose innocence and freedom made him singularly receptive to education in rational, humane behavior. Protect him, nurture him, and in his manhood he would create that bright new world of the Progressives' vision" (Wiebe 1967:169). During the Progressive era, both the states and the federal government adopted a variety of laws to protect children against dangerous labor and neglect, to require them to attend school, to secure for them a better future, and to influence immigrant children to adopt the American way of life (Rothman 1980).

The creation of the juvenile court and the emergence of institutional child care in the nineteenth and early twentieth centuries were simply outgrowths of the more comprehensive child-study movement, which viewed children as reformable innocents whose characters were malleable (Ryerson 1978; Tiffin 1982; Sutton 1988). Progressive programs were intended to structure child development, control and mold children, and protect them from exploitation. The goals and the methods of these programs, however, often reflected the Anglo-Americans' antipathy to the immigrant hordes, and a desire to save the second generation from perpetuating old-world ways (Empey 1979b). The principal child-saving reforms—child labor laws, child welfare laws, compulsory school attendance requirements, and the juvenile court system—reflected the central Progressive assumption that the ideal way to prepare children for life was to strengthen the nuclear family, shield children from adult roles, and formally educate them for upward mobility (Sutton 1988; Ainsworth 1991).

## SCIENTIFIC CRIMINOLOGY AND SOCIAL CONTROL

The development of new theories about human behavior and social deviance led Progressives to new views on criminal justice and social control policies (Rothman 1980; Allen 1981). The Progressives' reformulation of criminal justice strategies reflected basic changes in the ideological assumptions about the sources of crime and deviance. Positivism—the effort to identify the various factors that cause crime and deviance—challenged the classic formulations of crime as the product of free will choices (Matza 1964; Allen 1981). The Progressives saw crime not as a product of the deliberate exercise of an individual's free will but as a result of external, antecedent forces. The "new" criminology, as distinguished from the old theory of "free will," asserted a scientific determinism of deviance and sought to identify the causal variables producing crime and delinquency (Platt 1977; Rothman 1980).

In its quest for scientific legitimacy, criminology borrowed both methodology and vocabulary from the medical profession. With Pasteur's discovery of "germs," for the first time, physicians acquired the scientific ability to treat diseases effectively. The medical profession achieved a scientific aura, and patients passively submitted to the experts' ministrations (Bledstein 1976). Medical metaphors such as pathology, infection, diagnosis, and treatment provided popular analogues for criminal justice professionals, who also asserted a scientific approach to the diagnosis and cure of each offender (Allen 1964, 1981).

Progressives emphasized reforming the offender rather than punishing on the basis of the offense. The deterministic explanations of human behavior redirected research efforts to identify the causes of crime. Understanding scientifically the causes of crime also implied the correlative ability to "cure" the offender. Although early positivistic criminology attributed criminal behavior to hereditary and biological factors, social and environmental explanations soon supplanted these views (Ryerson 1978). Social science professionals graduating from colleges and universities with training in psychology, sociology, and social work acquired a professional stake in environmental explanations of deviance, because environmental factors allowed for greater possibilities of intervention and cure than did imperious biological determinism (Hawes 1971; Lubove 1965; Bledstein 1976).

The environmental explanations of deviance attributed delinquency to the social and economic conditions associated with modernization, such as immigrant ghettos and urban slums into which the benefits of the American society could not penetrate. Environmentalists emphasized the impacts of industrialization and urbanization in the processes of crime causation. Although there was always a touch of moralism condemning those who succumbed to these deleterious influences, there was also an appreciation of the vulnerability of the urban poor and young to economic forces and social conditions beyond their control (Ryerson 1978).

The influence of positive criminology resulted in the "rehabilitative ideal" that permeated all Progressive criminal justice reforms, including the increased use of probation and indeterminate sentencing, parole supervision following release, and the juvenile court (Allen 1964, 1981; Rothman 1980). The rehabilitative ideal emphasized open-ended, informal, and highly flexible policies so that the criminal justice professional had the discretion necessary to formulate individualized, case-by-case strategies for rehabilitating the deviant. Discretion was necessary because diagnosing the causes of and prescribing the cures for delinquency required an individualized approach that precluded uniformity of treatment or standardization of criteria (Rothman 1980). It is probably not coincidental that the increased flexibility, indeterminacy, and discretion in social control practices corresponded with the increasing volume and changing characteristics of offenders during this period (Fox 1970a; Sutton 1988).

A flourishing rehabilitative ideal requires both a belief in the malleability of human behavior and a basic moral consensus about the appropriate directions of human change (Allen 1964, 1981). It entails assumptions about means and ends, the goals of human change, and the availability of intervention strategies necessary to achieve them. Progressives believed that the new sciences of human behavior provided them with the tools for systematic human change. They also believed in the virtues of their social order and the propriety of imposing the values of a middle-class lifestyle on immigrants and the poor (Rothman 1980).

## COMBINING "CHILDHOOD" WITH SOCIAL CONTROL: THE PROGRESSIVE JUVENILE COURT

In the Progressives' vision, the juvenile court embodied the rehabilitative ideal. They created a specialized, bureaucratic agency, to be staffed by experts and designed to serve the needs of a specific category of client: the "child at risk," whether she was an offender, dependent, or neglected. "The desirability, even necessity, for a separate court system to address the problems of young people appeared obvious, given the newly emerging view of the adolescent as an immature creature in need of adult control. . . . By categorizing the adolescent as a subclass of the child rather than as a type of adult, the Progressive fashioned a discrete juvenile justice system premised upon the belief that, like other children, adolescents are not morally accountable for their behavior" (Ainsworth 1991:1097). The juvenile court professionals made discretionary, individualized treatment decisions to achieve benevolent goals and social uplift by substituting a scientific and preventative approach for the traditional punitive philosophy of the criminal law (Mennel 1983; Platt 1974).

Many of the characteristics of the Progressive juvenile court can be traced to the earlier "houses of refuge" that emerged in the first third of the nineteenth century. The houses of refuge were the first specialized agency for the control of youth (Finestone 1976; Hawes 1971; Kett 1977;

Mennel 1973; Pickett 1969; Rothman 1971; Fox 1970a). Sutton (1983:917) contends that

> developments in the 19th century laid the foundation for the subsequent development of the juvenile justice system in the United States. . . . [L]egislation establishing the juvenile court in Chicago did no more than formalize long-standing practices for dealing with juveniles in Illinois. . . . [I]n almost every state the legal and ideological innovations typically associated with the juvenile court (e.g., the extension of legal control over noncriminal children, the denial of due process, and the legalization of the rehabilitative ideal) had occurred before the advent of children's courts, as a result of earlier legislation establishing juvenile reformatories.

The legal justification for house of refuge and, later, juvenile court intervention was *parens patriae,* the right and responsibility of the state to substitute its own control over children for that of the natural parents when the latter were unable or unwilling to meet their responsibilities or when the child posed a community crime problem (Cogan 1970; Curtis 1976; Pisciotta 1982; Rendleman 1971). The leading case of the refuge period, *ex parte Crouse* (4 Whart. 9 [Pa. 1838]), reflected not only the ideology of environmentalism and preventive intervention, but also the breadth of the parens patriae doctrine and the futility of legal challenges to state intervention.

> The object of the charity is reformation, by training its inmates to industry, by imbuing their minds with principles of morality and religion, by furnishing them with means to earn a living, and, above all, by separating them from the corrupting influence of improper associates. To this end may not the natural parents, when unequal to the task of education, or unworthy of it, be superseded by the parens patriae, or common guardian of the community? It is to be remembered that the public has a paramount interest in the virtue and knowledge of its members, and that, of strict right, the business of education belongs to it. That parents are ordinarily intrusted with it is because it can seldom be put into better hands; but, where they are incompetent or corrupt, what is there to prevent the public from withdrawing their faculties, held, as they obviously are, at its sufferance? The right of parental control is a natural, but not an unalienable, one. . . . As to abridgment of indefeasible rights by confinement of the person, it is no more than what is born, to a greater or less extent, in every school; and we know of no natural right to exemption from restraints which conduce to an infant's welfare. Nor is there a doubt of the propriety of their application in the particular

instance. The infant has been snatched from a course which must have ended in confirmed depravity; and not only is the restraint of her person lawful, but it would be an act of extreme cruelty to release her from it.

The parens patriae doctrine, which underlay both house of refuge and juvenile court jurisdiction, drew no distinction between criminal and non-criminal youthful conduct. This supported the Progressives' position that juvenile court proceedings were civil rather than criminal in nature.

## PROCEDURAL INFORMALITY AND ACCESS TO COUNSEL

The civil nature of the proceedings fulfilled the reformers' desire to re-move children from the adult criminal system and allowed greater super-vision of the children and greater flexibility in treatment. The juvenile court reformers sought to aid children as well as to control their criminal behavior. Historically, controlling youth through the criminal law pre-sented the stark alternatives of a criminal conviction and punishment as an adult or an acquittal or dismissal that freed the youth from all super-vision (Hawes 1971; Kett 1977; Mennel 1973; Pickett 1969). Jury or judicial nullification to avoid punishment excluded many youths from control, particularly minor offenders (Rothman 1971; Fox 1970a). De-sires for greater supervision and control, rather than leniency, animated many reformers (Platt 1977; Ryerson 1978). They sought a system that would allow the law to intervene affirmatively in the lives of young of-fenders, rather than only to impose punishment. The rehabilitative juve-nile court provided Progressives with a middle ground between punishing behavior through the criminal process, thereby criminalizing a youth, or ignoring it altogether, thereby encouraging a resumption of a criminal career (Hawes 1971; Platt 1977; Rothman 1980; Ryerson 1978; Fox 1970a).

Because the reformers eschewed punishment, they could regulate be-havior such as smoking, "sexual precocity," truancy, immorality, stub-bornness, vagrancy, or living a wayward, idle, and dissolute life. While previous generations might have ignored such behaviors, the Progressives wished to eradicate them because in their ideology of "childhood," it be-tokened premature adulthood (Garlock 1979; Rosenberg and Rosenberg 1976; Schlossman and Wallach 1978). Such "status jurisdiction"—regu-lation of conduct that would not be criminal if engaged in by adults—reflected the dominant concept of childhood and adolescence that had taken root during the nineteenth century and authorized predelinquent intervention to forestall premature adulthood, enforce the dependent conditions of youth, and supervise children's moral upbringing. Because Progressive reformers believed that young girls needed more "moral" protection than did boys, females were especially at risk through the exercise of status jurisdiction (Schlossman and Wallach 1978).

Ironically, the juvenile court simultaneously affirmed the primacy of the nuclear family and expanded the power of the state to intervene in instances of parental inadequacy (Platt 1977; Rothman 1980). Child rearing had become too complex to relegate to unsupervised family control. Immigrant and lower-class families, caught in the conflict of cultures, could not be expected to adequately Americanize their children, and state supervision was imposed to assure that the next generation adopted an acceptable middle-class way of life. The juvenile court provided a primary agency through which Anglo-Protestant Americans defined the norms of family and childhood to which the outsiders were to adhere (Ryerson 1978; Platt 1977).

The Progressives envisioned a juvenile court administered by an expert judge and assisted by social service personnel, clinicians, and probation officers. They hoped judges would be specialists, trained in the social sciences and child development, whose empathic qualities and insight could aid in making individualized dispositions in the "best interests" of the child. One consequence of judicial discretion, however, "was a system that made the personality of the judge, his likes and dislikes, attitudes and prejudices, consistencies and caprices, the decisive element in shaping the character of his courtroom" (Rothman 1980:238). Progressives assumed that a rational, scientific analysis of facts would reveal the proper diagnosis and prescribe the cure, and the juvenile court's methodology encouraged collecting as much information as possible about the child. The resulting factual inquiry into the "whole child" accorded minor significance to the specific criminal offense since the offense was, at most, only a symptom of the child's "real needs."

A system of decision making in which literally everything is relevant to the ultimate determination of a child's "best interests" necessarily is heavily dependent on sound judgment and professional expertise. A well-trained probation staff schooled in the principles of psychology and social work, aided by mental hygiene clinics and psychological diagnostic services, would provide the scientific undergirding that assured consistency in dispositions (Rothman 1980; Ryerson 1978). Because the reformers' aims were benevolent, their solicitude individualized, and their intervention guided by science, they saw no reason to narrowly circumscribe the power of the state. They maximized discretion to provide flexibility in diagnosis and treatment and focused on the child and the child's character and lifestyle rather than on the crime.

In separating children from adult offenders, the juvenile court also rejected the procedures of criminal prosecutions. It introduced a euphemistic vocabulary and a physically separate court building to avoid the stigma of adult prosecutions, and it modified courtroom procedures to eliminate any implication of a criminal proceeding (President's Commission 1967a, 1967b). For example, proceedings were initiated by a petition in the welfare of the child, rather than by a criminal complaint or indictment. Because the important issues involved the child's background and welfare rather than the commission of a specific crime, courts dispensed with juries, lawyers, rules of evidence, and formal procedures. As the Pennsylvania Supreme Court noted, "Whether the child deserves to be saved by the state is no more a question for a jury than whether the father, if able to save it, ought to save it" (*Commonwealth v. Fisher*, 213 Pa. 48, 54 [Pa. Sup. Ct. 1905]).

To avoid stigmatizing youngsters, hearings were confidential and private, access to court records was limited, and youths were found to be "delinquent" rather than guilty of an offense. To make proceedings more personal and private, the judge was supposed to sit next to the child at a table, rather than elevated in robes. Court personnel presented a treatment plan to meet the child's needs based on a background investigation that identified the causes of the child's misconduct. Dispositions were indeterminate and nonproportional and could continue for the duration of minority. The events that brought the child before the court affected neither the degree nor the duration of intervention because each child's needs differed and no limits could be defined in advance. The goal was to determine why the child was in court in the first instance and what could be done to change the character, attitude, and behavior of the youth to prevent a reappearance (Mack 1909; Ryerson 1978).

From its inception, juvenile court judges were actively hostile to the presence of lawyers in delinquency proceedings:

> Although judges could not banish a lawyer from the courtroom altogether, they did not consider his presence either appropriate or necessary. Minnesota juvenile court judge Grier Orr boasted that in his courtroom "the lawyers do not do very much . . . and I do not believe I can recall any instance where the same attorney came back a second time; he found that it was useless for him to appear . . . for an attorney has not very much standing when it comes to the disposition of children in juvenile court. (Rothman 1980:216)

Juvenile court judges regarded lawyers as both irrelevant and an impediment to their "child-saving" mission.

As late as the Supreme Court's *Gault* decision in 1967, juvenile court judges still routinely discouraged the retention, appointment, or appearance of counsel. In one study, the authors report that

> [i]n the court itself, the parent's inquiry as to whether a lawyer is needed is often answered with the statement "that is a decision you must make for yourself," coupled with a reminder that if an attorney is to be retained the proceedings will have to be continued to another date (with the resulting inconvenience). Moreover, parents who are told by the judge that he is willing to proceed immediately and will make every effort himself to ensure that the rights of the child are protected may well fear that to bring in an attorney would be an implicit insult to the judge, an especially unattractive prospect when the judge has such wide discretion in making decisions. (Note 1966:796–97)

A California study concluded that

> [m]any judges discourage the presence of counsel in their courts in an effort to reduce the time devoted to the juvenile court assignment. . . . Some courts believe that attorneys have no place in the juvenile court and use coercive means to discourage their presence. (Handler 1965:32 n. 86)

Other studies contemporaneous with *Gault* reported colloquies between judges and juveniles that purported to advise the youths of their right to counsel but which were delivered in a manner designed to discourage the assertion of that right (Lefstein, Stapleton, and Teitelbaum 1969; Rubin 1977; Ferster, Courtless, and Snethen 1971).

## THE "CONSTITUTIONAL DOMESTICATION" OF THE JUVENILE COURT: PROCEDURAL FORMALITY AND THE RIGHT TO COUNSEL

Despite occasional challenges and criticism of some conceptual or administrative aspects of juvenile justice, no sustained and systematic examination of the juvenile court emerged until the 1960s (Handler 1965; Note 1966; President's Commission 1967a, 1967b). In 1967, however, *Gault* began a "due process revolution" that substantially transformed the juvenile court from a social welfare agency into a legal institution. The United States Supreme Court's "constitutional domestication" (*Gault*,

387 U.S. at 22) was the first step in the convergence of the procedures of the juvenile justice system with those of the adult criminal process (Feld 1981a, 1984; Paulsen 1966, 1967).

*Gault* involved the delinquency adjudication and institutional commitment of a youth who allegedly made a lewd telephone call of the "irritatingly offensive, adolescent, sex variety" to a neighbor (387 U.S. at 4). Fifteen-year-old Gerald Gault was taken into custody, detained overnight without notification of his parents, and made to appear at a hearing the following day. A pro forma petition alleged simply that he was a delinquent minor in need of the care and custody of the court. The complaining witness did not appear, no sworn testimony was taken, and no transcript or formal memorandum of the substance of the proceedings was made. The judge interrogated Gault, who apparently made incriminating responses. At no time was Gault assisted by an attorney or advised of a right to counsel. Following the hearing, the judge returned Gault to a detention cell for several days. At Gault's dispositional hearing the following week, the judge committed him as a juvenile delinquent to the state industrial school "for the period of his minority [that is, until twenty-one], unless sooner discharged by due process of law" (387 U.S. at 7–8). If Gault had been an adult, his offense would have resulted in no more than a fifty dollar fine or two months' imprisonment; as a juvenile, however, he was subject to incarceration for the duration of his minority, potentially as long as six years.

In reviewing the history of the juvenile court, the Court noted that the traditional rationales for denying procedural safeguards to juveniles included the belief that the proceedings were neither adversarial nor criminal and that, because the state acted as parens patriae, the child was entitled to custody rather than liberty. The Court rejected these assertions, however, because denial of procedures frequently resulted in arbitrariness rather than "careful, compassionate, individualized treatment" (387 U.S. at 18). Although the Court hoped to retain the potential benefits of the juvenile process, it insisted that the claims of the juvenile court process had to be candidly appraised in light of the realities of recidivism, the failures of rehabilitation, the stigma of a "delinquency" label, the breaches of confidentiality, and the arbitrariness of the process.

Rather than accepting the rehabilitative rhetoric of Progressive juvenile jurisprudence, the Supreme Court examined the realities of juvenile incarceration.

> The fact of the matter is that, however euphemistic the title, a "receiving home" or an "industrial school" for juveniles is an institution of confinement in which the child is incarcerated for a greater or lesser

time. His world becomes "a building with whitewashed walls, regimented routine, and institutional hours." Instead of mother and father and sisters and brothers and friends and classmates, his world is peopled by guards, custodians, state employees, and "delinquents" confined with him for anything from waywardness to rape and homicide. . . . [U]nder our Constitution, the condition of being a [child] does not justify a kangaroo court. (*Gault*, 387 U.S. at 27–28)

The Court cautioned that a juvenile justice process free of constitutional safeguards had not abated recidivism or lowered the high crime rates among juvenile offenders. Accordingly, the Court held that juveniles were entitled to advance notice of charges, a fair and impartial hearing, assistance of counsel, opportunity to confront and cross-examine witnesses, and the privilege against self-incrimination (*Gault*, 387 U.S. at 31–57; Rosenberg 1980; Feld 1984; McCarthy 1981).

Although the Court discussed the realities of the juvenile system and mandated procedural safeguards, it limited its holding to the adjudicatory hearing at which a child is determined to be a delinquent. The Court specifically held that "[w]e do not in this opinion consider the impact of these constitutional provisions upon the totality of the relationship of the juvenile and the state. We do not even consider the entire process relating to juvenile 'delinquents'" (*Gault*, 387 U.S. at 13). The Court's holding did not address a juvenile's rights in either the preadjudicatory (i.e., intake and detention) or postadjudicatory (i.e., disposition) stages of the proceeding, but narrowly confined itself to the actual adjudication of guilt or innocence in a trial-like setting (*Gault*, 387 U.S. at 13, 31 n. 48). It asserted that its decision would in no way impair the value of the unique procedures for processing and treating juveniles and that the procedural safeguards associated with the adversarial process were essential in juvenile proceedings, both to determine the truth and to preserve individual freedom by limiting the power of the state.

In contrast to the narrow holding, the basis for the Court's constitutional analysis of what rights must be afforded juveniles in adjudicatory hearings was broad. The Court based its decision to grant the rights to notice, counsel, and confrontation on the requirements of "fundamental fairness" implied in the Fourteenth Amendment's due process clause and did not even refer specifically to the explicit requirements of the Sixth Amendment. The Court did, however, explicitly invoke the Fifth Amendment to establish that juveniles were protected against self-incrimination in delinquency proceedings.

It would be entirely unrealistic to carve out of the Fifth Amendment all statements by juveniles on the ground that these cannot lead to "criminal" involvement. In the first place, juvenile proceedings to determine "delinquency," which may lead to commitment to a state institution, must be regarded as "criminal" for purposes of the privilege against self-incrimination. . . . [C]ommitment is a deprivation of liberty. It is incarceration against one's will whether it is called "criminal" or "civil." (*Gault*, 387 U.S. at 49–50)

As a consequence of the Court's decision in *Gault* recognizing the applicability of the privilege against self-incrimination, juvenile adjudications no longer could be characterized as either "noncriminal" or as "nonadversarial" because the Fifth Amendment privilege, more than any other provision of the Bill of Rights, is the fundamental guarantor of an adversarial process and the primary mechanism for maintaining a balance between the state and the individual.

The Court's extension of the self-incrimination protection provides the clearest example of the dual functions of such safeguards in juvenile court adjudications: assuring accurate fact-finding and protecting against government oppression. If the Court in *Gault* had been concerned solely with the reliability of juvenile confessions and the accuracy of fact-finding, safeguards other than the Fifth Amendment privilege, such as a requirement that all confessions must be shown to have been made "voluntarily," would have sufficed. In both *Gallegos v. Colorado* (370 U.S. 49 [1962]), and *Haley v. Ohio* (332 U.S. 596 [1948]), the Supreme Court considered the admissibility of confessions made by juveniles, employed the Fourteenth Amendment "voluntariness" test, and concluded that youthfulness was a special circumstance affecting the reliability of confession that required close judicial scrutiny. The Court, however, recognized that Fifth Amendment safeguards are not required simply because they ensure accurate fact-finding or reliable confessions, but also because they serve as a means of maintaining a proper balance between the individual and the state:

> The privilege against self-incrimination is, of course, related to the question of the safeguards necessary to assure that admissions or confessions are reasonably trustworthy, that they are not mere fruits of fear or coercion, but are reliable expressions of the truth. The roots of the privilege are, however, far deeper. They tap the basic stream of religious and political principle because the privilege reflects the limits of the individual's attornment to the state and—in a philosophical sense—insists upon the equality of the individual and the state. In other words, the privilege has a broader and deeper thrust than the rule which prevents the use of confessions which are the product of coercion because coercion is thought to carry with it

the danger of unreliability. One of its purposes is to prevent the state, whether by force or by psychological domination, from overcoming the mind and will of the person under investigation and depriving him of the freedom to decide whether to assist the state in securing his conviction. (*Gault*, 387 U.S. at 47)

In this respect, *Gault* is a premier example of the Warren Court's belief that expansion of constitutional rights and limitation on the coercive powers of the state could be obtained through the adversary process, which in turn would assure the regularity of law enforcement and reduce the need for continual judicial scrutiny (Allen 1975).

In subsequent juvenile court decisions, the Supreme Court further elaborated upon the essentially criminal nature of delinquency proceedings. In *In re Winship* (397 U.S. 358 [1970]), the Court decided that proof of delinquency must be established "beyond a reasonable doubt," rather than by lower civil standards of proof. Because there is no explicit provision of the Bill of Rights regarding the standard of proof in criminal cases, the *Winship* Court first held that proof beyond a reasonable doubt was a constitutional requirement in adult criminal proceedings. The Court then extended the same standard of proof to juvenile proceedings because of the standard's equally vital role there. In a later opinion, the Court amplified on its equation of delinquency cases with criminal prosecutions.

The Court [in *Winship*] saw no controlling difference in loss of liberty and stigma between a conviction for an adult and a delinquency adjudication for a juvenile. *Winship* recognized that the basic issue—whether the individual in fact committed a criminal act—was the same in both proceedings. There being no meaningful distinctions between the two proceedings, we required the state to prove the juvenile's act and intent beyond a reasonable doubt. (*Addington v. Texas*, 441 U.S. 418 at 427–28 [1979])

The *Winship* Court concluded that the need to prevent unwarranted convictions and to guard against government power was sufficiently important to outweigh the dissenters' concerns that the juvenile court's unique therapeutic function would be thwarted and that "differences between juvenile courts and traditional criminal courts [would be eroded]" (*Winship*, 397 U.S. at 377 [1970]). The *Winship* majority reasoned that while parens patriae intervention may be a desirable method of dealing with wayward youths, "that intervention cannot take the form of subjecting the child to the stigma of a finding that he violated a criminal law and to the possibility of institutional confinement on proof insufficient to convict him were he an adult." (397 U.S. at 367)

Five years later, the Court in *Breed v. Jones* (421 U.S. 519 [1975]) held that, after a conviction in juvenile court, the protections of the double jeopardy clause of the Fifth Amendment prohibit the adult criminal prosecution of a youth for the same offense. Although the Court framed the issue in terms of the applicability of an explicit provision of the Bill of Rights to state proceedings, it resolved the question by recognizing the functional equivalence and the identical interests of the defendants in a delinquency proceeding and an adult criminal trial. The Court reiterated:

> Although the juvenile-court system had its genesis in the desire to provide a distinctive procedure and setting to deal with the problems of youth, including those manifested by antisocial conduct, our decisions in recent years have recognized that there is a gap between the originally benign conception of the system and its realities.
> ... [I]t is simply too late in the day to conclude ... that a juvenile is not put in jeopardy at a proceeding whose object is to determine whether he has committed acts that violate a criminal law and whose potential consequences include both the stigma inherent in such a determination and the deprivation of liberty for many years. (*Breed*, 421 U.S. at 528–29)

The Court concluded that, with respect to the risks associated with double jeopardy, "we can find no persuasive distinction in that regard between the [juvenile] proceeding ... and a criminal prosecution, each of which is designed to 'vindicate [the] very vital interest in enforcement of criminal laws'" (*Breed*, 421 U.S. at 531).

Only in *McKeiver v. Pennsylvania* (403 U.S. 528 [1971]), which denied juveniles the right to a jury trial, did the Court decline to extend the procedural safeguards of adult criminal prosecutions to juvenile court proceedings. *McKeiver* was decided on the basis of Fourteenth Amendment due process and "fundamental fairness," rather than the Sixth Amendment jury trial guarantee which the Court had made applicable to adult criminal proceedings. The Court insisted, however, that "the juvenile court proceeding has not yet been held to be a 'criminal prosecution,' within the meaning and reach of the Sixth Amendment, and also has not yet been regarded as devoid of criminal aspects merely because it usually has been given the civil label" (*McKeiver*, 403 U.S. at 541). The Court cautioned that "[t]here is a possibility, at least, that the jury trial, if required as a matter of constitutional precept, will remake the juvenile proceeding into a fully adversary process and will put an effective end to what has been the idealistic prospect of an intimate, informal protective proceeding" (*McKeiver*, 403 U.S. at 545). The Court in *McKeiver* held that a jury is not required in a juvenile proceeding because the only requirement for "fundamental fairness" in such proceedings is "accurate fact finding," a requirement that can be as well satisfied by a judge as by a jury.

In concluding that due process required nothing more than accurate fact-finding, however, the Court departed significantly from its prior analyses in *Gault* (387 U.S. at 47) and *Winship* (397 U.S. at 363–64), which relied on the *dual* rationales of accurate fact-finding and protection against governmental oppression. Furthermore, in insisting that the only concern of fundamental fairness is accurate fact-finding, the Court ignored its analysis in *Gault*, which held that the Fifth Amendment's privilege against self-incrimination was necessary in order to protect against governmental oppression even though accurate fact-finding might be impeded. The Court, however, denied that protection against government oppression was required at all and, invoking the mythology of the sympathetic, paternalistic juvenile court judge, rejected the argument that the inbred, closed nature of the juvenile court could prejudice the accuracy of fact-finding (*McKeiver*, 403 U.S. at 547–48).

> Concern about the inapplicability of exclusionary and other rules of evidence, about the juvenile court judge's possible awareness of the juvenile's prior record and of the contents of the social file; about repeated appearances of the same familiar witnesses in the persons of juvenile and probation officers and social workers—all to the effect that this will create the likelihood of prejudgment—chooses to ignore, it seems to us, every aspect of fairness, of concern, of sympathy, and of paternal attention that the juvenile court system contemplates.

In denying juveniles the constitutional right to jury trials, the *McKeiver* Court departed from its earlier mode of constitutional analysis which recognized the dual functions of procedural safeguards—accurate fact-finding and preventing governmental oppression. Instead, it emphasized the adverse impact that jury trials might have on the informality, flexibility, and confidentiality of juvenile court proceedings. The result clearly was dictated by the Court's concern that the right to a trial by jury would be the procedural safeguard most disruptive of the traditional juvenile court and would require substantial alteration of traditional juvenile court practices because "it would bring with it . . . the traditional delay, the formality, and the clamor of the adversary system and, possibly, the public trial" (*McKeiver*, 403 U.S. at 550). Ultimately, the Court realized that imposing such a procedural requirement would render juvenile courts virtually indistinguishable from criminal courts and would raise the more basic question of whether there is any need for a separate juvenile court at all.

Rather than asking whether the constitutional right to a jury would have an adverse impact on any unique benefits of the juvenile court, the Court asked whether the right to a jury trial would positively aid or strengthen the functioning of the juvenile justice system. Although the *McKeiver* Court found faults with the juvenile process, it asserted that imposing jury trials would not correct those deficiencies and could make the juvenile process unduly formal and adversarial. The Court did not consider, however, whether there might be any offsetting advantages to increased formality in juvenile proceedings or to what extent its earlier decision in *Gault* had effectively foreclosed its renewed concern with flexibility and informality at the trial stage. Although the Court decried the possibility of a public trial, it presented neither evidence nor arguments to support its conclusion that publicity would be undesirable and that confidentiality was an indispensable element of the juvenile justice process.

The Supreme Court's decisions in *Gault*, *Winship*, and *McKeiver* precipitated a procedural revolution in the juvenile court system that unintentionally but inevitably transformed its original Progressive conception. For Progressive reformers, proof that the youth committed an offense was essentially secondary to a determination of the "real needs" of a child—the child's social circumstances and environment. Intervention was premised on the need for rehabilitation and social uplift, not on the commission of an offense. Although *McKeiver* refused to extend the right to a jury trial to juveniles, *Gault* and *Winship* imported the adversarial model, the privilege against self-incrimination, the right to an attorney, the criminal standard of proof, and the primacy of factual and legal guilt as a constitutional prerequisite to intervention. By emphasizing criminal procedural regularity in the determination of delinquency, the Supreme Court shifted the focus of the juvenile court from the Progressive emphasis on the "real needs" of the child to proof of the commission of criminal acts, thereby effectively transforming juvenile proceedings into criminal prosecutions.

## THE RIGHT TO COUNSEL IN JUVENILE COURT

The *Gault* Court based its decision to grant juveniles the right to counsel on the Fourteenth Amendment's due process clause, rather than the Sixth Amendment, asserting that as a matter of due process "the assistance of counsel is . . . essential for the determination of delinquency, carrying with it the awesome prospect of incarceration in a state institution" (387

U.S. at 36–37). The *Gault* Court's holding was strongly influenced by the recommendations of the President's Commission on Law Enforcement and the Administration of Justice (1967a, 1967b) that in order to assure procedural justice, the appointment of counsel is necessary "whenever coercive action is a possibility, without requiring any affirmative choice by child or parent." The Court quoted extensively from the commission's report:

> [N]o single action holds more potential for achieving procedural justice for the child in the juvenile court than provision of counsel. The presence of an independent legal representative of the child, or of his parent, is the keystone of the whole structure of guarantees that a minimum system of procedural justice requires. The rights to confront one's accusers, to cross-examine witnesses, to present evidence and testimony of one's own, to be unaffected by prejudicial and unreliable evidence, to participate meaningfully in the dispositional decision, to take an appeal have substantial meaning for the overwhelming majority of persons brought before the juvenile court only if they are provided with competent lawyers who can invoke those rights effectively. (*Gault*, 387 U.S. at 38, n. 65).

While *Gault* recognized that the presence of lawyers would make juvenile court proceedings more formal and adversarial, it asserted that their presence would impart "a healthy atmosphere of accountability" and that this was desirable, since "informality is often abused" (387 U.S. at 38). The President's Commission recommended the automatic appointment of counsel whenever coercive action by the juvenile court was possible. However, *Gault*'s actual holding was narrower and required only that "the child and his parents must be notified of the child's right to be represented by counsel retained by them, or if they are unable to afford counsel, that counsel will be appointed to represent the child" (387 U.S. at 41).

In granting the right to counsel, *Gault* manifested the Warren Court's belief that the adversary process could protect constitutional rights and limit the coercive powers of the state. The availability of counsel, in turn, would assure the regularity of law enforcement and reduce the need for continual judicial scrutiny (Allen 1975). Thus, *Gault* was simply another instance of the Warren Court's general broadening of the right to counsel to preserve individual liberty and autonomy.

The *Gault* Court quoted favorably from its 1932 decision in *Powell v. Alabama* (287 U.S. 45 [1932]), the first decision to hold that the Fourteenth Amendment's due process clause required the appointment of counsel in some state criminal proceedings. In a number of subsequent decisions, the Court elaborated on the "special circumstances" of a particular case that required the appointment of counsel (*Betts v. Brady*, 316 U.S. 455 [1942]; *Chewning v. Cunningham*, 368 U.S. 443 [1962]). Finally, in *Gideon v. Wainwright* (372 U.S. 335 [1963]), the Warren Court held that the Sixth Amendment's guarantee of counsel applied to state felony criminal proceedings as well as to prosecutions in federal courts. "[I]n our adversary system of criminal justice, any person haled into court, who is too poor to hire a lawyer, cannot be assured a fair trial unless counsel is provided for him" (372 U.S. at 342).

In *Argersinger v. Hamlin* (407 U.S. 25 [1972]), the Court considered whether an indigent defendant who was charged with and imprisoned for a minor offense was entitled to the appointment of counsel. In *Argersinger*, the Court held that "absent a knowing and intelligent waiver, no person may be imprisoned for any offense, whether classified as petty, misdemeanor or felony unless he was represented by counsel" (407 U.S. at 37 [1979]). Because Argersinger was actually imprisoned, it was unclear whether the line the Court drew for the right to appointed counsel was based on the type of charge—felony or misdemeanor—and the penalty *authorized* or on the *actual sentence* imposed. In *Scott v. Illinois* (440 U.S. 367 [1979]), the Court clarified any ambiguity when it held that in misdemeanor proceedings, the sentence the trial judge actually imposed (i.e., whether incarceration was ordered) rather than the one authorized by the statute, determined whether counsel must be appointed for the indigent. Basing the initial decision to appoint counsel on the eventual sentence, however, posed severe administrative problems. How could a judge decide what the eventual sentence likely would be without prejudging the defendant or prejudicing his right to a fair and impartial trial?

In *State v. Borst* (278 Minn. 388, 154 N.W.2d 888 [Minn. 1967]), the Minnesota Supreme Court, using its inherent supervisory powers, anticipated the United States Supreme Court's *Argersinger* and *Scott* decisions, and shortly after *Gideon* required the appointment of counsel even in misdemeanor cases "*which may lead to incarceration* in a penal institution" (*Borst*, 278 Minn. at 397, 154 N.W.2d at 894). The *Borst* Court relied, in part, upon *Gault*'s ruling on the need for counsel in delinquency cases to expand the scope of the right to counsel for adult defendants in any misdemeanor or ordinance prosecutions that could result in confinement. Like the Court in *Gault*, *Borst* recognized the adversarial reality of even "minor" prosecutions.

> [T]he possible loss of liberty by an innocent person charged with a misdemeanor, who does not know how to defend himself, is too sacred a right to be sacrificed on the altar of expedience. Any society that can afford a professional prosecutor to prosecute this type of

> crime must assume the burden of providing adequate defense, to the end that innocent people will not be convicted without having facilities available to properly present a defense. (278 Minn. at 397, 154 N.W.2d at 895)

*Scott* addressed the scope of the Sixth Amendment's right to counsel in minor cases in state proceedings. Since *Gault* decided the question of a juvenile's right to counsel under the Fourteenth Amendment's due process clause rather than the Sixth Amendment, the constitutional argument remains that "special circumstances" require the appointment of counsel even in minor nonincarceration cases where a juvenile may be unable to prepare an adequate defense because of the inherent disabilities of youth, substandard intelligence, or the complexities of the particular case.

## IMPLEMENTATION OF *GAULT*'S RIGHT TO COUNSEL IN STATE DELINQUENCY PROCEEDINGS

When *Gault* was decided, the presence of an attorney in delinquency proceedings was a rare event. By one estimate, attorneys appeared for juveniles in fewer than 5% of the cases (Note 1966:796–99). In the immediate aftermath of *Gault*, states that had not previously provided for counsel in juvenile court amended their statutes to do so. Despite the formal legal changes, however, the actual delivery of legal services to juveniles lagged behind. Lefstein, Stapleton, and Teitelbaum (1969) examined institutional compliance with the *Gault* decision and found that many juveniles were neither adequately advised of their right to counsel nor had counsel been appointed for them. Ferster and Courtless's (1972) analysis of court records showed that 27% of juveniles were represented, that observations of 64 hearings included 37.5% in which juveniles had counsel at the adjudicatory stage, and that in 66.7% of those cases in which lawyers were present, they did not participate in any way. Sarri and Hasenfeld's (1976:136) nationwide survey "revealed an astonishing disregard for due process by judges and very little activity by attorneys." In their national sample of 234 courts, only "17% employed lawyers full time and 11% employed them part time," and, in most instances, the lawyers were evaluated as having no influence whatever in the adjudicatory process (Sarri and Hasenfeld 1976:138).

In a more recent evaluation of legal representation, Clarke and Koch (1980) found that in North Carolina the juvenile defender project represented only 22.3% of juveniles in Winston-Salem, and only 45.8% in Charlotte. Aday (1986) found rates of representation of 26.2% and

38.7% in the jurisdictions he studied. Walter and Ostrander (1982) observed that only 32% of the juveniles in a large north-central city were represented by counsel. Bortner's (1982:139) evaluation of a large, midwestern county's juvenile court showed that "over half (58.2 percent) [the juveniles] were not represented by an attorney." Evaluations of rates of representation in Minnesota also indicate that a majority of youths are unrepresented (Feld 1984; Fine 1983). Feld reported enormous county-by-county variations within Minnesota in rates of representation, ranging from a high of over 90% to a low of less than 10% (Feld 1984, 1989). Nearly one-third of all youths removed from their homes and more than one-quarter of those confined in state juvenile correctional institutions lacked representation at the time of their adjudication and disposition (Feld 1989). Significant numbers of unrepresented juveniles continue to be incarcerated in other jurisdictions as well (Feld 1988a). A recent study in Missouri reported virtually identical findings: only 39.6% of urban youths and 5.3% of rural juveniles were represented, there were substantial disparities in rates of representation in different judicial circuits, and a substantial minority of all the youths who were removed from their homes were unrepresented (Kempf, Decker, and Bing 1990).

There are a variety of possible explanations for why so many youths are still unrepresented. Parents may be reluctant to retain an attorney or accept the appointment of a public defender for their child. If parents can afford to retain counsel but do not do so and counsel is appointed for the child at public expense, the county may seek reimbursement for the expenses and attorney's fees expended on behalf of the child (Minn. Stat. Ann. § 260.251, subd. 4 [1984]). In some cases, counties have sought reimbursement of thousands of dollars (*In re M.S.M.*, 387 N.W.2d 194, 200 [Minn. 1986]). As will be seen, public defender legal services are inadequate or nonexistent in nonurban areas (Kempf, Decker, and Bing 1990; Flicker 1977). Some judges may encourage and readily find a waiver of the right to counsel in order to ease the administrative burdens on the courts. In doing so, judges may give cursory and misleading advisories of rights that inadequately convey the importance of the right to counsel and suggest that the waiver litany is simply a meaningless technicality. For example, Sarri and Hasenfeld (1976:136) directly observed that "several judges gave such little attention to these memorized recitals of rights that they forgot where they were and had to start over."

Despite *Gault*, a continuing judicial hostility to an advocacy role in traditional treatment-oriented courts persists. For example, in *In re M.R.S.* (400 N.W.2d 147 at 152 [Minn. Ct. App., 1987]), the Court of Appeals reversed the trial court's summary dismissal of a juvenile's court appointed attorney for appealing its decision, noting that

[t]his kind of arbitrary action can have no other but a chilling effect on conscientious advocacy. To discharge an attorney without just cause simply because he or she challenges the court by seeking a writ of prohibition or appeal is manifestly improper.

Stapleton and Teitelbaum (1972:59–60) described the problem of integrating counsel into traditional juvenile court settings:

Empirical studies show what is to be expected—traditional courts and personnel are reluctant to adapt themselves to the new procedures now required by the due process clause, particularly as they require injection of elements of an adversary system into juvenile court proceedings. This, taken with the increasing appearance of counsel in juvenile court proceedings, undoubtedly will have consequences for the manner of legal representation. An attorney in traditional courts will find himself within a legal system which still considers itself non-adversary and seeks to serve goals not usually associated with other branches of law. It is only reasonable to anticipate that he will face formal and informal pressures to conform his manner of participation in delinquency hearings to the values of these courts—for example, to be less of an advocate for the child's best interests.

Finally, judges may decide not to appoint counsel if they predetermine that a sentence of probation or nonincarceration is the anticipated outcome (Lefstein, Stapleton, and Teitelbaum 1969; Bortner 1982). Whatever the reasons and despite *Gault*'s promise of counsel, many juveniles facing potentially coercive state action never see a lawyer, waive their right to counsel without consulting with an attorney or appreciating the legal consequences of relinquishing counsel, and face the prosecutorial power of the state alone and unaided.

The most common explanation for nonrepresentation is waiver of counsel. In most jurisdictions, including Minnesota, the validity of relinquishing a constitutional right is determined by using the *adult* legal standard to assess whether there was a "knowing, intelligent, and voluntary waiver" under the "totality of the circumstances" (*Johnson v. Zerbst*, 304 U.S. 458 [1938]; *Fare v. Michael C.*, 442 U.S. 707 [1979]; *State v. Nunn*, 297 N.W.2d 752 [Minn. 1980]; Feld 1984). While the United States Supreme Court has never ruled on the validity of a minor's waiver of the right to counsel in delinquency proceedings as such, it has upheld a minor's waiver of the *Miranda* right to counsel at the pretrial investigative stage under the "totality of the circumstances" (*Fare v. Michael C.*, 442 U.S. 707 [1979]). In *Fare*, the Court retreated from its earlier solicitude for youthfulness as a special circumstance at interrogation, at least when the defendant was a 16-year-old with experience with the police and who had "served time" in a youth camp (442 U.S. at 726–27). *Fare* reaffirmed that the adult "totality of the circumstances" test was the appropriate standard for evaluating the validity of waivers of rights and the admissibility of juvenile confessions. In so holding, *Fare* "represents a repudiation of the view that adult and child are members of binary, dichotomous categories whose inherently differing cognitive capacities justify separate waiver rules" (Ainsworth 1991:1116). To the contrary, cases like *Fare* represent a juridical erosion of the Progressives' assumption that children were different from and should be treated differently than adults.

The judicial position that a young minor can "knowingly and intelligently" waive constitutional rights is consistent with the Minnesota legislature's judgment that a youth can make an informed waiver decision without parental concurrence or consultation with an attorney. Minnesota's juvenile code provides that "waiver of any right . . . must be an express waiver intelligently made by the child after the child has been fully and effectively informed of the right being waived" (Minn. Stat. Ann. § 260.155(8) [1982]).

The right to waive counsel and appear as a *pro se* defendant follows from the United States Supreme Court's decisions in *Johnson v. Zerbst* (304 U.S. 458 [1938]) and *Faretta v. California* (422 U.S. 806 [1975]). In *Faretta*, the Court held that an adult defendant in a state criminal trial had a constitutional right to proceed without counsel when he or she voluntarily and intelligently elects to do so. The *Faretta* Court emphasized that the Sixth Amendment guarantees defendants the "assistance of counsel."

> It speaks of the "assistance" of counsel, and an assistant, however expert, is still an assistant. The language and spirit of the Sixth Amendment contemplate that counsel, like the other defense tools guaranteed by the Amendment, shall be an aid to a willing defendant—not an organ of the State interposed between an unwilling defendant and his right to defend himself personally. (422 U.S. at 820)

While recognizing an adult defendant's *Faretta* right to waive counsel and proceed *pro se*, the Minnesota Supreme Court has strongly encouraged trial courts to appoint standby counsel to assist an adult defendant at trial and temporary counsel to consult with an adult defendant prior to the entry of a guilty plea. In *State v. Rubin* (409 N.W.2d at 506 [Minn. 1987]), the supreme court ruled that "a trial court may not accept a guilty plea to a felony or gross misdemeanor charge made by an unrepresented defendant if the defendant has not consulted with counsel about waiving counsel and pleading guilty." Similarly, in *Burt v. State* (256 N.W.2d 633 [Minn. 1977]), the supreme court emphasized that "one way for a trial court to help ensure that a defendant's waiver of counsel is knowing and intelligent would be to provide a lawyer to consult with the defendant concerning his proposed waiver." In *Rubin*, the supreme court described the type of "penetrating and comprehensive examination" that must precede a "knowing and intelligent" waiver and strongly recommended the appointment of counsel "to advise and consult with the defendant as to the waiver" (409 N.W.2d at 506 [Minn. 1987]). In several earlier adult waiver cases, the Minnesota Supreme Court reversed defendants' convictions where their mental competency, youthfulness, or below average intelligence raised an issue about their capacity to knowingly and intelligently relinquish the assistance of counsel (*State v. Bauer*, 245 N.W.2d 848 [Minn. 1976]; *Burt v. State*, 256 N.W.2d 633 [Minn. 1977]).

The crucial issue for juveniles, as for adults, is whether such a waiver can occur "voluntarily and intelligently," particularly without prior consultation with counsel. The problem is particularly acute when the judges giving the judicial advisories seek a predetermined result—the waiver of counsel—which influences both the information they convey and their interpretation of the juvenile's response. As the Rhode Island Supreme Court noted in *In re John D.* (479 A.2d 1173 at 1178 [R.I. 1984]), "exceptional efforts must be made in order to be certain that an uncounselled juvenile fully understands the nature and consequences of his admission of delinquency."

The "totality" approach to waiver of rights by juveniles has been criticized extensively (Feld 1984; Grisso 1980, 1981). Empirical research suggests that juveniles simply are not as competent as adults to waive their rights in a "knowing and intelligent" manner (Grisso 1980, 1981; Lawrence 1983). Grisso (1980:1160) reports that the problems of understanding and waiving rights were particularly acute for younger juveniles:

> As a class, juveniles younger than fifteen years of age failed to meet both the absolute and relative (adult norm) standards for comprehension. . . . The vast majority of these juveniles misunderstood at least one of the four standard *Miranda* statements, and compared with adults, demonstrated significantly poorer comprehension of the nature and significance of the *Miranda* rights.

Grisso also reported that although "juveniles younger than fifteen manifest significantly poorer comprehension than adults of comparable intelligence," the level of comprehension exhibited by youths sixteen and older, although comparable to that of adults, was inadequate (Grisso 1980:1157). While several jurisdictions recognize this "developmental fact" and prohibit uncounseled waivers of the right to counsel or incarceration of unrepresented delinquents (Iowa Code Ann. § 232.11 [West Supp. 1985]; Wis. Stat. Ann. § 48.23 [West 1983]), the majority of states, including Minnesota, allow juveniles to waive their *Miranda* rights as well as their right to counsel in delinquency proceedings without an attorney's assistance.

## INCARCERATION WITHOUT REPRESENTATION

The questionable validity of many juveniles' waivers of the right to counsel raises collateral legal issues as well. In light of *Scott, Borst, Burt*, and *Rubin*, the initial confinement of an unrepresented juvenile may be improper. Under the Minnesota cases of *Borst* (154 N.W.2d 888 [1967]) and *Illingworth* (154 N.W.2d 687 [1967]), if the punishment is likely to be incarceration, then counsel must be provided to an indigent. Moreover, in Minnesota, there are no limitations on the dispositional authority of juvenile court judges. Any adjudication of delinquency for any underlying offense — felony, misdemeanor, or ordinance violation — may lead to removal from the home or confinement in the state Department of Corrections. Any delinquency dispositions may continue until the age of nineteen (Minn. Stat. Ann. § 260.181(4) [Supp. 1983]). Thus, every juvenile proceeding is potentially of considerable consequence.

## ENHANCEMENT OF SENTENCES BASED ON PRIOR UNCOUNSELED CONVICTIONS

It is also improper to consider prior uncounseled convictions for purposes of enhancing subsequent sentences. In *Baldasar v. Illinois* (446 U.S. 222 [1980]), the defendant's enhanced penalty was based upon a prior uncounseled misdemeanor conviction that had not resulted in incarceration. When Baldasar was convicted a second time for a similar offense, under the enhanced penalty statute, the prior conviction was used to convert the second conviction into a felony for which the defendant was imprisoned. In a *per curiam* opinion, the Supreme Court reversed Baldasar's felony conviction. Justice Stewart condemned the increased penalty, noting that the defendant "was sentenced to an increased term of imprisonment *only* because he had been convicted in a previous prosecution in which he had *not* had the assistance of appointed counsel in his defense" (446 U.S. at 224). Justice Marshall stated that a defendant's "prior uncounselled misdemeanor conviction could not be used collaterally to impose an increased term of imprisonment upon a subsequent conviction" (446 U.S. at 227).

*Baldasar* is consistent with earlier cases that held that an uncounseled felony conviction could not be used in a later trial to enhance punishments under recidivist statutes. In *United States v. Tucker* (404 U.S. 443 [1972]), the Supreme Court remanded for resentencing a defendant whose prior sentence was based upon uncounseled convictions. "The *Gideon* case established an unequivocal rule 'making it unconstitutional to try a person for a felony in a state court unless he had a lawyer or had validly waived one'" (404 U.S. at 448). In *Burgett v. Texas* (389 U.S. 109 [1967]), the Court noted that because it was unconstitutional to convict a person for a felony without benefit of a lawyer or the valid waiver of that right,

> [t]o permit a conviction obtained in violation of *Gideon v. Wainwright* to be used against a person either to support guilt or enhance punishment for another offense . . . is to erode the principle of that case. Worse yet, since the defect in the prior conviction was denial of the right to counsel, the accused in effect suffers anew from the deprivation of that Sixth Amendment right. (389 U.S. at 115)

Thus, unless there is a valid waiver of the right to counsel on the record when a guilty plea is entered, the conviction may not be used to enhance the term of incarceration for a subsequent offense (*Reeves v. Mabry*, 615 F.2d 489 [8th Cir. 1980]; *United States ex rel. Lasky v. LaVallee*, 472 F.2d 960 [2d Cir. 1973]).

The principle of *Baldasar, Tucker,* and *Burgett* that prior convictions obtained without representation by counsel or a valid waiver should not be used to enhance subsequent sentences has been applied in several sentencing contexts involving uncounseled juvenile convictions. In *Stockwell v. State* (207 N.W.2d 883 [Wisc. 1973]), the Wisconsin Supreme Court applied *Tucker* to *Gault* and held that juvenile adjudications in which the juvenile was denied the right to counsel could not be considered in subsequent sentencing proceedings. Similarly, in *Majchszak v. Ralston* (454 F. Supp. 1137 [1978]), where the defendant was denied parole release based on a salient factor score that included prior uncounseled delinquency adjudications, the court remanded for resentencing. In *Commonwealth v. Bivens* (486 A.2d 984 [Pa. 1985]), the court reversed the defendant's sentence when the sentencing judge used juvenile convictions obtained without the assistance of counsel in computing his adult criminal history score. And, in *Rizzo v. United States* (821 F.2d 1271 [7th Cir.

1987]), the court remanded for resentencing an adult defendant whose sentence was based, at least in part, on prior uncounseled juvenile adjudications.

Both the Federal and Minnesota Adult Sentencing Guidelines include prior juvenile felony convictions in the calculation of a defendant's current sentence (Minnesota Sentencing 1980). The courts have approved the use of convictions obtained in juvenile courts to enhance a subsequent sentence of an adult criminal defendant (*State v. Little*, 423 N.W.2d 722 [Minn. Ct. App., 1988]). In *State v. Nordstrom* (331 N.W.2d 90 [Minn. 1983]), the Minnesota Supreme Court held that a prior misdemeanor conviction based on an uncounseled guilty plea could not be used to convert a subsequent offense into a gross misdemeanor absent a valid waiver of counsel on the record at the prior proceeding. Similarly, in *State v. Edmison* (379 N.W.2d 85 [Minn. 1985]), the Minnesota Supreme Court based its decision on *Baldasar* and *Tucker*, and held that a sentencing court may not use a defendant's prior misdemeanor convictions to determine the presumptive sentence under the Guidelines unless the state proved that the prior conviction was obtained with the assistance of counsel or a valid waiver of the right. Thus, whether a juvenile's prior convictions were obtained without the assistance of counsel or a valid waiver remains an issue in the context of subsequent sentences.

While juvenile court judges in most states neither follow formal sentencing guidelines nor numerically weight a youth's prior record (Feld 1988b), their use of prior uncounseled adjudications in sentencing juveniles upon a subsequent conviction implicates the same issues that *Baldasar* and *Edmison* condemned for adults. "It makes little difference whether an enhanced penalty provision mandates an increased term of imprisonment or whether a judge imposed it exercising his sentencing discretion. As long as the prior uncounselled conviction leads to the increased incarceration, the defendant is being deprived of his liberty because of that conviction" (Rudstein 1982:536). Indeed, because of juvenile court judges' virtually unrestricted sentencing discretion, the *Baldasar* issues are especially problematic in the sentencing of juveniles. If a juvenile who is convicted without counsel and placed on probation is subsequently adjudicated delinquent for a new offense and committed to an institution, is the latter sentence "enhanced" based on the prior, uncounseled conviction, or does it simply reflect the judge's assessment of the juvenile's "treatment needs" as reflected in the subsequent delinquency?

The Minnesota Supreme Court affords adult defendants a right to counsel even for minor offenses that may lead to incarceration. Every delinquency proceeding in Minnesota carries with it the possibility of removal from the child's home or incarceration (Minn. Stat. Ann. § 260.185, subd. 1(c),(d) [1982]). Moreover, the Minnesota Supreme Court has urged extreme caution in recognizing the validity of waivers of counsel by young, inexperienced, or impressionable defendants, with obvious implications for the capacity of juveniles to waive their rights. Finally, the court has held that prior uncounseled convictions may not be used to enhance subsequent sentences unless there was a valid waiver of counsel at the earlier proceeding. Chapter Four analyzes empirically the availability of counsel and sentencing practices in delinquency proceedings, and explores the extent to which these well-established legal principles for adults are implemented in juvenile courts.

Even when juveniles are represented, attorneys may not be capable of or committed to representing their juvenile clients in an effective adversarial manner. Institutional pressures to maintain stable, cooperative working relations with other personnel in the system may be inconsistent with effective adversarial advocacy. These constraints may include organizational pressures to cooperate, judicial hostility toward adversarial litigants, role ambiguity created by the dual goals of rehabilitation and punishment, reluctance to help juveniles "beat a case," or an internalization of a court's treatment philosophy which may compromise the role of counsel in juvenile court (Duffee and Siegel 1971; Platt and Friedman 1968; Platt, Schechter, and Tiffany 1968; Stapleton and Teitelbaum 1972; Lefstein, Stapleton, and Teitelbaum 1969; Ferster, Courtless, and Snethen, 1971; Kay and Segal 1973; McMillian and McMurtry, 1970; Bortner 1982; Clarke and Koch 1980; Knitzer and Sobie 1984; Blumberg 1967).

Several studies have questioned whether lawyers can actually perform as advocates in a system rooted in parens patriae and benevolent rehabilitation (Stapleton and Teitelbaum 1972; Fox 1970a; Kay and Segal 1973). One study observed and interviewed juvenile justice personnel in several jurisdictions and reported that

> an overzealous defense attorney may produce an adverse reaction in the court. Even judges who are not actually hostile to the presence of an attorney may expect him to assume a different role in the juvenile court from the one he would have in criminal court. He is not to utilize "technical objections" to obtain a finding of no delinquency. Rather he is to act as the servant of the court in the process of ascertaining the truth—a function that seems to entail actively encouraging his client to confess. (Note 1966:797)

Indeed, there are some indications that lawyers representing juveniles in more traditional "therapeutic" juvenile courts may actually disadvantage their clients in adjudications or dispositions (Stapleton and Teitelbaum 1972; Clarke and Koch 1980; Bortner 1982). One observer concluded that "in an informal court in which an aggressive adversary attitude may well hurt his client's interests, an attorney should probably conform to the reigning conventions as much as possible; he might be wise to insist on a strict adherence to the rules of evidence only in those particular instances when their relaxation would be clearly detrimental to his client" (Note 1966:798). Duffee and Siegel (1971), Clarke and Koch (1980), Stapleton and Teitelbaum (1972), Hayeslip (1979), and Bortner (1982), all reported that juveniles with counsel are more likely to be incarcerated than juveniles without counsel. Bortner (1982:139–40), for example, found that

> [w]hen the possibility of receiving the most severe dispositions (place-ment outside the home in either group homes or institutions) is ex-amined, those juveniles who were represented by attorneys were more likely to receive these dispositions than were juveniles not rep-resented (35.8 percent compared to 9.6 percent). Further statistical analysis reveals that, regardless of the types of offenses with which they were charged, juveniles represented by attorneys receive more severe dispositions.

Research on legal representation in Canadian juvenile courts also reports a negative impact of counsel on juveniles' sentencing in some settings (Carrington and Moyer, 1988a, 1988b).

Chapters Three and Four provide opportunities to examine the cir-cumstances under which attorneys are appointed and the consequences of representation for processing and disposing of cases in different types of juvenile courts. In Chapter Three, the determinants and impact of counsel are examined in a six-state comparison. In Chapter Four, the determinants and impact of counsel are examined in one state, Minne-sota, by analyzing juvenile justice administration in counties with high, medium, and low rates of representation.

## VARIETIES OF JUVENILE JUSTICE

With *Gault*'s imposition of procedural formality and the emergence of punitive as well as therapeutic goals (Feld 1984, 1988b), a state's juvenile courts can no longer be assumed to conform with the traditional, reha-bilitative model or even to be similar to one another. Intensive ethno-graphic studies that focus on a single juvenile court cannot be generalized to other courts in other settings (Bortner 1982; Cicourel 1968; Emerson

1969). Indeed, most juvenile court ethnographies do not provide enough information about a court's legal orientation or social or political context to explain its behavior. The few comparative studies of juvenile courts reveal some of the complexities of goals, philosophies, court structures, and procedures that characterize the juvenile court as an institution (Cohen and Kluegel 1978, 1979; Sarri and Hasenfeld 1976).

Recent comparative research indicates that juvenile courts are variable organizations that differ on a number of structural and procedural dimensions such as status offender orientation, centralization of authority, formalization of procedure, and intake screening discretion (Stapleton, Aday, and Ito 1982; Hasenfeld and Cheung 1985). Contrasting traditional therapeutic courts with those holding a more legalistic, due process orientation captures many of the major variations in juvenile justice administration (Sarri and Hasenfeld 1976). "[T]he empirical typology of metropolitan juvenile courts reflects the existence of the two major types of juvenile courts ('traditional' and 'due process') suggested in the literature. More important, however, it reveals variations in court structure and procedure that are not captured adequately by existing simplistic typologies" (Stapleton, Aday, and Ito 1982:559). Traditional courts emphasize intervening in a child's "best interests" on an informal, discretionary basis, while the legalistic courts emphasize more formal, rule-oriented decision making and protection of a juvenile's legal rights. "Traditional" and "due process" courts may be arrayed across a continuum from informal to formal with corresponding procedural and structural differences. "At one extreme lies the system best described by the concept of *parens patriae*, with an emphasis on 'helping' the child, intervening in his or her best interest. At the other lies the more formal, legalistic system, with a due process model of restricted information flow and precise rules of adjudication" (Stapleton, Aday, and Ito 1982:550).

The presence of an attorney is one important indicator of procedural and structural variations among juvenile courts. Traditional therapeutic and formal due process courts will differ considerably in the presence of counsel (Handler 1965; Cohen and Kluegel 1978; Stapleton and Teitelbaum 1972; Feld 1984; Sarri and Hasenfeld 1976). Whether or not attorneys are present routinely, in turn, affects every other aspect of juvenile justice administration. Recent studies of the impact of counsel in juvenile courts indicate that the presence of counsel, which is associated with a formal, due process orientation, is also related to differences in pretrial detention, sentencing, and case-processing practices (Cohen and Kluegel 1978; Carrington and Moyer 1988a, 1988b; Kempf, Decker, and Bing 1990). One goal of this study is to account for variations in rates of representation in different juvenile courts by exploring the social and legal variables that influence the procedural and substantive orientation of a court. Recognizing that states' juvenile courts are not a single, uniform justice system vastly complicates research that must identify and account for these systemic differences as well.

While the presence or absence of defense attorneys is associated with differences in juvenile justice administration, what accounts for these systemic differences? Despite their procedural and philosophical differences, courts within a state typically operate under laws and rules of procedure of general applicability. What external political, social structural, and legal variables influence the procedural and substantive orientations of these courts? What are the comparative costs and benefits of formal versus informal dispute resolution? How do different juvenile courts administer justice and intervene in the lives of young people?

Although the same statutes and court rules of procedure typically apply to all juvenile courts within a state, there is substantial geographic variation in juvenile justice administration (Feld 1991; Mahoney 1987; Kempf, Decker, and Bing 1990). For example, whether youths live in metropolitan areas with full-time juvenile courts or in rural areas with part-time juvenile judges affects how their cases are processed and the sentences they receive (Kempf, Decker, and Bing 1990). The geographic and structural influences on formal versus informal means of control result in differences in the selection of delinquents and in the administration of justice. For example, attorneys appear much more frequently in urban courts and a more formal, due process model of justice obtains, whereas rural juvenile courts adhere to a more traditional, informal model of justice (Feld 1991; Kempf, Decker, and Bing 1990). In turn, the bases of decisions in the various settings differ. In the traditional juvenile court, decisions are

> guided by reference to a substantive goal or by the best decision in the individual case [i.e. "the child's best interests"], not by the application of abstract rules. The ideal in the juvenile court has been one of "individualized" justice whereby each offender should be treated as unique and as deserving such treatment. The framework of relevant criteria of decision-making is far broader than only the "legal" factors relevant in adult courts, and encompasses a variety of social background variables that are indicative of the offender's personal, home, and community situations. (Horowitz and Wasserman 1980:417)

There also appears to be a relationship between social structure, procedural formality, and severity of sanctions. The more formal, urban courts held larger proportions of youths in pretrial detention and sentenced similarly charged offenders more severely than did the suburban or rural courts (Feld 1991; Kempf, Decker, and Bing 1990). Chapter Six examines the relationships between social structure, procedural formality, and juvenile justice administration.

Chapter Eight concludes with a consideration of the policy implications of delivery of legal services, procedural formality, and justice by geography for justice administration and juvenile court reform. At a practical level, the analyses focus on the types of legislative and judicial reforms that are necessary to successfully transform the juvenile court into a legal institution rather than a social welfare agency. At a more theoretical level, however, Chapter Nine questions whether it is either possible or even desirable to reform the juvenile court within its present institutional setting. Despite decades of statutory and judicial reforms and an empirical record of proven failure, the ideologies of childhood and therapeutic justice persist tenaciously and may constitute an insuperable barrier to the court's "constitutional domestication."

# chapter two

# DATA AND METHODOLOGY

There have been remarkably few studies of the delivery of legal services in juvenile courts and even fewer that examine the presence or role of attorneys in more than one courtroom or county. Almost all of the comparative studies of juvenile justice administration were conducted in the aftermath of *Gault* (Chused 1973; Stapleton and Teitelbaum 1972). Prior to this research, the most recent comparative study of lawyers in juvenile courts compared two North Carolina counties in 1975–76 (Clarke and Koch 1980).

This study reports the first and only comparative analyses of variations in rates of representation for entire states, as well as for subsets within one state, Minnesota. Chapter Three examines variations in the implementation of the right to counsel in six states—California, Minnesota, New York, Nebraska, North Dakota, and Pennsylvania. Chapter Four examines variations in juvenile justice administration in Minnesota by analyzing data for the entire state and for counties aggregated on the basis of high, medium, and low rates of representation. Chapter Six examines variations in juvenile justice administration in Minnesota by analyzing data for the entire state and for counties aggregated on the basis of their urban, suburban, and rural social structural characteristics. These strategies—analyzing general variations in juvenile justice administration in six states and in depth within one state—provide the basis for a comparative examination of the circumstances under which lawyers are appointed to represent juveniles, the case characteristics and social structural variables associated with rates of representation, and the effects of representation on case processing and dispositions.

## CREATING A FORMAL JUVENILE COURT FILE

Typically, juvenile delinquency cases begin with a juvenile's referral by police, parents, probation officers, or school officials to either the county prosecuting attorney, a county's juvenile court, or the court's juvenile probation or intake department. These "gatekeepers" screen cases on a discretionary basis for legal sufficiency or social welfare needs to determine whether formal juvenile court intervention is appropriate. Many of these referrals are closed by the social services staff at intake with some type of *informal* disposition—dismissal, counseling, warning, referral to another agency, or informal probation—that does not result in the filing of a petition. In the remaining cases, a petition—the formal initiation of the juvenile process—is filed by the county attorney.

Informal screening and formal charging practices vary considerably among states and even among counties within a state. Between 1957 and 1982, for example, approximately half of all delinquency referrals nationwide were handled by formal petition, ranging from a high of 54% in some years to a low of 41% in others (Nimick et al. 1985a:12) In 1988, 48% of all delinquency referrals and 22% of all status referrals resulted in the filing of a formal petition (Snyder et al. 1990:14, 99). In four of the states examined in Chapter Three, the proportion of referrals resulting in petitions ranges from 10.7% to 62.8% (Table 3-1).

A petition is the formal charging document in juvenile courts and is comparable legally to the prosecutor's issuance of a complaint or a grand jury's indictment in the adult criminal process (Feld 1984; Sonsteng and Scott 1985). The relationship between a juvenile court intake staff's screening functions and a county attorney's charging practices vary from county to county and state to state. While the county attorney has the ultimate authority to file formal delinquency petitions (*In re Maricopa County, Juvenile Action*, 594 P.2d 506 [Ariz. Sup. Ct. 1979]), in those states and counties with juvenile court intake units, informal arrangements between prosecutors and social services personnel or administrative guidelines may govern the screening of cases, with minor offenses typically routed initially through intake. Since different court intake or probation staff as well as county attorneys use different criteria to decide whether or not to file a formal delinquency or status petition, the selection of delinquent populations may vary considerably in different counties. The common denominator of all the cases in this study is that formal charges were filed in their respective counties.

A juvenile offender will be arraigned on the petition. The constitutional right to counsel announced in *Gault* attaches only at the filing of the petition and this is the practice in most states as well. The Minnesota Supreme Court in *In re M.A.* (310 N.W.2d 699 at 701 [Minn. 1981]), for example, ruled that "the right to counsel attaches at the time the formal petition is filed. At this point, there is a definite commencement of the adversary proceedings." If counsel is appointed at all to represent a juvenile, it typically occurs at the arraignment. At the arraignment, the juvenile may admit or deny the allegations in the petition. In many cases, juveniles may waive their right to counsel at the arraignment, admit the allegations of the petition, and their cases are disposed of without the assistance of an attorney. In other cases, a public defender or court-appointed lawyer may be appointed at the arraignment who confers briefly with the juvenile before admitting or denying the allegations. In rare instances, a private attorney retained by the child's family may appear to represent the juvenile. In the very small fraction of cases that actually result in formal, contested hearings, counsel may be present more often. Following an adjudication for a delinquency or status offense, a juvenile may have her case disposed, that is, sentenced. Routine sentencing may occur either immediately after adjudication or following one or two weeks' delay during which time a social worker prepares a social report evaluating the youth's treatment needs.

This study entails a secondary analysis of data originally collected and stored at the National Juvenile Court Data Archive (NJCDA). Many state juvenile court systems maintain automated reporting or case management information systems. The validity of the data is high because the data sets were developed originally for information systems designed by state and local juvenile courts to meet their own administrative, courtroom calendar, and planning and evaluation needs.

Beginning in 1978, the National Center for Juvenile Justice (NCJJ), the research division of the National Council of Juvenile and Family Court Judges, obtained support from the Office of Juvenile Justice and Delinquency Prevention, U.S. Department of Justice, to collect and store the computerized case records developed by the individual states. Each year, data contributed to the NJCDA are merged to create a national data set containing detailed descriptions of cases handled by the states' juvenile courts. Although the individual states collect, code, and report different types of information about a case, the NJCDA has developed a standardized, national coding format that enables it to recode the raw data provided by the states into a more uniform format. The NJCDA staff studied codebooks and operation manuals, interviewed data suppliers, and analyzed data files to maximize their understanding of each information system and to assure the comparability of the data sets.

Because the various states collect different types of information, this study is constrained by the data available. Moreover, cross-state comparative analyses necessarily impose a least common denominator on the numbers and types of variables that can be examined. While thirty states now contribute their annual juvenile court data tapes to the NJCDA, the six states analyzed in Chapter Three were selected solely because they were the only states whose data files included information on representation by counsel.

## DATA IN CHAPTER THREE—"CASES DISPOSED"

The NJCDA's unit of count, "case disposed," represents a youth whose case is disposed of by the juvenile court for a new delinquency or status referral. A case is "disposed" when some definite action is taken, whether dismissal, warning, informal counseling or probation, referral to a treatment program, adjudication as a delinquent with some disposition, or transfer to an adult criminal court (Nimick et al. 1985a:3). As a result of multiple referrals, one child may be involved in several "cases" during a calendar year. Moreover, each "case" referral may contain more than one offense or charge. The multiple referrals of an individual child may tend to overstate the numbers of youths handled annually. Multiple charges in one petition may appear to understate the volume of delinquency in a jurisdiction. Because the unit of count is "case disposed," one cannot generalize from this data either the number of individual youths who are processed by the court annually or the number of separate offenses with which juveniles are charged.

The multistate comparative data analyzed in Chapter Three were originally collected by the California Bureau of Criminal Statistics and Special Services,[1] the Minnesota Supreme Court's Judicial Information System,[2] the Nebraska Commission on Law Enforcement and Criminal Justice,[3] the New York Office of Court Administration,[4] the North Dakota Office of State Court Administrator,[5] and the Pennsylvania Juvenile Court Judges' Commission.[6]

The data reported in Chapter Three include all delinquency and status offense cases disposed of in the six jurisdictions in 1984. While many referrals may be closed at intake with some type of informal disposition, the sample in Chapter Three consists exclusively of *petitioned* delinquency and status cases. It excludes all juvenile court referrals or petitions for abuse, dependency, or neglect, as well as routine traffic violations. Because the right to counsel announced in *Gault* attaches only after the formal initiation of delinquency proceedings, only formally *petitioned* delinquency and status cases are analyzed.

## DATA IN CHAPTERS FOUR THROUGH SEVEN—
## CASES OF INDIVIDUAL JUVENILES

The data analyzed in Chapters Four through Seven were collected by the Minnesota Supreme Court's Judicial Information System (SJIS) for delinquency and status offense cases processed in 1986. Like the data analyzed in Chapter Three, all juvenile court referrals for abuse, dependency, or neglect, and routine traffic violations are excluded. Because the right to counsel announced in *Gault* attaches only after the formal initiation of delinquency proceedings, only formally *petitioned* delinquency and status cases are analyzed.[7] The data were collected from each county in which the juvenile was charged.

Unlike the data in Chapter Three, which involve "cases disposed," the data in Chapters Four through Seven consist of *individual juveniles* against whom *petitions* were filed. The SJIS data in Chapters Four through Seven is a youth-based data file, rather than a case-based data file. It consists of 17,195 individual juveniles whose cases were formally petitioned in Minnesota's juvenile courts in 1986. Unfortunately, the annual data collected by the Minnesota SJIS do not include any family, school, or socioeconomic status variables, or a youth's prior record of offenses, adjudications, or dispositions. However, each youth processed in a county's juvenile court receives a unique identifying number which is used for all subsequent purposes. The NJCDA created a youth-based file by merging the 1984, 1985, and 1986 annual data tapes and matching the county/youth identification number across years to reconstruct a juvenile's prior record of petitions, adjudications, and dispositions. Thus, the data reported herein reflect a youth's most current referral to juvenile court as well as all prior petitions, adjudications, and dispositions for at least the preceding two years or more.[8]

Chapters Six and Seven also use 1980 Minnesota county census data to provide indicators of social structure. To facilitate analyses between the census and SJIS data sets, the county is the unit of analysis, and counties are then aggregated as urban, suburban, or rural.

## DATA CODING PROTOCOLS

In Chapters Three through Seven, the offenses reported by the various states were regrouped into six analytical categories. The National Juvenile Court Data Archive developed a seventy-eight-item coding protocol to recode raw offense data provided by the individual states into a uniform national format. This permits delinquency offense data from several different original formats to be recoded for analysis using a single conversion program.

The felony/misdemeanor offense distinction provides both an indicator of a crime's seriousness and legally is relevant for the right to counsel (*Gideon v. Wainwright*, 372 U.S. 335 [1963]; *Scott v. Illinois*, 440 U.S. 367 [1979]).[9] Offenses are also classified as person, property, other delinquency, and status. Combining person and property with the felony and misdemeanor distinctions produces a six-item offense scale. "Felony offenses against person" generally correspond to the FBI's Uniform Crime Report classification of Part I violent felonies against the person—homicide, rape, robbery, and aggravated assault. "Felony offenses against property" generally include FBI Part I property offenses—burglary, felony theft, and auto theft. "Minor offenses against person" consist primarily of simple assaults, and "minor offenses against property" consist primarily of larceny, shoplifting, or vandalism. "Other delinquency" includes a mixed bag of residual offenses—minor drug offenses such as possession of marijuana, public order offenses, as well as offenses against the administration of justice, primarily contempt of court. "Status" offenses are the juvenile offenses that are not criminal for adults—running away from home, truancy, curfew violation, ungovernability and the like.

When a petition alleges more than one offense, the youth is classified on the basis of the most serious charge. When a petition contains multiple allegations, there is no way to separate whether they are multiple charges arising out of the same offense transaction or whether they represent several offenses committed on different occasions which were simply petitioned in the same document.

This study uses two indicators of the severity of dispositions: out-of-home placement and secure confinement. Using the severity of sanctions as a measure of juvenile court action or attorney effectiveness reflects an assumption that a verdict of "not guilty" or a nominal disposition generally is, at least from the defendant's point of view, a positive result and conversely, removal or incarceration, a negative one (Kelley and Ramsey 1982). The NJCDA developed a twenty-two-item conversion program to transform state-specific dispositions into a uniform national format. The NJCDA staff speak directly with the states' data collectors and reporters to determine how specific dispositions or programs should be classified—out-of-home and secure—within the national format. Out-of-home placement includes any disposition in which the child is removed from his or her home and placed, for example, in a group home, foster care, in-patient psychiatric or chemical dependency treatment facility, or a secure institution. While many in-patient psychiatric or chemical dependency placements are secure facilities, these commitments are classified as out-of-home placements to distinguish them from more traditional institutional confinement in training schools. Secure confinement is a substantial subset of all out-of-home placements, but includes only confinement in county-level institutions or state training schools. In the juvenile justice context, secure confinement is somewhat of a misnomer, since most juvenile training schools and institutions do not rely upon locks, bars, fences, or armed guards to the same degree as do adult maximum security institutions (Feld 1977). Both home removal and secure confinement dispositions entail the types of liberty infringements that trigger the right to counsel under *Gault* and *Scott*. Moreover, such court interventions are unambiguous for purposes of interstate and intrastate comparisons.

## PRESENTATION OF DATA

The comparative analyses in Chapter Three array the data in the tables by state. The comparative analyses in Chapters Four and Five report the data for the entire state and separately for the counties aggregated on the basis of high, medium, and low rates of representation. While the overall rate of representation in Minnesota in 1986 was 45.3%, there was substantial variation among the eighty-seven counties. In four counties, more than 90% of juveniles were represented, whereas in six other counties, less than 10% of juveniles had lawyers. The five counties in which 66.7% or more juveniles were represented in juvenile courts were classified as "high" representation counties.[10] The fourteen counties in which more than 33.3% but less than 66.7% of juveniles had lawyers were classified as containing "medium" representation courts.[11] The remaining sixty-eight counties in which less than 33.3% of juveniles had lawyers were classified as "low" representation counties.

The comparative analyses in Chapters Six and Seven report the data for the entire state and separately for counties aggregated on the basis of their urban, suburban, and rural social structural characteristics. The classification of counties as urban, suburban and small urban, and rural uses the census concept of Standardized Metropolitan Statistical Area (SMSA) and youth-population density.[12] In this study, counties were classified as *urban* if they were located within an SMSA, had one or more cities of 100,000 inhabitants, and had a juvenile population aged ten to seventeen of at least 50,000.[13] Counties were classified as either *suburban* or *small urban* if they were located within a metropolitan SMSA (suburban) or, if within their own SMSA (small urban), had one or more cities of 25,000 to 100,000, and had a juvenile population aged ten to seventeen of more than 7,500 but less than 50,000.[14] The remaining counties in Minnesota were classified as rural because they are located outside of an SMSA, had no principal city of 25,000 or greater, and had less than 7,500 juveniles aged ten to seventeen.

The analyses in the following chapters attempt to answer two interrelated questions. First, what case characteristics determine when lawyers appear on behalf of juveniles? Second, what effect does representation have on the way that a case is handled and disposed? The former will examine the relationships between certain independent variables such as offense seriousness, prior record, pretrial detention, and variations in rates of representation. The latter will examine the impact of counsel on the sentences juveniles receive and the ways in which their cases are processed, after controlling for the influence of other independent legal variables. The analyses will also examine the determinants and impact of counsel in different contexts. Chapters Four and Five focus on the impact of counsel on juvenile justice administration when lawyers often, occasionally, or seldom appear. Chapter Six examines the relationship between social structure—urban, suburban, or rural setting—and juvenile justice administration including the impact of counsel.

## NOTES

1. California's Bureau of Criminal Statistics and Special Services (the Bureau) compiles and publishes California's juvenile court data (NJCDA 1986a). The Bureau, through its Juvenile Court and Probation Statistical System (JCPSS), collects information as a juvenile progresses through the juvenile justice system from referral to probation intake to a final court disposition. Case processing begins with a referral to a county juvenile probation department. Many delinquency and status cases are handled informally at the intake level and proceed no further. These cases are reported to the Bureau as "referral" actions. All formally petitioned delinquency and status offense cases are reported only after the court's disposition is known. The data collected by the Bureau include the date of referral, the county and source of referral, the referral offense(s), the offense(s) for which the youth was ultimately adjudicated, the youth's detention status, whether the prosecutor filed a petition, the nature of the juvenile's defense representation, the eventual disposition, the juvenile's birth date, race, sex, prior delinquency status, and current status at the conclusion of the proceedings.

2. The Minnesota Supreme Court's Judicial Information System (SJIS) compiles statewide statistical data on juvenile delinquency and status petitions filed annually. The data are based on the petitions filed; there is no data base that includes the cases referred to intake, county probation, or juvenile courts that were handled informally. The data collected on a case-specific basis are similar to those collected in California and include offense behavior, representation by counsel, court

processing information, entries each time a court activity occurs, any continuation or change in the status of a case, and types of dispositions. In most counties, this information is obtained from the juvenile courts' own computer system and is entered by court administrators in each county who are trained by the state court administrator. Since the juvenile courts themselves rely upon this computerized information for record keeping, scheduling hearings, maintaining court calendars, and monitoring cases, it is generally reliable.

3. The Nebraska Commission on Law Enforcement and Criminal Justice (the Commission), through its Juvenile Court Reporting System, collects data from the state's juvenile justice agencies (NJCDA 1986b). The county courts that handle juvenile cases as well as the separate juvenile courts report to the Commission monthly by completing a Juvenile Court Statistical (JCS) Form when a case is disposed. Except for Douglas and Sarpy counties which report only petitioned cases, the Nebraska data include both cases processed formally with a petition as well as those handled informally. In addition to the information that is collected in California and Minnesota, the Nebraska records also include a youth's school attainment, living arrangements at referral, number of prior referrals, and manner of handling (formal/informal). Where a referral involves more than one offense, the most serious offense is recorded. The Commission reviews the JCS forms forwarded from the counties for internal validity. When errors are discovered, the submitting court is contacted and the error is corrected.

4. The New York Office of Court Administration (OCA) collects data from the sixty-two family courts statewide that handle petitioned delinquency and status (PINS) cases (NJCDA 1986c). The courts report to the OCA after the disposition of a case by completing disposition reporting cards. The records include the same information collected in California and Minnesota. Upon receipt of the disposition reports, the OCA checks the data for internal validity and contacts the submitting court to correct any errors found. New York, like Minnesota, only records petitioned cases; there is no reporting of delinquency or status referrals that are handled informally by county probation departments.

5. The fifty-three counties in North Dakota report all delinquency and status referrals to the Office of State Court Administrator (OSCA) on a weekly or bimonthly basis. The county juvenile probation offices complete a juvenile court "face sheet form" which includes the filing information, social history, and disposition of each case referred to the juvenile court as well as a separate change-of-status form. While the social history information is not entered in the OSCA's computers, the other information collected is similar to that obtained in California and Minnesota.

6. Juvenile court data in Pennsylvania are collected by the Juvenile Court Judges' Commission (JCJC). A statistical card is submitted when a referral is received by the county probation department, if a youth is detained, and when the case is finally disposed. Like the other jurisdictions, the unit of count is the case disposed, a referral disposed of informally by the probation department or formally by the court. In addition to the types of offender and offense information collected by California and Minnesota, the JCJC reporting forms also include substantial in-

formation on a juvenile's educational status, family status, living arrangements, family income, and additional indicators of offense seriousness such as injury to victim, use of weapons, or the total value of property stolen or damaged.

Philadelphia uses a separate reporting system from the rest of Pennsylvania. It records information only on petitioned cases and does not include the information collected by the other Pennsylvania counties on school attainment, family status or income, the additional offense seriousness indicators, or a youth's pretrial detention status.

7. The United States Supreme Court has not decided whether noncriminal status offenders are constitutionally entitled to representation by counsel. The delinquency proceeding in *Gault* involved conduct that would be a crime if committed by an adult and that could result in institutional confinement. Federal and state legislation and court opinions severely restrict pretrial detention and institutional confinement of status offenders (Rubin 1985:70–73). Thus, the Supreme Court could conclude that since status offenses do not involve criminal behavior that could lead to incarceration, there is no constitutional right to counsel. Under Minnesota state law, however, the right to counsel attaches in status or "petty" matters as well as in delinquency proceedings (Minn. Stat. Ann. § 260.155, subd. 2 [1986]; Minn. R.P. Juv. Ct. 1.01; 4.01, subd. 1).

8. The youth identification numbers are unique within a county, but not within the entire state. A youth who has delinquency referrals in several different counties will receive separate identification numbers in each county. Thus, the variable "prior referrals" may be slightly inflated by a juvenile with multiple referrals in several counties, and slightly reduced by juveniles whose prior records consist of only one referral in each of several counties. Such multiple cases appear to be rare. A cross-tabulation of youths' county of residence with the county of adjudication reveals between 95% to 98% overlap. Because Minnesota lacks a statewide juvenile information system, a juvenile court at sentencing normally has information regarding only prior referrals in its own county. Thus, the variable "prior referrals" includes the information routinely available to and relied upon by the courts themselves.

9. The Minnesota Criminal Code contains three categories of offenses: felony (punishable by more than one year of imprisonment); misdemeanor (punishable by less than ninety days); and gross misdemeanor (an intermediate offense that is neither a felony nor a misdemeanor) [Minn. Stat. § 609.02, subd. 2–4]. The Minnesota Sentencing Guidelines (1980:27–28) treat misdemeanors and gross misdemeanors as one-quarter and one-half of a point and felonies as one point in the computation of an offender's criminal history score. In the present coding schema, gross misdemeanors were classified as "minor" offenses to preserve the felony distinction.

10. The "high" representation counties and their primary legal service delivery systems—public defender (PD) or court appointed (CA)—include: Anoka (97.9%, PD), Dakota (100.0%, CA), Goodhue (92.7%, PD), LeSuer (68.5%, PD), and Ramsey (92.3%, PD).

11. The "medium" representation counties and their primary mechanism for de-

livering legal services—public defender (PD) or court appointed (CA)—include: Cass (45.2%, CA), Douglas (42.5%, CA), Hennepin (47.7%, PD), Lake (38.7%, CA), Lincoln (45.8%, CA), Lyon (42.9%, CA), McLeod (43.3%, CA), Mille Lacs (40.1%, CA), Nobles (39.0%, CA), Pine (44.4%, CA), St. Louis (49.9%, PD), Todd (37.0%, CA), Wadena (65.9%, CA), and Washington (40.1%, CA).

12.  An SMSA is an integrated economic and social unit with a large population nucleus. An SMSA always includes a central city of specified population (50,000 or greater), and the remainder of the county in which it is located. In addition, an SMSA also includes contiguous counties and their smaller cities (generally with populations of less than 50,000) when the economic and social relationships between the central and contiguous counties meet specified criteria of metropolitan character and integration.

One consequence of using SMSAs is that it does not separate the component central cities from their suburban periphery with the consequence that the suburbs tend to dilute the central urban problem zones. Thus, within the same "urban" county, the characteristics of a city and its suburb may be substantially different and summary statistics may not be representative of either. Since the SJIS data are collected on a county-specific basis, however, it is necessary to use aggregated county-level census data for comparisons.

13.  Hennepin County (Minneapolis) and Ramsey County (St. Paul) are classified as urban counties.

14.  The Twin Cities metropolitan-area suburban counties meeting the SMSA and juvenile population criteria include: Anoka, Dakota, Scott, Washington, and Wright counties. The small urban counties and their principal cities include: Olmsted (Rochester), St. Louis (Duluth), and Stearns (St. Cloud).

# chapter three ───────────────────────────────

# A COMPARATIVE EVALUATION OF THE
# IMPLEMENTATION OF *GAULT* IN SIX STATES

## The Presence of Lawyers in Juvenile Courts

This chapter provides the first opportunity to analyze systematically the delivery of legal services in juvenile courts. It presents the first statewide and multistate data to assess the determinants of representation and the impact of counsel in juvenile courts in more than one jurisdiction. As described in Chapter Two, the data in this chapter reflect all delinquency and status offense cases formally petitioned in the juvenile courts of California, Minnesota, Nebraska, New York, North Dakota, and Pennsylvania. Part of the analyses treats the availability of counsel as a dependent variable using case characteristics and court processing factors as independent variables. Other parts treat counsel as an independent variable, assessing the impact of lawyers on juvenile court case processing and dispositions. These analyses attempt to answer the interrelated questions, when are attorneys appointed to represent juveniles, why are they appointed, and what difference does it make whether or not a youth is represented?

## PETITIONS AND OFFENSES

Initially, the appearance of counsel must be placed in the larger context of juvenile justice administration in the respective states. Table 3-1 introduces the six states' juvenile justice systems, reports the total number of referrals where available, the total number of petitions, the percentage of

**Table 3-1  Petitions and Petitioned Offenses**

| | California | Minnesota | Nebraska | New York | North Dakota | Pennsylvania | Philadelphia |
|---|---|---|---|---|---|---|---|
| Number of Referrals | 147,422 | — | 6,091 | — | 7,741 | 18,926 | — |
| Number of Petitions | 68,227 | 15,304 | 3,830 | 21,383 | 831 | 10,168 | 6,812 |
| % Referrals Petitioned | 46.3 | — | 62.8 | — | 10.7 | 53.7 | — |
| Felony Offense Against Person | | | | | | | |
| % | 8.7 | 2.2 | 1.0 | 8.2 | 0.2 | 13.0 | 38.1 |
| N | (5,946) | (338) | (39) | (1,764) | (2) | (1,320) | (2,592) |
| Felony Offense Against Property | | | | | | | |
| % | 27.2 | 14.3 | 11.1 | 14.9 | 15.8 | 25.9 | 19.7 |
| N | (18,571) | (2,196) | (427) | (3,192) | (131) | (2,653) | (1,339) |
| Minor Offense Against Person | | | | | | | |
| % | 6.1 | 5.0 | 3.7 | 6.6 | 2.8 | 12.5 | 3.7 |
| N | (4,166) | (766) | (143) | (1,414) | (23) | (1,275) | (255) |
| Minor Offense Against Property | | | | | | | |
| % | 17.1 | 29.9 | 43.9 | 18.8 | 29.8 | 24.9 | 24.9 |
| N | (11,700) | (4,574) | (1,680) | (4,019) | (248) | (2,532) | (1,694) |
| Other Delinquency | | | | | | | |
| % | 38.7 | 20.6 | 9.5 | 7.6 | 16.7 | 23.5 | 13.7 |
| N | (26,376) | (3,148) | (364) | (1,631) | (139) | (2,386) | (932) |
| Status Offense | | | | | | | |
| % | 2.2 | 28.0 | 30.7 | 43.8 | 34.7 | — | — |
| N | (1,468) | (4,282) | (1,177) | (9,363) | (288) | — | — |

referrals to petitions, and the types of offenses for which petitions were filed.

On the basis of the delinquency petitions filed, the juvenile courts in the various states confront very different delinquent populations. In part, these differences reflect the nature of the prepetition screening. While California, Nebraska, and Pennsylvania courts formally petition approximately half of the cases referred to their juvenile courts, North Dakota juvenile courts formally charge only 10.7% of their referrals. The juvenile courts in Minnesota and New York do not maintain records of court referrals that are closed informally without the filing of a petition.

The numbers of petitions filed differ substantially. Reflecting the obvious differences in their youth population bases, the larger, urban states process far more cases than do the more rural, midwestern states. Recall that the data for Philadelphia and the remainder of Pennsylvania are collected separately. Philadelphia by itself processes more delinquency petitions than do Nebraska and North Dakota together.

The nature of the offenses petitioned also differs substantially among the states. Serious crimes are much more prevalent in the large, urban jurisdictions. For example, larger proportions of juveniles in California, New York, and Pennsylvania are charged with felony offenses against the person—homicide, rape, aggravated assault, and robbery—than in the midwestern states. In Philadelphia, 38.1% of the juvenile court's caseload involves violent offenses against the person, primarily robbery. By contrast, a substantial portion of the midwestern states' caseloads consists of minor property offenses such as theft and shoplifting. Despite the public and political concern about serious youth crime, however, a relatively small proportion of most juvenile courts' dockets in all the states are concerned with felony crimes and most of that misconduct involves felony offenses involving property, such as burglary and car theft, rather than violence.

The states also differ markedly in their treatment of noncriminal status offenders. Pennsylvania/Philadelphia juvenile courts do not have jurisdiction over status offenders. In California, status offenders appear to be referred to juvenile courts only as a last resort. By contrast, in the midwestern states, status offenses are the first or second most common type of juvenile court matters handled. In New York, the maximum age of juvenile court jurisdiction is sixteen years of age, rather than eighteen as in the other states. Accordingly, the New York juvenile justice system deals with a significantly younger population that includes a substantially larger proportion of status offenders.

## RATES OF REPRESENTATION

Table 3-2 shows the overall rates of representation by counsel in the respective states, the percentages of private attorneys and public attorneys—court appointed or public defender—and the rates of representation by type of offense. Although *Gault* held that *every* juvenile was constitutionally entitled to "the guiding hand of counsel at every step of the process," *Gault*'s promise remains unrealized in half of these jurisdictions.

The large, urban states are far more successful in assuring that juveniles receive the assistance of counsel than are the midwestern states. Overall, between 84.9% and 95.9% of the juveniles in the large, urban states receive the assistance of counsel as contrasted with between 37.5% and 52.7% of the juveniles in the midwestern states. Indeed, these data may actually understate the larger, urban state/smaller, rural state disparities. The California Bureau of Criminal Statistics and Special Services cautions that a coding error may be responsible for some of the juveniles who were reported to be unrepresented.[1]

The first rows of Table 3-2 report the percentages of private attorneys and public attorneys reflected in the overall rates of representation. In every jurisdiction and regardless of the overall rate of representation, public attorneys handle the vast bulk of delinquency petitions by ratios of between 3:1 and 10:1.

Table 3-2 clearly shows that it is possible to provide very high levels of defense representation to juveniles adjudicated delinquent. More than 95% of the juveniles in Philadelphia and New York State, and 85% or more in Pennsylvania and California were represented. Since the large urban states process a greater volume of delinquency cases, their success in delivering legal services is all the more impressive. While it may be somewhat more difficult to deliver legal services easily in all parts of the rural midwestern states, that can hardly account for the disparities reflected in Table 3-2. As will be seen in Chapter Four, county by county analyses in Minnesota show substantial disparities within the state; even the largest and most populous county in the state with a well-developed public defender system provides representation to less than half the juveniles. These variations among and within states suggest that rates of representation reflect deliberate judicial and legislative policy decisions. California, New York, and Pennsylvania simply have made the commitment to a full-representation juvenile justice system.

Table 3-2 also shows the rates of representation by type of offense. One pattern that emerges in all of the states is a direct relationship between the seriousness of the offense and the rates of representation. Ju-

**Table 3-2  Representation by Counsel (Private, Public Defender/Court Appointed)**

| | California | Minnesota | Nebraska | New York | North Dakota | Pennsylvania | Philadelphia |
|---|---|---|---|---|---|---|---|
| **% Counsel** | 84.9[a] | 47.7[c] | 52.7 | 95.9 | 37.5 | 86.4 | 95.2 |
| Private | 7.6 | 5.3 | 13.3 | 5.1 | 10.5 | 14.5 | 22.0 |
| CAPD[b] | 77.3 | 42.3 | 39.4 | 90.8 | 27.1 | 71.9 | 73.2 |
| **Felony Offense Against Person—% Counsel** | 88.7 | 66.1 | 58.8 | 98.5 | 100.0 | 91.4 | 96.3 |
| Private | 11.2 | 9.9 | 14.7 | 4.3 | — | 22.0 | 29.9 |
| CAPD | 77.5 | 56.3 | 44.1 | 94.2 | 100.0 | 69.4 | 66.4 |
| **Felony Offense Against Property—% Counsel** | 86.8 | 60.6 | 59.9 | 98.1 | 38.9 | 87.1 | 95.0 |
| Private | 9.0 | 6.2 | 14.4 | 8.3 | 12.2 | 15.1 | 20.5 |
| CAPD | 77.8 | 54.4 | 45.5 | 89.7 | 26.7 | 72.0 | 74.5 |
| **Minor Offense Against Person—% Counsel** | 86.7 | 73.5 | 41.3 | 99.0 | 47.8 | 89.3 | 96.1 |
| Private | 8.6 | 7.3 | 14.9 | 9.5 | 17.4 | 16.4 | 22.4 |
| CAPD | 78.1 | 66.1 | 26.4 | 89.5 | 30.4 | 72.9 | 73.7 |
| **Minor Offense Against Property—% Counsel** | 83.8 | 46.8 | 49.6 | 96.2 | 38.3 | 85.5 | 94.7 |
| Private | 6.1 | 5.3 | 14.1 | 6.5 | 12.5 | 11.9 | 16.1 |
| CAPD | 77.7 | 41.4 | 35.5 | 89.7 | 25.8 | 73.6 | 78.7 |
| **Other Delinquency—% Counsel** | 83.4 | 55.5 | 48.9 | 96.8 | 33.1 | 82.1 | 93.2 |
| Private | 6.4 | 5.9 | 16.0 | 8.0 | 10.8 | 10.8 | 12.3 |
| CAPD | 77.0 | 49.6 | 32.8 | 88.7 | 22.3 | 71.4 | 80.9 |
| **Status Offense—% Counsel** | 74.1 | 30.7 | 56.6 | 93.8 | 37.2 | — | — |
| Private | 3.3 | 3.9 | 10.3 | 2.3 | 7.3 | | |
| CAPD | 70.8 | 26.9 | 46.3 | 91.6 | 29.9 | | |

a. The California Bureau of Criminal Statistics and Special Services cautions that this percentage may *understate* the actual rate of representation.
b. Court Appointed; Public Defender.
c. Discrepancies are due to rounding.

veniles charged with felonies or with offenses against the person generally have higher rates of representation than the state's overall rate. These differences in rates of representation by offense are typically greater in the states with lower rates of representation than in those with higher rates because of the latter group's smaller overall variation. In Minnesota, for example, while only 47.7% of all cases entail juveniles who are represented, 66.1% of those charged with felony offenses against the person, 73.5% of those charged with minor offenses against the person, and 60.6% of those charged with felony offenses against property are represented.

A second and similar pattern is the appearance of larger proportions of private attorneys on behalf of juveniles charged with felony offenses—person and property—and offenses against the person than appear in the other offense categories. Perhaps the greater seriousness of those offenses and their potential consequences encourage juveniles or their families to seek the assistance of private counsel. Conversely, private attorneys are least likely to be retained by parents to represent the status offenders with whom the parents are often in conflict.

## OFFENSE AND DISPOSITION

There is extensive research on the determinants of juvenile court dispositions (Fagan, Slaughter, and Hartstone 1987; McCarthy and Smith 1986; Dannefer and Schutt 1982; Thomas and Cage 1977). However, "even a superficial review of the relevant literature leaves one with the rather uncomfortable feeling that the only consistent finding of prior research is that there are no consistencies in the determinants of the decision-making process" (Thomas and Sieverdes 1975:416). In general, the seriousness of the present offense and the length of the prior record—the so-called "legal variables"—explain most of the variance that can be accounted for in juvenile sentencing, with some additional influence of race (Fagan, Slaughter, and Hartstone 1987; McCarthy and Smith 1986). However, in most of these sentencing studies, the legal variables only account for about 25% to 30% of the variance in dispositions (Thomas and Cage 1977; Clarke and Koch 1980; McCarthy and Smith 1986; Horowitz and Wasserman 1980).

Because of limited data on prior records and personal or social characteristics, this cross-state comparison cannot identify fully the determinants of dispositions. However, the data do lend themselves to some exploration of the relationships between offenses, dispositions, and representation by an attorney. Table 3-3 uses two measures of juvenile court dispositions: 1) out-of-home placements, and 2) secure confine-

**Table 3-3  Present Offense and Disposition: Out-of-Home Placement/Secure Confinement**

| | California | Minnesota | Nebraska | New York | North Dakota | Pennsylvania | Philadelphia |
|---|---|---|---|---|---|---|---|
| **Overall** | | | | | | | |
| Home | | | | | | | |
| % | 30.8 | 17.2 | 15.2 | 16.1 | 28.0 | 22.1 | 10.3 |
| N | (21,048) | (2,631) | (584) | (3,255) | (233) | (2,213) | (628) |
| Secure | | | | | | | |
| % | 14.5 | 3.3 | 5.2 | 7.1 | 9.6 | 1.3 | 1.1 |
| N | (9,902) | (504) | (199) | (1,423) | (80) | (132) | (76) |
| Felony Offense Against Person | | | | | | | |
| Home (%) | 39.5 | 30.2 | 28.2 | 22.3 | 50.0 | 28.7 | 12.6 |
| Secure (%) | 20.4 | 9.5 | 15.4 | 19.2 | 50.0 | 2.5 | 1.7 |
| Felony Offense Against Property | | | | | | | |
| Home (%) | 31.2 | 27.4 | 18.5 | 18.6 | 35.1 | 21.3 | 11.3 |
| Secure (%) | 15.7 | 9.2 | 12.2 | 12.0 | 17.6 | 0.9 | 0.8 |
| Minor Offense Against Person | | | | | | | |
| Home (%) | 25.8 | 21.5 | 21.7 | 12.7 | 39.1 | 13.5 | 5.7 |
| Secure (%) | 11.5 | 3.3 | 9.1 | 9.6 | 13.0 | 0.2 | 0.4 |
| Minor Offense Against Property | | | | | | | |
| Home (%) | 24.3 | 14.6 | 8.5 | 14.1 | 28.6 | 18.8 | 5.9 |
| Secure (%) | 10.1 | 3.5 | 4.5 | 9.6 | 8.1 | 0.6 | 0.6 |
| Other Delinquency | | | | | | | |
| Home (%) | 32.5 | 20.2 | 15.9 | 16.1 | 27.3 | 27.5 | 11.4 |
| Secure (%) | 15.2 | 1.9 | 8.8 | 10.6 | 14.4 | 2.4 | 1.0 |
| Status Offense | | | | | | | |
| Home (%) | 27.9 | 10.7 | 22.3 | 15.6 | 23.6 | — | — |
| Secure (%) | 1.0 | 0.5 | 1.8 | 1.3 | 4.5 | — | — |

ment. These categories provide clear-cut delineations that lend themselves to cross-state comparisons. They also have legal significance for the appointment of counsel, since the Supreme Court has held, at least for adults, that all persons charged with felonies must be afforded the right to counsel (*Gideon v. Wainwright*, 373 U.S. 335 [1963]), and that no person convicted of a misdemeanor may be incarcerated unless he or she was afforded or validly waived the assistance of counsel (*Scott v. Illinois*, 440 U.S. 367 [1979]).

Table 3-3 shows both the overall rates of out-of-home placements and secure confinement in the respective states as well as by categories of offenses. The states differ markedly in their overall use of out-of-home placements and secure confinement, ranging from a high of 30.8% home removal and 14.5% incarceration in California to a low of 10.3% home removal and 1.1% confinement in Philadelphia. The ratio of out-of-home placement to secure confinement also varies from about 16:1 in Pennsylvania to about 2:1 in California.

As might be expected, the seriousness of the present offense substantially alters a youth's risk of removal and confinement. In every state, felony offenses against the person garner both the highest rates of out-of-home placement and secure confinement, typically followed either by minor offenses against the person or felony offenses against property, for example, burglary. Conversely, minor property offenses—primarily petty theft and shoplifting—and status offenses, the modal forms of delinquency, typically have the lowest rates of home removal or confinement.

## OFFENSE AND DISPOSITION BY COUNSEL

Table 3-4 adds the effects of counsel to the information contained in Table 3-3. Within each offense category of youths who receive out-of-home or secure dispositions, Table 3-4 shows the disposition rates for those youths who were represented by counsel and those who were not. For example, Table 3-3 shows that of juveniles charged with felonies against the person in California, 39.5% receive out-of-home placement and 20.4% receive secure confinement dispositions. The same cell in Table 3-4 shows that youths *with counsel* were somewhat more likely to receive severe dispositions than those *without counsel*—40.0% versus 35.5% out-of-home and 21.0% versus 15.4% secure confinement.

Except for North Dakota, with its very small numbers and low rates of representation, a comparison of the two columns in each state and at each offense level reveals that youths with lawyers almost always receive more severe dispositions than do those without lawyers. With twelve possible comparisons in each state—six offense categories times two dispo-

**Table 3-4  Representation by Counsel and Rate of Disposition (Home/Secure)**

| Counsel | California Yes | California No | Minnesota Yes | Minnesota No | Nebraska Yes | Nebraska No | New York Yes | New York No | North Dakota Yes | North Dakota No | Pennsylvania Yes | Pennsylvania No | Philadelphia Yes | Philadelphia No |
|---|---|---|---|---|---|---|---|---|---|---|---|---|---|---|
| **Felony Offense Against Person** | | | | | | | | | | | | | | |
| Home (%) | 40.0 | 35.5 | 32.8 | 21.4 | 25.0 | 28.6 | 22.6 | — | 50.0 | — | 31.0 | 16.8 | 12.9 | 4.9 |
| Secure (%) | 21.0 | 15.4 | 9.5 | 4.9 | 15.0 | 21.4 | 19.5 | — | 50.0 | — | 2.8 | 0.9 | 1.7 | 2.1 |
| **Felony Offense Against Property** | | | | | | | | | | | | | | |
| Home (%) | 32.0 | 26.1 | 31.6 | 19.1 | 24.9 | 11.1 | 19.0 | — | 47.1 | 27.5 | 24.9 | 8.2 | 11.7 | 4.8 |
| Secure (%) | 16.5 | 10.6 | 10.4 | 5.0 | 16.2 | 7.8 | 12.2 | — | 11.8 | 21.3 | 1.1 | — | 0.9 | — |
| **Minor Offense Against Person** | | | | | | | | | | | | | | |
| Home (%) | 26.8 | 19.2 | 22.3 | 14.9 | 20.0 | 28.2 | 12.7 | 7.1 | 45.5 | 33.3 | 22.0 | 7.8 | 5.5 | 10.0 |
| Secure (%) | 12.3 | 6.1 | 3.5 | 1.1 | 12.0 | 9.9 | 9.7 | — | 9.1 | 16.7 | 0.4 | — | 0.4 | — |
| **Minor Offense Against Property** | | | | | | | | | | | | | | |
| Home (%) | 25.5 | 17.9 | 18.8 | 9.6 | 12.5 | 5.7 | 14.6 | — | 38.9 | 22.2 | 24.9 | 4.8 | 5.9 | 6.3 |
| Secure (%) | 10.8 | 6.4 | 4.2 | 2.0 | 7.3 | 2.4 | 9.1 | — | 8.4 | 7.8 | 0.8 | — | 0.7 | — |
| **Other Delinquency** | | | | | | | | | | | | | | |
| Home (%) | 34.4 | 22.8 | 28.1 | 9.8 | 24.2 | 9.0 | 16.7 | — | 32.6 | 24.7 | 37.6 | 17.4 | 11.4 | 11.1 |
| Secure (%) | 16.5 | 9.1 | 2.2 | 0.8 | 13.3 | 2.2 | 11.0 | — | 13.0 | 15.1 | 3.5 | 0.9 | 0.6 | 6.3 |
| **Status Offense** | | | | | | | | | | | | | | |
| Home (%) | 30.4 | 20.8 | 16.5 | 7.6 | 34.1 | 14.2 | 16.6 | 1.0 | 32.7 | 18.2 | — | — | — | — |
| Secure (%) | 6.3 | 7.1 | 0.9 | 0.4 | 2.1 | 1.4 | 1.4 | — | 1.9 | 6.7 | — | — | — | — |

sitions—represented youths received more severe dispositions than unrepresented youths in every category in Minnesota, New York, and Pennsylvania, in all but one in California and in all but three in Nebraska. Even in the highest representation jurisdictions—New York and Pennsylvania—this pattern prevails; there was virtually no secure confinement of unrepresented juveniles in these locales.

While the relationship between representation and more severe disposition is consistent in the different jurisdictions, the explanation of this relationship is not readily apparent. Clarke and Koch (1980) speculate that the presence of lawyers may antagonize traditional juvenile court judges and subtly influence the eventual disposition imposed. However, the pattern also prevails in the jurisdictions with very high rates of representation where the presence of counsel is not unusual. Perhaps judges discern the eventual disposition early in the proceedings and appoint counsel more frequently when an out-of-home placement or secure confinement is anticipated (Aday 1986). Conversely, judges may exhibit more leniency if a youth is not represented. Or, perhaps, other variables besides the seriousness of the present offense influence both the appointment of counsel and the eventual disposition.

## DETENTION BY OFFENSE

Table 3-5 shows the overall percentage and numbers of juveniles against whom petitions were filed who were held in pretrial detention, as well as the numbers and rates of detention by offense category. Detention, as used here, refers to a juvenile's custody status following referral but prior to court action. It is important to note, however, that detention is coded differently in various jurisdictions. In California, for example, which appears to have a very high rate of pretrial detention, any juvenile brought to a detention facility is logged in and counted as detained, even if he or she is only held for a short while until a parent arrives. By contrast, Minnesota, which appears to have a very low rate of pretrial detention, uses a very conservative definition of detention. Juveniles in Minnesota are coded as detained only if a detention hearing is held, which normally occurs thirty-six hours—about two court days—after apprehension (Feld 1984). Thus, the data in Table 3-5, while suggestive, are not directly comparable. Unfortunately, Philadelphia does not provide information on a juvenile's pretrial detention status.

Regardless of the jurisdictional definition of detention, the use of detention follows similar patterns. Juveniles committing felonies against the person are most likely to be detained, followed either by those committing minor offenses against the person or felony offenses against prop-

**Table 3-5** Pretrial Detention Rates by Present Offense

| | California | Minnesota | Nebraska | New York | North Dakota | Pennsylvania |
|---|---|---|---|---|---|---|
| **Overall** | | | | | | |
| % Detained | 54.0 | 9.4 | 12.6 | 18.0 | 14.7 | 29.0 |
| N | (36,100) | (1,443) | (483) | (3,841) | (122) | (2,946) |
| Felony Offense Against Person | | | | | | |
| % Detained | 68.1 | 24.6 | 46.2 | 22.3 | 50.0 | 43.6 |
| N | (4,013) | (83) | (18) | (393) | (1) | (576) |
| Felony Offense Against Property | | | | | | |
| % Detained | 56.6 | 15.0 | 20.1 | 17.5 | 15.3 | 30.6 |
| N | (10,353) | (329) | (86) | (560) | (20) | (806) |
| Minor Offense Against Person | | | | | | |
| % Detained | 52.0 | 16.1 | 25.2 | 15.2 | 21.7 | 22.0 |
| N | (2,129) | (123) | (36) | (215) | (5) | (281) |
| Minor Offense Against Property | | | | | | |
| % Detained | 45.5 | 7.1 | 9.8 | 16.1 | 11.3 | 27.4 |
| N | (5,222) | (326) | (165) | (646) | (28) | (693) |
| Other Delinquency | | | | | | |
| % Detained | 54.7 | 10.6 | 13.7 | 20.2 | 20.1 | 24.7 |
| N | (14,047) | (335) | (50) | (330) | (28) | (590) |
| Status Offense | | | | | | |
| % Detained | 24.1 | 5.8 | 10.9 | 18.1 | 13.9 | — |
| N | (336) | (247) | (128) | (1,697) | (40) | — |

erty. Since the evidentiary distinctions between a felony and a minor offense against the person, the degree of injury to the victim, for example, may not be apparent at the time of detention, these patterns are not surprising.

Despite the seeming "legal rationality" of detention reflected in Table 3-5, most multivariate studies (Coates, Miller, and Ohlin 1978; Clarke and Koch 1980; Frazier and Bishop 1985), as well as the more detailed analyses in Chapters Four and Six can account for very little of the variance in detention decision making. While larger proportions of juveniles charged with serious offenses are detained than are those charged with trivial offenses, in most states the majority of all youths are released immediately. Moreover, since most juvenile court dockets consist of youths charged with minor offenses, their seemingly smaller percentage rates of detention mask the larger absolute numbers of youths detained. For example, in Minnesota, while a larger proportion of youths charged with felony offenses against property are detained (15.0%) than are those charged with minor offenses against property (7.1%) because there are so many more of the latter (Table 3-1), the absolute numbers of youths detained are almost identical (329 vs. 326). In absolute terms, Nebraska, New York, and North Dakota each detain more youths charged with status offenses than they do youths charged with felony offenses.

## DETENTION AND COUNSEL

Table 3-6 examines the relationship between a youth's detention status and representation by counsel. Detention, particularly if it continues for more than a day, is a legally significant juvenile court intervention which also requires the assistance of counsel (Feld 1984; *Schall v. Martin*, 104 S. Ct. 2403 [1984]). Every jurisdiction provides for a prompt detention hearing to determine the existence of probable cause, the presence of grounds for detention, and the child's custody status pending trial (Feld 1984).

Table 3-6 reports the rate of representation at each offense level for those youths who were detained and for those who were not detained. For example, in Minnesota, 66.1% of the juveniles charged with a felony offense against the person were represented (Table 3-2) and 24.6% of them were detained (Table 3-5). However, of those charged with felony offenses against the person, 75.0% who also were detained were represented, as contrasted with 63.8% of those with similar charges but who were not detained.

For each state, a comparison of the two columns reveals a consistent pattern—youths who were held in detention had higher rates of represen-

**Table 3-6 Rate of Pretrial Detention and Representation by Counsel**

| Detention | California | | Minnesota | | Nebraska | | New York | | North Dakota | | Pennsylvania | |
|---|---|---|---|---|---|---|---|---|---|---|---|---|
| | Yes | No | Yes | No | Yes | No | Yes | No | Yes | No | Yes | No |
| Felony Offense Against Person— % Counsel | 90.8 | 84.9 | 75.0 | 63.8 | 46.7 | 68.4 | 99.7 | 98.1 | 100.0 | 100.0 | 96.4 | 87.4 |
| Felony Offense Against Property— % Counsel | 90.2 | 83.5 | 72.7 | 58.9 | 65.4 | 58.6 | 99.8 | 97.7 | 30.0 | 40.5 | 94.0 | 83.8 |
| Minor Offense Against Person— % Counsel | 89.9 | 84.2 | 82.4 | 72.2 | 47.2 | 38.8 | 99.5 | 98.9 | 80.0 | 38.9 | 95.0 | 86.4 |
| Minor Offense Against Property— % Counsel | 87.5 | 82.1 | 74.6 | 45.2 | 68.9 | 47.0 | 99.1 | 95.7 | 35.7 | 38.6 | 95.4 | 80.9 |
| Other Delinquency— % Counsel | 89.1 | 79.1 | 78.5 | 53.2 | 72.1 | 44.3 | 99.4 | 96.1 | 17.9 | 36.9 | 92.5 | 77.6 |
| Status Offense— % Counsel | 88.4 | 72.1 | 70.3 | 28.5 | 89.7 | 51.1 | 99.4 | 92.6 | 32.5 | 37.9 | — | — |

tation than did juveniles who were not. In four of the six states at every level of offense, detained youths were more likely to be represented. In Nebraska, in five of the six levels of offenses, detained youths were more likely to be represented. Again, only in North Dakota, with its small numbers and low rates of representation, does the pattern break down.

While the differences between detained and nondetained youths are smaller in the three jurisdictions with the highest rates of representation, in Minnesota and Nebraska they are substantial, especially as the seriousness of the offense decreases. Comparing the overall rate of representation at different offense levels (Table 3-2) with the rates of representation for detained youths (Table 3-6) shows that detention provides a significant additional impetus for the appointment of counsel particularly for less serious offenders.

## DETENTION AND DISPOSITIONS

Several studies have examined the determinants of detention and the relationship between a child's pretrial detention status and subsequent disposition (Krisberg and Schwartz 1983; Frazier and Bishop 1985; Clarke and Koch 1980; McCarthy 1987). These studies report that while several of the same variables affect both rates of detention and subsequent disposition, after appropriate controls, detention per se exhibits an independent effect on dispositions.

Because of the cross-state data limitations, this study cannot control for several variables simultaneously. However, Table 3-7 shows the relationship between a youth's offense, detention status, and eventual disposition. Table 3-7 reports the percentages of youths within each offense category who were detained and who were not detained who received out-of-home placement and secure confinement. For example, in Nebraska, of youths charged with a felony against the person, 55.6% of those who were detained were eventually removed from their homes as contrasted with only 4.8% of those similarly charged but not detained. Again, the results are remarkably consistent; in five of the six jurisdictions and at every offense level, youths who were detained received more severe dispositions than did those who were not. Even in North Dakota with its small numbers, the relationship between detention and secure confinement appears in most offense categories.

What Table 3-7 shows, then, is that the same factors that determine the initial detention decision appear to influence the ultimate disposition as well. However, when one compares the zero-order relationship between offense and disposition (Table 3-3) with the relationship between offense/detention and disposition (Table 3-7), it is apparent that detained

**Table 3-7  Impact of Pretrial Detention on Disposition (Home/Secure)**

| Detention | California | | Minnesota | | Nebraska | | New York | | North Dakota | | Pennsylvania | |
|---|---|---|---|---|---|---|---|---|---|---|---|---|
| | Yes | No | Yes | No | Yes | No | Yes | No | Yes | No | Yes | No |
| Felony Offense Against Person | | | | | | | | | | | | |
| Home (%) | 51.3 | 14.9 | 53.0 | 22.7 | 55.6 | 4.8 | 57.6 | 11.9 | — | 100.0 | 50.3 | 11.9 |
| Secure (%) | 26.3 | 8.0 | 20.5 | 5.9 | 33.3 | — | 50.3 | 10.1 | — | 100.0 | 5.2 | 0.4 |
| Felony Offense Against Property | | | | | | | | | | | | |
| Home (%) | 42.2 | 17.1 | 46.5 | 24.0 | 51.2 | 10.3 | 49.6 | 11.7 | 30.0 | 36.0 | 47.0 | 10.0 |
| Secure (%) | 19.6 | 11.0 | 22.5 | 6.9 | 36.0 | 6.2 | 32.0 | 7.5 | 30.0 | 15.3 | 2.2 | 0.3 |
| Minor Offense Against Person | | | | | | | | | | | | |
| Home (%) | 38.9 | 11.6 | 46.3 | 16.8 | 41.7 | 15.0 | 45.4 | 6.8 | 60.0 | 33.3 | 40.4 | 5.9 |
| Secure (%) | 16.6 | 6.3 | 6.5 | 2.6 | 22.2 | 4.7 | 39.0 | 4.3 | 60.0 | 5.6 | 0.7 | 0.1 |
| Minor Offense Against Property | | | | | | | | | | | | |
| Home (%) | 37.1 | 13.7 | 40.2 | 12.7 | 35.8 | 5.5 | 45.4 | 7.9 | 28.6 | 28.6 | 48.5 | 7.5 |
| Secure (%) | 12.8 | 8.2 | 15.3 | 2.6 | 22.4 | 2.5 | 31.5 | 4.3 | 7.1 | 8.2 | 2.0 | 0.1 |
| Other Delinquency | | | | | | | | | | | | |
| Home (%) | 44.3 | 18.6 | 43.9 | 17.4 | 50.0 | 10.5 | 44.2 | 8.9 | 28.6 | 27.0 | 55.4 | 18.3 |
| Secure (%) | 17.9 | 12.5 | 7.5 | 1.3 | 24.0 | 6.4 | 31.1 | 5.4 | 17.9 | 13.5 | 5.8 | 1.3 |
| Status Offense | | | | | | | | | | | | |
| Home (%) | 31.5 | 25.4 | 37.2 | 9.1 | 59.4 | 17.7 | 40.2 | 10.2 | 17.5 | 24.6 | — | — |
| Secure (%) | 8.6 | 6.1 | 4.0 | 0.3 | 7.8 | 1.0 | 2.8 | 1.0 | 5.0 | 4.4 | — | — |

youths are significantly more at risk for out-of-home placement and secure confinement than are nondetained youths. Generally, pretrial detention more than doubles a youth's probability of receiving a secure confinement disposition.

## COUNSEL, DETENTION, AND DISPOSITION

Table 3-5 reported the percentages of youths who were detained at each
offense level. Table 3-6 examined the relationship between detention
status and representation and reported that detention increased the likelihood of representation. Table 3-7 examined the relationship between
detention status and disposition and showed that detention also increased
the likelihood of a youth receiving more severe dispositions.

Table 3-8 reports the relationship between detention and disposition
when youth are represented by counsel to see whether the presence or
absence of counsel affects their dispositions. Table 3-8 indicates that a
detained youth who is represented by counsel is more likely to receive a
severe disposition than a detained youth who is not represented. In New
York, California, and Pennsylvania, which had very high rates of representation, the represented/detained youths consistently received more severe dispositions than did the small group of unrepresented/detained juveniles, as was also the case in Nebraska. Only in Minnesota and North
Dakota was the presence of counsel not an "aggravating" factor at the
sentencing of detained youth. Again, this may simply be the result of
dwindling numbers, or perhaps the factors that influenced the initial detention decision took precedence over the presence of counsel in those
states.

The data in Table 3-8 for New York and Pennsylvania, to a lesser
degree, further reinforce the findings reported in Table 3-4 that there was
virtually no removal from the home or incarceration of unrepresented
youths. By contrast, substantial numbers and proportions of youths unrepresented by counsel in the midwestern states were being detained and
later removed from their homes or placed in secure confinement.

## PRIOR REFERRALS

Another legal variable that affects a juvenile's eventual disposition is a
prior history of delinquency referrals (Clarke and Koch 1980; Henretta,
Frazier, and Bishop 1986). The next analyses assess the relationships between prior referrals and dispositions, prior referrals and representation
by counsel, and prior referrals, representation by counsel, and dispositions.

**Table 3-8 Representation by Counsel for Detained Juveniles and Rate of Disposition (Home/Secure)**

| Counsel | California Yes | California No | Minnesota Yes | Minnesota No | Nebraska Yes | Nebraska No | New York Yes | New York No | North Dakota Yes | North Dakota No | Pennsylvania Yes | Pennsylvania No |
|---|---|---|---|---|---|---|---|---|---|---|---|---|
| **Felony Offense Against Person** | | | | | | | | | | | | |
| Home (%) | 51.3 | 51.5 | 52.1 | 62.5 | 57.1 | 50.0 | 57.7 | — | — | — | 50.6 | 42.9 |
| Secure (%) | 27.0 | 19.9 | 18.8 | 12.5 | 42.9 | 37.5 | 50.4 | — | — | — | 5.2 | 4.8 |
| **Felony Offense Against Property** | | | | | | | | | | | | |
| Home (%) | 42.9 | 36.1 | 47.2 | 42.4 | 60.8 | 40.7 | 49.6 | — | 16.7 | 35.7 | 47.7 | 35.4 |
| Secure (%) | 20.9 | 8.3 | 18.8 | 22.7 | 37.3 | 37.0 | 32.0 | — | 16.7 | 35.7 | 2.4 | — |
| **Minor Offense Against Person** | | | | | | | | | | | | |
| Home (%) | 39.5 | 34.0 | 44.0 | 50.0 | 41.2 | 42.1 | 45.6 | — | 50.0 | 100.0 | 41.4 | 21.4 |
| Secure (%) | 17.5 | 8.8 | 5.3 | 12.5 | 29.4 | 15.8 | 39.2 | — | 25.0 | 100.0 | 0.7 | — |
| **Minor Offense Against Property** | | | | | | | | | | | | |
| Home (%) | 38.5 | 26.8 | 37.6 | 35.6 | 40.4 | 23.4 | 45.8 | — | 40.0 | 22.2 | 49.4 | 29.0 |
| Secure (%) | 14.0 | 4.1 | 11.0 | 11.9 | 25.0 | 14.9 | 31.8 | — | — | 11.1 | 2.1 | — |
| **Other Delinquency** | | | | | | | | | | | | |
| Home (%) | 45.4 | 35.3 | 44.3 | 37.9 | 58.1 | 33.3 | 44.5 | — | 60.0 | 21.7 | 57.9 | 25.0 |
| Secure (%) | 19.2 | 7.0 | 3.8 | 8.6 | 29.0 | 8.3 | 31.3 | — | 40.0 | 13.0 | 6.0 | 2.3 |
| **Status Offense** | | | | | | | | | | | | |
| Home (%) | 32.0 | 28.2 | 36.5 | 34.8 | 61.9 | 41.7 | 40.2 | 44.4 | 30.8 | 11.1 | — | — |
| Secure (%) | 9.4 | 2.6 | 3.2 | 6.1 | 3.8 | 33.3 | 2.9 | — | — | 7.4 | — | — |

Nebraska is the only state in this six-state sample that routinely records information about a juvenile's prior referrals at the time of a current referral. However, the other states' data tapes include youth identification numbers. By combining several years of annual data tapes and matching the county/youth identification number across years, it is possible to reconstruct a youth's prior record of offenses and dispositions.

The Minnesota data included in Tables 3-9 through 3-11 are from the data set that will be analyzed more extensively in Chapters Four through Seven. As described more fully in Chapter Two, the Minnesota data is a youth-based file, rather than a case-based file. For purposes of these analyses, however, the differences are not important. The Minnesota data involves individual juveniles whose cases were charged in 1986 and whose prior records were acquired in 1984, 1985, and 1986. In 1986, 45.3% of Minnesota's juveniles were represented (Table 4-3), as compared with 47.7% of the cases disposed in 1984 (Table 3-2), and the pattern of representation by offense was similar. The distribution of offenses in Minnesota in 1986 was also similar to that recorded in 1984 (Tables 3-1 and 4-1). Using these Minnesota data permits a cross-state comparison of the relationship between prior referrals, dispositions, and the presence of counsel. In both Minnesota and Nebraska, the records of prior referrals were recoded as 0, 1–2, 3–4, and 5 or more.[2]

## PRIOR REFERRALS AND DISPOSITION

Table 3-9 reports the relationship between prior referrals and out-of-home placements and secure confinement dispositions. Within each offense level, there is a nearly perfect linear relationship between additional prior referrals and the likelihood of more severe dispositions.

For example, in Minnesota, 35.7% of those juveniles with no prior record who commit a felony offense against the person receive an out-of-home placement, as compared with 51.9% of those with one or two priors, 84.8% of those with three or four priors, and 100.0% of those with five or more priors. The same pattern obtains for secure confinement dispositions. A similar direct relationship between prior referrals and dispositions is evident in Nebraska as well. Clearly then, after controlling for the seriousness of the present offense, the addition of a prior record strongly influences the sentencing practices of juvenile courts.

## PRIOR REFERRALS AND RATES OF REPRESENTATION

It will be recalled from Table 3-2 that overall, 52.7% of youths in Nebraska and 47.7% of youths in Minnesota (45.3% in 1986) were repre-

**Table 3-9   Prior Referral and Rate of Disposition (Home/Secure)**

| | Minnesota | | | | Nebraska | | | |
|---|---|---|---|---|---|---|---|---|
| Prior Referrals | 0 | 1–2 | 3–4 | 5+ | 0 | 1–2 | 3–4 | 5+ |
| Felony Offense Against Person | | | | | | | | |
| Home (%) | 35.7 | 51.9 | 84.8 | 100.0 | 18.8 | 20.0 | 50.0 | 66.7 |
| Secure (%) | 22.9 | 33.3 | 60.6 | 100.0 | 6.3 | 13.3 | — | 50.0 |
| Felony Offense Against Property | | | | | | | | |
| Home (%) | 21.7 | 46.4 | 76.5 | 72.0 | 7.7 | 25.2 | 40.0 | 48.3 |
| Secure (%) | 16.0 | 31.9 | 67.0 | 54.0 | 2.1 | 19.1 | 30.0 | 44.8 |
| Minor Offense Against Person | | | | | | | | |
| Home (%) | 14.2 | 38.5 | 62.2 | 73.3 | 9.8 | 26.0 | 23.8 | 70.0 |
| Secure (%) | 8.0 | 22.6 | 40.5 | 66.7 | 3.3 | 12.0 | 9.5 | 30.0 |
| Minor Offense Against Property | | | | | | | | |
| Home (%) | 10.4 | 27.3 | 49.0 | 65.2 | 4.7 | 12.8 | 19.0 | 25.3 |
| Secure (%) | 6.6 | 18.8 | 39.5 | 52.2 | 1.5 | 7.5 | 14.3 | 16.9 |
| Other Delinquency | | | | | | | | |
| Home (%) | 12.4 | 31.5 | 46.9 | 55.0 | 8.7 | 25.3 | 36.8 | 18.2 |
| Secure (%) | 6.7 | 19.2 | 31.9 | 50.0 | 1.7 | 18.9 | 21.1 | 9.1 |
| Status Offense | | | | | | | | |
| Home (%) | 8.7 | 19.3 | 38.9 | 48.8 | 19.8 | 27.7 | 31.8 | 47.6 |
| Secure (%) | 1.6 | 5.8 | 23.5 | 30.2 | 0.9 | 3.6 | 6.8 | 9.5 |

**Table 3-10   Rate of Representation by Prior Referral**

| | Minnesota | | | | Nebraska | | | |
|---|---|---|---|---|---|---|---|---|
| Prior Referrals | 0 | 1–2 | 3–4 | 5+ | 0 | 1–2 | 3–4 | 5+ |
| Felony Offense Against Person (%) | 73.6 | 81.5 | 89.3 | 100.0 | 76.9 | 64.3 | 50.0 | — |
| Felony Offense Against Property (%) | 57.1 | 71.2 | 78.2 | 84.1 | 59.6 | 67.9 | 65.4 | 26.1 |
| Minor Offense Against Person (%) | 55.0 | 69.5 | 88.9 | 71.4 | 51.0 | 26.8 | 38.9 | 50.0 |
| Minor Offense Against Property (%) | 39.5 | 58.8 | 75.1 | 82.6 | 46.8 | 57.6 | 53.0 | 35.9 |
| Other Delinquency (%) | 38.9 | 59.2 | 75.0 | 89.7 | 46.3 | 53.4 | 60.0 | 28.6 |
| Status Offense (%) | 23.3 | 40.3 | 62.9 | 66.7 | 57.7 | 58.5 | 34.4 | 43.8 |

sented by counsel. Table 3-10 shows, within each offense level, the relationship between prior delinquency referrals and the likelihood of representation.

The aggregate rates of representation reported in Tables 3-2 and 4-3 are the composite of juveniles with and without prior referrals. For example, in Minnesota, in 1986, 77.3% of all juveniles charged with felony offenses against the person were represented. However, this proportion of representation consisted of 73.6% with no priors, 81.5% with one or two, 89.3% with three or four, and 100.0% percent with five or more priors. A similar relationship between prior referrals and rates of representation prevails in Minnesota at all offense levels. Thus, in Minnesota prior referrals increase both the likelihood of out-of-home placement and secure confinement (Table 3-9) as well as the appointment of counsel (Table 3-10). In Nebraska, by contrast, the relationship between prior referrals and rates of representation is not nearly as consistent. The major difference in rates of representation occurs between youths with no prior referrals and those with one or two priors. Perhaps this is because in Nebraska, prior referrals include informal as well as formal referrals, whereas in Minnesota, prior referrals consist exclusively of previously petitioned cases.

## DISPOSITION BY ATTORNEYS BY PRIORS

Tables 3-9 and 3-10 show that prior referrals are associated with receiving more severe dispositions as well as with the likelihood of having an attorney. Table 3-11 examines the relationship between prior referrals and receiving an out-of-home placement or secure confinement disposition when an attorney is present or absent. The percentages within offense categories, dispositions, and priors are those for youths receiving an out-of-home placement or secure confinement when an attorney is present and when one is not.

As can be seen by row comparisons at each offense level and type of disposition across priors, youths with attorneys are more likely to receive out-of-home placement and secure confinement than are those without counsel. In effect, controlling for present offense and prior record simultaneously, larger proportions of youths with lawyers receive out-of-home placements and secure confinement than do those without. In Minnesota, with forty-eight possible comparisons—six categories of offense times two types of disposition times four of priors—represented youths received more severe dispositions in forty-four instances, or 91.7% of the time. In Nebraska, represented youths received more severe dispositions in thirty-nine comparisons, or 81.3% of the time.

**Table 3-11   Rate of Disposition (Home/Secure) by Counsel by Prior Referral**

| | Minnesota | | | | Nebraska | | | |
|---|---|---|---|---|---|---|---|---|
| Prior Referrals | 0 | 1–2 | 3–4 | 5+ | 0 | 1–2 | 3–4 | 5+ |
| **Felony Offense Against Person** | | | | | | | | |
| Home (%) | | | | | | | | |
| Counsel | 39.5 | 49.5 | 84.0 | 100.0 | 10.0 | 33.3 | 100.0 | — |
| No Counsel | 23.1 | 54.5 | 66.7 | — | — | — | — | 80.0 |
| Secure (%) | | | | | | | | |
| Counsel | 24.3 | 32.0 | 56.0 | 100.0 | 10.0 | 22.2 | — | — |
| No Counsel | 15.4 | 31.8 | 66.7 | — | — | — | — | 60.0 |
| **Felony Offense Against Property** | | | | | | | | |
| Home (%) | | | | | | | | |
| Counsel | 25.2 | 53.4 | 76.9 | 75.0 | 10.8 | 35.5 | 58.8 | 100.0 |
| No Counsel | 15.2 | 27.7 | 68.2 | 42.9 | 2.3 | 8.3 | 22.2 | 47.1 |
| Secure (%) | | | | | | | | |
| Counsel | 18.9 | 37.2 | 66.7 | 55.6 | 3.1 | 26.3 | 41.2 | 100.0 |
| No Counsel | 10.4 | 16.8 | 54.5 | 28.6 | 1.1 | 5.6 | 22.2 | 41.2 |
| **Minor Offense Against Person** | | | | | | | | |
| Home (%) | | | | | | | | |
| Counsel | 19.4 | 41.5 | 65.6 | 90.0 | — | 36.4 | 42.9 | 60.0 |
| No Counsel | 7.5 | 31.7 | 50.0 | 50.0 | 20.0 | 30.0 | 18.2 | 80.0 |
| Secure (%) | | | | | | | | |
| Counsel | 11.1 | 22.2 | 40.6 | 80.0 | — | 18.2 | 28.6 | 40.0 |
| No Counsel | 3.5 | 21.7 | 50.0 | 50.0 | 8.0 | 13.3 | — | 20.0 |
| **Minor Offense Against Property** | | | | | | | | |
| Home (%) | | | | | | | | |
| Counsel | 14.8 | 32.8 | 50.7 | 68.4 | 7.6 | 17.2 | 31.8 | 17.4 |
| No Counsel | 7.5 | 20.1 | 37.8 | 50.0 | 2.2 | 5.8 | 10.3 | 36.6 |
| Secure (%) | | | | | | | | |
| Counsel | 9.1 | 23.8 | 39.1 | 57.9 | 3.0 | 9.7 | 29.5 | 17.4 |
| No Counsel | 4.9 | 11.7 | 33.3 | 25.0 | 0.2 | 3.6 | 2.6 | 19.5 |
| **Other Delinquency** | | | | | | | | |
| Home (%) | | | | | | | | |
| Counsel | 20.2 | 39.3 | 59.0 | 55.9 | 16.0 | 38.5 | 44.4 | — |
| No Counsel | 6.8 | 20.1 | 14.8 | 50.0 | 5.7 | 8.8 | 16.7 | 40.0 |
| Secure (%) | | | | | | | | |
| Counsel | 11.6 | 23.5 | 42.3 | 50.0 | 4.0 | 30.8 | 22.2 | — |
| No Counsel | 3.1 | 11.5 | 7.4 | 50.0 | — | 2.9 | — | 20.0 |
| **Status Offense** | | | | | | | | |
| Home (%) | | | | | | | | |
| Counsel | 17.3 | 30.0 | 53.4 | 64.3 | 32.2 | 38.8 | 36.4 | 57.1 |
| No Counsel | 6.5 | 13.8 | 19.2 | 14.3 | 11.1 | 16.4 | 23.8 | 44.4 |
| Secure (%) | | | | | | | | |
| Counsel | 3.2 | 10.6 | 30.7 | 42.9 | 1.2 | 1.9 | 18.2 | 28.6 |
| No Counsel | 1.1 | 2.8 | 13.5 | 7.1 | 1.2 | 1.4 | 4.8 | — |

## CONCLUSION

Nearly twenty years after *Gault* held that juveniles are constitutionally entitled to the assistance of counsel, half of the jurisdictions for which data are available still are not in compliance. In Nebraska, Minnesota, and North Dakota, nearly half or more of delinquent and status offenders appear in juvenile courts without lawyers (Table 3-2). Moreover, many juveniles who receive out-of-home placement and even secure confinement were adjudicated delinquent and sentenced without the assistance of counsel (Table 3-4). One may speculate whether the midwestern states are more representative of most juvenile courts in other parts of the country than are the large urban states. However, in light of the more limited findings from other jurisdictions (Clarke and Koch 1980; Bortner 1982; Aday 1986), it is apparent that many juveniles are unrepresented.

Clearly, it is possible to provide counsel for the vast majority of young offenders. California, Pennsylvania and Philadelphia, and New York do so routinely. What is especially impressive in those jurisdictions is the very low numbers of uncounseled juveniles who receive out-of-home placement or secure confinement dispositions (Tables 3-4 and 3-8). While this chapter shows substantial differences in rates of representation among the different states, it cannot account for the greater availability of counsel in some of the jurisdictions than in others.

One can only speculate as to why *Gault*'s mandate is implemented more fully in some jurisdictions than in others. One avenue for inquiry concerns when the right to counsel was originally recognized in the juvenile courts of the various states. It may be, for example, that the states in which lawyers are routinely available provided counsel to juveniles even prior to *Gault*. As a consequence, the Supreme Court's decision would have had relatively little practical impact on justice administration. On the other hand, those states whose legislation did not provide for counsel prior to *Gault* may be more grudging in their subsequent compliance. California, for example, provided for appointment of counsel in juvenile courts in 1961 (Cal. Welf. & Inst. Code § 634; Lemert 1970). Similarly, New York provided for counsel in juvenile courts in 1962 (N.Y. Fam. Ct. Act § 741(a)). By contrast, jurisdictions that did not provide "due process" in juvenile courts prior to *Gault*, amended their juvenile codes thereafter. For example, North Dakota legislation did not provide for appointment of counsel until 1969, in reaction to *Gault* (N.D. Cent. Code § 27–20–26). It may be, then, that successful implementation of a legal reform depends upon whether the impetus is generated from within a state or imposed upon the state.

Apart from simply documenting variations in rates of representation, this comparison also examined the determinants of representation. It examined the relationship between "legal variables"—seriousness of offense, detention status, and prior referrals—and the appointment of counsel. In each analysis, it showed the zero-order relationship between the legal variables and dispositions, the legal variables and the appointment of counsel, and the effect of representation on dispositions.

There is obviously a relationship between the factors that produce more severe dispositions and the factors that influence the appointment of counsel. Each legal variable associated with more severe dispositions is also associated with greater rates of representation. And yet, within the limitations of this research design, it appears that in virtually every jurisdiction, representation by counsel is an aggravating factor in a juvenile's disposition. When controlling for the seriousness of the present offense, unrepresented juveniles seem to fare better at sentencing than those with lawyers (Tables 3-3 and 3-4). When controlling for offense and detention status, unrepresented juveniles again fare better than those with representation (Tables 3-7 and 3-8). When controlling for the seriousness of the present offense and prior referrals, the presence of counsel produces more severe dispositions (Tables 3-10 and 3-11). In short, while the legal variables enhance the probabilities of representation, the fact of representation appears to exert an independent effect on the severity of dispositions.

Although other studies have alluded to this phenomenon (Bortner 1982; Clarke and Koch 1980; Carrington and Moyer 1988a, 1988b), this research provides additional evidence that representation by counsel redounds to the disadvantage of a juvenile. Chapters Four and Five will attempt to explain why this might be so. One possible explanation is that attorneys in juvenile court are simply incompetent and prejudice their clients' cases (Stapleton and Teitelbaum 1972; Lefstein, Stapleton, and Teitelbaum 1969; Fox 1970a; Platt, Schechter, and Tiffany 1968; Platt and Friedman 1968; Ferster, Courtless, and Snethen 1971; McMillian and McMurtry 1970; Kay and Segal 1973; Bortner 1982; Clarke and Koch 1980; Knitzer and Sobie 1984). Or perhaps the relationship between the presence of counsel and the increased severity of dispositions is spurious. It may be that early in a proceeding, a juvenile court judge's greater familiarity with a case may alert him or her to the eventual disposition that will be imposed and counsel may be appointed in anticipation of more severe consequences (Aday 1986). In many jurisdictions, the same judge who presides at a youth's arraignment and detention hearing will later decide the case on the merits and then impose a sentence. Perhaps the initial decision to appoint counsel is based upon the same evidence developed at those earlier stages which also influences later dispositions.

Another possible explanation is that juvenile court judges may treat more formally and severely juveniles who appear with counsel than those without. Within statutory limits, judges may feel less constrained when sentencing a youth who is represented. While not necessarily punishing juveniles who are represented, judges may incline toward leniency toward those youths who appear unaided and "throw themselves on the mercy of the court." Such may be the price of formal procedures.

The relationship between the presence of counsel, procedural formality, and sentencing severity raises a host of issues about juvenile justice administration. Intrastate variations in judicial waiver (Hamparian et al. 1982; Feld 1990), sentencing practices (Feld 1991), and the rates and effects of representation indicate that juvenile courts are highly variable organizations that differ on many dimensions (Stapleton, Aday, and Ito 1982; Hasenfeld and Cheung 1985; Feld 1989, 1991). With *Gault*'s imposition of formal procedures and the emergence of punitive sentencing goals, juvenile courts no longer can be assumed either to conform to the traditional, therapeutic model or even to be similar to one another (Feld 1984, 1988b).

A court's social context may strongly influence the ways in which cases are selected, heard, and disposed. Social structure is associated consistently with differences in juvenile crime rates, the degree of procedural formality, and juvenile justice administration. These differences are reflected in prepetition screening of cases, the presence of counsel, pretrial detention, and sentencing practices. The data in this chapter provide some macrolevel evidence from which to infer a relationship between procedural formality and sentencing severity in juvenile courts. The rates of representation in more urban, industrial states—California, Pennsylvania, and New York—are about double the rates in more rural, midwestern states—Minnesota, North Dakota, and Nebraska. Perhaps related to its greater procedural formality, California is one of the leaders in "cracking down" on youth crime (Forst and Blomquist 1991; Private Sector Task Force, 1987), and New York's "designated felony" legislation is characterized as "one of the harshest juvenile justice [sentencing] systems in the country" (Woods 1980:2). In short, structural features associated with juvenile crime and its repression may also be associated with procedural formality and severity in juvenile justice administration. These patterns are similar to studies of adult criminal courts that analyze the effects of urbanization and other contextual variables on sentencing decisions (Meyers and Talarico 1986, 1987).

Recent trends in juvenile justice emphasize punishment over rehabilitation with a corresponding increase in procedural formality (Feld 1984, 1987, 1988b). Is there a relationship between procedural formality and sentencing severity? Does greater urban crime engender more punitive responses, which then require more formal procedural safeguards as a prerequisite? Or does urban bureaucratization lead to more formal procedural safeguards, which then enable judges to exact a greater toll than they otherwise might? Perceived increases in urban crime may foster a "war-on-crime" mentality that places immense pressures on the juvenile justice system to "get tough" and furthers the convergence between juvenile and criminal courts. The in-depth analyses of the determinants and impact of counsel in Minnesota in Chapters Four and Five will attempt to untangle further this complex web.

## NOTES

1. According to the Bureau, the coding forms used in 1984 classified defense representation as (1) none, (2) private counsel, (3) court appointed counsel, and (4) public defender. In some instances, although a juvenile may have been represented, the court personnel who completed the forms reported "none" if they did not know which type of counsel appeared. The reporting form was revised in 1986 to include an additional category of "unknown."

2. In Minnesota, the prior record consists exclusively of previously petitioned cases. In Nebraska, the prior referrals include both formally petitioned cases and those referred to intake which were disposed of informally. As indicated in Table 3-1, 62.8% of referrals in Nebraska result in formal petitions.

# chapter four ──────────────────────────

## DO LAWYERS MAKE A DIFFERENCE?

The Impact of Counsel in Minnesota's Juvenile Courts

Chapter Four examines the determinants and impact of counsel on juvenile justice administration in Minnesota in 1986. The analyses attempt to answer two interrelated questions. First, what factors determine when lawyers appear on behalf of juveniles? Second, what effect does representation have on the way that a juvenile's case is handled and disposed? The first question involves examining the relationships between certain independent variables such as offense seriousness, prior record, and pretrial detention, and variations in rates of representation. The second question involves examining the impact of counsel on the sentences juveniles receive or the ways in which their cases are processed, after controlling for the influence of other independent, legal variables. Since Minnesota is a state in which somewhat less than half of all petitioned youths are represented (Table 3-2), it provides a natural, quasi-experiment that is a research design in which subjects are not randomly assigned to experimental groups, but in which statistical controls can hold constant many of the relevant independent variables. Thus, Chapter Four will examine the determinants and influence of counsel on juvenile justice administration in counties in which lawyers routinely appear, often appear, and seldom appear.

## OFFENSES, ATTORNEYS, AND DISPOSITIONS

Tables 4-1 to 4-4 introduce the Minnesota juvenile justice system. They examine the types of offenses juveniles commit, the sources of referral to juvenile courts, rates of representation, and the effect of counsel on juveniles' dispositions. The tables in this chapter and the following chapter report row or column percentages and the sample size (N =) where appropriate for the entire state and separately for counties that have been aggregated on the basis of their high, medium, or low rates of representation. As described in greater detail in Chapter Two, counties were classified as high representation if more than 67% of youths were represented, medium if between 33% and 66% were represented, and low if less than 33% of youths had counsel. Because of the large overall sample size (N = 17,195), and the nonrandom assignment of subjects to various categories, tests of significance are omitted.

## PETITIONS AND OFFENSES

Initially, the appearance of counsel must be placed in the larger context of juvenile justice administration in Minnesota. Table 4-1 reports the total

**Table 4-1    Petitions and Offenses**

|  | Statewide | High | Medium | Low |
|---|---|---|---|---|
| **Felony** | | | | |
| % | 18.4 | 20.1 | 19.6 | 16.6 |
| N | 3,153 | 711 | 1,243 | 1,199 |
| Felony Offense Against Person | | | | |
| % | 4.0 | 4.8 | 4.3 | 3.2 |
| N | 680 | 169 | 276 | 235 |
| Felony Offense Against Property | | | | |
| % | 14.4 | 15.3 | 15.2 | 13.2 |
| N | 2,473 | 542 | 967 | 964 |
| **Misdemeanor** | | | | |
| % | 54.4 | 59.0 | 53.4 | 53.0 |
| N | 9,298 | 2,084 | 3,383 | 3,831 |
| Minor Offense Against Person | | | | |
| % | 5.2 | 6.6 | 5.5 | 4.2 |
| N | 889 | 234 | 348 | 307 |
| Minor Offense Against Property | | | | |
| % | 32.3 | 32.0 | 28.3 | 35.9 |
| N | 5,554 | 1,137 | 1,799 | 2,618 |
| Other Delinquency | | | | |
| % | 16.6 | 20.1 | 19.4 | 12.4 |
| N | 2,855 | 713 | 1,236 | 906 |
| **Status** | | | | |
| % | 27.2 | 20.9 | 27.0 | 30.5 |
| N | 4,649 | 737 | 1,708 | 2,204 |

number of juveniles against whom petitions were filed and the types of offenses with which they were charged in the state and in the aggregated counties with high, medium, and low rates of representation. Throughout the state, 18.4% of juveniles were charged with offenses that would be felonies if committed by adults, 54.4% were charged with minor offenses—misdemeanors and gross misdemeanors—and 27.2% were charged with noncriminal status offenses, those forms of juvenile misconduct that would not be criminal if committed by an adult, such as truancy, running away, alcohol consumption and the like (Minn. Stat. § 260.015, subd. 19–24). Within the felony category, offenses against property predominated, primarily burglary. Similarly, within the minor offense category, property offenses such as shoplifting, theft, and vandalism predominated. Less than 10% of Minnesota's delinquency cases involved felony or minor offenses against the person, and slightly more than 25% of the cases involved noncriminal status offenses.

When juveniles' petitions are examined separately for the counties with high, medium, and low rates of representation, somewhat different offense patterns emerge. In general, the counties with low rates of representation, which are primarily but not exclusively rural counties, deal with somewhat less serious delinquency. They process 3% to 4.5% fewer juveniles charged with felony offenses and a correspondingly larger proportion of status offenders. Only 7.4% of juveniles in counties with low rates of representation were charged with felony or minor offenses against the person, as contrasted with 9.8% and 11.4% of juveniles in counties with medium and high rates of representation. While minor offenses against property are the most prevalent form of delinquency throughout the state, property offenses and status offenses constitute about two-thirds of the dockets of juvenile courts in low representation counties. As later analyses will demonstrate, there is a direct relationship between the seriousness of the offense and rates of representation. Counties with lower rates of representation handle somewhat less serious types of offenders, which is consistent with their predominantly rural character (Nimick et al. 1985a:13). By contrast, the counties with high rates of representation handle about 10% fewer juveniles charged with status offenses and proportionally more youths charged with misdemeanor and felony offenses.

## SOURCE OF REFERRAL

Juvenile delinquency and status offense cases are referred to juvenile courts from a variety of sources: police, probation officers, parents, schools, welfare departments, and others. Table 4-2 reports the sources of referral to juvenile courts in Minnesota.

While police are the primary source of juvenile referrals in the state for all offense categories, probation officers and "other"—primarily schools—refer many juveniles in the "other delinquency" and status offense categories. Other delinquency includes drug offenses such as possession of marijuana, disorderly conduct and public order offenses, and, most significantly, contempt of court and violations of probation. These latter offenses account for the predominance of probation officers as sources of referral. The status offense category includes 1,187 cases of truancy, which are referred primarily by the schools. While schools are the obvious source of referrals for truancy, school districts receive state educational funding on a per capita basis and have a substantial fiscal, as well as educational, incentive to keep the largest numbers of students enrolled in school (Minn. Stat. Ann. § 124.17 [1986]).

The proportion of referrals by sources other than police differ in the counties with high, medium, and low rates of representation. While referrals by schools are the largest source of nonpolice referrals in all three types of counties, they differ in the relative makeup of probation and parental referrals. In the high representation counties, about one out of ten delinquents (10.9%) are referred by probation officers, primarily in the "other delinquency" category, presumably for probation violations (38.3%). By contrast, in the medium and low representation counties, probation is an insignificant source of referral, contributing only 0.1% of cases, with proportionally more referrals by parents. As will be seen, the source of a referral, especially from a probation officer, strongly influences the actions of courts.

The substantially greater role of probation officers as sources of referral, especially for other delinquency and status offenses, in the high representation counties than in the medium and low representation counties suggests a greater degree of formality and bureaucratization in the high representation settings. The greater prevalence of counsel in these settings is simply another indicator of courtroom processes with greater procedural formality and role differentiation.

## RATES OF REPRESENTATION

Tables 4-3 and 4-4 report the overall rates of representation by counsel, the percentages of private attorneys and public attorneys—court appointed or public defender—and the rates of representation by type of offense. Although *Gault* held that *every* juvenile is constitutionally enti-

**Table 4-2 Offense and Petitioner**

| Petitioner | Statewide | | | | High | | | | Medium | | | | Low | | | |
|---|---|---|---|---|---|---|---|---|---|---|---|---|---|---|---|---|
| | Police | Prob. Officer | Parent | Other | Police | Prob. Officer | Parent | Other | Police | Prob. Officer | Parent | Other | Police | Prob. Officer | Parent | Other |
| **Overall (%)** | 89.2 | 2.3 | 1.5 | 7.0 | 72.8 | 10.9 | 1.3 | 15.0 | 92.0 | 0.1 | 2.3 | 5.6 | 94.6 | 0.1 | 0.9 | 4.3 |
| Felony Offense Against Person (%) | 94.6 | 0.1 | 0.3 | 5.0 | 84.6 | — | 0.6 | 14.8 | 97.8 | 0.4 | — | 1.8 | 97.9 | — | 0.4 | 1.7 |
| Felony Offense Against Property (%) | 96.1 | 0.2 | — | 3.7 | 94.8 | 0.6 | — | 4.6 | 93.7 | — | — | 6.3 | 99.3 | 0.1 | 0.1 | 0.5 |
| Minor Offense Against Person (%) | 95.7 | 0.3 | 0.2 | 3.7 | 91.0 | 0.9 | 0.4 | 7.7 | 95.7 | 0.3 | 0.3 | 3.7 | 99.3 | — | — | 0.7 |
| Minor Offense Against Property (%) | 95.8 | 0.3 | 0.4 | 3.6 | 92.7 | 1.0 | 0.1 | 6.2 | 95.0 | — | 0.3 | 4.7 | 97.6 | 0.1 | 0.6 | 1.6 |
| Other Delinquency (%) | 82.8 | 9.7 | 0.8 | 6.8 | 46.6 | 38.3 | 3.1 | 12.1 | 93.0 | — | — | 7.0 | 97.2 | 0.3 | — | 2.4 |
| Status (%) | 79.8 | 2.2 | 4.4 | 13.7 | 43.4 | 12.9 | 2.7 | 41.0 | 85.9 | 0.2 | 8.1 | 5.9 | 87.3 | 0.1 | 2.0 | 10.6 |
| **Representation by Counsel (%)** | 43.1 | 89.9 | 50.4 | 56.2 | 96.0 | 91.2 | 84.8 | 90.6 | 47.5 | 80.0 | 40.1 | 37.8 | 19.0 | 44.4 | 48.4 | 18.2 |

**Table 4-3 Rate of Representation and Offense**

| Attorney | Statewide | | High | | Medium | | Low | |
|---|---|---|---|---|---|---|---|---|
| | Yes | No | Yes | No | Yes | No | Yes | No |
| **Overall** | | | | | | | | |
| % Counsel at Adjudication | 45.3 | 54.7 | 94.5 | 5.5 | 46.8 | 53.2 | 19.3 | 80.7 |
| **Felony (%)** | 66.1 | 33.9 | 98.1 | 1.9 | 71.2 | 28.8 | 41.1 | 58.9 |
| Felony Offense Against Person (%) | 77.3 | 22.7 | 97.5 | 2.5 | 81.5 | 18.5 | 56.8 | 43.2 |
| Felony Offense Against Property (%) | 63.0 | 37.0 | 98.3 | 1.7 | 68.2 | 31.8 | 37.3 | 62.7 |
| **Misdemeanor (%)** | 46.4 | 53.6 | 95.2 | 4.8 | 47.4 | 52.6 | 18.2 | 81.8 |
| Minor Offense Against Person (%) | 62.4 | 37.6 | 96.5 | 3.5 | 66.2 | 33.8 | 30.5 | 69.5 |
| Minor Offense Against Property (%) | 44.6 | 55.4 | 97.2 | 2.8 | 52.3 | 47.7 | 15.8 | 84.2 |
| Other Delinquency (%) | 44.9 | 55.1 | 91.5 | 8.5 | 34.7 | 65.3 | 21.3 | 78.7 |
| **Status (%)** | 28.9 | 71.1 | 89.1 | 10.9 | 27.2 | 72.8 | 9.3 | 90.7 |
| **Overall** | | | | | | | | |
| % Counsel at Disposition | 38.9 | 61.1 | 66.7 | 33.3 | 45.3 | 54.7 | 20.0 | 80.0 |

tled to "the guiding hand of counsel at every step of the process," *Gault*'s mandate remains unrealized in Minnesota.

Overall, only 45.3% of juveniles in Minnesota receive the assistance of counsel at their adjudication, that is, their arraignment, plea, or trial. However, in the five counties with high rates of representation, 94.5% of juveniles have counsel; in the fourteen counties with medium rates, 46.8% have counsel; and in the remaining sixty-eight counties with low rates, only 19.3% have counsel. While these categories—high, medium, and low—were created by classifying counties on the basis of their rates of representation, the substantial differences in aggregate rates of representation lend themselves to a variety of comparative analyses of the determinants and impact of counsel in delinquency proceedings in different types of juvenile courts within the state.

Table 4-3 reports aggregate rates of representation regardless of the type of attorney. These summary rates will facilitate subsequent analyses that report both the effects of representation versus nonrepresentation as well as representation by different types of lawyers. It is noteworthy to compare the rates of representation reported in Table 4-3 with those for different types of petitioners reported in the last row of Table 4-2. While the overall rate of representation of juveniles in the state is 45.3%, a slightly lower proportion of juveniles referred by police are represented. By contrast, when juveniles are referred by probation officers a much larger proportion, nearly double the overall state rate, are represented. In part, the greater rate of representation for probation referrals reflects the fact that such juveniles have prior records and perhaps already have an ongoing relationship with an attorney from their prior appearances. The rate is further inflated because a large proportion of cases referred by probation officers are in high representation counties, although the same pattern prevails in the medium or low representation counties. Subsequent analyses will show a consistent relationship between rates of representation and the severity of dispositions (Tables 4-9, 4-14, and 4-18). Many referrals by probation officers involve juveniles who have failed in a previous placement or who are being brought back to court for a new disposition. Such juveniles are already considerably more at risk to be removed from their homes and thus more likely to have counsel appointed. There are no other consistent patterns in the rates of representation by sources of referral from parents or schools.

The last row of Table 4-3 reports the rates of representation of juveniles at the time of their disposition. Comparing the rates of representation at adjudication (arraignment, plea, or trial) with those at disposition reveals that 6.4% fewer juveniles have counsel when they are sentenced than at the earlier stages of delinquency proceedings. Virtually all of the decrease in representation at disposition occurs in the counties with high rates of representation (94.5% versus 66.7%). Perhaps defense lawyers are more comfortable functioning in a procedurally formal adjudicative context than they are in the "messy" social services-dominated dispositional setting. Or perhaps defense attorneys appreciate that their presence or participation at disposition may be an exercise in futility or may even adversely affect the eventual disposition. Throughout these analyses, juveniles are classified as represented if an attorney appeared on their behalf during the adjudicatory phase of the proceedings.

Like the findings in Chapter Three from California, New York, and Pennsylvania, Table 4-3 clearly shows that it is possible to provide high levels of defense representation to all juveniles charged with delinquency. In the high representation counties which process more than one-fifth of Minnesota's delinquents, more than 98% of youths charged with felony offenses, and almost 95% of those charged with minor criminal offenses are represented. While it may be somewhat more difficult to deliver legal services easily in the rural counties of the state, these aggregate county variations suggest that differences in rates of representation reflect deliberate policy decisions by the juvenile court judges about the appointment of counsel rather than any inherent difficulty in providing counsel or the competence of juveniles to waive representation.

Table 4-3 also shows the rates of representation by type of offense. One pattern that emerges is a direct relationship between the seriousness of the present offense and rates of representation. Juveniles charged with felony offenses and with minor offenses against the person generally have higher rates of representation than the overall rate. Thus, while only 45.3% of juveniles in the state have lawyers, nearly two-thirds (66.1%) of those charged with felony offenses are represented by counsel—77.3% of those charged with felony offenses against the person, and 63.0% of those charged with felony offenses against property—as are 62.4% of those charged with minor offenses against the person. However, these types of offenses constitute less than one-quarter of the juvenile courts' dockets (Table 4-1). In no other offense categories are even a majority of youths represented. These variations in rates of representation by offense further reinforce the view that the decision to appoint counsel reflects deliberate judicial policies rather than differences in minors' competence to waive the assistance of lawyers.

In the high representation counties, as would be expected, there is only minor variation by offenses with somewhat lower rates of representation for juveniles charged with the least serious types of delinquency and status offenses. In the medium and low representation counties, felony offenses and offenses against the person also garner the highest rates of representation. Indeed, in the low representation counties, the only offense category in which even a majority of juveniles are represented (56.8%) are those charged with felony offenses against person, that is, 3.2% of the delinquency petitions filed in those counties (Table 4-1). By contrast, nearly two-thirds (62.7%) of those charged with felony offenses against property, such as burglary, appear without counsel. Even though Table 4-1 reported some differences in offense patterns in high, medium, and low representation counties, Table 4-3 effectively controls for the seriousness of the present offense. Thus, the variations in rates of representation clearly *are not* a function of differences in the distribution of offenses in the counties.

The first row of Table 4-4 reports the proportion of private attorneys and public attorneys (court appointed or public defenders) reflected in the overall rates of representation. Private attorneys are those lawyers directly retained and paid for by the juvenile or his or her parents. Public defenders and court appointed counsel are paid for by the county and appointed by the court; juveniles have virtually no choice in who will represent them. In a very few instances in some counties, a court may appoint a guardian *ad litem*, an adult who is neither a lawyer nor the

**Table 4-4  Attorney Type and Offense**

| | Statewide | | | | High | | | | Medium | | | | Low | | | |
|---|---|---|---|---|---|---|---|---|---|---|---|---|---|---|---|---|
| | Private | PD[a] | CA[b] | None | Private | PD | CA | None | Private | PD | CA | None | Private | PD | CA | None |
| **Overall (%)** | 5.1 | 28.5 | 11.7 | 54.7 | 2.4 | 76.9 | 15.2 | 5.5 | 8.5 | 30.8 | 7.5 | 53.2 | 3.4 | 2.3 | 13.6 | 80.7 |
| **Felony (%)** | 8.1 | 36.0 | 21.9 | 33.9 | 2.8 | 72.8 | 22.5 | 1.9 | 13.3 | 43.9 | 14.0 | 28.8 | 5.9 | 5.4 | 29.8 | 58.9 |
| Felony Offense Against Person (%) | 11.2 | 43.5 | 22.7 | 22.7 | 4.3 | 73.0 | 20.2 | 2.5 | 16.6 | 54.1 | 10.8 | 18.5 | 9.9 | 8.0 | 39.0 | 43.2 |
| Felony Offense Against Property (%) | 7.2 | 34.0 | 21.7 | 37.0 | 2.3 | 72.7 | 23.2 | 1.7 | 12.4 | 40.9 | 14.9 | 31.8 | 4.9 | 4.8 | 27.6 | 62.7 |
| **Misdemeanor (%)** | 5.5 | 29.4 | 11.5 | 53.6 | 2.5 | 76.2 | 16.5 | 4.8 | 9.6 | 30.8 | 7.0 | 52.6 | 3.4 | 2.1 | 12.8 | 81.8 |
| Minor Offense Against Person (%) | 6.4 | 40.5 | 15.5 | 37.6 | 4.4 | 75.8 | 16.3 | 3.5 | 9.8 | 47.8 | 8.6 | 33.8 | 3.9 | 3.5 | 23.0 | 69.5 |
| Minor Offense Against Property (%) | 4.9 | 27.5 | 12.2 | 55.4 | 2.1 | 74.6 | 20.5 | 2.8 | 10.1 | 34.0 | 8.2 | 47.7 | 2.4 | 2.0 | 11.4 | 84.2 |
| Other Delinquency (%) | 6.5 | 29.7 | 8.7 | 55.1 | 2.6 | 78.8 | 10.1 | 8.5 | 8.8 | 21.3 | 4.7 | 65.3 | 6.3 | 1.7 | 13.4 | 78.7 |
| **Status (%)** | 2.1 | 21.6 | 5.1 | 71.1 | 1.8 | 82.6 | 4.6 | 10.9 | 2.5 | 20.9 | 3.7 | 72.8 | 2.0 | 1.0 | 6.4 | 90.7 |

a.  Public Defender.
b.  Court Appointed.

juvenile's parent, to appear with the juvenile. Since such guardians are not licensed attorneys and do not act to represent the child's preferences but rather their own assessment of the child's "best interests," those juveniles with whom guardians occasionally appear are classified as unrepresented.

While most of Minnesota's juveniles are unrepresented (54.7%), when they do have lawyers, their lawyers are most likely to be public defenders (28.5%). Public defenders are the primary legal services delivery system in most of the "high" and "medium" representation counties whereas the "low" representation counties rely upon court appointed counsel. Since privately retained counsel appear in only 5.1% of all delinquency and status cases in the state, public defenders and court appointed attorneys handle the bulk of lawyer-represented petitions. The heavy reliance on "public" attorneys is consistent with the experience in other states (Table 3-2), where public lawyers also predominated in the representation of juvenile offenders.

While the seriousness of the offense increases the likelihood of representation, larger proportions of private attorneys appear on behalf of juveniles charged with felony offenses—person and property—and offenses against the person than appear in the other offense categories. Comparing the overall rate of appearance of private attorneys with the rates when juveniles are charged with felonies against the person shows that the seriousness of the offense doubles the presence of private attorneys. Perhaps the greater seriousness of those offenses and their potential consequences encourage juveniles and/or their families to retain the assistance of private counsel. Conversely, private attorneys are least likely to be retained by parents to represent the status offenders that the parents have referred and with whom they are often in conflict.

## REPRESENTATION BY COUNSEL AND AGE OF JUVENILES

One of the traditional and common explanations for why so many juveniles are unrepresented is that they "waive" their right to counsel. Since legal competency—the capacity to make a "knowing, intelligent, and voluntary" waiver of the right to counsel—presumably correlates with age, one would expect younger juveniles to have higher rates of representation than do older youths. Juvenile court jurisdiction in Minnesota includes any person under the age of eighteen as well as any person who is alleged to have committed their offense prior to age eighteen (Minn. Stat. Ann. § 260.015, subd. 2 [1986]). In some instances, a youth who committed an offense at age seventeen may become eighteen by the time he or she is charged as a delinquent. The dispositional authority of Minnesota's juvenile courts continues until age nineteen (Minn. Stat. Ann. § 260.181, subd. 4 [1986]).

Table 4-5 reports that for the state overall, juveniles aged sixteen and seventeen, presumably the most mature and therefore competent to waive their rights, have somewhat lower rates of representation than do their younger counterparts, although the rate of representation for the eighteen-year-old juveniles is somewhat higher. Moreover, the rate of representation for even the youngest juveniles—those twelve and under—is virtually indistinguishable from the overall state average, 46.3% representation versus 45.3% representation, respectively.

When the data are examined separately in counties with high, medium, and low rates of representation, no clear patterns emerge. In the counties with high rates of representation, there is no discernible relationship between a juvenile's age and rates of representation, which presumably reflects the general policy to appoint lawyers in all instances. While juveniles aged twelve or younger have the second lowest proportion of representation, those aged thirteen have the highest. The sixteen and seventeen-year-old juveniles have higher rates of representation than do the fourteen or fifteen-year-olds. In the counties with medium rates of representation, the youngest juveniles—twelve and under and thirteen—have the highest rates of representation, followed by the sixteen and seventeen-year-old juveniles, while juveniles fourteen and fifteen have the lowest rates of representation. In the counties with low rates of representation, there is no apparent relationship between age and representation by counsel. The youngest juveniles, those twelve and under, have the second lowest rate of representation (18.6%), only seventeen-year-old juveniles having a lower rate (17.8%). In short, any relationship between a juvenile's age and a juvenile court judge's determination that a minor is competent to make a "knowing, intelligent, and voluntary" waiver of constitutional rights is purely coincidental. Later analyses will examine

Table 4-5   Representation by Counsel and Age of Juvenile

| Age | Statewide (%) | High (%) | Medium (%) | Low (%) |
|---|---|---|---|---|
| 12 and Under | 46.3 | 92.8 | 56.3 | 18.6 |
| 13 | 48.9 | 97.8 | 49.3 | 19.9 |
| 14 | 47.7 | 94.6 | 45.7 | 20.9 |
| 15 | 47.4 | 93.2 | 45.0 | 19.2 |
| 16 | 44.1 | 94.8 | 46.2 | 19.8 |
| 17 | 41.9 | 94.9 | 46.1 | 17.8 |
| 18 | 45.0 | 91.2 | 45.5 | 22.8 |

the relationships between age, offenses, and dispositions to determine whether other variables account for the high rates of waivers of counsel by even the youngest juveniles.

## PRESENT OFFENSE AND DISPOSITION

Although there is extensive research on juvenile court sentencing practices, a review of the literature concludes that there are no consistent factors that determine the outcomes of the decision-making process (Thomas and Sieverdes 1975:416). The studies—conducted in different jurisdictions at different times and employing different methodologies and theoretical perspectives—yield contradictory results (Fagan, Slaughter, and Hartstone 1987; McCarthy and Smith 1986).

Juvenile court judges answer the question "what should be done with this child," in part, by reference to explicit statutory mandates (Feld 1988b). However, practical and bureaucratic considerations influence their discretionary decision making as well (Cicourel 1968; Emerson 1969; Bortner 1982; Matza 1964). Juvenile justice practitioners enjoy greater discretion than do their adult-process counterparts because of their presumed need to look beyond the present offense to the "best interests of the child" and paternalistic assumptions about the control of children. Thomas and Fitch (1975:64) note that

> the juvenile justice system differs significantly from its adult counterpart in its express incorporation of highly differential processing of alleged delinquents. The separate juvenile court system emerged from a pervasive belief that the goal of rehabilitation best could be served by permitting juvenile courts to maximize flexibility, informality, and discretion, especially at the dispositional or sentencing stage. Thus, the dispositional alternatives available to the juvenile court are extremely broad.

An obvious question, then, is to what extent do legal factors such as the present offense and prior record, or social characteristics, such as race, sex, family status, or social class, influence dispositional decision making. Juvenile justice personnel make dispositional decisions throughout the process. Police officers may refer a case to intake for formal processing, adjust it informally on the street or at the station house, or divert it (Bittner 1976; Black and Reiss 1970). Intake, in turn, may refer a youth to the juvenile court for formal adjudication or dispose of the case through informal supervision or diversion (Bell and Lang 1985). Finally, even after formal adjudication, the juvenile court judge may choose from a wide array of dispositional alternatives ranging from a continuance without a finding of delinquency, probation, or commitment to a state training school. Recent research indicates that the dispositional decision-making process is cumulative; decisions made by the initial participants— police, intake, or participants at detention—affect the types of decisions made by subsequent participants (McCarthy and Smith 1986; Barton 1976; Phillips and Dinitz 1982). Thus, assessing judicial decision making implicates decision making by other juvenile justice actors.

Evaluations of dispositional practices by police, intake, and the juvenile court suggest that, despite the nominal commitment to individualized justice, the principle of offense pervades practical decision making throughout the process (Feld 1987, 1988b). Matza (1964: 113–14) has described the principle of offense as a principle of equality, treating similar cases in a similar fashion based on a relatively narrowly defined frame of legal relevance.

> The principle of [offense or] equality refers to a specific set of substantive criteria that are awarded central relevance and, historically, to a set of considerations that were specifically and momentously precluded. Its meaning, especially in criminal [and juvenile] proceedings, has been to give a central and unrivaled position in the framework of relevance to considerations of offense and conditions closely related to offense like prior record, and to more or less preclude considerations of status and circumstance.

Traditionally, juvenile courts pursued substantive justice in which characteristics of the offender, rather than the offense, determined dispositional decisions. Substantive decision making is designed to achieve the best decision in the individual case rather than to apply abstract legal principles or guidelines to recurring factual situations. The "rehabilitative ideal" of the juvenile court is one of individualized justice that encompasses a variety of social background variables rather than simply legal factors (Horowitz and Wasserman 1980).

Despite the juvenile court's traditional commitment to the "best interests" of the child, however, recent evaluation research suggests an increased emphasis on characteristics of the offense as a determinant of sentences (Feld 1988b). As a corollary of the procedural formality imposed by *Gault*, juvenile courts increasingly seek formal rationality by using general rules applicable to categories of cases rather than pursuing individualized substantive justice.

The President's Commission on Law Enforcement and the Administration of Justice in 1967 (President's Commission 1967b), which influenced the Supreme Court's *Gault* decision, also provided a theoretical imprimatur for offense-based sentencing when it explicitly acknowledged the punitive character of juvenile court intervention:

> Court adjudication and disposition of those offenders should no longer be viewed solely as a diagnosis and prescription for cure, but should be frankly recognized as an authoritative court judgment expressing society's claim to protection. While rehabilitative efforts should be vigorously pursued in deference to the youth of the offenders and in keeping with a general commitment to individualized treatment of all offenders, the incapacitative, deterrent, and condemnatory aspects of the judgment should not be disguised. (President's Commission 1967b:2)

Subsequently, several juvenile justice policy groups have recommended the abolition of indeterminate sentences and their replacement with formal dispositional criteria and sentences proportional to the seriousness of the offense—in short, a shift from substantive justice to formal legal rationality (American Bar Association 1980a; National Advisory Committee 1976).

The elevation of the principle of offense receives practical impetus from bureaucratic imperatives. One is the desire of juvenile and criminal justice agencies to avoid "scandal" and unfavorable political and media attention (Cicourel 1968; Emerson 1969; Bortner 1982; Matza 1964). Emerson (1974:624) observes that

> juvenile court decision-making comes to be pervaded by a sense of vulnerability to adverse public reaction for failing to control or restrain delinquent offenders. [Fear of scrutiny and criticism increases pressures] to impose maximum restraints on the offender—in most instances incarceration. Anything less risks immediate criticism. But more than this, it also exposes the court to the possibility of even stronger reaction in the future. For given any recurrence of serious illegal activity, former decisions that can be interpreted as "lenient" become difficult to defend.

Similarly, Matza (1964:122) notes that ultimately, the juvenile court judge must be responsive to public concerns about safety.

> He will have to explain . . . why the 17-year-old murderer of an innocent matron was allowed to roam the streets, on probation, when just last year he was booked for mugging. This is no easy question to answer. Somehow, an invoking of the principle of individualized justice and a justification of mercy on the basis of accredited social-work theory hardly seems appropriate on these occasions.

These organizational factors encourage courts to attach more formal and restrictive responses to more serious forms of juvenile deviance. "[W]hether a juvenile goes to some manner of prison or is put on some manner of probation . . . depends first, on a traditional rule-of-thumb assessment of the total risk of danger and thus scandal evident in the juvenile's current offense and prior record of offenses" (Matza 1964:125).

Finally, juvenile courts necessarily develop bureaucratic strategies to cope with the requirements of contradictory formal goals and highly individualized assessments.

> Time after time after time procedures emerge which permit officials . . . to classify and categorize those who come to their attention as swiftly and simply as they can. The form of these categorization processes is commonly defined by the types of information which organizations routinely capture as a basis for forming or, equally often, defending the decisions they are obligated to make. (Marshall and Thomas 1983:55–57)

Since the present offense and the prior record of delinquency are among the types of information routinely and necessarily collected in juvenile court processing, it is hardly surprising that they provide a type of decisional rule. As the juvenile court balances its internal, clinical and administrative concerns with external public relations considerations, it restores the principle of offense, at least in part, as a form of decisional rule. Matza (1964:124–25) argues that

> [t]he court's solution [to its dispositional dilemma] contains two elements. One, the main part of the solution, is to more or less reinstore—*sub rosa*—the *principle of offense*. . . . [T]he concern with individual characteristics and with treatment is not completely surrendered by the court . . . but they are transformed. . . . The workable bureaucratic equivalents of the stress on extraordinary individual characteristics—equity—and the philosophy of treatment are the doctrines of *parental sponsorship* and *residential availability*.

Unfortunately, the SJIS data do not include information on several of the personal and social variables characteristically used in juvenile sentencing research, and this study cannot analyze fully the determinants of dispositions. However, the data do lend themselves to an exploration of the relationships between legal variables, dispositions, and representation by an attorney. Table 4-6 uses two measures of juvenile court dispositions: 1) out-of-home placement, and 2) secure confinement. Out-of-home placement involves any disposition in which the child is removed from his or her home and placed, for example, in a group home, foster care, in-patient psychiatric or chemical dependency treatment facility, or secure institution. Secure confinement is a substantial subset of all out-of-home placement, but consists exclusively of commitments to the county-level institutions or state training schools. While out-of-home placement is not the functional equivalent of adult penal confinement, it constitutes a very severe intervention in the life of a child and family and may continue for a significant period. Both of these forms of intervention provide clear-cut delineations that lend themselves to cross-county comparisons. They are legally significant for the appointment of counsel, because the Supreme Court has held, at least for adults, that all persons charged with felonies must be afforded the right to counsel and that no person convicted of a misdemeanor may be incarcerated unless he or she was afforded or waived the assistance of counsel (*Gideon v. Wainwright*, 372 U.S. 335 [1963]; *Scott v. Illinois*, 440 U.S. 367 [1979]).

Table 4-6 reports the rates of out-of-home placement and secure confinement dispositions in the state and in the respective counties, overall as well as by categories of offenses. The high, medium, and low representation counties differ markedly in their use of out-of-home placement and secure confinement. For the whole state, 18.5% of all petitioned juveniles are removed from their homes, and 11.1% of all juveniles are incarcerated in state or local institutions. However, in high representation counties, about one of four juveniles is removed from home, in medium representation counties, about one of five, while in low representation counties, only about one out of seven is removed. Juveniles prosecuted in the high representation counties are nearly twice as likely to be removed or confined as those in low representation counties. These differences in sentencing patterns raise questions about the relationships between procedural formality and sentencing severity that will be explored further in Chapter Six.

As might be expected, the seriousness of the present offense substantially alters a youth's risk of removal and confinement. Despite the juvenile court's theoretical commitment to individualized dispositions in which there is no necessary relationship between the seriousness of a juvenile's offense, his "real needs" and the ultimate sentence, the actual practices evidence a strong element of proportionality. Juveniles charged with felony offenses against person and property or minor offenses against the person have the highest rates of out-of-home placement and secure confinement. For the state as a whole, of all the juveniles charged with a felony offense against the person, 42.2% are removed from their homes, and 27.5% are incarcerated. Overall, about one-third (34.3%) of

**Table 4-6   Offense and Disposition: Out-of-Home Placement/Secure Confinement**

| | Statewide | High | Medium | Low |
|---|---|---|---|---|
| **Overall** | | | | |
| % Home | 18.5 | 25.1 | 20.0 | 13.9 |
| N | (3,168) | (882) | (1,274) | (1,012) |
| % Secure | 11.1 | 15.8 | 12.3 | 7.8 |
| N | (1,903) | (555) | (780) | (568) |
| **Felony** | | | | |
| % Home | 34.3 | 35.5 | 38.2 | 29.0 |
| % Secure | 24.4 | 25.9 | 28.8 | 18.5 |
| Felony Offense Against Person | | | | |
| % Home | 42.2 | 44.2 | 46.0 | 35.9 |
| % Secure | 27.5 | 29.5 | 32.1 | 20.2 |
| Felony Offense Against Property | | | | |
| % Home | 32.1 | 33.1 | 35.9 | 27.4 |
| % Secure | 23.6 | 25.0 | 27.9 | 18.1 |
| **Misdemeanor** | | | | |
| % Home | 17.6 | 25.3 | 18.0 | 13.4 |
| % Secure | 11.3 | 16.4 | 11.7 | 8.3 |
| Minor Offense Against Person | | | | |
| % Home | 24.0 | 29.5 | 24.6 | 19.6 |
| % Secure | 14.5 | 19.7 | 13.1 | 12.7 |
| Minor Offense Against Property | | | | |
| % Home | 16.0 | 19.3 | 19.6 | 12.0 |
| % Secure | 10.8 | 13.3 | 13.9 | 7.6 |
| Other Delinquency | | | | |
| % Home | 18.9 | 33.6 | 14.0 | 15.0 |
| % Secure | 11.3 | 20.3 | 8.4 | 8.6 |
| **Status** | | | | |
| % Home | 12.4 | 23.1 | 12.5 | 8.9 |
| % Secure | 3.5 | 9.7 | 2.3 | 2.5 |
| | **Source of Referral and Disposition** | | | |
| Police | | | | |
| % Home | 17.0 | 20.3 | 20.0 | 13.3 |
| % Secure | 10.7 | 14.1 | 12.6 | 7.8 |
| Probation Officer | | | | |
| % Home | 53.0 | 52.0 | 80.0 | 77.7 |
| % Secure | 28.7 | 28.4 | 20.0 | 44.4 |
| Parents | | | | |
| % Home | 34.0 | 38.6 | 25.2 | 47.7 |
| % Secure | 7.4 | 15.9 | 1.4 | 14.9 |
| Other | | | | |
| % Home | 22.3 | 28.5 | 17.7 | 17.2 |
| % Secure | 11.2 | 15.2 | 11.0 | 4.8 |

all juvenile offenders charged with felony offenses are removed from their homes and about one-quarter (24.4%) of all juveniles charged with felony offenses are confined. Conversely, misdemeanor offenders, such as shoplifters or thieves, are removed from their homes (17.6%) or placed in secure confinement (11.3%) at about half the rate of those charged with felony offenses. As a result of legal restrictions on the placement of status offenders, they have the lowest proportion of removal from their homes or secure confinement (Minn. Stat. Ann. § 260.194 [1982]; *L.E.A. v. Hammergren*, 294 N.W.2d 705 [Minn. 1980]). Significantly, even though institutional confinement of status offenders is not permitted (Minn. Stat. Ann. § 260.185, subd. 1(c)(5)(d)[1986]), 3.5% of the status offenders in the state and 9.7% of those in the high representation counties still are being incarcerated in county or state institutions. The sentences imposed on juveniles charged with other delinquency are inflated by the substantially higher rates of out-of-home placement and confinement dispositions imposed in the counties with high rates of representation. In those counties, 38.3% of other delinquency referrals, primarily for contempt or probation violations, were made by probation officers (Table 4-2). As Table 4-6 indicates, referrals by probation officers in all counties characteristically garner higher rates of severe sentences.

While there is a clear and direct relationship between the seriousness of the present offense and the severity of disposition, there are also marked differences between the sentences imposed in the high and medium representation counties when compared with those in the low representation counties. At nearly every level of offense, judges in the low representation counties impose less severe dispositions. These differences are most conspicuous in the sentencing of juveniles charged with the most serious offenses, where almost 10% fewer juveniles charged with felony offenses receive secure confinement dispositions than do those in the medium or high representation counties.

Table 4-6 also reports on the rates of out-of-home placement and secure confinement dispositions by sources of referral. Recall that Table 4-2 reported that most of the nonpolice referrals occurred in the categories of other delinquency and status offenses, that in the counties with high rates of representation, probation officers referred a substantial proportion of juveniles for probation violations and schools referred a large proportion of status offenders as truants, and that in the medium and low rates of representation counties, school referrals for truancy predominated. Comparing the rates of out-of-home placement and secure confinement by the type of petitioner with the overall rates of dispositions and, especially, with the disposition rates for the other delinquency and status offense categories indicates that the source of a petition strongly influences the disposition of a case. In general, somewhat fewer referrals by police than by other petitioners result in significant interventions by juvenile courts even though police predominate in the referrals of serious criminal offenses (Table 4-2). By contrast, courts react very severely to referrals by probation officers with over half of all such juveniles removed from their homes and more than one-quarter incarcerated. Because probation officers generally refer less serious types of offenses—the other delinquency and status offense categories (Table 4-2)—than do police officers, these differences are even more substantial. Similarly, complaints by parents and schools are given great credence by juvenile courts. About one-third of all referrals by parents result in the removal of the juvenile from the home as do more than one-fifth of the referrals from schools. Of course, to the extent that "parental sponsorship," the willingness of parents to have their child returned home, modifies the principle of offense as a sentencing principle (Matza 1964), the high rate of home removal for parental referrals is understandable.

## AGE, OFFENSE, AND DISPOSITION (HOME/SECURE)

As might be expected, juveniles aged fifteen to seventeen predominate in the juvenile court, and the length of a youth's prior record increases with age. Table 4-7 summarizes the relationships between age, delinquency, and prior referrals.

For the state as a whole, juveniles aged fourteen and under constitute 27.7% of all delinquents. In the counties with high, medium, and low rates of representation, these younger juveniles constitute 27.7%, 30.6%, and 25.1%, respectively, of the juvenile court dockets. Comparing juveniles' proportional contributions to the juvenile courts' population with their contribution to the various offense categories indicates that these younger juveniles are charged with about as many felony offenses against the person and against property as their overall percentage of the court population. If anything, the younger juveniles tend to be underrepresented only in the less serious categories of offenses. This suggests that the seriousness of the offense influences the prepetition screening and charging decisions in the cases of younger juveniles. By contrast, the eighteen-year-old juveniles contribute to the more serious offenses slightly less than their proportional makeup of the juvenile court's population.

Although slightly more younger juveniles are charged with serious offenses, they tend to have fewer prior referrals. This is primarily a function of age. Thus, in the state, about 10% fewer juveniles aged twelve and under have prior referrals when compared with fifteen-year-old youths,

# Table 4-7a  Age, Offense, and Prior Referral

| Age | Statewide | | | | | | | High | | | | | | |
|---|---|---|---|---|---|---|---|---|---|---|---|---|---|---|
| | 12 and Under | 13 | 14 | 15 | 16 | 17 | 18 | 12 and Under | 13 | 14 | 15 | 16 | 17 | 18 |
| % Delinquents | 6.1 | 7.8 | 13.8 | 21.1 | 22.6 | 25.8 | 2.8 | 4.7 | 7.9 | 15.1 | 25.0 | 21.6 | 23.1 | 2.7 |
| **Present Offense** | | | | | | | | | | | | | | |
| Felony Offense Against Person (%) | 8.8 | 10.7 | 13.5 | 21.2 | 20.1 | 23.2 | 2.4 | 8.9 | 13.6 | 13.0 | 24.9 | 13.0 | 24.9 | 1.8 |
| Felony Offense Against Property (%) | 6.6 | 7.3 | 13.7 | 21.6 | 25.2 | 23.0 | 2.6 | 4.6 | 6.3 | 15.1 | 24.9 | 22.1 | 24.4 | 2.6 |
| Minor Offense Against Person (%) | 5.8 | 12.0 | 13.9 | 19.0 | 21.9 | 25.1 | 2.1 | 5.6 | 11.5 | 14.1 | 18.8 | 20.9 | 27.8 | 1.3 |
| Minor Offense Against Property (%) | 8.7 | 8.3 | 14.4 | 20.0 | 22.1 | 23.8 | 2.8 | 6.1 | 7.4 | 14.2 | 23.3 | 23.9 | 22.6 | 2.6 |
| Other Delinquency (%) | 2.6 | 5.7 | 11.6 | 19.9 | 24.1 | 31.7 | 4.3 | 2.8 | 7.4 | 16.0 | 27.8 | 21.6 | 20.9 | 3.5 |
| Status Offense (%) | 4.3 | 7.5 | 14.5 | 23.5 | 21.5 | 26.5 | 2.1 | 3.3 | 7.6 | 16.7 | 27.0 | 19.7 | 23.1 | 2.7 |
| **Prior Referrals** | | | | | | | | | | | | | | |
| 0 | 79.6 | 72.7 | 69.0 | 68.9 | 72.5 | 73.4 | 70.2 | 68.7 | 69.0 | 64.6 | 59.1 | 63.5 | 67.1 | 62.1 |
| 1–2 | 16.5 | 22.5 | 24.6 | 24.5 | 22.8 | 22.7 | 25.0 | 23.5 | 24.2 | 27.6 | 29.5 | 28.7 | 26.8 | 29.5 |
| 3–4 | 2.9 | 4.1 | 4.9 | 4.8 | 3.6 | 3.0 | 4.2 | 5.4 | 5.3 | 5.6 | 8.4 | 5.2 | 4.8 | 7.4 |
| 5+ | 1.1 | 0.7 | 1.5 | 1.7 | 1.1 | 0.9 | 0.6 | 2.4 | 1.4 | 2.2 | 3.0 | 2.6 | 1.3 | 1.1 |

Table 4-7b  Age, Offense, and Prior Referral

| Age | Medium | | | | | | | Low | | | | | | |
|---|---|---|---|---|---|---|---|---|---|---|---|---|---|---|
| | 12 and Under | 13 | 14 | 15 | 16 | 17 | 18 | 12 and Under | 13 | 14 | 15 | 16 | 17 | 18 |
| % Delinquents | 6.8 | 9.0 | 14.8 | 21.5 | 21.6 | 23.8 | 2.5 | 6.1 | 6.7 | 12.3 | 19.0 | 24.0 | 28.9 | 3.0 |
| **Present Offense** | | | | | | | | | | | | | | |
| Felony Offense Against Person (%) | 8.3 | 10.5 | 12.7 | 19.6 | 23.2 | 22.8 | 2.9 | 9.4 | 8.9 | 14.9 | 20.4 | 21.7 | 22.6 | 2.1 |
| Felony Offense Against Property (%) | 7.8 | 7.7 | 12.6 | 19.2 | 26.9 | 23.2 | 2.7 | 6.4 | 7.6 | 14.1 | 22.1 | 25.1 | 22.1 | 2.6 |
| Minor Offense Against Person (%) | 8.6 | 15.8 | 16.4 | 18.7 | 17.2 | 22.1 | 1.1 | 2.9 | 8.1 | 11.1 | 19.5 | 28.0 | 26.4 | 3.9 |
| Minor Offense Against Property (%) | 8.9 | 7.6 | 13.3 | 19.8 | 22.1 | 25.6 | 2.7 | 9.6 | 9.2 | 15.2 | 18.7 | 21.4 | 23.1 | 2.9 |
| Other Delinquency (%) | 2.2 | 4.7 | 10.1 | 18.4 | 24.7 | 35.2 | 4.7 | 3.1 | 5.7 | 10.3 | 15.7 | 25.4 | 35.3 | 4.5 |
| Status Offense (%) | 6.7 | 12.9 | 21.1 | 27.6 | 16.5 | 14.2 | 1.0 | 2.9 | 3.4 | 8.7 | 19.1 | 26.0 | 37.3 | 2.7 |
| **Prior Referrals** | | | | | | | | | | | | | | |
| 0 | 76.2 | 65.4 | 62.9 | 66.8 | 70.8 | 71.6 | 72.2 | 86.9 | 83.1 | 78.1 | 77.2 | 77.8 | 77.1 | 72.1 |
| 1–2 | 19.0 | 28.1 | 28.2 | 26.6 | 24.6 | 24.1 | 22.8 | 11.5 | 15.0 | 19.0 | 19.2 | 18.8 | 20.2 | 24.7 |
| 3–4 | 3.9 | 5.9 | 7.1 | 4.9 | 3.8 | 3.2 | 4.3 | 0.9 | 1.2 | 2.2 | 2.5 | 2.7 | 2.1 | 2.7 |
| 5+ | 0.9 | 0.5 | 1.8 | 1.6 | 0.8 | 1.1 | 0.6 | 0.7 | 0.6 | 0.7 | 1.0 | 0.7 | 0.6 | 0.5 |

the group with the most extensive record of prior referrals. The relationship between age and prior record is the same in the state overall and in the counties with high, medium, and low rates of representation, with the youngest juveniles usually having fewer prior referrals and the older juveniles having more.

Subsequent analyses will show a strong relationship between the seriousness of a juvenile's present offense, the length of the prior record, and the eventual sentence that is imposed. While younger juveniles' present offenses are often comparable with those of their older colleagues, their somewhat less extensive prior records and their extreme youth may provide some protection at the time of sentencing.

Table 4-8 shows the relationship between juveniles' age and disposition. A comparison of the overall rates of out-of-home placement (18.5%, Table 4-6) and secure confinement dispositions (11.1%, Table 4-6) with the rates by age indicates that a substantially lower percentage of juveniles twelve or younger are removed from their homes or confined. However,

**Table 4-8   Age and Rate of Disposition (Home/Secure)**

| Age | Statewide | High | Medium | Low |
|---|---|---|---|---|
| **12 and Under** | | | | |
| % Home | 13.4 | 16.8 | 15.2 | 10.4 |
| % Secure | 4.4 | 8.4 | 3.9 | 3.4 |
| **13** | | | | |
| % Home | 21.5 | 27.0 | 22.9 | 16.7 |
| % Secure | 9.4 | 12.6 | 10.3 | 6.5 |
| **14** | | | | |
| % Home | 21.0 | 26.7 | 21.6 | 16.8 |
| % Secure | 11.6 | 16.5 | 12.1 | 8.1 |
| **15** | | | | |
| % Home | 21.2 | 29.3 | 20.3 | 16.8 |
| % Secure | 12.7 | 19.5 | 12.2 | 8.8 |
| **16** | | | | |
| % Home | 18.8 | 26.7 | 21.4 | 13.4 |
| % Secure | 11.7 | 15.9 | 14.6 | 7.6 |
| **17** | | | | |
| % Home | 15.8 | 20.8 | 18.5 | 11.9 |
| % Secure | 11.4 | 14.7 | 13.4 | 8.6 |
| **18** | | | | |
| % Home | 10.8 | 9.5 | 14.9 | 8.3 |
| % Secure | 9.3 | 8.4 | 13.0 | 6.9 |

by age fourteen, youthfulness is no longer a mitigating factor in the sentencing of juveniles. In addition, the ratio of out-of-home placement to secure confinement decreases with age. Thus, for juveniles twelve or younger, about one-third of those removed from home are confined. For the eighteen-year-old juveniles, if a sentence is imposed, in about nine of ten cases it will be for secure confinement. The likely explanation is that for older juveniles with prior referrals, previous noninstitutional placements, and only a limited time remaining within juvenile court jurisdiction, a more severe consequence is required.

## OFFENSES AND DISPOSITIONS BY COUNSEL

Table 4-9 amplifies the information contained in Table 4-6 and provides the first assessment of the impact of counsel on delinquency dispositions. Within each offense category, Table 4-9 shows the disposition rates—out-of-home placement and secure confinement—for those juveniles who were represented and those who were not. Thus, Table 4-6 reports that for the entire state, 18.5% of all juveniles received out-of-home placements and 11.1% of all youths received secure confinement dispositions. The same cell in Table 4-9 shows that youths *with counsel* are nearly three times more likely to receive severe dispositions than are those *without counsel*—28.1% of represented juveniles versus 10.3% of unrepresented youths received out-of-home placement and 17.6% versus 5.2% secure confinement.

A comparison of the two columns in the state and in the high, medium, and low representation counties at each offense level reveals that youths with lawyers consistently receive more severe dispositions than do those without attorneys. With twelve possible comparisons—six offense categories times two dispositions—represented youths received more severe dispositions than unrepresented youth at every offense level in the state overall and in the counties with medium rates of representation, and in eleven out of twelve comparisons in the counties with low rates of representation. Although a similar pattern was revealed in the counties with high rates of representation (eight out of twelve comparisons), as the footnotes in Table 4-9 indicate, in several cells there were so few unrepresented youths that any out-of-home placement or secure confinement disposition produced anomalous results. Since the data reported in Table 4-9 control for the seriousness of the present offense, it appears that youths *with* attorneys are between two and three times more likely to receive severe dispositions than are those youths *without* counsel.

While the relationship between representation and more severe disposition is consistent, the explanation of this relationship is not readily

**Table 4-9   Representation by Counsel and Rate of Disposition (Home/Secure)**

| Counsel | Statewide Yes | Statewide No | High Yes | High No | Medium Yes | Medium No | Low Yes | Low No |
|---|---|---|---|---|---|---|---|---|
| **Overall** | | | | | | | | |
| % Home | 28.1 | 10.3 | 25.9 | 12.9 | 29.4 | 10.8 | 30.5 | 9.9 |
| % Secure | 17.6 | 5.2 | 16.2 | 7.5 | 18.6 | 5.6 | 18.8 | 5.0 |
| **Felony** | | | | | | | | |
| % Home | 39.6 | 20.8 | 34.6 | 60.0 | 42.8 | 19.1 | 40.4 | 21.3 |
| % Secure | 28.2 | 13.9 | 24.8 | 40.0 | 32.2 | 14.4 | 24.7 | 13.4 |
| Felony Offense Against Person | | | | | | | | |
| % Home | 44.8 | 29.5 | 43.4 | 100.0[a] | 49.0 | 28.3 | 37.2 | 29.3 |
| % Secure | 28.3 | 19.4 | 28.7 | — | 33.3 | 19.6 | 17.0 | 19.5 |
| Felony Offense Against Property | | | | | | | | |
| % Home | 37.9 | 19.3 | 32.3 | 50.0[b] | 40.6 | 17.6 | 41.5 | 20.0 |
| % Secure | 28.1 | 13.0 | 23.8 | 50.0 | 31.8 | 13.6 | 27.4 | 12.5 |
| **Misdemeanor** | | | | | | | | |
| % Home | 25.8 | 10.2 | 25.7 | 20.0 | 24.8 | 10.7 | 28.1 | 9.6 |
| % Secure | 16.7 | 6.1 | 16.6 | 12.9 | 16.1 | 6.6 | 18.6 | 5.6 |
| Minor Offense Against Person | | | | | | | | |
| % Home | 30.7 | 13.6 | 29.5 | — | 31.4 | 11.7 | 31.5 | 14.8 |
| % Secure | 18.0 | 8.5 | 19.9 | — | 15.5 | 7.2 | 20.5 | 9.3 |
| Minor Offense Against Property | | | | | | | | |
| % Home | 22.8 | 10.2 | 19.5 | 20.0[c] | 24.8 | 13.1 | 26.8 | 8.8 |
| % Secure | 15.7 | 6.5 | 13.6 | 12.0 | 17.3 | 9.2 | 17.7 | 5.4 |
| Other Delinquency | | | | | | | | |
| % Home | 29.4 | 9.5 | 34.8 | 20.9 | 21.8 | 8.0 | 29.2 | 10.5 |
| % Secure | 18.2 | 4.8 | 20.8 | 14.0 | 13.7 | 3.9 | 19.4 | 5.3 |
| **Status** | | | | | | | | |
| % Home | 24.8 | 8.1 | 25.2 | 9.4 | 23.5 | 9.2 | 26.6 | 7.3 |
| % Secure | 8.3 | 1.7 | 10.7 | 3.1 | 3.8 | 1.7 | 10.6 | 1.6 |

a. Of the 123 juveniles charged with a felony offense against person, only 1 (or 0.8% of the total) was unrepresented and received an out-of-home placement.

b. Of the 454 juveniles charged with felony offenses against property, 4 (or 0.9% of the total) were unrepresented. Two of them (or 1.8% of the total) received institutional confinement dispositions.

c. Of the 1,058 juveniles charged with minor offenses against property, only 25 (or 2.4% of the total), were unrepresented of whom 5 (or 2.4% of the total) received out-of-home placements.

apparent. It may be that the presence of lawyers antagonizes traditional juvenile court judges and subtly influences the eventual disposition imposed. Judges may treat more formally and severely juveniles who appear with counsel than those without and may feel less constrained when sentencing a youth who is represented. Adherence to the forms of due process may insulate sentences from appellate reversal. Conversely, while not necessarily "punishing" juveniles who appear with counsel, judges may exhibit more leniency to an unrepresented, repentant youth who "throws himself on the mercy of the court." However, the pattern also prevails in the counties with high rates of representation where the presence of counsel is not unusual. Or perhaps judges discern the eventual disposition early in the proceedings and appoint counsel more frequently when an out-of-home placement or secure confinement is anticipated. In many counties, the same judge who presides at a youth's arraignment and detention hearing will later decide the case on the merits and ultimately impose the sentence (Feld 1984). Perhaps the initial decision to appoint counsel is based upon the evidence developed at those earlier stages which also influences later dispositions. If judges try to tailor their initial appointment decision to the eventual sentence they impose, however, they may be prejudging the case and prejudicing the interests of the defendant. Still another possibility is that other variables besides the seriousness of the present offense may influence both the initial decision to appoint counsel as well as the ultimate disposition.

While Table 4-9 reports the rates of disposition for represented and unrepresented juveniles, Table 4-10 reports the proportions of juveniles who received out-of-home placement and secure confinement dispositions who were or were not represented. Again, Table 4-6 reports that for the whole state, 18.5% and 11.1% of juveniles received out-of-home and secure confinement dispositions. Table 4-10 reports that of the 18.5% of juveniles removed from their home, 69.3% were represented and 30.7% were not. Similarly, of the 11.1% of juveniles who were incarcerated, 73.5% had counsel and 26.5% did not. In short, nearly one-third of the youths in the state who were removed from their homes and more than one-quarter of the juveniles in secure confinement *did not* have counsel. In purely numerical terms, 910 juveniles removed from their homes and 464 who were incarcerated *were not represented*. In the absence of a valid waiver of counsel on the record by each of those youths, such home removal or incarceration violates the constitution (*Scott v. Illinois*, 440 U.S. 367 [1979]).

In light of the differences in counties with high, medium and low rates of representation as well as in rates of representation by offense (Table 4-3), the results reported in Table 4-10 follow predictable patterns.

**Table 4-10   Disposition (Home/Secure) of Juveniles and Rate of Representation by Counsel**

| Counsel | Statewide Yes | No | High Yes | No | Medium Yes | No | Low Yes | No |
|---|---|---|---|---|---|---|---|---|
| **Overall** | | | | | | | | |
| % Home | 69.3 | 30.7 | 97.2 | 2.8 | 70.4 | 29.6 | 42.4 | 57.6 |
| N | (2,051) | (910) | (829) | (24) | (824) | (346) | (398) | (540) |
| % Secure | 73.5 | 26.5 | 97.4 | 2.6 | 74.6 | 25.4 | 47.4 | 52.6 |
| N | (1,285) | (464) | (518) | (14) | (522) | (178) | (245) | (272) |
| **Felony** | | | | | | | | |
| % Home | 78.2 | 21.8 | 98.5 | 1.5 | 84.8 | 15.2 | 53.6 | 46.4 |
| % Secure | 79.2 | 20.8 | 98.6 | 1.4 | 84.8 | 15.2 | 52.9 | 47.1 |
| Felony Offense Against Person | | | | | | | | |
| % Home | 83.2 | 16.8 | 98.1 | 1.9 | 88.5 | 11.5 | 59.3 | 40.7 |
| % Secure | 82.6 | 17.4 | 100.0 | — | 88.3 | 11.7 | 50.0 | 50.0 |
| Felony Offense Against Property | | | | | | | | |
| % Home | 76.5 | 23.5 | 98.6 | 1.4 | 83.3 | 16.7 | 52.1 | 47.9 |
| % Secure | 78.2 | 21.8 | 98.2 | 1.8 | 83.6 | 16.4 | 53.6 | 46.4 |
| **Misdemeanor** | | | | | | | | |
| % Home | 69.0 | 31.0 | 97.1 | 2.9 | 67.9 | 32.1 | 41.0 | 59.0 |
| % Secure | 70.7 | 29.3 | 97.1 | 2.9 | 68.8 | 31.2 | 44.1 | 55.9 |
| Minor Offense Against Person | | | | | | | | |
| % Home | 77.8 | 22.2 | 100.0 | — | 83.3 | 16.7 | 46.0 | 54.0 |
| % Secure | 76.6 | 23.4 | 100.0 | — | 80.0 | 20.0 | 46.9 | 53.1 |
| Minor Offense Against Property | | | | | | | | |
| % Home | 65.0 | 35.0 | 97.6 | 2.4 | 67.8 | 32.2 | 37.7 | 62.3 |
| % Secure | 66.5 | 33.5 | 97.9 | 2.1 | 67.8 | 32.2 | 39.5 | 60.5 |
| Other Delinquency | | | | | | | | |
| % Home | 72.2 | 27.8 | 96.1 | 3.9 | 60.6 | 39.4 | 46.0 | 54.0 |
| % Secure | 76.0 | 24.0 | 95.6 | 4.4 | 66.3 | 33.7 | 53.2 | 46.8 |
| **Status** | | | | | | | | |
| % Home | 55.3 | 44.7 | 96.2 | 3.8 | 48.8 | 51.2 | 27.2 | 72.8 |
| % Secure | 66.9 | 33.1 | 97.0 | 3.0 | 45.7 | 54.3 | 40.8 | 59.2 |

Overall, less than 3% of unrepresented juveniles in the high representation counties were removed from their homes or incarcerated. In the medium representation counties, more than one-quarter of the juveniles removed from their homes (29.6%) or incarcerated (25.4%) did not have counsel. In the sixty-eight low representation counties, more than half of the youths removed (57.6%) or incarcerated (52.6%) were unrepresented. Indeed, in the low representation counties, only a bare majority of the juveniles charged with felony offenses who were removed from home or confined were represented. In every other offense category, the majority of juveniles removed or incarcerated were sentenced without the assistance of an attorney.

Table 4-3 reported higher rates of representation for juveniles charged with more serious offenses. When the disposition rates are analyzed by offense, it appears that the largest proportions of unrepresented juveniles who are removed or incarcerated are those who are charged with the less serious offenses. For the whole state, 20.8% of unrepresented juveniles charged with a felony offense were incarcerated. By contrast, 29.3% of the juveniles who were charged with misdemeanors and institutionalized were unrepresented. Indeed, 33.5% of those incarcerated for minor offenses against property, the most common delinquency allegation in the state, and 33.1% of those incarcerated for status offenses were unrepresented. Recall, only 18.4% of Minnesota's juveniles were charged with felony offenses; the greatest concentrations of delinquents were in the minor property offense—shoplifting, theft, vandalism and the like—and status offense categories (Table 4-1). Juveniles charged with those minor offenses had lower rates of representation (Tables 4-3 and 4-4). As a result, these minor offense categories were the ones in which the largest proportions of unrepresented juveniles were removed from their homes and incarcerated. In short, both absolutely and proportionally, incarceration without representation occurs most frequently among the least serious part of the juvenile court population.

These findings are especially important in light of the United States and Minnesota Supreme Courts' rulings in *Scott* (440 U.S. at 373–74 [1979]) and *Borst* (278 Minn. 388, 154 N.W.2d at 894 [1967]) that adult misdemeanor defendants cannot be incarcerated without the appointment of counsel or a record of a valid waiver. There are many counties in Minnesota in which half or more of the youths who are charged with seemingly minor, misdemeanor offenses are removed from their homes or incarcerated without the assistance of counsel. It is highly questionable whether the juvenile court judges who sentenced the young juveniles in these minor nuisance cases engaged in and created a record of the type of "penetrating and comprehensive examination" that must precede a "knowing and intelligent" waiver of the right to counsel (*State v. Rubin*, 409 N.W.2d 504, 506 [Minn. 1987]).

Tables 4-9 and 4-10 report the proportions of represented and unrepresented juveniles charged with different types of offenses who received out-of-home placement and secure confinement dispositions. Table 4-11 reports on juveniles' dispositions when represented by different types of attorneys—private, public defender, court appointed attorney, or none. Thus, Table 4-9 reports that in the state overall, of those juveniles who were represented by counsel and charged with a felony offense against the person, 44.8% and 28.3% respectively received out-of-home placement and secure confinement dispositions. Table 4-11 indicates that the 44.8% overall rate differs by type of attorney, with 30.3% of juveniles represented by private counsel removed from their homes as contrasted with 49.0% of those represented by public defenders and 44.3% of those represented by court appointed lawyers.

It is difficult to assess the impact of different types of attorneys because the methods of delivering legal services are associated closely with counties, which in turn vary in rates of representation (Table 4-3) and on other dimensions. While private attorneys are a relative rarity in juvenile courts, they also appear least frequently in the county courts with high rates of representation. By contrast, public defenders predominate in the counties with high and medium rates of representation—primarily urban and suburban county courts—while court appointed lawyers predominate in the rural counties with lowest rates of representation. Despite these variations in legal services systems by county rate of representation, rank ordering the different types of attorneys within an offense category by dispositions provides a crude indicator of the effectiveness of counsel.

Table 4-9 reported that generally smaller proportions of unrepresented juveniles than represented juveniles received the most severe dispositions. For the state as a whole, juveniles represented by private attorneys have the lowest rates of out-of-home placement and secure confinement dispositions of represented juveniles; those represented by court appointed attorneys have intermediate rates; and those represented by public defenders appear to have the highest rates of removal. Of course, these findings are only suggestive, because court appointed lawyers predominate in rural counties with low rates of representation where the judges also impose less severe sentences for offenses of comparable severity (Table 4-6 and Chapter Six).

Table 4-11 indicates that when the data are examined separately by county according to the rates of representation, the pattern remains. In counties with high rates of representation, the 2.4% of juveniles who retain private counsel (Table 4-4) have the lowest rate of out-of-home placement and secure confinement of all represented juveniles. In the counties with medium rates of representation, juveniles with private counsel have the lowest rates of out-of-home placement but the highest proportion of secure confinement dispositions. And in the counties with low rates of representation, the 3.4% of juveniles who retain private counsel (Table 4-4) have the lowest proportions of out-of-home place-

**Table 4-11  Type of Counsel and Rate of Disposition (Home/Secure)**

| Counsel | Statewide | | | | High | | | | Medium | | | | Low | | | |
|---|---|---|---|---|---|---|---|---|---|---|---|---|---|---|---|---|
| | Private | PD[a] | CA[b] | None | Private | PD | CA | None | Private | PD | CA | None | Private | PD | CA | None |
| **Overall** | | | | | | | | | | | | | | | | |
| % Home | 19.5 | 28.8 | 30.0 | 10.3 | 14.5 | 27.3 | 20.8 | 12.9 | 22.9 | 30.9 | 30.4 | 10.8 | 13.6 | 29.4 | 34.9 | 9.9 |
| % Secure | 15.5 | 17.9 | 17.6 | 5.2 | 8.4 | 17.1 | 12.9 | 7.5 | 19.4 | 18.9 | 16.4 | 5.6 | 9.2 | 20.9 | 20.8 | 5.0 |
| **Felony Offense Against Person** | | | | | | | | | | | | | | | | |
| % Home | 30.3 | 49.0 | 44.3 | 29.5 | 16.7 | 44.1 | 47.8 | 100.0 | 36.4 | 53.7 | 46.2 | 28.3 | 18.8 | 33.3 | 42.4 | 29.3 |
| % Secure | 25.8 | 34.3 | 17.4 | 19.4 | 16.7 | 31.2 | 21.7 | — | 31.8 | 36.6 | 19.2 | 19.6 | 12.5 | 33.3 | 15.2 | 19.5 |
| **Felony Offense Against Property** | | | | | | | | | | | | | | | | |
| % Home | 30.4 | 40.6 | 36.0 | 19.3 | 12.5 | 36.5 | 21.6 | 50.0 | 35.9 | 43.5 | 36.4 | 17.6 | 18.9 | 48.7 | 44.3 | 20.0 |
| % Secure | 27.0 | 30.7 | 24.4 | 13.0 | — | 27.3 | 15.5 | 50.0 | 34.0 | 33.4 | 25.6 | 13.6 | 13.5 | 33.3 | 28.9 | 12.5 |
| **Minor Offense Against Person** | | | | | | | | | | | | | | | | |
| % Home | 15.4 | 33.6 | 30.4 | 13.6 | 22.2 | 32.1 | 21.2 | — | 12.9 | 36.7 | 23.1 | 11.7 | 16.7 | — | 39.6 | 14.8 |
| % Secure | 5.8 | 20.2 | 17.9 | 8.5 | 11.1 | 23.1 | 9.1 | — | 3.2 | 18.7 | 11.5 | 7.2 | 8.3 | — | 26.4 | 9.3 |
| **Minor Offense Against Property** | | | | | | | | | | | | | | | | |
| % Home | 20.2 | 21.9 | 25.7 | 10.2 | 16.0 | 19.9 | 18.1 | 20.0 | 21.7 | 24.7 | 28.9 | 13.1 | 17.5 | 20.8 | 29.7 | 8.8 |
| % Secure | 16.7 | 15.3 | 16.4 | 6.5 | 12.0 | 14.3 | 11.0 | 12.0 | 18.9 | 16.8 | 17.6 | 9.2 | 12.3 | 12.5 | 19.7 | 5.4 |
| **Other Delinquency** | | | | | | | | | | | | | | | | |
| % Home | 11.1 | 33.7 | 28.7 | 9.5 | 13.3 | 37.6 | 21.6 | 20.9 | 12.5 | 25.4 | 23.4 | 8.0 | 7.5 | 40.9 | 35.5 | 10.5 |
| % Secure | 8.9 | 20.3 | 17.7 | 4.8 | — | 22.2 | 15.9 | 14.0 | 10.7 | 15.3 | 12.5 | 3.9 | 7.5 | 36.4 | 21.3 | 5.3 |
| **Status** | | | | | | | | | | | | | | | | |
| % Home | 14.7 | 24.5 | 30.8 | 8.1 | 18.2 | 25.4 | 24.2 | 9.4 | 17.9 | 23.3 | 28.6 | 9.2 | 11.1 | 16.7 | 33.6 | 7.3 |
| % Secure | 7.4 | 8.1 | 9.8 | 1.7 | 18.2 | 10.5 | 12.1 | 3.1 | 7.7 | 4.0 | — | 1.7 | 4.4 | 5.6 | 13.6 | 1.6 |

a. Public Defender.
b. Court Appointed.

ment or secure confinement dispositions and enjoy a distinct advantage over their counterparts who are represented by other types of attorneys. Despite the relative success of private attorneys vis-a-vis other types of lawyers, unrepresented juveniles in the state and in all types of counties still have lower rates of removal and confinement.

The comparative success of private attorneys versus public attorneys in juvenile courts is somewhat surprising. Private practitioners are not attracted to juvenile court practice (Platt 1977). The disincentives for private attorneys' representation of juveniles are substantial: juveniles are not a significant source of fee-paying clients. If a private attorney is retained, most likely it will be by the child's parents, a situation which potentially puts the attorney in the middle of a conflict between the interests of the juvenile-client on the one hand and those of the fee-paying parents on the other. Moreover, most juvenile courts do not give private practitioners priority on the calendar, which increases the costs of representation. Private attorneys also may have less access to court personnel than do the public lawyer regulars (Platt and Friedman 1968). In addition, private lawyers may be discouraged from juvenile practice because of the inherent difficulty of working with unpredictable young people and the frustration of practicing law in a highly discretionary environment (Feld 1984). In light of the amorphous nature of a delinquency charge, there are few opportunities for outright "victory" and these are further diminished by the unreliability of young witnesses and the comparative credibility of adults versus juveniles. Ultimately, lawyers manipulate symbols and create an appearance of action which justifies their fees (Blumberg 1967). In juvenile courts, there are fewer opportunities for "mystification" since there are fewer rules or administrative guidelines to manipulate and less opportunity for plea and sentence bargaining than in the adult system (Bortner 1982; Emerson 1969; Matza 1964). Finally, private attorneys, as adults, share the juvenile court's view of their clients as immature children, experience dilemmas when representing youngsters that do not occur when defending presumptively competent adults, and internalize the court's theoretical commitment to the rehabilitative ideal. As an arcane legal specialty area marked by informality and confidentiality, juvenile courts are typically closed, inbred, and inhospitable to the occasional outsiders who invade their province.

In the present study, however, this may be a blessing in disguise. A private attorney with relatively little regular involvement in juvenile court proceedings may have a smaller stake in conforming to the traditional expectations of the court or social services personnel and thus may be more independent on behalf of his client (Nardulli 1986). Wheeler and Wheeler (1980:325–26), for example, conclude that "it appears that clients of retained and appointed attorneys have similar conviction rates but the retained attorneys' clients receive less serious dispositions. These findings indicate that type of attorney has a greater impact on sentencing than on conviction." By contrast, attorneys immersed more routinely in the juvenile justice process may be more responsive to institutional expectations and more inclined to value stable long-term relations with the court and its personnel.

Although the SJIS data do not include information on parental socioeconomic status, the appearance of a private attorney may be an indirect indicator of a somewhat more affluent family background. If so, then the relative success of private practitioners may be less a tribute to their legal acumen than to the parental wherewithal that led to their retention. When the parents pay the fees, a private attorney may be more responsive to their interests. In the juvenile court context, this may mean that the private attorney shares the parents' interest in seeking a disposition that will further the child's "best interest." The coalition of a private attorney and parents pursuing the child's welfare may provide evidence of "family sponsorship" that justifies a more lenient disposition. Matza (1964:125), for example, contends that dispositional decision making is strongly influenced by the ability of parents to supervise their child so as to avoid subsequent "scandal." "If the reckoning of danger [of scandal] is moderate then the decision will turn on an assessment of the presence, the amount, the quality, and the dependability of parental sponsorship. . . . [T]hose with adequate sponsorship will be rendered onto probation, and those inadequately sponsored to prison." Thus, the variations in rates of disposition by type of attorney may reflect social characteristics of juveniles for which this study cannot account and for which the type of attorney is an indirect indicator.

## PRIOR REFERRALS, ATTORNEYS, AND DISPOSITIONS

In addition to the seriousness of the present offense, a prior history of delinquency referrals affects the eventual disposition that a juvenile receives (Clarke and Koch 1980; Henretta, Frazier, and Bishop 1986). The next analyses control for the present offense and assess the relationships between prior referrals and dispositions, prior referrals and representation by counsel, and prior referrals, representation by counsel, and dispositions. As described in Chapter Two, a juvenile's prior record in 1986 was constructed by merging 1984, 1985, and 1986 annual data tapes and matching a youth's identification numbers across the years. Records could not be constructed for earlier years because Hennepin County (Minneapolis), the most populous county in the state and which processes about one-quarter of all delinquency cases, only integrated its computerized court-processing data into the SJIS data system in 1984. In these analyses, the records of prior referrals are coded as 0, 1–2, 3–4, and 5 or more. Prior records include only previous cases that resulted in *formal petitions* and do not reflect police contacts or juvenile referrals to court intake that did not result in the filing of formal charges.

## PRIOR REFERRALS AND DISPOSITIONS

Table 4-12 reports both the overall percentages of juveniles with prior records as well as the relationship between the present offense, prior referrals, and out-of-home placement and secure confinement dispositions. For the entire state, 71.9% of the youths against whom petitions were filed appeared in juvenile court for the first time. When the prior referrals in the counties with high, medium, and low representation are examined separately, however, about 10% more of the juveniles in the low representation counties were making their first appearance with correspondingly fewer recidivists than in the other types of counties. This reinforces the observation based on Table 4-1 that juveniles in the low representation, predominantly rural, counties were relatively less involved in criminal activity.

Table 4-12 also reports the relationship between a prior record of delinquency and out-of-home placement and secure confinement dispositions. Quite clearly, both overall and within categories of offenses, a record of previously petitioned offenses substantially alters a youth's likelihood of receiving a more severe disposition. In the aggregate, each additional one or two prior referrals increases the proportion of juveniles' receiving out-of-home placements and secure confinements, with the largest increase occurring between those juveniles with one or two prior referrals and those with three or four. Regardless of the nature of the present offense, by the time a juvenile appears in juvenile court on his or her third or fourth delinquency petition, more than half (52.9%) will be removed from the home and more than one-third (39.9%) will be confined.

Within each offense level, there appears to be a nearly perfect linear relationship between additional prior referrals and more severe dispositions. For example, Table 4-6 reports that 42.2% of the juveniles who commit a felony offense against the person receive out-of-home placement. Table 4-12 shows that the 42.2% overall rate is composed of 35.7% of those with no prior referrals, 51.9% of those with one or two, 84.8% of those with three or four and 100% of those with five or more

**Table 4-12  Present Offense, Prior Record, and Rate of Disposition (Home/Secure)**

| Priors | Statewide | | | | High | | | | Medium | | | | Low | | | |
|---|---|---|---|---|---|---|---|---|---|---|---|---|---|---|---|---|
| | 0 | 1–2 | 3–4 | 5+ | 0 | 1–2 | 3–4 | 5+ | 0 | 1–2 | 3–4 | 5+ | 0 | 1–2 | 3–4 | 5+ |
| **Prior Overall** | | | | | | | | | | | | | | | | |
| % | 71.9 | 23.0 | 3.9 | 1.2 | 64.0 | 27.7 | 6.0 | 2.2 | 68.9 | 25.3 | 4.6 | 1.2 | 78.3 | 18.8 | 2.2 | 0.7 |
| N | (12,359) | (3,962) | (669) | (205) | (2,274) | (984) | (214) | (79) | (4,378) | (1,610) | (293) | (74) | (5,707) | (1,368) | (162) | (52) |
| **Disposition Overall** | | | | | | | | | | | | | | | | |
| % Home | 12.4 | 29.5 | 52.9 | 61.6 | 13.8 | 37.5 | 68.3 | 80.5 | 14.6 | 28.1 | 47.8 | 56.8 | 10.1 | 25.4 | 42.2 | 40.4 |
| % Secure | 6.8 | 17.7 | 39.9 | 48.8 | 7.1 | 24.1 | 52.9 | 64.9 | 8.8 | 16.0 | 36.5 | 43.2 | 5.2 | 15.3 | 29.2 | 32.7 |
| **Felony Offense Against Person** | | | | | | | | | | | | | | | | |
| % Home | 35.7 | 51.9 | 84.8 | 100.0 | 33.3 | 60.7 | 88.9 | 100.0 | 42.6 | 44.1 | 88.9 | — | 28.7 | 57.1 | 66.7 | — |
| % Secure | 22.9 | 33.3 | 60.6 | 100.0 | 16.7 | 50.0 | 77.8 | 100.0 | 31.4 | 25.4 | 61.1 | — | 16.0 | 33.3 | 33.3 | — |
| **Felony Offense Against Property** | | | | | | | | | | | | | | | | |
| % Home | 21.7 | 46.4 | 76.5 | 72.0 | 16.8 | 55.6 | 83.3 | 85.7 | 26.1 | 46.3 | 83.3 | 90.5 | 19.6 | 41.3 | 62.2 | 33.3 |
| % Secure | 16.0 | 31.9 | 67.0 | 54.0 | 11.9 | 42.1 | 76.7 | 50.0 | 20.8 | 31.7 | 75.0 | 81.0 | 12.9 | 26.1 | 48.6 | 20.0 |
| **Minor Offense Against Person** | | | | | | | | | | | | | | | | |
| % Home | 14.2 | 38.5 | 62.2 | 73.3 | 14.5 | 44.7 | 78.6 | 100.0 | 15.2 | 40.7 | 55.0 | 75.0 | 13.0 | 34.2 | 33.3 | 50.0 |
| % Secure | 8.0 | 22.6 | 40.5 | 66.7 | 8.2 | 27.8 | 57.1 | 80.0 | 8.5 | 18.5 | 30.0 | 75.0 | 7.3 | 23.3 | 33.3 | 50.0 |
| **Minor Offense Against Property** | | | | | | | | | | | | | | | | |
| % Home | 10.4 | 27.3 | 49.0 | 65.2 | 10.5 | 31.3 | 67.3 | 83.3 | 13.9 | 28.2 | 45.1 | 58.8 | 8.4 | 24.0 | 40.0 | 45.5 |
| % Secure | 6.6 | 18.8 | 39.5 | 52.2 | 5.6 | 23.1 | 55.1 | 77.8 | 9.8 | 19.3 | 37.4 | 35.3 | 5.1 | 15.6 | 30.0 | 36.4 |
| **Other Delinquency** | | | | | | | | | | | | | | | | |
| % Home | 12.4 | 31.5 | 46.9 | 55.0 | 19.4 | 45.7 | 70.8 | 68.4 | 10.2 | 22.3 | 30.4 | 33.3 | 11.6 | 27.6 | 26.3 | 55.6 |
| % Secure | 6.7 | 19.2 | 31.9 | 50.0 | 10.8 | 26.9 | 47.9 | 57.9 | 5.2 | 14.4 | 28.3 | 33.3 | 6.5 | 16.5 | — | 55.6 |
| **Status** | | | | | | | | | | | | | | | | |
| % Home | 8.7 | 19.3 | 38.9 | 48.8 | 13.1 | 31.9 | 61.2 | 86.7 | 9.0 | 18.6 | 26.5 | 31.6 | 7.5 | 13.7 | 31.3 | 22.2 |
| % Secure | 1.6 | 5.8 | 23.5 | 30.2 | 2.9 | 12.6 | 42.9 | 66.7 | 1.1 | 3.7 | 10.3 | 10.5 | 1.5 | 5.0 | 21.9 | 11.1 |

priors. The same pattern prevails at all offense levels and prior referrals and for both types of dispositions.

Even though there is a direct relationship between prior referrals and increasing severity of intervention in all types of counties, the juvenile court judges in the low representation counties consistently remove and confine smaller proportions of juveniles than do their counterparts in the medium and high representation counties. This pattern, initially observed in Table 4-6, persists. After controlling simultaneously for the seriousness of the present offense and prior referrals, the juvenile court judges in the low representation counties generally sentence less severely. Juvenile court judges' dispositions may also reflect budgetary constraints, since the costs of placements are borne by the welfare funds of the county (Minn. Stat. Ann. § 260.251 [1986]). In the low representation counties, with small populations and tax bases, extensive and therefore expensive intervention simply may be fiscally prohibitive. Indeed, the same cost considerations may limit both the appointment of counsel and sentencing options.

Examining the ratios of out-of-home placement to secure confinement indicates that as a juvenile accumulates prior referrals the likelihood that the eventual disposition will entail secure confinement increases. For example, for the state overall, of the juveniles with no prior referrals who were removed from their home, 54.8% received institutional commitments (6.8/12.4%). By contrast, of those with five or more priors, 79.2% were confined in secure settings (48.8/61.6%). Comparing the dispositions of juveniles making their first appearance with those of juveniles with five or more prior referrals suggests that prior referrals exert a stronger influence on the sentences received by juveniles charged with less serious offenses than those charged with more serious offenses.

Table 4-12 provides strong evidence that despite the juvenile court's nominal commitment to individualized sentencing, the judges have reintroduced de facto the "principle of offense" as a dispositional guideline. The seriousness of a youth's present offense and the length of the prior record—the primary factors included in the Minnesota Adult Sentencing Guidelines (1980) as well—both exert substantial influences on the eventual disposition. These findings are consistent with a survey of juvenile court sentencing practices in California which also reported that, despite claims of individualization, juvenile dispositions appear to be based primarily on the youth's present offense and prior record. That study concluded that

> comparisons of juvenile and adult sentencing practices suggest that
> juvenile and criminal courts in California are much more alike than

statutory language would suggest, in the degree to which they focus on aggravating circumstances of the charged offense and the defendant's prior record in determining the degree of confinement that will be imposed. (Greenwood et al. 1983:51)

## PRIOR REFERRALS AND RATES OF REPRESENTATION

Tables 4-3 and 4-4 report that for the state as a whole, 45.3% of juveniles were represented. In the counties with high, medium, and low rates of representation, the rates were 94.5%, 46.8%, and 19.3%, respectively. The aggregate rates and the rates for the different types of offenses are the composites for all juveniles. Table 4-13 shows, overall and within each offense level, the relationship between prior delinquency referrals and representation.

There is a direct relationship between additional prior referrals and increased rates of representation. For example, while, for the state as a whole, the rate of representation is 45.3%, only 39.3% of juveniles appearing for the first time have counsel, as contrasted with 57.8% of those with one or two prior referrals, 74.0% of those with three or four, and 80.8% of those with five or more prior referrals. The relationship between prior referrals and rates of representation prevails at all offense levels and in all types of counties. The minor deviations that occur only appear for those juveniles with five or more referrals and can be attributed to the diminishing numbers of youths in those cells. The relationship between prior referrals and appointment of counsel occurs even in the high representation counties where there is very little overall variation in rates of representation. Since larger proportions of juveniles charged with serious offenses are represented in all types of counties, the influence of priors on rates of representation appears to be stronger for youths charged with less serious types of offenses.

The findings in Table 4-12 and 4-13 implicate the United States and Minnesota Supreme Courts' rulings in *Baldasar* (446 U.S. 222 [1980]) and *Edmison* (379 N.W.2d 85 [Minn. 1985]) that prohibit the use of prior uncounseled convictions to enhance subsequent sentences. Overall, more than half the juveniles in the state are unrepresented. If, as Table 4-13 indicates, an even lower proportion of first offenders are represented by counsel, then many of those juveniles who are sentenced subsequently as repeat offenders have had their dispositions based, at least in part, on prior uncounseled convictions. Because the use of prior uncounseled convictions to enhance later sentencing is prohibited for adults, one can only speculate about juvenile court judges' apparent heavy reliance on uncoun-

**Table 4-13   Rate of Representation and Prior Referral**

| Priors | Statewide | | | | High | | | | Medium | | | | Low | | | |
|---|---|---|---|---|---|---|---|---|---|---|---|---|---|---|---|---|
| | 0 | 1–2 | 3–4 | 5+ | 0 | 1–2 | 3–4 | 5+ | 0 | 1–2 | 3–4 | 5+ | 0 | 1–2 | 3–4 | 5+ |
| **Overall % Counsel** | 39.3 | 57.8 | 74.0 | 80.8 | 93.5 | 95.6 | 97.0 | 100.0 | 40.7 | 57.7 | 72.4 | 75.4 | 16.1 | 29.0 | 43.8 | 57.1 |
| Felony Offense Against Person | 75.5 | 80.3 | 89.7 | 100.0 | 97.4 | 97.3 | 100.0 | 100.0 | 79.5 | 84.5 | 93.8 | — | 55.6 | 61.7 | 50.0 | — |
| Felony Offense Against Property | 57.6 | 72.9 | 77.6 | 85.7 | 97.9 | 100.0 | 93.1 | 100.0 | 62.7 | 78.9 | 82.5 | 93.8 | 31.2 | 49.1 | 60.5 | 64.7 |
| Minor Offense Against Person | 57.2 | 71.0 | 89.5 | 71.4 | 95.2 | 98.4 | 100.0 | 100.0 | 60.3 | 77.1 | 85.7 | 75.0 | 26.6 | 39.4 | 66.7 | 40.0 |
| Minor Offense Against Property | 38.9 | 57.6 | 75.9 | 83.0 | 96.9 | 97.7 | 97.9 | 100.0 | 44.8 | 64.9 | 83.5 | 77.8 | 12.8 | 25.1 | 40.8 | 63.6 |
| Other Delinquency | 37.3 | 60.3 | 73.8 | 89.2 | 89.0 | 93.2 | 98.0 | 100.0 | 30.3 | 44.7 | 55.0 | 77.8 | 19.0 | 29.0 | 38.5 | 71.4 |
| Status | 23.6 | 40.1 | 62.5 | 69.0 | 87.3 | 90.9 | 96.0 | 100.0 | 20.2 | 39.2 | 53.0 | 55.6 | 8.0 | 14.2 | 25.0 | 37.5 |

seled prior adjudications as a major determinant of many juveniles' subsequent sentences.

## DISPOSITIONS BY ATTORNEYS BY PRIORS

Tables 4-12 and 4-13 show that a record of prior referrals is associated with receiving more severe dispositions as well as with a greater likelihood of having an attorney. Table 4-14 examines the relationship between prior referrals and receiving an out-of-home placement or secure confinement disposition when an attorney is present or absent. The row percentages within offense categories, dispositions, and prior referrals are those for youths placed out-of-home or securely confined when an attorney is present and when one is not.

As can be seen by row comparisons at each offense level and type of disposition across priors, youths with attorneys are more likely to receive out-of-home placement and secure confinement dispositions than are those without counsel. In Table 4-14, which controls for the seriousness of the present offense and the prior record simultaneously, larger proportions of youths with lawyers receive out-of-home placement and secure confinement than do those without. For the state as a whole, with forty-eight possible comparisons—six categories of offense times two types of disposition times four degrees of priors—represented youths received more severe dispositions in forty-four instances, or 91.7% of the cases.

When the effects of representation are analyzed separately in the counties with high, medium, and low rates of representation, the same pattern prevails—represented youths consistently fare worse than unrepresented ones. In the counties with high rates of representation, one would expect very little variation in dispositions because nearly all juveniles had attorneys and virtually no unrepresented youths were removed or confined. Of the forty-eight comparisons, there were only seven instances in which a larger proportion of unrepresented juveniles received more severe dispositions than their represented counterparts. And, in five of those seven instances, there was only one juvenile in the comparison cell who was unrepresented and who received an out-of-home or secure disposition. What is especially impressive about the dispositional practices in the high representation counties is the extremely low percentages and absolute numbers of juveniles who were removed from their homes or confined without counsel (Table 4-10).

The same pattern of represented youths receiving more severe sentences than unrepresented youths prevailed in the medium and low representation counties as well. In the medium rate counties, in thirty-six of forty-eight comparisons, or 75% of the cases, represented juveniles fared worse. And in six of the twelve comparisons in which larger proportions of unrepresented juveniles received more severe sentences, there was only one case in the unrepresented cell. In the low rate counties, the pattern was somewhat less strong, probably because only 19.3% of all the juveniles were represented (Table 4-3). Even so, there were only fourteen comparisons in which unrepresented juveniles received more severe sentences, and in four of those instances, there were no represented juveniles in the comparison cell.

Thus, for juveniles in Minnesota, after controlling for the seriousness of the present offense and prior record, the presence of an attorney seems to be an aggravating factor at sentencing. Both in the state as a whole, as well as in the counties with high, medium, and low rates of representation, the same pattern prevails; larger proportions of represented juveniles than unrepresented youths received severe dispositions. Since most of the deviations from this pattern are the result of small numbers, that is, only one juvenile in the unrepresented comparison cell, the apparent adverse impact of counsel may be even stronger.

Although a lengthy prior record increases both the likelihood of representation and of receiving a severe disposition, the absence of counsel by no means protects a juvenile from harsh dispositions. While larger proportions of represented youths may be removed from their homes or confined, a substantial proportion of unrepresented juveniles, including many with extensive records of delinquency, are also removed or confined (Tables 4-12 and 4-13). Since *Scott v. Illinois* (440 U.S. at 373) and *State v. Borst* (278 Minn. 388, 154 N.W.2d at 398) alerted trial judges to the need to appoint counsel when incarceration is anticipated, it is difficult to explain why so many youths charged with a serious present offense and with an extensive prior record appear in court without counsel when a severe sentence is so likely.

While the relationship between representation and more severe dispositions is consistent in the state and in the different types of counties, the explanation of this relationship is not readily apparent. Perhaps still other variables besides the seriousness of the present offense and the length of the prior record influence both the initial appointment of counsel and the eventual disposition.

## PRETRIAL DETENTION, ATTORNEYS, AND DISPOSITIONS

Several studies have examined the determinants of detention and the relationship between a child's pretrial detention status and subsequent disposition (Krisberg and Schwartz 1983; Frazier and Bishop 1985; Clarke

**Table 4-14  Rate of Disposition (Home/Secure) by Counsel by Prior Referral**

| Priors | Statewide | | | | High | | | | Medium | | | | Low | | | |
|---|---|---|---|---|---|---|---|---|---|---|---|---|---|---|---|---|
| | 0 | 1–2 | 3–4 | 5+ | 0 | 1–2 | 3–4 | 5+ | 0 | 1–2 | 3–4 | 5+ | 0 | 1–2 | 3–4 | 5+ |
| **Felony Offense Against Person** | | | | | | | | | | | | | | | | |
| % Home | | | | | | | | | | | | | | | | |
| Counsel | 39.5 | 49.5 | 84.0 | 100.0 | 32.9 | 59.3 | 87.5 | 100.0 | 47.1 | 42.9 | 86.7 | 30.9 | 32.4 | 52.4 | 50.0 | — |
| No Counsel | 23.1 | 54.5 | 66.7 | — | 100.0[a] | — | — | — | 24.3 | 37.5 | 100.0[a] | 14.6 | 21.2 | 64.3 | 50.0 | — |
| % Secure | | | | | | | | | | | | | | | | |
| Counsel | 24.3 | 32.0 | 56.0 | 100.0 | 16.5 | 48.1 | 75.0 | 100.0 | 35.0 | 22.4 | 53.3 | — | 12.7 | 33.3 | — | — |
| No Counsel | 15.4 | 31.8 | 66.7 | — | — | — | — | — | 16.2 | 25.0 | 100.0[a] | — | 15.2 | 35.7 | 50.0 | — |
| **Felony Offense Against Property** | | | | | | | | | | | | | | | | |
| % Home | | | | | | | | | | | | | | | | |
| Counsel | 25.2 | 53.4 | 76.9 | 75.0 | 16.2 | 54.5 | 83.3 | 85.7 | 30.9 | 49.4 | 82.4 | 85.7 | 28.8 | 59.6 | 60.0 | 37.5 |
| No Counsel | 15.2 | 27.7 | 68.2 | 42.9 | — | — | 100.0[a] | — | 14.6 | 21.7 | 71.4 | 100.0[a] | 15.5 | 30.3 | 61.5 | 33.3 |
| % Secure | | | | | | | | | | | | | | | | |
| Counsel | 18.9 | 37.2 | 66.7 | 55.6 | 11.0 | 41.3 | 75.0 | 50.0 | 25.5 | 33.9 | 70.6 | 78.6 | 18.3 | 38.2 | 50.0 | 25.0 |
| No Counsel | 10.4 | 16.8 | 54.5 | 28.6 | — | — | 100.0[a] | — | 11.0 | 15.2 | 71.4 | 100.0[a] | 10.1 | 17.4 | 38.5 | 16.7 |
| **Minor Offense Against Person** | | | | | | | | | | | | | | | | |
| % Home | | | | | | | | | | | | | | | | |
| Counsel | 19.4 | 41.5 | 65.6 | 90.0 | 14.0 | 42.0 | 78.6 | 100.0 | 21.9 | 41.7 | 62.5 | 66.7 | 25.0 | 40.0 | — | 100.0 |
| No Counsel | 7.5 | 31.7 | 50.0 | 50.0 | — | — | — | — | 5.7 | 31.6 | 33.3 | 100.0[a] | 8.8 | 31.7 | 100.0[a] | 33.3 |

| | | | | | | | | | | | | | | | | |
|---|---|---|---|---|---|---|---|---|---|---|---|---|---|---|---|---|
| **% Secure** | | | | | | | | | | | | | | | | |
| Counsel | 11.1 | 22.2 | 40.6 | 80.0 | 8.4 | 28.0 | 57.1 | 80.0 | 11.7 | 16.7 | 31.3 | 66.7 | 15.9 | 24.0 | — | 100.0 |
| No Counsel | 3.5 | 21.7 | 50.0 | 50.0 | — | — | — | — | 3.4 | 15.8 | 33.3 | 100.0ᵃ | 3.6 | 24.4 | 100.0ᵃ | 33.3 |
| **Minor Offense Against Property** | | | | | | | | | | | | | | | | |
| **% Home** | | | | | | | | | | | | | | | | |
| Counsel | 14.8 | 32.8 | 50.7 | 68.4 | 10.7 | 31.2 | 68.9 | 83.3 | 18.1 | 31.3 | 41.7 | 61.5 | 19.5 | 40.0 | 42.9 | 42.9 |
| No Counsel | 7.5 | 20.1 | 37.8 | 50.0 | 5.3 | 60.0 | 100.0ᵃ | — | 10.0 | 22.6 | 50.0 | 50.0 | 6.6 | 18.3 | 30.0 | 50.0 |
| **% Secure** | | | | | | | | | | | | | | | | |
| Counsel | 9.1 | 23.8 | 39.1 | 57.9 | 5.7 | 23.6 | 57.8 | 77.8 | 12.4 | 21.5 | 33.3 | 38.5 | 11.7 | 30.0 | 19.0 | 42.9 |
| No Counsel | 4.9 | 11.7 | 33.3 | 25.0 | 5.3 | 20.0 | 100.0ᵃ | — | 7.2 | 14.4 | 42.9 | 25.0 | 4.1 | 10.3 | 26.7 | 25.0 |
| **Other Delinquency** | | | | | | | | | | | | | | | | |
| **% Home** | | | | | | | | | | | | | | | | |
| Counsel | 20.2 | 39.3 | 59.0 | 55.9 | 20.1 | 46.0 | 73.9 | 68.4 | 18.7 | 25.0 | 42.3 | 37.5 | 24.2 | 45.7 | 16.7 | 42.9 |
| No Counsel | 6.8 | 20.1 | 14.8 | 50.0 | 10.7 | 40.0 | — | — | 5.7 | 17.0 | 10.5 | — | 7.9 | 21.8 | 25.0 | 100.0 |
| **% Secure** | | | | | | | | | | | | | | | | |
| Counsel | 11.6 | 23.5 | 42.3 | 50.0 | 10.9 | 26.5 | 50.0 | 57.9 | 10.3 | 14.8 | 38.5 | 37.5 | 15.3 | 32.6 | — | 42.9 |
| No Counsel | 3.1 | 11.5 | 7.4 | 50.0 | 7.1 | 26.7 | — | — | 2.1 | 10.5 | 10.5 | — | 3.9 | 10.9 | — | 100.0 |
| **Status** | | | | | | | | | | | | | | | | |
| **% Home** | | | | | | | | | | | | | | | | |
| Counsel | 17.3 | 30.0 | 53.4 | 64.3 | 14.0 | 35.2 | 65.2 | 86.7 | 19.2 | 25.6 | 34.3 | 40.0 | 23.9 | 27.3 | 71.4 | 33.3 |
| No Counsel | 6.5 | 13.8 | 19.2 | 14.3 | 8.0 | 15.4 | — | — | 7.2 | 14.5 | 19.4 | 12.5 | 6.1 | 13.0 | 20.0 | 16.7 |
| **% Secure** | | | | | | | | | | | | | | | | |
| Counsel | 3.2 | 10.6 | 30.7 | 42.9 | 2.8 | 14.5 | 45.7 | 66.7 | 1.4 | 4.9 | 8.6 | 20.0 | 6.7 | 18.2 | 42.9 | — |
| No Counsel | 1.1 | 2.8 | 13.5 | 7.1 | 4.0 | — | — | — | 1.1 | 2.3 | 12.9 | — | 1.0 | 3.3 | 15.0 | 16.7 |

a. There was only one (1) unrepresented juvenile in this cell.

and Koch 1980; McCarthy 1987). These studies report that while several of the same variables affect both rates of detention and subsequent disposition, after appropriate controls, detention per se exhibits an independent effect on dispositions. Clarke and Koch (1980:294) observe that, after controlling for the effects of present offense and prior record, "the commitment rate remained much greater for children held in detention, except at the highest level of record and offense seriousness. . . . We conclude that being detained before adjudication had an independent effect on the likelihood of commitment, entirely apart from the fact that both detention and commitment had some common causal antecedents." They attribute the independent, negative effects of detention on rates of adjudication and commitment to the fact that "[t]he child's ability to defend himself may have been impaired by detention, either because he was prejudged by the same court that later decided his case, or because it was harder for him to talk to his lawyer and otherwise prepare his defense" (Clarke and Koch 1980:295). It may be that the apparent relationship between representation by counsel and more severe dispositions is influenced by differences in rates of pretrial detention. The next set of analyses examine the relationships between detention and offenses, detention and counsel, detention and dispositions, and detention, counsel, and dispositions.

## DETENTION BY OFFENSE

Table 4-15 shows the overall numbers and percentages of juveniles against whom petitions were filed and who were detained and the rates of pretrial detention by present offense category and the number of prior referrals. Detention, as used here, refers to a juvenile's custody status following arrest or referral but prior to formal court action—adjudication or disposition. Detention, as distinguished from shelter care, connotes a physically restricting facility which may include a detention center, state institution, or even adult jail (Minn. Stat. Ann. § 260.015, subd. 16, 17 [1986]; Schwartz, Harris, and Levi 1988).

The Minnesota detention statutes and Juvenile Court Rules governing detention procedures authorize pretrial preventive detention if "the child would endanger self or others, not return for a court hearing, nor remain in the care or control of the person to whose lawful custody the child is released, or that the child's health or welfare would be immediately endangered" (Minn. Stat. Ann. §§ 260.171, subd. 1; 260.172, subd. 1 [1986]; Minn. R.P. Juv.Ct. 18.02(2)(A)(i); 18.06(5)(b)(i); 18.09(2)(D)(i)). The specific offense that a juvenile allegedly committed is not an explicit statutory criterion for detention except insofar as a juve-

**Table 4-15    Rate of Detention by Offense and Prior Record**

|  | Statewide | High | Medium | Low |
|---|---|---|---|---|
| **Overall** | | | | |
| % Detention | 7.6 | 6.7 | 12.2 | 4.0 |
| N | (1,309) | (239) | (775) | (295) |
| **Felony** | | | | |
| % | 14.9 | 9.1 | 23.7 | 9.2 |
| N | (470) | (65) | (295) | (110) |
| Felony Offense Against Person | | | | |
| % | 24.3 | 20.7 | 35.1 | 14.0 |
| N | (165) | (35) | (97) | (33) |
| Felony Offense Against Property | | | | |
| % | 12.3 | 5.5 | 20.5 | 8.0 |
| N | (305) | (30) | (198) | (77) |
| **Misdemeanor** | | | | |
| % | 6.5 | 5.2 | 11.1 | 3.1 |
| N | (606) | (109) | (377) | (120) |
| Minor Offense Against Person | | | | |
| % | 11.4 | 6.4 | 19.8 | 5.5 |
| N | (101) | (15) | (69) | (17) |
| Minor Offense Against Property | | | | |
| % | 6.0 | 3.5 | 12.5 | 2.6 |
| N | (332) | (40) | (224) | (68) |
| Other Delinquency | | | | |
| % | 6.1 | 7.6 | 6.8 | 3.9 |
| N | (173) | (54) | (84) | (35) |
| **Status** | | | | |
| % | 4.8 | 8.7 | 5.8 | 2.6 |
| N | (221) | (64) | (99) | (58) |
| | **Detention and Priors** | | | |
| 0 | 5.5 | 4.7 | 8.9 | 3.3 |
| 1–2 | 11.3 | 9.3 | 16.9 | 6.2 |
| 3–4 | 19.9 | 12.6 | 30.0 | 11.1 |
| 5+ | 20.5 | 16.5 | 33.8 | 7.7 |

nile court judge views it as evidence of "endangering" others. The vague, overly inclusive criteria in the Minnesota juvenile detention statute have been criticized extensively:

> In Minnesota, the detaining court need only find "probable cause that . . . others would be *endangered* if [the defendant were] released," and eligibility for detention is neither limited to the type of crime charged nor based on an examination of the accused's individual circumstances. Although continued detention is authorized based on an individual judge's conclusion that the community would be "endangered" by a youth's release, "endangerment" is not statutorily defined or circumscribed. The Minnesota rule lacks even the New York statutory requirement [upheld in *Schall v. Martin*, 467 U.S. 253 (1984)] that the risk be that of "an act which if committed by an adult would constitute a crime.". . . Minnesota requires only a finding of probable cause that a youth committed a delinquent act, which can include a violation of "any state or local law" as well as of many ordinances. Presumably, every juvenile court judge in the state may apply this same lower standard of proof on any individual, idiosyncratic basis with virtually no means of effective appellate supervision. (Feld 1984:206–7)

Minnesota appears to have a low overall rate of pretrial detention. Based on the 1984 data reported in Chapter Three, only 9.4% of all cases referred in Minnesota resulted in pretrial detention, the lowest rate in the six-state comparison (Table 3-5), and in 1986, only 7.6% of all juveniles were detained (Table 4-15). However, the SJIS uses a very restrictive definition of "detention." Juveniles in Minnesota are classified as detained only if a detention hearing is held within thirty-six hours—about two court days—after the juvenile was placed in custody (Minn. R.P. Juv. Ct. 18; Minn. Stat. §§ 260.171(1); 260.172(1) [1986]). Many more juveniles who are detained briefly pending the arrival of their parents or released within one or two days but prior to a detention hearing are not counted as detained.

The use of pretrial detention follows a similar pattern in the state as a whole as well as in the counties categorized on the basis of rates of representation. While only a small proportion of all juveniles in the state receive a detention hearing (7.6%), the seriousness of the present offense and the length of the prior record both appear to alter substantially a youth's likelihood of being detained. Several studies have noted the significance of a prior record for the decision to detain (Bailey 1981; Cohen and Kluegel 1979; McCarthy 1987). For the entire state, nearly one-quarter (24.3%) of youths charged with a felony offense against the person are detained. Juveniles charged with felony offenses against property and those charged with minor offenses against the person also have higher than baseline rates of detention.

The bivariate analyses—offense by detention—reported here suggest a greater degree of "legal rationality" than do other studies which report insignificant relationships between legal variables and detention decisions. Coates, Miller, and Ohlin (1978:101–4) report that current offense history and prior experience in youth corrections do not appear to be strongly related to the detention decision. Clarke and Koch (1980) conclude that the initial detention decision is not based on offense criteria or other rational factors. Frazier and Bishop (1985:1143) succinctly conclude that "neither legal variables nor socio-demographic characteristics can predict the probability of being detained." While there is some relationship among the seriousness of the offense, prior referrals, and rates of detention in this study, it does not appear to be a strong one. For example, more than three-quarters of the youths charged with even the most serious offenses are not detained. As will be seen, the regression analyses of detention decisions (Tables 4-23 through 4-26), are more consistent with other research that suggests that there is very little apparent rationale for the initial decision to detain a juvenile.

When the data are examined for counties with high, medium, and low rates of representation, similar patterns emerge. Youths charged with felony offenses, offenses against the person, and those with lengthier prior records are consistently detained at higher rates than their less delinquent counterparts. While the pattern is the same, the overall use of detention differs substantially. Detention is used most heavily in the counties with medium rates of representation in which Hennepin County (Minneapolis) predominates. By contrast, the counties with low rates of representation employ pretrial detention far less often. Their rates of detention are typically only one-third to one-half of those in the medium representation counties. The most likely explanation for differences in overall rates of detention is the availability of detention facilities. There is substantial evidence that the primary determinant of rates of detention in a state or county is the availability of detention bedspace (Krisberg and Schwartz 1983; Kramer and Steffensmeier 1978; Lerman 1977; Pawlak 1977; Bookin-Weiner 1984). This phenomenon suggests a penological paraphrase of Parkinson's Law, that bodies expand to fill the bedspace allotted. Frazier and Bishop (1985:1136) summarize these studies charitably and note that "a juvenile's detention status may be based on illegitimate factors such as the organization of the decision-making process or the philosophies of justice held by officials."

## PRETRIAL DETENTION AND REPRESENTATION BY COUNSEL

Table 4-16 examines the relationship between juveniles' detention status and rates of representation by counsel. Detention, particularly if it continues for more than a day and results in a hearing, is a legally significant juvenile court intervention that also requires the assistance of counsel (*Schall v. Martin*, 467 U.S 253 [1984]; Feld 1984). Every jurisdiction provides for a prompt detention hearing to determine the existence of probable cause, the presence of substantive grounds for detention, and the child's custody status pending trial.

Table 4-16 reports the rates of representation overall and at each offense level for juveniles who were detained and for those who were not. Overall, only 45.3% of juveniles in the state were represented (Table 4-3). However, the rate of representation for the 7.6% of juveniles who were detained was 75.4% as contrasted with 43.0% for those who remained at liberty. Similarly, 77.3% of all juveniles charged with a felony offense against the person were represented (Table 4-3) and nearly a quarter of them were detained (Table 4-15). Of those who were detained, 87.2% were represented, as contrasted with 74.5% of those who were not detained.

Controlling for the offense, a comparison of the two columns for the state as a whole and for the counties grouped by rates of representation reveals a very consistent pattern—youths who were held in detention had substantially higher rates of representation than did juveniles who were not (compare Table 4-3 with Table 4-16). While there is virtually no difference between detained and nondetained youths in the counties with

**Table 4-16   Pretrial Detention and Rate of Representation by Counsel**

| Detention | Statewide | | High | | Medium | | Low | |
|---|---|---|---|---|---|---|---|---|
| | Yes | No | Yes | No | Yes | No | Yes | No |
| **Overall % Counsel** | 75.4 | 43.0 | 96.0 | 94.4 | 73.7 | 43.4 | 60.6 | 17.8 |
| Felony Offense Against Person | 87.2 | 74.5 | 96.9 | 97.7 | 86.7 | 79.0 | 76.9 | 54.0 |
| Felony Offense Against Property | 82.0 | 60.8 | 100.0 | 98.2 | 84.2 | 65.0 | 68.9 | 35.0 |
| Minor Offense Against Person | 77.5 | 60.6 | 100.0 | 96.2 | 73.0 | 64.6 | 75.0 | 28.5 |
| Minor Offense Against Property | 72.3 | 42.9 | 97.4 | 97.2 | 71.9 | 49.6 | 55.8 | 14.9 |
| Other Delinquency | 76.1 | 43.2 | 91.8 | 91.5 | 66.7 | 32.8 | 70.4 | 19.7 |
| Status | 62.3 | 27.2 | 95.3 | 88.4 | 53.3 | 25.5 | 37.3 | 8.6 |

high rates of representation, in the other types of counties as well as for the state as a whole, the differences in rates are considerable, especially as the seriousness of the present offense decreases. While a majority of all the juveniles charged with minor offenses against property, other delinquency, and status offenses are unrepresented (Table 4-3), the situation is reversed for the small group who are held in detention. In the low representation counties, where only 19.3% of all juveniles have counsel, of the 4.0% of youths who are detained, more than 60% are represented. Comparing the overall rates of representation at different offense levels (Table 4-3) with the rates of representation for detained youths (Table 4-16) shows that detention provides a significant additional impetus for the appointment of counsel, particularly for less serious offenders. For example, while only 15.8% of juveniles in low representation counties charged with a minor offense against property have counsel (Table 4-3), 55.8% of those held in detention do.

## DETENTION AND DISPOSITIONS

Several studies that examined the determinants of detention and the relationship between pretrial detention and subsequent dispositions report that while the two decisions share common variables, detention appears to exhibit an independent effect on the severity of dispositions (Krisberg and Schwartz 1983; Frazier and Bishop 1985; Clarke and Koch 1980; McCarthy 1987). Table 4-17 shows the relationship between a youth's present offense, detention status, and eventual disposition. It reports the percentages of youths within each offense category who were detained and who were not detained who received out-of-home placement and secure confinement dispositions.

Again, the results are remarkably consistent; in the state as a whole, in the counties grouped by rates of representation, and at every offense level, substantially larger proportions of youths who were detained received more severe dispositions than did those who were not detained. When compared with the overall disposition rates by offense (Table 4-6), detained youths were about three times more likely to receive severe dispositions than their counterparts who were not held in detention. For example, while 18.5% of all juveniles were removed from their homes (Table 4-6), 57.3% of detained juveniles were removed as contrasted with 15.3% of those who were not detained. In part, the differences in sentences between detained and nondetained youths may reflect the somewhat larger proportion of juveniles with prior records who were held in pretrial detention (compare Table 4-12, prior record and disposition, with Table 4-15, detention of juveniles with priors). This suggests that

**Table 4-17    Impact of Pretrial Detention on Disposition (Home/Secure)**

| Detention | Statewide | | High | | Medium | | Low | |
|---|---|---|---|---|---|---|---|---|
| | Yes | No | Yes | No | Yes | No | Yes | No |
| **Overall** | | | | | | | | |
| % Home | 57.3 | 15.3 | 56.7 | 22.8 | 56.6 | 15.0 | 59.7 | 12.0 |
| % Secure | 35.3 | 9.1 | 32.0 | 14.6 | 35.7 | 9.0 | 36.6 | 6.6 |
| Felony Offenses Against Person | | | | | | | | |
| % Home | 65.2 | 35.0 | 62.5 | 40.0 | 61.5 | 37.9 | 80.8 | 29.1 |
| % Secure | 46.1 | 21.7 | 41.7 | 26.7 | 48.4 | 23.6 | 42.3 | 16.9 |
| Felony Offense Against Property | | | | | | | | |
| % Home | 71.0 | 26.8 | 85.7 | 30.7 | 69.9 | 26.9 | 69.0 | 24.3 |
| % Secure | 53.3 | 19.5 | 57.1 | 23.5 | 53.4 | 21.2 | 51.7 | 15.6 |
| Minor Offense Against Person | | | | | | | | |
| % Home | 54.2 | 19.8 | 64.3 | 26.6 | 48.5 | 18.6 | 68.8 | 16.6 |
| % Secure | 32.3 | 12.0 | 35.7 | 18.3 | 30.3 | 8.7 | 37.5 | 11.2 |
| Minor Offense Against Property | | | | | | | | |
| % Home | 53.4 | 13.6 | 60.5 | 17.8 | 49.3 | 15.4 | 63.5 | 10.7 |
| % Secure | 33.9 | 9.4 | 36.8 | 12.5 | 30.3 | 11.6 | 44.4 | 6.7 |
| Other Delinquency | | | | | | | | |
| % Home | 59.7 | 15.9 | 60.0 | 31.3 | 58.6 | 10.3 | 61.5 | 12.4 |
| % Secure | 36.4 | 9.4 | 36.4 | 19.0 | 36.4 | 6.1 | 36.5 | 7.0 |
| Status | | | | | | | | |
| % Home | 47.9 | 10.6 | 51.7 | 20.4 | 49.0 | 10.2 | 42.1 | 8.0 |
| % Secure | 11.4 | 3.1 | 17.2 | 9.0 | 6.3 | 2.0 | 14.0 | 2.1 |

similar factors influence both the initial detention decision and the ultimate disposition. However, when one compares the relationship between present offense and disposition (Table 4-6) with the relationship between offense/detention and disposition (Table 4-17), it is apparent that detained youths are substantially more at risk of receiving out-of-home placement and secure confinement dispositions than are nondetained youths. While pretrial detention increases a youth's probability of receiving more severe dispositions, the impact of detention on dispositions increases as the seriousness of the offense declines (compare Table 4-6 with Table 4-17).

## REPRESENTATION BY COUNSEL OF DETAINED JUVENILES AND DISPOSITION

Table 4-15 reported the percentages of youths who were detained at each offense level. Table 4-16 examined the relationship between detention status and representation, and reported that detention substantially increased the likelihood of representation. Table 4-17 examined the relationship between detention status and disposition and showed that detention increased the likelihood of a youth receiving more severe dispositions. Table 4-18 reports the relationship between offense and disposition of detained youths who are represented by counsel and those who are not, to investigate whether the presence of counsel affects their sentences.

Even though pretrial detention increases the likelihood that a youth will have counsel (Table 4-16), Table 4-18 indicates that a detained youth

**Table 4-18   Representation of Detained Juveniles and Rate of Disposition (Home/Secure)**

| Attorney | Statewide | | High | | Medium | | Low | |
|---|---|---|---|---|---|---|---|---|
| | Yes | No | Yes | No | Yes | No | Yes | No |
| **Overall** | | | | | | | | |
| % Home | 57.8 | 50.4 | 56.5 | 33.3 | 56.4 | 47.7 | 64.5 | 57.3 |
| N | (484) | (138) | (117) | (3) | (278) | (84) | (89) | (51) |
| % Secure | 35.7 | 24.8 | 30.9 | 11.1 | 35.3 | 24.4 | 44.2 | 27.0 |
| N | (299) | (68) | (64) | (1) | (174) | (43) | (61) | (24) |
| Felony Offense Against Person | | | | | | | | |
| % Home | 64.8 | 53.3 | 59.1 | — | 63.2 | 40.0 | 80.0 | 80.0 |
| % Secure | 43.8 | 40.0 | 36.4 | — | 48.5 | 30.0 | 33.3 | 60.0 |
| Felony Offense Against Property | | | | | | | | |
| % Home | 70.0 | 59.4 | 83.4 | — | 68.3 | 52.2 | 69.7 | 70.5 |
| % Secure | 52.2 | 43.2 | 55.6 | — | 51.2 | 43.5 | 54.5 | 42.9 |
| Minor Offense Against Person | | | | | | | | |
| % Home | 57.1 | 45.0 | 58.3 | — | 51.1 | 41.1 | 87.5 | 66.6 |
| % Secure | 31.7 | 25.0 | 33.3 | — | 30.2 | 23.5 | 37.5 | 33.3 |
| Minor Offense Against Property | | | | | | | | |
| % Home | 51.7 | 59.0 | 60.0 | 100.0[a] | 47.9 | 50.0 | 60.0 | 84.2 |
| % Secure | 34.3 | 29.5 | 37.1 | — | 29.7 | 25.9 | 53.3 | 42.1 |
| Other Delinquency | | | | | | | | |
| % Home | 56.2 | 59.5 | 66.7 | 20.0 | 50.0 | 61.6 | 51.6 | 72.7 |
| % Secure | 35.4 | 26.2 | 37.8 | 20.0 | 29.6 | 30.8 | 41.9 | 18.2 |
| Status | | | | | | | | |
| % Home | 55.8 | 35.5 | 52.7 | 33.3 | 56.3 | 38.1 | 64.7 | 32.4 |
| % Secure | 13.3 | 8.9 | 18.2 | — | 4.2 | 7.1 | 23.5 | 11.8 |

a. There was only one (1) unrepresented juvenile in this cell.

who is represented by counsel is somewhat more likely to receive a severe disposition than a detained youth who is not represented. For the state as a whole, out of twelve comparisons—six categories of offense times two dispositions—larger proportions of detained juveniles who were represented received more severe dispositions in ten instances. In the counties with high rates of representation, the represented/detained youths received more severe dispositions simply because there were so few cases of unrepresented detained juveniles (Table 4-9). In the counties with medium rates of representation, in 75% of the comparisons, detained juveniles with lawyers received more severe sentences than did their unrepresented counterparts, as was also the case in 58.3% of the counties with low rates of representation. When the focus is only on the most severe disposition—secure confinement—larger proportions of detained juveniles with lawyers than those without lawyers were institutionalized in twenty-one out of the twenty-four comparisons. Thus, the presence of counsel appears to be an "aggravating" factor in the sentencing of detained youths, although it may also reflect the influence of other factors, such as prior record, that affect the initial detention decision, rates of representation, and the ultimate disposition.

The data in Table 4-18 also reinforce the findings reported in Table 4-9; in the counties with high rates of representation, there was virtually no detention, removal from home, or incarceration of unrepresented juveniles. By contrast, even allowing for the "aggravating" effect of counsel, substantial proportions of youths in the other counties in Minnesota were being detained and removed from their homes or incarcerated without the assistance of counsel. For the whole state, more than one-fifth (22.2%, N = 138) of the juveniles who were held in detention and removed from their homes, and nearly that proportion who were detained and incarcerated (18.5%, N = 68) were unrepresented throughout the process.

## MULTIPLE REGRESSION EQUATIONS FOR APPOINTMENT OF COUNSEL, PRETRIAL DETENTION, AND OUT-OF-HOME PLACEMENT AND SECURE CONFINEMENT DISPOSITIONS

The preceding analyses focused on bivariate relationships between selected variables while controlling for the effects of one or more other variables. The next analyses use ordinary least squares multiple regression procedures to analyze the relationships among a number of independent variables and to assess the relative impact of each independent variable on the dependent variable while controlling for the effects of other variables. Using regression techniques allows one to estimate and evaluate the strength and significance of the independent contributions of a number of factors to the explanation or prediction of a dependent variable (Kerlinger and Pedhazur 1973; Kleinbaum and Kupper 1978; Lewis-Beck 1980). Multiple regression estimates the relationships between the dependent variable and the independent variables by extracting from each variable the effects of the others. Thus, for example, the unique effect of the presence of an attorney on dispositions can be measured while taking into account or controlling for the effect of other variables.

The standardized regression coefficient for each independent variable ("beta" in Tables 4-19 through 4-30) expresses the relationship between each independent variable and the dependent variable once the effects of the other variables have been taken into account. The relative importance of each independent variable in predicting the dependent variable is determined by the size of the beta, or standardized regression, coefficient. Where two or more independent variables are measured in different units, standardized coefficients provide the only way to compare the relative effect on the dependent variable of each independent variable. Tables 4-19 through 4-30 also report the zero-order correlation coefficient (r) between each independent variable and the dependent variable, the multiple regression correlation coefficient (R), and $R^2$. The $R^2$ summarizes the amount of variation in the dependent variable that is explained by the independent variables included in the regression equation. The $R^2$ has the additional virtue of being interpretable as a straightforward percentage. For example, an $R^2 = .20$ means that 20% of the variation in the dependent variable is explained by the joint operation of the independent variables.

Forward stepwise regression equations were computed using Statistical Package for the Social Sciences (SPSS) for the entire state and separately for counties with high, medium, and low rates of representation (Nie et al. 1975). Using standard regression techniques, each variable is added to the regression equation in a separate step after the influence of all other variables has been calculated. The increment in $R^2$ due to the addition of that variable is taken as the component of variation attributable to that variable. Forward stepwise inclusion enters independent variables only if they meet certain statistical criteria (e.g., $p < .05$) and the order of inclusion is determined by the respective contribution of each variable to the explained variance (Nie et al. 1975:345). Regression equations were calculated for the following dichotomous dependent variables: representation; detention; out-of-home placement; and secure confinement.[1] The independent variables and their coding, which affects the signs of the beta coefficients, include: representation (1 = yes, 2 = no); secure confinement (1 = yes, 2 = no); a previous secure confinement disposition (1 = yes, 2 = no); out-of-home placement (1 = yes, 2 = no); a previous out-of-home placement (1 = yes, 2 = no); age (1 = twelve or younger, through 7 = eighteen years of age); gender (1 = male, 2 = female); detention (1 = no, 2 = yes); priors (1 = none, through 4 = five or more); present offense (1 = felony offense against person, through 6 = status); and number of offenses at disposition ( 1 = none, through 6 = five or more). As previously noted, the SJIS data include only court-processing variables. Thus, the study cannot control for the influence of many of the substantive factors that juvenile courts may also deem relevant such as family status, socioeconomic status, clinical evaluations, and school progress or involvement in work.

## REGRESSING APPOINTMENT OF COUNSEL FOR INDEPENDENT VARIABLES

The first regression equations are designed to determine which factors relate to the initial decision to appoint an attorney for a juvenile. Tables 4-19 through 4-22 summarize the regression equations for the state and for the counties with high, medium, and low rates of representation. In the state and in all types of counties, the most significant independent variable affecting the appointment of counsel is the seriousness of a juvenile's present offense. The length of the prior record, a juvenile's pretrial detention status, and severity of the eventual sentence, that is, receiving an out-of-home placement, also influence the appointment of counsel.

Table 4-19  **Regression Model of Factors Influencing the Appointment of Counsel (Statewide)**

| Independent Variables | Zero-Order r | Standardized Beta Coefficient | Multiple R | R² |
|---|---|---|---|---|
| Offense Severity | .253* | .216* | .253 | .064 |
| Prior Record | −.205* | −.128* | .320 | .102 |
| Out-of-Home Disposition | .229* | .120* | .350 | .122 |
| Detention | −.164* | −.082* | .359 | .129 |
| Prior Out-of-Home Disposition | .193* | .039* | .360 | .130 |
| Age | .040* | .017*** | .361 | .130 |

*p < .001
**p < .01
***p < .05

For the state as a whole, the present offense and prior record explain most of the variance that can be accounted for in rates of representation (10.2%). The beta coefficient indicates that the seriousness of the present offense (.216) has almost twice the influence of the prior record ($-.128$). Whether a juvenile eventually is removed from his or her home accounts for an additional 2% of the variance in rates of representation and has nearly the same impact as the prior record (.120) on the appointment decision. Obviously, an event such as removal from the home, which may occur several months after the initial decision to appoint counsel, does not *cause* that earlier decision. Regression simply describes the association between the eventual disposition, such as removal from the home, and the presence of counsel. While the present offense and prior record are also associated with removal from the home (Tables 4-6, 4-12), multiple regression has already factored those variables into the equation and the impact of the disposition represents the residual effect after accounting for the partial influence of those other variables.

The relationship between the initial decision to appoint counsel for a juvenile and the later decision to remove him or her from home may reflect a process in which the initial appointment decision is dictated by the anticipated home removal decision. Finally, as earlier analyses suggested (Table 4-16), a juvenile's pretrial detention status is also associated with the appointment of counsel. Here, the causal ordering is clearer—if a juvenile is detained initially, then an attorney is more likely to be appointed both for the detention hearing as well as for subsequent proceedings. The cumulative $R^2$ for the statewide regression equation is .130, which means that 13% of the variance in the appointment of counsel can be explained by the six independent variables in this equation.

Because nearly 95% of the juveniles in the counties with high rates of representation had attorneys (Table 4-3), there is very little variation in

**Table 4-20   Regression Model of Factors Influencing the Appointment of Counsel (High Representation Counties)**

| Independent Variables | Zero-Order r | Standardized Beta Coefficient | Multiple R | $R^2$ |
|---|---|---|---|---|
| Offense Severity | .115* | .101* | .115 | .013 |
| Prior Record | −.102* | −.071* | .156 | .024 |
| Out-of-Home Disposition | .111* | .077* | .170 | .029 |
| Gender | .077* | .051** | .177 | .031 |

*p < .001
**p < .01
***p < .05

the dependent variable. While the present offense, prior record, and home removal disposition enter the regression equation, together they explain very little of the variance in the appointment of counsel, only 2.9%, and the beta weights for those variables are only about half of those for the entire state. There is also a slight tendency for male delinquents to have higher rates of representation than females. However, when nearly every juvenile has a lawyer, there is very little systematic variation that explains those few who do not.

The regression equation for the appointment of counsel in counties with medium rates of representation mirrors that for the state as a whole. The independent variables of present offense, prior record, home removal disposition, and pretrial detention enter the equation in the same order and account for more of the variance in appointment of counsel, 15.1%. Of these factors, the seriousness of the present offense is clearly the most influential (.291 versus .116 for prior record).

In the counties with low rates of representation, the order in which the independent variables enter the equation is somewhat different from those in the high and medium representation counties. While the seriousness of the present offense remains the strongest influence on the appointment of counsel, removal from the home is second, detention third, and a prior record is fourth. Moreover, the beta weights of home removal, detention, and prior record are about the same, indicating that each has about the same association with variance in representation. While the length of the prior record is associated with a juvenile's age (Table 4-7), after controlling for that relationship, older youths are somewhat more likely to be represented than their younger counterparts (Table 4-5).

These multiple regression equations confirm the earlier bivariate

**Table 4-21  Regression Model of Factors Influencing the Appointment of Counsel (Medium Representation Counties)**

| Independent Variables | Zero-Order r | Standardized Beta Coefficient | Multiple R | R² |
|---|---|---|---|---|
| Offense Severity | .324* | .291* | .324 | .105 |
| Prior Record | −.169* | −.116* | .366 | .133 |
| Out-of-Home Disposition | .208* | .091* | .383 | .147 |
| Detention | −.172* | −.066* | .388 | .151 |
| Prior Out-of-Home Disposition | .178* | .041** | .389 | .152 |

*$p < .001$
**$p < .01$
***$p < .05$

**Table 4-22 Regression Model of Factors Influencing the Appointment of Counsel (Low Representation Counties)**

| Independent Variables | Zero-Order r | Standardized Beta Coefficient | Multiple R | R² |
|---|---|---|---|---|
| Offense Severity | .248* | .207* | .248 | .062 |
| Out-of-Home Disposition | .236* | .144* | .318 | .101 |
| Detention | −.195* | −.133* | .343 | .118 |
| Prior Record | −.175* | −.112* | .361 | .130 |
| Age | .008* | −.027*** | .362 | .131 |

*p < .001
**p < .01
***p < .05

analyses. In the state and in all types of counties, juveniles charged with more serious offenses are more likely to be represented (Tables 4-3 and 4-4), as are those with lengthier prior records (Table 4-13), those who are held in pretrial detention (Table 4-16), and those who are removed from their homes following adjudication (Tables 4-10, 4-11, and 4-14). What is most surprising, however, is that after factoring into the regression equation all of the legally relevant variables—present offense, prior record, pretrial detention, and postadjudication disposition—only 13% of the variance in appointment of counsel can be explained. While the very low R² in the high representation counties is understandable, even in the medium representation counties, only 15.2% of the variance in representation can be explained. Though it is possible that other variables for which this study cannot account—parental socioeconomic status, family structure, educational attainment, or the like—may explain some additional variance in representation, a very large amount of the variation in representation seems to be random. The very substantial aggregate county variations in rates of representation suggest that after identifying the relevant legal variables, idiosyncratic judicial policies within each county regarding waivers of rights are the major, albeit unmeasurable, factor in the appointment decision.

## REGRESSING PRETRIAL DETENTION ON INDEPENDENT VARIABLES

In the next set of regression equations, the dependent variable is pretrial detention (1 = no, 2 = yes). The independent variables are those used in the preceding analyses as well as the presence of an attorney. The regression equations attempt to identify which factors influence the decision to place a juvenile in pretrial detention. As the earlier analyses of detention indicated (Tables 4-15 through 4-18), while a juvenile's detention status exerts a strong influence on case processing and dispositions, identifying the factors that lead to the initial decision to detain juveniles is more problematic. Several studies suggest that there is no formal rationale for the detention decision or that the primary determinate is the availability of detention bedspaces (Coates, Miller, and Ohlin 1978; Frazier and Bishop 1985).

Tables 4-23 through 4-26 summarize the regression equations for pretrial detention for the state and for counties with high, medium, and low rates of representation. As will be seen in the regression analyses for out-of-home placement and secure confinement (Tables 4-27 through 4-30), after controlling for the present offense and prior record, a juvenile's pretrial detention status is a significant factor in dispositions. Given the impact of pretrial detention on subsequent sentencing, the issue is what factors influence the initial decision to detain.

Table 4-23 reports the independent variables entering the regression equation for pretrial detention for the entire state. Recall that 1,309, or 7.6%, of all juveniles in Minnesota had one or more detention hearings (Table 4-15). Interestingly, a subsequent event, receiving an out-of-home placement, accounts for most of the variance in pretrial detention, 7% (beta = −.211). The next most influential variable is the presence of an attorney, which accounts for an additional 1.1% of variance (beta = −.086). A comparison of the beta coefficient for out-of-home placement with the betas of the other variables indicates that the eventual disposition exerts three or more times as much influence as any of the other variables on detention. Similarly, the association between representation and de-

**Table 4-23   Regression Model of Factors Influencing the Detention Decision (Statewide)**

| Independent Variables | Zero-Order r | Standardized Beta Coefficient | Multiple R | R² |
|---|---|---|---|---|
| Out-of-Home Disposition | −.265* | −.211* | .265 | .070 |
| Representation | −.164* | −.086* | .285 | .081 |
| Offense Severity | −.117* | −.068* | .290 | .084 |
| Prior Record | .140* | .048* | .296 | .087 |
| Gender | .020** | .046* | .299 | .090 |
| Age | −.039* | −.019*** | .300 | .090 |

*p < .001
**p < .01
***p < .05

tention probably results from detention increasing the likelihood of representation, rather than from representation increasing a juvenile's likelihood of being detained (Tables 4-16 and 4-19). While both out-of-home placement and the appointment of counsel are influenced by the seriousness of the present offense and the prior record, the residuals of those variables also enter the regression equation for pretrial detention. Finally, after controlling for the influence of those other variables, it appears that juveniles who are female and those who are younger are somewhat more likely to be detained than are male or older juveniles. Being female explains an additional .3% of variance in pretrial detention. While the beta coefficient for gender is small (.046) it is comparable in influence to having a prior record (.048) or a more serious offense (−.068).

Because the eventual disposition occurs weeks or months after the initial decision to detain, one possible inference is that out-of-home placement and pretrial detention share underlying common elements. The detention statute focuses on a juvenile's danger to others, danger to self, or likelihood of absconding (Minn. Stat. Ann. §§ 260.171, 260.172 [1986]; Feld 1984). While the sentencing statute does not include specific criteria (Minn. Stat. Ann. § 260.185 [1986]), one interpretation is that the same subjective, discretionary factors that animate the initial detention decision later influence a judge's decision to remove a juvenile from the home.

An equally plausible interpretation, which draws on the findings of other research, is that there is very little rationale for the initial detention decision, but that it, in turn, may exert an independent effect on eventual dispositions apart from any common elements (Clarke and Koch 1980; Krisberg and Schwartz 1983; Pawlak 1977; Kramer and Steffensmeier 1978; McCarthy 1987). Frazier and Bishop (1985:1150–51), for example, provide alternative interpretations for their inability to explain the detention decision.

> The fact that we were unable to model detention decisions in these data may mean that courts detain juveniles based on legitimate considerations supplied to the judge in ad hoc fashion, although we have no evidence to suggest that this occurs. Alternatively, this inability to model detention decisions may mean that the process is idiosyncratic, causing some juveniles to suffer significant deprivations of liberty based on considerations that are irrelevant to the approved purposes of detention. If this latter explanation is correct, the problem may lie in the fact that statutory detention criteria are too broad and/or that detention statutes offer too little guidance regarding whether youths meet the stated criteria.

In the counties with high rates of representation, the regression equation can only account for 5.1% of the variance in rates of detention, and

**Table 4-24   Regression Model of Factors Influencing the Detention Decision (High Representation Counties)**

| Independent Variables | Zero-Order r | Standardized Beta Coefficient | Multiple R | R² |
|---|---|---|---|---|
| Out-of-Home Disposition | −.189* | −.193* | .189 | .036 |
| Prior Out-of-Home Disposition | −.146* | −.139* | .198 | .039 |
| Prior Secure Confinement Disposition | −.082* | .119* | .212 | .045 |
| Gender | .050** | .041*** | .217 | .047 |
| Secure Confinement Disposition | −.106* | .062*** | .220 | .048 |
| Prior Record | .128* | .056*** | .224 | .050 |
| Age | −.047** | −.033*** | .226 | .051 |

*p < .001
**p < .01
***p < .05

most of that is explained by the eventual sentence imposed in the present proceeding or by previous out-of-home or secure confinement dispositions. A relationship between previous sentences, current pretrial detention, and the eventual disposition is understandable. A record of prior referrals influences a juvenile's present detention status (Table 4-15). A prior out-of-home placement or secure confinement disposition represents a previous judicial determination that the juvenile should not remain at home, whether because of the nature of the prior offense or perceived treatment needs. Thus, when a juvenile on probation or parole is reapprehended, police and probation officers as well as the juvenile court judge are likely to incorporate their earlier decisions into their current ones.

Table 4-25 reports the regression equation for pretrial detention in the counties with medium rates of representation where juveniles were detained at around two or three times the rate as in other parts of the state (12.2% versus 6.7% and 4.0%, Table 4-15). Again, eventual out-of-home placement, the seriousness of the present offense, the length of the prior record, and the presence of an attorney explain most (12.1%) of the variance, of which the out-of-home placement exerts the most influence (beta = −.272). Female juveniles are somewhat more likely to be detained than are their male counterparts after controlling for the other independent variables (beta = .051).

Table 4-26 reports the regression equation for the detention decision

**Table 4-25    Regression Model of Factors Influencing the Detention Decision (Medium Representation Counties)**

| Independent Variables | Zero-Order r | Standardized Beta Coefficient | Multiple R | R² |
|---|---|---|---|---|
| Out-of-Home Disposition | −.304* | −.272* | .304 | .092 |
| Offense Severity | −.177* | −.121* | .327 | .107 |
| Prior Record | .158* | .076* | .342 | .117 |
| Representation | −.172* | −.067* | .348 | .121 |
| Gender | −.006 | .051* | .352 | .123 |
| Prior Secure Confinement Disposition | −.165* | −.052* | .354 | .124 |
| Secure Confinement Disposition | −.224* | .044*** | .355 | .125 |

*$p < .001$
**$p < .01$
***$p < .05$

**Table 4-26    Regression Model of Factors Influencing the Detention Decision (Low Representation Counties)**

| Independent Variables | Zero-Order r | Standardized Beta Coefficient | Multiple R | R² |
|---|---|---|---|---|
| Out-of-Home Disposition | −.255* | −.192* | .256 | .065 |
| Representation | −.195* | −.143* | .291 | .085 |
| Gender | .028*** | .037** | .293 | .086 |
| Secure Confinement Disposition | −.207* | −.041*** | .294 | .087 |

*$p < .001$
**$p < .01$
***$p < .05$

in the counties with low rates of representation where comparatively few juveniles are detained (Table 4-15). As in other settings, pretrial detention is most strongly associated with an eventual out-of-home placement and the presence of an attorney ($R^2 = .085$). Perhaps more surprising, how- ever, is the absence of either the present offense or prior record from the regression equation. For the reasons indicated previously, neither the eventual disposition nor the appointment of counsel cause the initial pre- trial detention. Yet this data and the regression equation do not identify any other significant causal variables that logically explain detention. The inability of this study to model the initial detention decision is consistent with other recent research findings. Again, Frazier and Bishop (1985:1143) conclude that "neither standard sociodemographic variables nor theoretically important legal variables are related to detention decisions. These findings suggest that courts do not make detention decisions based on the juvenile's age, gender or race and that courts are influenced neither by the seriousness of the current charges nor by prior records of offending." After additional analyses, they conclude that "detention decisions are systematically related neither to characteristics of juveniles nor to the offenses of juveniles about which decision-makers are routinely informed" (Frazier and Bishop 1985:1150).

These data, and similar findings in other jurisdictions, raise troubling questions about the determinants and uses of detention. Very little of the variance in the use of detention can be explained by traditional legal variables. Only .6% of the detention decision can be explained by the seriousness of the present offense and prior record independently of a home removal disposition and the presence of counsel (Table 4-23). The variations in the use of detention in different parts of the state suggest that the vague and general statutory criteria are susceptible to many differing local interpretations and applications.

Pretrial, preventive detention is a very onerous imposition, and its overuse and abuse in the juvenile justice process has been criticized extensively (Guggenheim 1977; Feld 1984; Krisberg and Schwartz 1983; Comment 1983). The vast majority of juveniles' institutional experiences occur in pretrial detention centers rather than in postadjudication commitments to training schools or other correctional facilities (Sarri and Hasenfeld 1976; Sarri 1974). Moreover, many juvenile court jurisdictions do not have juvenile detention facilities, in which case juveniles are preventively detained in adult jails (Schwartz, Harris, and Levi 1988; Goldfarb 1975). Cases like *D.B. v. Tewksbury* (545 F. Supp. 896 [D.Or. 1983]), provide graphic descriptions of the deplorable conditions under which juveniles are confined in adult jails. Commentators have described the realities of juvenile confinement thusly:

> Over half a million juveniles annually detained in "junior jails," another several hundred thousand held in adult jails, penned like cattle, demoralized by lack of activities and trained staff. Often brutalized. Over half the facilities in which juveniles are held have no psychiatric or social work staff. A fourth have no school program. The median age of detainees is fourteen; the novice may be sodomized within a matter of hours. Many have not been charged with a crime at all. (Wald 1976:119)

It is this institutional reality that Justice Rehnquist in *Schall v. Martin* (467 U.S. at 265 [1984]) characterized as the functional equivalent of parental supervision.

Quite apart from the obviously injurious consequences of pretrial imprisonment, such as deprivation of liberty, stigmatization, and negative self-labeling, detention may also impair a juvenile's ability to prepare legal defenses and may increase both a juvenile's probability of conviction and the likelihood of institutional confinement following adjudication (Coates, Miller, and Ohlin 1978; Clarke and Koch 1980; Frazier and Bishop 1985).

## REGRESSING OUT-OF-HOME PLACEMENT AND SECURE CONFINEMENT DISPOSITIONS ON INDEPENDENT VARIABLES

This study uses two alternative measures of dispositions—out-of-home placement and secure confinement. The next sets of regression equations examine the independent variables associated with the juvenile court's sentencing decision to remove a juvenile from his or her home and to institutionalize. Tables 4-27 through 4-30 summarize the regression equations for the state as a whole and separately for the counties with high, medium, and low rates of representation.

Table 4-27 reports the regression variables for juvenile court sentencing decisions—out-of-home placement and secure confinement—for the entire state. All of the independent variables together account for 24.5% of the variance in home removal and 22.4% of the variance in institutionalization. Of the independent variables, a previous disposition of removal from the home is the most powerful determinant of the present decision to remove a juvenile from home (beta = .357). Similarly, a previous secure confinement disposition is the most powerful determinant of the present decision to incarcerate a youth (beta = .354).

Two relatively recent studies examined the impact of prior juvenile court sentences on the present one. Thornberry and Christenson (1984) report that the dispositions for prior offenses exert a strong influence on current dispositions and that repeat offenders are likely to receive the same type of disposition for subsequent offenses—that is to say, there is stability in sentencing. By contrast, Henretta, Frazier, and Bishop (1986) analyze the effects of previous sentences on the present disposition while controlling for other variables and report evidence of progression or escalation, rather than stability, in sentencing. They conclude that

> prior dispositions exert a fairly strong influence on the disposition of new offenses. . . . [O]nly severity of the current offense proved to be

**Table 4-27    Regression Model of Factors Influencing Out-of-Home Placement and Secure Confinement Dispositions (Statewide)**

| Independent Variables | Zero-Order r | Standardized Beta Coefficient | Multiple R | R² |
|---|---|---|---|---|
| | | **Out-of-Home Placement** | | |
| Prior Out-of-Home Disposition | .422* | .357* | .422 | .179 |
| Detention | −.265* | −.175* | .467 | .218 |
| Representation | .229* | .107* | .483 | .233 |
| Offense Severity | .157* | .077* | .490 | .240 |
| Number of Offenses at Disposition | −.084* | −.060* | .494 | .244 |
| Age | .039* | .018** | .494 | .244 |
| Prior Record | −.282* | −.019*** | .494 | .244 |
| Gender | .023** | −.014*** | .494 | .245 |
| | | **Secure Confinement** | | |
| Prior Secure Confinement Disposition | .414* | .354* | .414 | .171 |
| Offense Severity | .191* | .120* | .445 | .198 |
| Detention | −.194* | −.115* | .462 | .214 |
| Representation | .197* | .081* | .469 | .220 |
| Number of Offenses at Disposition | −.086* | −.050* | .471 | .222 |
| Prior Record | −.260* | −.040* | .473 | .223 |
| Age | −.023** | −.040*** | .474 | .224 |

*$p < .001$
**$p < .01$
***$p < .05$

a stronger predictor of case outcomes. . . . [W]e did not find only stability in dispositional outcomes over repeat offenses. In our data, there is evidence of progression or escalation in the severity of disposition of subsequent offenses. (Henretta, Frazier, and Bishop 1986:561)

Although this study was not designed to replicate those of Thornberry or Henretta, it does provide evidence of the strong influence of prior dispositions on later sentences. The high zero-order correlations ("r") between prior home removal and present home removal, and between prior secure confinement and present secure confinement show the strong relationship between the two decisions. For the state as a whole and in all types of counties, a previous sentence of the same type as the current sentence is the first variable to enter the regression equation, has a beta weight that is double or triple that of the next variable, and explains about two-thirds to three-quarters of the total explained variance in sentencing.

The relationship between the previous disposition and the present one is consistent with the traditional, rehabilitative juvenile court sentencing philosophy. If sentencing decisions are individualized to fit the offender rather than the offense, then, absent a significant change in individual circumstances, a repeat involvement calls for a similar or greater intervention, regardless of the nature of the present offense. A juvenile's recidivism provides strong evidence to a sentencing judge that the child has failed to "learn his lesson." The previous disposition serves as a minimum constraint on the severity of the present sentence. To intervene less stringently is to give up and admit failure.

The next three variables to enter the equations for home removal and secure confinement, albeit in somewhat different order, are the seriousness of the present offense, pretrial detention, and the presence of an attorney. A relationship between the seriousness of the present offense and the more severe sentences reflects a modicum of proportionality in individualized dispositions (Table 4-6). Comparing the beta weights for the present offense (out-of-home = .077, institutional = .120) with those of previous dispositions indicates that the latter are three to five times more powerful in explaining the present sentence.

Pretrial detention also exerts a significant influence on the eventual sentence imposed on a juvenile (out-of-home beta = −.175, institutional beta = −.115). The presence of detention in the regression equations means that after controlling for the effects of the present offense, prior record and other variables that detention and the dispositions may share in common, the fact of detention per se exerts an additional and substantial effect on sentences. Indeed, a juvenile's pretrial detention status is about as influential as the present offense (beta = −.115 vs. .120) in the decision to confine and about twice as important (beta = −.175 vs. .077) in the decision to remove a juvenile from home. Other studies have noted the deleterious impact of pretrial detention on postadjudication dispositions.

Other than noting the strong and consistent relationship between pretrial detention and eventual out-of-home placement, the preceding regression analyses (Tables 4-23 through 4-26) could not identify causal variables that explained much of the variance in detention. The presence of detention in the disposition regression equations indicates that after controlling for the influences of the other independent variables, the fact of detention itself has a substantial impact on the sentences that youths receive. It is possible that both detention and the disposition decisions share common factors other than legal variables for which this study cannot control but which explain the strong relationship between the two. It is at least as likely, however, that the initial decision to detain is "irrational," meaning it has no formal legal rational basis, but that it then strongly influences subsequent decisions (McCarthy and Smith 1986:55–60). If process variables such as detention have no objective bases but strongly influence subsequent decision making, then it is important that juvenile courts and legislatures scrutinize more closely and regulate more explicitly those earlier decisions that may cumulate to a juvenile's later detriment.

The regression equations indicate that the presence of an attorney is an aggravating factor in a juvenile's disposition, accounting for about 1.5% of the variance in home removal and about .6% of the variance in secure confinement. While the overall explained variance is small, the beta coefficient indicates that the presence of an attorney has more influence on a youth's removal from home than does the seriousness of the offense (representation beta = .107, offense beta = .077). Thus, earlier observations that the presence of an attorney seems to be an aggravating factor at sentencing (Tables 4-9, 4-10, 4-14, and 4-18) are borne out by the regression equations. Again, there is the interpretive problem of causal ordering. While the simple presence of an attorney may produce more severe sentences, alternatively, the judge's anticipation of a more severe sentence may increase the likelihood of appointment of counsel.

The other variables in the regression equation explain very little additional variance in sentencing. The beta signs associated with the variable "age" indicate a slight tendency to remove younger juveniles from their homes (beta = .018) and to institutionalize older juveniles (−.040). Similarly, the beta sign for gender (−.014) indicates a very weak tendency to remove more female offenders than males from their homes after controlling for other variables. However, while statistically significant, none of these other variables explain even .1% of the variance in sentencing.

Table 4-28 reports the regression equations for home removal and secure confinement in counties with high rates of representation. A previous sentence of home removal or institutional confinement is the variable that is most powerfully associated with a current home removal or secure placement. Although pretrial detention, a prior record, and the severity of the present offense also influence both decisions, their relative contributions are distinctly subordinate to the juvenile justice system's

**Table 4-28  Regression Model of Factors Influencing Out-of-Home Placement and Secure Confinement Dispositions (High Representation Counties)**

| Independent Variables | Zero-Order r | Standardized Beta Coefficient | Multiple R | R² |
|---|---|---|---|---|
| | | **Out-of-Home Placement** | | |
| Prior Out-of-Home Disposition | .498* | .347* | .498 | .248 |
| Detention | −.189* | −.115* | .511 | .261 |
| Prior Record | −.407* | −.112* | .519 | .270 |
| Number of Offenses at Disposition | −.083* | −.068* | .525 | .276 |
| Offense Severity | .055* | .075* | .530 | .281 |
| Representation | .111* | .054* | .532 | .283 |
| Gender | −.014 | −.054** | .535 | .286 |
| | | **Secure Confinement** | | |
| Prior Secure Confinement Disposition | .478* | .325* | .478 | .228 |
| Prior Record | −.393* | −.134* | .494 | .244 |
| Offense Severity | .099* | .109* | .507 | .257 |
| Detention | −.106* | −.050* | .510 | .260 |
| Prior Out-of-Home Disposition | .444* | .083** | .511 | .262 |
| Number of Offenses at Disposition | −.064* | −.040** | .513 | .263 |

$*p < .001$
$**p < .01$
$***p < .05$

ratification of its own prior decisions. Somewhat surprisingly, even in counties where virtually all youths are represented, the presence of an attorney is still a statistically significant, aggravating factor in the decision to remove a juvenile from home (beta = .054).

Table 4-29 presents the regression statistics for out-of-home placement and secure confinement of juveniles in counties with medium rates of representation. A prior home removal disposition and pretrial detention status are the most influential determinants of a current home removal, and a prior institutional commitment, the seriousness of the present offense, and pretrial detention are the most significant determinants of current institutional confinement. The relationship between out-of-home placement and pretrial detention was noted earlier (Tables 4-23

**Table 4-29  Regression Model of Factors Influencing Out-of-Home Placement and Secure Confinement Dispositions (Medium Representation Counties)**

| Independent Variables | Zero-Order r | Standardized Beta Coefficient | Multiple R | R² |
|---|---|---|---|---|
| | | **Out-of-Home Placement** | | |
| Prior Out-of-Home Removal Disposition | .373* | .371* | .373 | .139 |
| Detention | −.304* | −.213* | .443 | .196 |
| Offense Severity | .197* | .098* | .461 | .213 |
| Representation | .208* | .082* | .467 | .218 |
| Number of Offenses at Disposition | −.087* | −.051* | .470 | .221 |
| Prior Secure Confinement Disposition | .279* | −.076* | .472 | .223 |
| | | **Secure Confinement** | | |
| Prior Secure Confinement Disposition | .364* | .311* | .364 | .133 |
| Offense Severity | .255* | .156* | .424 | .180 |
| Detention | −.224* | −.134* | .445 | .197 |
| Gender | .137* | .052* | .448 | .201 |
| Representation | .182* | .056* | .451 | .203 |
| Number of Offenses at Disposition | −.101* | −.048* | .454 | .206 |
| Age | −.056* | −.041* | .455 | .207 |

*p < .001
**p < .01
***p < .05

through 4-26). In Table 4-29, detention emerges as a strong influence on out-of-home placement and a somewhat lesser influence on secure confinement (out-of-home beta = −.213, institutional beta = −.134). While a juvenile's detention status explains more of the variance in home removal than does either the present offense or number of prior offenses, it will be recalled that there was no apparent explanation for the initial decision to detain. As in previous analyses, the presence of an attorney is an aggravating factor at sentencing (out-of-home beta = .082, institutional beta = .056). After controlling for other variables, older males are somewhat more at risk for secure confinement than are other juveniles.

**Table 4-30  Regression Model of Factors Influencing Out-of-Home Placement and Secure Confinement Dispositions (Low Representation Counties)**

| Independent Variables | Zero-Order r | Standardized Beta Coefficient | Multiple R | R² |
|---|---|---|---|---|
| | | **Out-of-Home Placement** | | |
| Prior Out-of-Home Removal Disposition | .388* | .338* | .388 | .151 |
| Detention | −.255* | −.184* | .443 | .197 |
| Representation | .236* | .120* | .464 | .215 |
| Offense Severity | .163* | .072* | .471 | .222 |
| Number of Offenses at Disposition | −.116* | −.060* | .474 | .225 |
| Gender | .001 | −.025*** | .475 | .226 |
| Age | .039* | .022*** | .475 | .226 |
| | | **Secure Confinement** | | |
| Prior Secure Confinement Disposition | .391* | .351* | .391 | .153 |
| Detention | −.207* | −.141* | .426 | .181 |
| Offense Severity | .177* | .106* | .446 | .199 |
| Representation | .205* | .099* | .457 | .209 |
| Number of Offenses at Disposition | −.118* | −.054* | .460 | .212 |
| Age | −.022*** | −.034** | .461 | .213 |

$*p < .001$
$**p < .01$
$***p < .05$

In the counties with low rates of representation, the previous home removal or confinement disposition, pretrial detention, the seriousness of the offense, and the presence of an attorney explain most of the variance in dispositions. Of these, the previous sentence is clearly the dominant influence (out-of-home beta = .338, institutional beta = .351) followed by pretrial detention. A comparison of the beta weights for attorney representation in the high, medium, and low representation counties suggests that in the low representation counties, where attorneys appear infrequently, their presence makes a larger contribution to the severity of the eventual sentences imposed than in settings where they appear more commonly.

## CONCLUSION

Grouping counties on the basis of their rates of representation reveals that high, medium, and low representation counties differ significantly in the administration of juvenile justice. The presence of an attorney provides an important indicator of a county court's formal, due-process orientation which, in turn, is associated with differences in pretrial detention, sentencing, and case-processing practices. The courts in the high representation counties handle more juveniles charged with criminal offenses and correspondingly fewer charged with status offenses than do those in low representation counties. Moreover, the procedurally more formal courts have higher rates of pretrial detention and more severe sentencing practices than do the low representation courts. Chapter Five explores additional indicators of the effects of counsel on juvenile justice administration. It reveals that attorneys have a different impact on the ways in which cases are processed in settings where they always, occasionally, and seldom appear.

## NOTE

1. Because the four dependent variables are dichotomous, categorical variables rather than interval variables, log linear or logit approaches to multivariate analyses may be preferable to ordinary least squares regression. For example, Cohen and Kluegel (1978) criticized earlier research on juvenile justice decision making for using inadequate data-analytic techniques. Thornberry (1979:170) reanalyzed the data in his earlier study and concluded that the findings "are remarkably similar to the ones reached in this author's earlier study, even though the earlier work was based on less sophisticated analytic techniques." Because the sample size in this study is very large (N = 17,195), the data robust, and the complexity of the data requires multivariate analyses, ordinary least squares regression was used (Kleinbaum and Kupper 1978).

# chapter five

# THE IMPACT OF COUNSEL ON JUVENILE JUSTICE ADMINISTRATION

Chapter Four analyzed the relationships between certain legal variables and the initial decision to appoint an attorney as well as the effect of the presence of counsel on juveniles' dispositions. Those analyses indicate that each legal variable—seriousness of present offense, prior referrals, and pretrial detention status—appears to be associated with both higher rates of representation and more severe dispositions. The regression analyses, which simultaneously controlled for the effects of all the other legal variables, indicate that the presence of an attorney makes an additional, independent contribution to the severity of sentences juveniles receive. The analyses in Chapter Five seek additional ways of measuring the determinants and impact of representation in juvenile court proceedings.

## REPRESENTATION BY COUNSEL AND NUMBER OF OFFENSES AT DISPOSITION

Table 5-1 reports on the number of charges that remain at the time of a juvenile's disposition. As the note to Table 5-1 indicates, juveniles are acquitted or have all charges dismissed in a very small proportion of delinquency and status cases, only 3.3% of the total. In most instances, a delinquency determination is based on only one sustained charge, and two or more offenses are proved in only 14.0% of the cases. A substantially larger proportion of cases involving felony offenses and offenses against the person involve multiple offenses at disposition, 30.4% of fel-

**Table 5-1   Number of Offenses at Disposition**

| Number of Offenses | Statewide | | High | | Medium | | Low | |
|---|---|---|---|---|---|---|---|---|
| | 1 | 2+ | 1 | 2+ | 1 | 2+ | 1 | 2+ |
| **Overall %**[a] | 82.7 | 14.0 | 85.7 | 8.0 | 84.8 | 13.8 | 79.4 | 17.1 |
| **Felony** | 69.7 | 30.3 | 82.3 | 17.7 | 69.9 | 30.1 | 62.1 | 37.9 |
| Felony Offense Against Person | 69.6 | 30.4 | 79.8 | 21.2 | 68.3 | 31.7 | 64.7 | 35.3 |
| Felony Offense Against Property | 69.8 | 30.2 | 83.0 | 17.0 | 70.4 | 29.6 | 61.5 | 38.5 |
| **Misdemeanor** | 84.8 | 15.2 | 92.0 | 8.0 | 85.7 | 14.3 | 80.1 | 19.9 |
| Minor Offense Against Person | 82.0 | 18.0 | 91.3 | 8.7 | 81.5 | 18.5 | 76.5 | 23.5 |
| Minor Offense Against Property | 85.0 | 15.0 | 90.0 | 10.0 | 86.3 | 13.7 | 82.0 | 18.0 |
| Other Delinquency | 85.0 | 15.0 | 95.2 | 4.8 | 85.8 | 14.2 | 76.4 | 23.6 |
| **Status** | 96.7 | 3.3 | 97.8 | 2.2 | 97.9 | 2.0 | 95.5 | 4.5 |

a. The overall percentages for the total number of offenses at disposition do not equal 100% because of the small fraction of cases in which there were no offenses at disposition, that is, cases ending in acquittal or dismissal of all charges. For the state as a whole, and for the high, medium, and low representation counties, the rates were, respectively: 3.3%, 6.3%, 1.4%, and 3.5%.

ony offenses against the person, 30.2% of felony offenses against property, and 18.0% of minor offenses against the person. By contrast, for the state overall, only 3.3% of juveniles charged with status offenses have more than one offense at disposition.

Table 5-1 reports that more serious offenses often are associated with several offenses remaining at disposition. More serious offenses also engender higher rates of representation (Tables 4-3 and 4-4). Thus, a comparison of juveniles with multiple offenses at dispositions both with counsel and without counsel provides an additional opportunity to assess the determinants and impact of counsel.

Although the differences are often quite small, for the counties with high, medium, and low rates of representation, a larger proportion of juveniles who are represented by attorneys had multiple charges at disposition than did the unrepresented youths. The number of petitions with sustained charges at disposition are reduced by those resulting in acquittals or dismissals. The note to Table 5-1 reported that in the counties with high rates of representation, 6.3% of all juveniles were acquitted or had all charges dismissed. These dismissals were confined primarily to those few juveniles who appeared without counsel. While 5.0% of represented juveniles had all charges dismissed, 23.8% of the unrepresented ones did.

**Table 5-2   Representation by Counsel and Number of Offenses at Disposition**

| Counsel | Statewide | | High | | Medium | | Low | |
|---|---|---|---|---|---|---|---|---|
| | Yes | No | Yes | No | Yes | No | Yes | No |
| **Number of Offenses at Disposition[a] Overall %** | | | | | | | | |
| 1 | 81.8 | 83.8 | 86.9 | 72.5 | 81.6 | 87.4 | 69.8 | 82.1 |
| 2+ | 14.7 | 13.5 | 8.1 | 3.7 | 17.0 | 11.3 | 25.6 | 15.2 |
| Felony Offense Against Person | | | | | | | | |
| 1 | 70.2 | 69.5 | 80.3 | 100.0[b] | 66.7 | 76.1 | 64.9 | 65.5 |
| 2+ | 29.8 | 30.5 | 19.7 | — | 33.3 | 23.9 | 35.1 | 34.5 |
| Felony Offense Against Property | | | | | | | | |
| 1 | 73.0 | 63.5 | 82.5 | 75.0 | 71.9 | 66.3 | 59.3 | 61.9 |
| 2+ | 27.0 | 36.5 | 17.5 | 25.0[b] | 28.1 | 33.7 | 40.7 | 38.1 |
| Minor Offense Against Person | | | | | | | | |
| 1 | 83.8 | 80.4 | 92.1 | 100.0 | 80.2 | 82.9 | 74.3 | 78.7 |
| 2+ | 16.2 | 19.6 | 7.9 | — | 19.8 | 17.1 | 25.7 | 21.3 |
| Minor Offense Against Property | | | | | | | | |
| 1 | 85.4 | 84.7 | 90.0 | 92.3 | 85.8 | 87.0 | 72.4 | 83.7 |
| 2+ | 14.6 | 15.3 | 10.0 | 7.7 | 14.2 | 13.0 | 27.6 | 16.3 |
| Other Delinquency | | | | | | | | |
| 1 | 89.1 | 81.9 | 95.5 | 95.6 | 86.0 | 85.8 | 76.5 | 76.7 |
| 2+ | 10.9 | 18.1 | 4.5 | 4.4 | 14.0 | 14.2 | 23.5 | 23.3 |
| Status | | | | | | | | |
| 1 | 97.0 | 96.6 | 98.0 | 96.9 | 97.1 | 98.0 | 93.6 | 95.6 |
| 2+ | 3.0 | 3.4 | 2.0 | 3.1 | 2.9 | 2.0 | 6.4 | 4.4 |

a. The overall percentages for the total number of offenses at disposition do not equal 100% because of the small fraction of cases in which there were no offenses at disposition, that is, cases ending in acquittal or dismissal of all charges. See Table 5-1, note a. For the state as a whole and for the high, medium, and low representation counties, the acquittal/dismissal rates for represented and unrepresented youth were, respectively: 3.5% and 2.7%; 5.0% and 23.8%; 1.4% and 1.3%; and 4.6% and 2.8%.

b. There was only 1 unrepresented juvenile in this cell.

Though the counties with medium and low rates of representation did not differ as dramatically in the rates of dismissal for represented and unrepresented juveniles, 5.7% and 10.4% more of the represented juveniles in those counties had multiple charges at disposition than did their unrepresented counterparts. Thus, as evidenced by multiple charges, represented juveniles had somewhat more complex cases than did unrepresented youths. This is consistent with the only other study that attempted to identify the factors associated with representation and to gauge the complexity of cases as they influenced the severity of dispositions (Stapleton and Teitelbaum 1972:72–79).

Comparing the proportion of represented and unrepresented juveniles with two or more charges at disposition in the counties with high, medium, and low rates of representation also confirms that represented juveniles had somewhat more complex cases. In the counties with high and medium rates of representation, a larger proportion of represented juveniles had more charges than their unrepresented colleagues in four of six comparisons. In the counties with low rates of representation, the represented juveniles exceeded their unrepresented counterparts in all six comparisons.

## REPRESENTATION BY COUNSEL AND REDUCTION IN CHARGES

Whether a juvenile was convicted of the original and most serious offense for which the petition was filed provides another way to assess the performance of attorneys. Unfortunately, the SJIS data tapes do not permit direct tracking of each discrete offense from filing to disposition. Fortunately, however, for the vast majority of juveniles, 82.7%, only one offense is alleged (Table 5-1).

Table 5-3 compares the most serious offense initially alleged in the petition with the most serious offense remaining at the time of disposition to determine in what proportion of cases the original charge was reduced. The percentages represent the proportion of juveniles convicted of the

**Table 5-3    Representation by Counsel and Proportion of Charges Reduced**

| | Statewide | | High | | Medium | | Low | |
|---|---|---|---|---|---|---|---|---|
| Counsel | Yes | No | Yes | No | Yes | No | Yes | No |
| Felony Offense Against Person | 82.9 | 88.9 | 73.0 | 25.0 | 93.4 | 95.8 | 77.7 | 88.0 |
| Felony Offense Against Property | 86.8 | 89.5 | 84.6 | 44.4 | 93.6 | 94.0 | 77.6 | 87.9 |
| Minor Offense Against Person | 84.5 | 91.8 | 77.2 | 25.0 | 92.4 | 95.6 | 82.6 | 92.3 |
| Minor Offense Against Property | 92.3 | 94.1 | 90.6 | 80.6 | 96.0 | 95.7 | 88.4 | 93.7 |
| Other Delinquency | 91.5 | 94.6 | 90.1 | 72.4 | 95.4 | 97.3 | 87.2 | 93.4 |
| Status | 94.2 | 96.4 | 93.9 | 82.1 | 95.8 | 97.0 | 92.2 | 96.7 |

same type of offense that they were originally charged with when they did or did not have a lawyer. Quite clearly, juveniles charged with a serious offense have a greater likelihood of having their charges reduced than do those charged with less serious offenses. Thus, about 15% of the juveniles charged with a felony offense against the person have their top charge reduced as compared with only about 5% of those charged with a status offense. In part, the greater reduction of serious offenses reflects the fact that the more serious offenses encompass a greater number of possible "lesser included" offenses as well as a larger proportion of cases with multiple allegations (Table 5-1), both of which permit pleas to other less serious offenses.

Comparing the proportions of reduced charges when juveniles are or are not represented by counsel provides another basis for assessing the performance of attorneys. In the state overall and in the counties with medium and low rates of representation, a larger proportion of juveniles who appear with counsel are convicted of offenses less serious than those with which they were originally charged (Table 5-3). As expected, the amount of reduction is greatest for those charged with felony offenses and offenses against the person and less for those charged with the more numerous but less serious minor offenses against property, other delinquency, and status violations.

When the counties with high, medium, and low rates of representation are examined separately, attorneys show the greatest impact in those counties where they are least common (i.e., low representation counties) and the least impact in the counties where they appear most frequently. In the counties with high rates of representation, the 5.5% of unrepresented juveniles (Table 4-4) have much greater rates of charge reduction than do their represented colleagues. The greater rate of charge reduction and dismissal (Table 5-2) suggests that the juvenile court judges in the high representation counties are especially conscious of these juveniles' lack of representation, indulge a presumption for leniency in their favor, and impose very few out-of-home placement or secure confinement dispositions on them (Tables 4-9 and 4-10).

By contrast, the presence of lawyers has the greatest impact on charge reduction in the low representation counties where attorneys appeared in less than 20% of cases. For juveniles charged with the most serious felony offenses, attorneys were able to effect about a 10% reduction when compared with the unrepresented juveniles. Even for the less serious offenses, represented juveniles enjoyed about a 5% reduction in charges as compared with the unrepresented youths. In the counties with medium rates of representation, there was a modest 1% to 2% difference in reduced charges in favor of represented juveniles.

Table 5-4 reports the proportional reduction in charges by the type of attorney. As in Table 5-3, the percentages represent the proportion of juveniles convicted of the same type of offense with which they were originally charged, depending on the type of attorney who represented them. Slightly more than 5% of juveniles had a private attorney while the bulk of juveniles were represented either by public defenders or court appointed attorneys depending upon the legal services delivery system in the particular county (Tables 4-3 and 4-4). Examining charge reduction by type of attorney for the state as a whole, it appears that a juvenile fares somewhat better when represented by a public attorney rather than a private attorney. For the six offense comparisons, in no instance did a private attorney garner a greater proportion of charge reductions than did at least one of the public attorney types, and in two-thirds of the comparisons private attorneys did worse than both. Setting aside the data from the counties with high rates of representation where there were very few private attorneys (2.4%, Table 4-4) or unrepresented juveniles, it appears from the medium and low representation counties that if a juvenile seeks counsel at all, a public sector attorney who is more familiar with the system may provide greater assistance. Interestingly, in many of the comparisons, unrepresented juveniles enjoyed a larger proportional reduction in charges than did those who retained private counsel. Recall, however, as measured by the dispositions their clients received (Table 4-11), private attorneys were somewhat more effective than public attorneys. While a record of convictions for more serious offenses may affect a youth's subsequent sentences both as a juvenile and as an adult, for the majority of juveniles who do not recidivate, the disposition of their present case is the most crucial decision.

## FINDING OF DELINQUENCY

In Minnesota, one of a juvenile court judge's dispositional options is to find the facts to be proven but then continue the case for ninety days "before a finding of delinquency has been entered" (Minn. Stat. Ann. § 260.185, subd. 3 [1982]). Even without finding delinquency, a judge may order many of the same dispositions. The option of continuing a case without a formal finding of delinquency provides a dispositional alternative to intake screening for those county juvenile courts that do not screen cases extensively prior to filing a petition. A finding of delinquency, however, constitutes a more formal determination that may be counted as part of the adult criminal history score for subsequent sentencing purposes (Minnesota Sentencing 1980).

What factors influence a judge's decision whether or not to make a

**Table 5-4  Attorney Type and Proportion of Charges Reduced**

| Counsel | Statewide | | | | High | | | | Medium | | | | Low | | | |
|---|---|---|---|---|---|---|---|---|---|---|---|---|---|---|---|---|
| | Private | PD[a] | CA[b] | None | Private | PD | CA | None | Private | PD | CA | None | Private | PD | CA | None |
| Felony Offense Against Person (%) | 90.1 | 82.6 | 79.9 | 88.9 | 71.4 | 73.9 | 69.7 | 25.0 | 100.0 | 91.4 | 92.9 | 95.8 | 76.2 | 70.6 | 79.5 | 88.0 |
| Felony Offense Against Property (%) | 84.4 | 89.3 | 83.7 | 89.5 | 41.7 | 83.8 | 91.7 | 44.4 | 91.0 | 94.8 | 92.5 | 94.0 | 79.5 | 90.7 | 75.0 | 87.9 |
| Minor Offense Against Person (%) | 90.7 | 83.4 | 84.7 | 91.8 | 80.0 | 74.4 | 89.2 | 25.0 | 93.9 | 92.5 | 89.7 | 95.6 | 90.9 | 90.0 | 80.0 | 92.3 |
| Minor Offense Against Property (%) | 94.2 | 92.9 | 90.2 | 94.1 | 87.0 | 90.7 | 90.6 | 80.6 | 97.7 | 96.1 | 93.7 | 95.7 | 86.2 | 92.0 | 88.2 | 93.7 |
| Other Delinquency (%) | 93.1 | 91.7 | 89.5 | 94.6 | 77.8 | 90.6 | 89.9 | 72.4 | 100.0 | 93.6 | 94.5 | 97.3 | 84.9 | 100.0 | 86.7 | 93.4 |
| Status (%) | 95.7 | 94.9 | 91.0 | 96.4 | 84.6 | 94.6 | 84.8 | 82.1 | 97.4 | 95.7 | 94.8 | 97.0 | 97.6 | 90.0 | 90.9 | 96.7 |

a. Public Defender.
b. Court Appointed.

**Table 5-5    Factors Associated with a Finding of Delinquency**

| | Statewide | High Representation | Medium Representation | Low Representation |
|---|---|---|---|---|
| **Finding of Delinquency Overall %** | 55.2 | 53.3 | 56.0 | 55.5 |
| **Offense %** | | | | |
| Felony Offense Against Person | 65.0 | 63.6 | 67.2 | 63.1 |
| Felony Offense Against Property | 65.9 | 57.1 | 70.3 | 66.1 |
| Minor Offense Against Person | 54.8 | 46.4 | 59.0 | 55.3 |
| Minor Offense Against Property | 55.2 | 48.8 | 60.6 | 54.3 |
| Other Delinquency | 54.4 | 49.1 | 55.1 | 57.2 |
| Status | 54.6 | 75.9 | 44.3 | 55.8 |
| **Detention %** | | | | |
| Yes | 78.3 | 69.0 | 83.9 | 71.2 |
| No | 53.4 | 52.3 | 52.1 | 54.8 |
| **Disposition Overall %** | | | | |
| Home | 79.1 | 76.5 | 82.6 | 77.0 |
| Secure | 84.6 | 80.4 | 89.6 | 81.7 |
| **Attorney %** | | | | |
| Present | 61.2 | 56.0 | 66.3 | 63.0 |
| Absent | 53.3 | 40.7 | 48.4 | 56.5 |

formal finding of delinquency? The obvious candidates are the seriousness of the present offense, pretrial detention, the severity of the eventual disposition, and the presence of an attorney. Table 5-5 summarizes the relationships between these variables and a finding of delinquency.

For the state as a whole and in the counties with high, medium, and low rates of representation, juvenile court judges make a finding of delinquency in 55.2% of all petitioned cases. The legal variables all influence the judges' propensity to make a formal finding of delinquency in the expected directions. Judges make a finding of delinquency in about 10% more of the cases in which a juvenile is convicted of a felony offense than for the less serious offenses. The only surprising result is the very high rate (75.9%) of findings of delinquency for juveniles convicted of status offenses in the counties with high rates of representation.

Similarly, a juvenile's pretrial detention status influences the judge's eventual decision to make a finding of delinquency. Recall from Table 4-15 that only 7.6% of juveniles in the state were detained, and that those charged with more serious offenses and with more extensive prior records had higher rates of detention. Thus, in the state as a whole, 78.3% of those juveniles held in detention were formally found to be delinquent as compared with 53.4% of those who were not held in detention. The relationship between pretrial detention and the greater likelihood of a finding of delinquency prevailed in all types of counties with the greatest impact in the counties with medium rates of representation, which used pretrial detention more extensively (Table 4-15).

There was also a direct relationship between a formal finding of delinquency and the severity of the eventual disposition a juvenile received. In the state as a whole, judges made a formal finding of delinquency in 79.1% of cases in which juveniles were removed from their homes, and in 84.6% of cases in which a secure confinement disposition was imposed.

In light of the previously described relationships between offenses, detention, representation by counsel, and dispositions (Tables 4-3 through 4-18), it is not surprising that judges entered findings of delinquency in larger proportions of cases where juveniles were represented by an attorney than when they were not. In the state as a whole, judges made a formal finding of delinquency almost 10% more often when juveniles were represented (61.2%) than when they were not (53.3%). In the counties with high, medium, and low rates of representation the same pattern prevailed with larger proportions of represented juveniles than unrepresented juveniles found to be delinquent. In light of the associations between the legal variables and rates of representation, and the legal variables and formal delinquency determinations, it is difficult to attribute the differences in rates of finding delinquency to the presence of counsel as such. Rather, the presence of lawyers probably mirrors the other variables that increase the likelihood of a formal delinquency determination.

## CASE-PROCESSING TIME AND THE IMPACT OF COUNSEL

Whether attorneys expedite or retard the rapidity of juvenile justice administration is another way of assessing their impact on the process. The next analyses summarize the relationships between the amount of time it takes to process a case and detention, type of offense, and the presence of an attorney. The amount of time a juvenile spends in the system is measured from the date the petition is filed to the date of disposition. Throughout these analyses, time in the system is reported for cases that take less than eight weeks to process and those that take more than twenty-one weeks.

Table 5-6 reports on the amount of time it takes to process delinquency cases by the type of offense. Overall, juvenile justice appears to be very expeditious—more than half of the cases are disposed of in less than two months and only about one case in five is still pending five months after the petition was filed. The counties with low rates of representation appear to dispose of cases somewhat faster than do the counties with medium and high rates of representation, with about 8% more cases disposed of within eight weeks and about 5% fewer still pending in the system after five months.

There is a direct relationship between the seriousness of the offense and the amount of time a youth spends in the juvenile justice process. A smaller proportion of felony offenses and offenses against the person are disposed of quickly and a larger proportion of those cases are still active after twenty-one weeks. For example, of juveniles charged with a felony offense against the person, about one-third (33.4%) have their cases resolved in less than two months, whereas 37.3% of the cases are still active after five months. By contrast, more than half of the juveniles charged with minor property offenses, other delinquency, and more than two-thirds of those charged with status offenses have their cases resolved quickly; only about one out of six of those cases is still in the system after five months. When the processing times are analyzed separately for the

**Table 5-6   Offense and Case-Processing Time**

| Time | Statewide | | High | | Medium | | Low | |
|---|---|---|---|---|---|---|---|---|
| | 8 Wks or Less | 21 Wks or More | 8 Wks or Less | 21 Wks or More | 8 Wks or Less | 21 Wks or More | 8 Wks or Less | 21 Wks or More |
| **Overall %** | 57.9 | 18.3 | 54.1 | 20.4 | 54.4 | 20.6 | 62.8 | 15.4 |
| Felony Offense Against Person | 33.4 | 37.3 | 43.4 | 20.9 | 27.5 | 44.2 | 34.8 | 38.8 |
| Felony Offense Against Property | 47.3 | 25.5 | 54.6 | 21.2 | 41.9 | 27.7 | 49.0 | 25.6 |
| Minor Offense Against Person | 43.3 | 26.6 | 48.4 | 22.3 | 34.0 | 32.8 | 50.9 | 22.0 |
| Minor Offense Against Property | 56.3 | 18.5 | 54.1 | 19.5 | 50.0 | 24.6 | 61.7 | 13.9 |
| Other Delinquency | 61.1 | 16.9 | 56.6 | 21.2 | 64.6 | 14.1 | 59.8 | 17.7 |
| Status | 68.8 | 11.6 | 54.3 | 20.9 | 65.9 | 11.5 | 75.7 | 8.6 |

counties with high, medium, and low rates of representation, it appears that the high representation counties dispose of felony cases most efficiently and the counties with low rates of representation dispose of the less serious cases most expeditiously.

Previous analyses reported a relationship between offenses and rates of representation (Table 4-3) as well as between detention and rates of representation (Table 4-16). In order to ascertain the impact of attorneys on case-processing time, it is also necessary to analyze the effects of detention on case processing. Table 5-7 reports the amount of time it takes to process cases when juveniles are held in detention and when they are

**Table 5-7   Offense, Detention, and Case-Processing Time**

| | Statewide | | High | | Medium | | Low | |
|---|---|---|---|---|---|---|---|---|
| Detention | Yes | No | Yes | No | Yes | No | Yes | No |
| **Overall %** | | | | | | | | |
| 8 Weeks or Less | 35.1 | 59.8 | 40.2 | 55.1 | 29.5 | 57.9 | 45.8 | 63.5 |
| 21 Weeks or More | 38.6 | 16.7 | 33.5 | 19.5 | 42.6 | 17.5 | 32.2 | 14.7 |
| Felony Offense Against Person | | | | | | | | |
| 8 Weeks or Less | 35.7 | 32.7 | 41.7 | 43.8 | 30.8 | 25.9 | 46.4 | 32.9 |
| 21 Weeks or More | 38.5 | 36.9 | 33.3 | 18.1 | 41.8 | 45.4 | 32.1 | 39.9 |
| Felony Offense Against Property | | | | | | | | |
| 8 Weeks or Less | 40.7 | 48.2 | 52.4 | 54.7 | 37.8 | 43.0 | 45.8 | 49.2 |
| 21 Weeks or More | 34.4 | 24.3 | 14.3 | 21.5 | 36.8 | 25.3 | 33.9 | 24.9 |
| Minor Offense Against Person | | | | | | | | |
| 8 Weeks or Less | 32.7 | 44.8 | 46.7 | 48.5 | 25.8 | 36.1 | 47.1 | 51.2 |
| 21 Weeks or More | 49.0 | 23.4 | 40.0 | 20.7 | 53.0 | 27.8 | 41.2 | 20.8 |
| Minor Offense Against Property | | | | | | | | |
| 8 Weeks or Less | 27.6 | 58.2 | 34.2 | 54.8 | 22.2 | 54.0 | 42.2 | 62.2 |
| 21 Weeks or More | 47.4 | 16.7 | 42.1 | 18.7 | 52.0 | 20.7 | 34.4 | 13.4 |
| Other Delinquency | | | | | | | | |
| 8 Weeks or Less | 36.7 | 63.0 | 44.1 | 57.7 | 32.3 | 67.3 | 36.5 | 61.1 |
| 21 Weeks or More | 36.7 | 15.5 | 32.2 | 20.2 | 37.4 | 12.1 | 40.4 | 16.4 |
| Status | | | | | | | | |
| 8 Weeks or Less | 29.9 | 70.7 | 23.0 | 57.3 | 22.9 | 68.5 | 49.1 | 76.4 |
| 21 Weeks or More | 33.2 | 10.5 | 39.3 | 19.1 | 34.4 | 10.1 | 24.6 | 8.2 |

at liberty. Recall 7.6% of juveniles received one or more detention hearings and that the seriousness of the present offense affected rates of detention (Table 4-15). Table 5-7 controls for the present offense and reports the case-processing times of detained and nondetained juveniles.

Quite clearly, detaining a juvenile dramatically alters the rapidity with which juvenile courts process his or her case. For the state overall, only 35.1% of detained juveniles have their cases disposed of within eight weeks, as contrasted with 59.8% of those who were not detained. Conversely, detention more than doubles the proportion of cases that are still active after five months, 38.6% versus 16.7% percent. The finding that detention substantially *slows* the processing of a case is especially troubling, since the Minnesota juvenile court rules require more expeditious processing of juveniles held in detention (Minn. R. P. Juv. Ct. 27.02, subd. 1). Feld's analysis of these provisions notes that

> [t]he Rules establish two timetables for processing juvenile offenders through the various stages of the justice system. The timetables vary depending upon whether the youth is being held in detention. . . . For a youth who is taken into custody and held in detention, the sequence and timing of the stages of the process are accelerated and a detention hearing is required. . . . Following arraignment, a detained youth must be brought to trial within 30 days rather than the 60 days provided for youths who remain at liberty, and the various notice, discovery, and pretrial proceedings must be completed during this period. (Feld 1984:165 n. 87)

Similarly, the American Bar Association's Juvenile Justice Standards (1980b, 1980c) recommend the expedited hearing and disposition of cases of detained juveniles.

When the impact of detention on case processing is analyzed for the high, medium, and low representation counties, the deleterious effect of detention is most conspicuous in the counties with medium rates of representation. In those counties, about 10% fewer cases are disposed of quickly and about 10% more are still active later than in the high or low representation counties. Recall also that the counties with medium rates of representation had the highest rates of pretrial detention (Table 4-15, 12.2% vs. 6.7% (high) and 4.0% (low)).

Although the seriousness of a juvenile's offense substantially alters the likelihood of detention (Table 4-15), the fact of detention as such exerts a relatively constant effect on the time required to process cases; roughly the same proportion of cases are still active after five months at all levels of offense. However, when detained cases are compared with nondetained cases, the retarding effect of detention on processing is most apparent for juveniles charged with less serious types of offenses. Thus, for juveniles charged with minor property and status offenses, about three times as many cases of those who were detained initially as contrasted with those who were not detained were still active after five months (compare Table 5-6 with 5-7).

Throughout these analyses, many of the indicators that a case is more complex—seriousness of present offense (Table 4-3), a prior record (Table 4-13), pretrial detention (Table 4-16), the number of offenses at disposition (Table 5-2)—have been associated with higher rates of representation. Table 5-8 reports on the effects of an attorney on case-processing time while controlling for the seriousness of the offense.

For the state overall, 57.9% of all delinquency cases were resolved in less than eight weeks and only 18.3% were still active after twenty-one weeks (Table 5-6). Table 5-8 reports those rates for juveniles with and without counsel. Quite clearly, the presence of an attorney substantially slows the speed with which a case is disposed. While 57.9% of all cases are disposed of in less than two months, only 45.6% of represented cases as contrasted with 66.7% of unrepresented cases are. Similarly, nearly twice as many of the cases of represented youths as unrepresented youths are still active after five months. Although Table 5-6 reported that much larger proportions of the less serious cases—minor property, other delinquency, and status offenses—were resolved quickly, when juveniles were represented by counsel, nearly twice as many cases remained active after five months as compared with the unrepresented youths.

The impact of an attorney differs when the data are examined separately for counties with high, medium, and low rates of representation. In counties where virtually all juveniles have lawyers, it takes somewhat longer to process the cases of unrepresented juveniles. In those counties, a larger proportion of unrepresented cases are still active after five months for juveniles charged with all but status offenses. In the counties with medium and low rates of representation, however, about 25% more of the cases of unrepresented juveniles are closed early while twice as many cases of represented juveniles remain active after five months. Thus, the impact of counsel on juvenile justice administration depends upon whether the courts have adapted to their presence. When lawyers appear routinely, they help the courts administer their dockets expeditiously. Where their presence is less common, it may indicate that a case is more complicated. However, regardless of the complexity of the case, the presence of the lawyer is an additional complication that may retard the administration of juvenile justice.

**Table 5-8   Case-Processing Time and Representation by Counsel**

| Counsel | Statewide | | High | | Medium | | Low | |
|---|---|---|---|---|---|---|---|---|
| | Yes | No | Yes | No | Yes | No | Yes | No |
| **Overall %** | | | | | | | | |
| 8 Weeks or Less | 45.6 | 66.7 | 54.4 | 42.9 | 39.2 | 65.5 | 37.8 | 68.2 |
| 21 Weeks or More | 25.3 | 13.0 | 20.2 | 26.5 | 29.8 | 13.3 | 28.5 | 12.3 |
| Felony Offense Against Person | | | | | | | | |
| 8 Weeks or Less | 28.1 | 39.7 | 41.8 | — | 23.0 | 34.8 | 21.3 | 42.9 |
| 21 Weeks or More | 41.0 | 32.1 | 20.5 | 100.0ᵃ | 48.0 | 32.6 | 52.1 | 31.0 |
| Felony Offense Against Property | | | | | | | | |
| 8 Weeks or Less | 42.1 | 53.3 | 54.0 | 25.0 | 35.6 | 52.0 | 35.7 | 54.2 |
| 21 Weeks or More | 28.7 | 21.2 | 20.8 | 50.0 | 32.0 | 19.0 | 34.6 | 22.1 |
| Minor Offense Against Person | | | | | | | | |
| 8 Weeks or Less | 35.6 | 55.4 | 47.5 | 50.0 | 25.6 | 50.5 | 35.1 | 58.5 |
| 21 Weeks or More | 30.1 | 20.9 | 22.0 | 50.0 | 36.7 | 24.3 | 31.1 | 18.6 |
| Minor Offense Against Property | | | | | | | | |
| 8 Weeks or Less | 45.1 | 64.8 | 54.6 | 26.9 | 39.1 | 60.9 | 33.8 | 66.9 |
| 21 Weeks or More | 24.3 | 14.0 | 19.5 | 26.9 | 30.5 | 18.4 | 23.1 | 12.0 |
| Other Delinquency | | | | | | | | |
| 8 Weeks or Less | 49.3 | 70.5 | 57.1 | 44.4 | 43.7 | 76.2 | 37.8 | 65.6 |
| 21 Weeks or More | 23.7 | 11.6 | 21.0 | 26.7 | 24.8 | 8.1 | 29.5 | 14.5 |
| Status | | | | | | | | |
| 8 Weeks or Less | 53.2 | 73.7 | 53.3 | 60.9 | 52.8 | 67.3 | 53.7 | 78.0 |
| 21 Weeks or More | 19.9 | 8.5 | 21.8 | 12.5 | 18.5 | 10.2 | 17.0 | 7.4 |

a. There was only 1 unrepresented juvenile in this cell.

## CONCLUSION

Quite clearly, as Chapters Four and Five demonstrate, the high, medium, and low representation counties differ significantly in the administration of juvenile justice. Grouping counties on the basis of their rates of representation provides an indicator of a formal, due-process orientation which, in turn, is associated with differences in pretrial detention, sentencing, and case-processing practices. The courts in the high representation counties handle more juveniles charged with criminal offenses and correspondingly fewer charged with status offenses than do those in low representation counties. Moreover, the procedurally more formal courts have higher rates of pretrial detention and more severe sentencing practices than do the low representation courts.

Although all of these juvenile courts operate under the same statutes and rules of procedure, quite clearly the delivery of legal services and the resulting administration of juvenile justice is highly variable. While certain legal variables affect rates of representation in all types of settings, and the presence of defense attorneys is closely associated with differences in justice administration, the foregoing analyses do not account for the county-level variations in rates of representation. The presence of attorneys, as an indicator of a juvenile court's procedural and substantive orientations, varies. Chapter Six examines the social structural factors that influence rates of representation and juvenile justice administration.

## chapter six

# THE SOCIAL CONTEXT OF JUVENILE COURTS

Urban, Suburban, and Rural Variations in Juvenile Justice
Administration

Although the same statutes and court rules of procedure apply in Minnesota's eighty-seven counties, as Chapter Four revealed, there is substantial variation in the availability of counsel which, in turn, has important consequences for juvenile justice administration. Chapter Six examines one source of those procedural and substantive variations, the social structural characteristics of the counties, and reports that there is "justice by geography"—where youths live affects how their cases are processed and the severity of the sentences they receive.

The juvenile courts in urban, suburban, and rural locales appear to pursue different substantive ends and use different procedural means. Because this study focuses on the impact of lawyers and procedural formality on juvenile justice administration, it uses the presence of counsel as one indicator of a court's traditional, informal or formal, due-process orientation. The geographical and structural influences on formal versus informal means of control result in differences in the selection of delinquents and the administration of justice.

The urban juvenile courts operate in milieus that provide fewer mechanisms for informal social control than do rural courts and, consequently, they place greater emphasis on formal social control. As will be seen, attorneys appear in urban courts more than twice as often as they do in rural courts. Urban courts appear to cast a broader, more inclusive net of control that encompasses proportionally more and younger youths than do suburban or rural courts. There also appears to be a relationship between social structure, procedural formality, and severity of sanctions. The more formal, urban courts hold larger proportions of youths in pretrial detention and sentence similarly charged offenders more severely than do the suburban or rural courts. Chapter Six analyzes the relationships between social structure, procedural formality, and juvenile justice administration.

## SOCIAL STRUCTURE, CRIME, AND JUSTICE ADMINISTRATION

Crime and delinquency are disproportionately urban phenomena (Laub and Hindelang 1981; Blau and Blau 1982). Criminology uses social structural features to explain variations in the distribution of crime. Classical sociological theory, for example, attributes the greater prevalence of crime in cities to urban anomie. In traditional rural communities, homogeneity and uniformity of beliefs foster informal social control, whereas in modern urban settings, anonymity, population density, and heterogeneity weaken social cohesion and increase reliance on formal social control (Durkheim 1964; Clinard and Abbot 1973; Shelley 1981). The emergence of the houses of refuge on the East Coast in the early nineteenth century and of the juvenile court in Chicago at the end of the nineteenth century are specific instances of the general phenomenon of greater reliance on formal mechanisms of control as more traditional, informal mechanisms weaken (Rothman 1971, 1980; Finestone 1976; Sutton 1988). Social ecology, associated with the Chicago School, relates urban structural features such as income inequality, family structure, or racial composition to variations in crime rates (Shaw and McKay 1942; Sampson 1986a, 1986b; Byrne and Sampson 1985).

Urbanization is associated with greater bureaucratization and formal social control as well as with higher rates of crime (Meyers and Talarico 1986, 1987). Weber (1947, 1954) associated the formal rationalization of social life with urbanization and bureaucratization and argued that abstract rules would supplant more traditional methods of dispute resolution as law becomes increasingly rational and functionally specialized. Presumably, urban courts would be more formal and bureaucratized, emphasize rationality and efficiency, and sentence on the basis of legally relevant factors such as present offense and prior record. By contrast, more traditional, rural courts would be less formal or bureaucratized, and would sentence on the basis of nonlegal, ascriptive considerations.

Surprisingly, very little research has been done on the relationships between urbanization, bureaucratization, and criminal and juvenile justice administration. The few studies available document significant urban-rural differences in sentencing. Hagan (1974) found that differential treatment of racial minorities was more pronounced in rural courts than in bureaucratized urban ones. Tepperman (1973) reported that rural juvenile courts treated female offenders more leniently than males, but that gender differences declined with urbanization. Austin (1981) found rural criminal courts considered social background factors more extensively, sentencing blacks more harshly and females more leniently, while urban courts adhered to a more legalistic model of sentencing. Paternoster (1983) found that social context influenced adult charging decisions; rural prosecutors were more likely to seek the death penalty than urban ones. Meyers and Talarico (1986, 1987) report that urbanization and social context affect criminal court sentencing decisions. In short, these studies support Weberian expectations that similarly situated offenders may be treated differently based on their locale and that differential processing is more prevalent in rural settings and declines with urbanization and bureaucratization.

Criminology also attempts to explain variations in the administration of justice. Organizations interact with and are influenced by their external environments; for example, the expectations of police, political officials, appellate courts, news media, and the public all affect how courts perform (Eisenstein and Jacob 1977; Sampson 1986). Criminal justice agencies operate within differing sociopolitical environments and depend upon their environment for legitimation, resources, and clients. As a result, external social, economic, and political variables constrain even ostensibly similar organizations. Wilson (1968), Smith (1984), and Crank's (1990) analyses of police practices attribute differences in the exercises of police discretion to variations in community social structure. Levin (1977) compared criminal sentencing outcomes in two large metropolitan areas and attributed differences in sentencing practices to differences in the cities' political cultures. Eisenstein and Jacob (1977) identified the pivotal roles of courtroom work groups on judicial sentencing decisions in different jurisdictions.

## SOCIAL STRUCTURAL VARIATIONS IN JUVENILE JUSTICE ADMINISTRATION— FORMAL VERSUS INFORMAL SOCIAL CONTROL

The traditional juvenile court's emphasis on rehabilitating offenders rather than punishing for offenses fostered judicial discretion, procedural informality, and organizational diversity (Rothman 1980; Feld 1988b; Mack 1909). The broad legal framework associated with individualized justice allowed judges to apply the same law very differently to ostensibly similar juvenile offenders. Descriptions of contemporary juvenile courts continue to emphasize judicial diversity (Rubin 1985). Recognizing that a state's juvenile courts are not a single, uniform justice system vastly complicates research analyzing courts' behavior. Recent research that recognizes courts' diversity does not explore either the social structural sources or the administrative consequences of formal-informal or "due process"-"traditional" organizational variation.

The few studies that compare juvenile courts in different locales indicate that they are variable organizations that differ on several structural and procedural dimensions (Stapleton, Aday, and Ito 1982; Hasenfeld and Cheung 1985). Contrasting traditional therapeutic courts with those holding a more legalistic, due-process orientation captures much of the variation in juvenile justice administration. The former intervene in a child's "best interests" on an informal, discretionary basis, while the latter emphasize more formal, rule-oriented decision making. "At one extreme lies the system best described by the concept of *parens patriae*, with an emphasis on 'helping' the child, intervening in his or her best interest. At the other lies the more formal, legalistic system, with a due process model of restricted information flow and precise rules of adjudication" (Stapleton, Aday, and Ito 1982:550). "Traditional" and "due process" courts may be arrayed across a continuum from informal to formal with corresponding procedural and substantive differences. Recent research in Missouri confirms the structural and procedural relationship and reports that rural courts still adhere to a pre-*Gault*, informal parens patriae approach while urban courts are more legalistic and process cases according to offense criteria (Kempf, Decker, and Bing 1990).

As Chapters Four and Five revealed, the appearance of an attorney provides an important indicator of substantive and procedural variation among juvenile courts, and their relative emphases on traditional informality or "due process" (Handler 1965; Cohen and Kluegel 1978; Stapleton and Teitelbaum 1972; Feld 1984). In turn, the informal and due-process variations in juvenile justice administration, as reflected in the presence of counsel, are associated with differences in pretrial detention, sentencing, and case-processing practices (Feld 1989, 1991; Cohen and Kluegel 1978; Carrington and Moyer 1988a, 1988b; Kempf, Decker, and Bing 1990). Chapter Six attempts to account for variations in rates of representation in different juvenile courts by exploring the social structural and legal variables that influence the procedural and substantive orientation of a court.

Although the presence or absence of defense attorneys is associated with differences in juvenile justice administration, what accounts for these systematic differences? Despite their procedural and philosophical differences, these courts operate under laws and rules of procedure of state-wide applicability. How does social structure influence the procedural and substantive orientations of juvenile courts? Are there different costs and benefits of formal versus informal dispute resolution? How do different juvenile courts administer justice and intervene in the lives of young people?

In order to analyze the relationships between social structure and juvenile justice administration, this study uses data from two sources: Minnesota county census data from 1980 provide indicators of social structure, and the Minnesota Supreme Court's Judicial Information System (SJIS) data for delinquency and status offense cases processed in 1986 provide information on juvenile justice administration. To facilitate analyses between census and SJIS data sets, counties are the unit of analysis which are then aggregated as urban, suburban, or rural. Chapter Two describes the SJIS data and coding protocols more fully.

The SJIS juvenile-court processing data are in the same form as reported in Chapters Four and Five. In this chapter, however, county juvenile court data are aggregated on the basis of their urban, suburban, or rural location, rather than on the basis of high, medium, or low rates of representation. The classification of counties as urban, suburban and small urban, and rural uses the census concept of Standardized Metropolitan Statistical Area (SMSA) and youth-population density. Counties were classified as *urban* if they were located within an SMSA, had one or more cities of 100,000 inhabitants, and had a juvenile population aged ten to seventeen of at least 50,000. By these criteria, Hennepin County (Minneapolis) and Ramsey County (St. Paul) were classified as urban counties. Counties were classified as either *suburban* or *small urban*, if they were located within a metropolitan SMSA (suburban) or, if within their own SMSA (small urban), had one or more cities of 25,000 to 100,000, and had a juvenile population aged ten to seventeen of more than 7,500 but less than 50,000. There were five suburban counties and three small urban counties that were combined in these analyses. The remaining counties in Minnesota were classified as rural because they were outside of an SMSA, had no principal city of 25,000 or greater, and had fewer than 7,500 juveniles aged ten to seventeen.

This chapter explores the effects of social context on juvenile justice administration. How do counties' social structures influence the juvenile delinquency problems they encounter and their responses to it? To the extent that the implementation of law reflects the social organization of the communities in which the courts are embedded and operate, are there discernible variations in juvenile justice administration?

## URBAN, SUBURBAN, AND RURAL SOCIAL STRUCTURAL CHARACTERISTICS

Tables 6-1 and 6-2 introduce Minnesota's urban, suburban, and rural social structure, and the counties' crime rates and allocations of law enforcement resources. Based on the census classification criteria, Minnesota has two urban counties, eight suburban and small urban counties, and seventy-seven rural counties. More than one-third (34.4%) of the population lives in the two urban counties, about one-quarter (25.2%) in the eight suburban or small urban settings, and the remainder (40.4%) in rural counties.

## JUVENILE AND FAMILY POPULATION CHARACTERISTICS

Juvenile courts deal almost exclusively with delinquent youths aged ten to seventeen. Table 6-1 reports the number and percentage of those young people in the general population. While 14.0% of Minnesota's population falls within the age jurisdiction of juvenile courts, the geographic distribution is uneven: suburban counties have the largest proportion of juvenile-court-eligible youths (15.7%); rural counties have the second largest (14.3%); and urban counties have the smallest proportion (12.5%). There is a similar pattern for family households with children under eighteen as a proportion of the total households in the state. While nearly 40% of all households include children under eighteen, substantially larger proportions of suburban (47.6%) and rural (40.3%) households include children than do urban households (34.2%).

Sampson (1986b) emphasizes the theoretical importance of family organization as a criminogenic variable since family disruption may decrease the effectiveness of both informal and formal social controls. Sampson (1986b) contends that cohesive, two-parent families assume responsibility for other youths as well as their own children and provide increased supervision of children and property as well as public activities in the neighborhood. The social-control effectiveness of cohesive families may derive less from intervention in criminal acts than from awareness of and control over peer-group activities. As a result, youths in areas characterized by stable families—regardless of their own family situation—probably have more informal controls placed on their activities. By contrast, Blau and Blau (1982) reason that divorce and separation in a population may indicate instability and conflict in personal relations, which also may be reflected in social disorganization and criminal violence. While the urban counties have the lowest proportion of juveniles aged ten

**Table 6-1    Urban, Suburban, and Rural County Population and Economic Characteristics (1980 Census, Except as Indicated)**

|  | State | Urban | Suburban | Rural |
|---|---|---|---|---|
| Total Number of Counties | 87 | 2 | 8 | 77 |
| Population | 4,076,070 | 1,401,195 | 1,028,709 | 1,646,066 |
| Proportion of Total Population | 100.0 | 34.4 | 25.2 | 40.4 |
| Juvenile Population Age 10–17 | 571,648 | 175,152 | 161,345 | 235,151 |
| Juvenile % of Total Population | 14.0 | 12.5 | 15.7 | 14.3 |
| Family Households with Children <18 as Proportion of Total Households (%) | 39.7 | 34.2 | 47.6 | 40.3 |
| Female-headed Households with Own Child as Proportion of Total Households (%) | 4.5 | 5.7 | 4.8 | 3.3 |
| Black Households as Proportion of Total Households (%) | 1.3 | 3.2 | 0.3 | 0.1 |
| Hispanic Households as Proportion of Total Households (%) | 0.6 | 0.9 | 0.5 | 0.4 |
| Non-White[a] Population as Proportion of Total Population (%) | 3.4 | 6.7 | 1.8 | 1.7 |
| Households with Income <$10,000 as Proportion of Total Households (%) | 27.1 | 23.5 | 20.8 | 34.1 |
| Persons Below Poverty Level (1979) as Proportion of Total Persons (%) | 9.5 | 7.7 | 6.6 | 12.8 |
| Children <18 Below Poverty Level (1979) as Proportion of All Children (%) | 10.2 | 9.0 | 6.4 | 13.7 |
| Owner-Occupied House as Proportion of Occupied Housing (%) | 71.7 | 62.1 | 76.6 | 77.7 |
| Persons Born in State as Proportion of Total Persons (%) | 74.9 | 69.6 | 76.6 | 78.2 |

a.  Nonwhite population includes blacks, Native Americans, Asians, Hispanics, and other races.

to seventeen, they have the highest proportion of children in female-headed households. Although 4.5% of all the households in Minnesota are female-headed with children, the percentage varies significantly within the geographic paradigm. In the urban counties, 5.7% are female-headed households with children, compared with 4.8% in the suburban counties and 3.3% in the rural counties. If family disruption weakens informal social control, then urban counties may need more alternative formal controls.

## RACIAL DIVERSITY

Racial diversity is relevant both to crime rates and justice administration. Variations in racial composition are associated with differences in crime rates (Blau and Blau 1982; Hindelang 1978). Moreover, population heterogeneity decreases shared common traits and experiences, relates negatively to social integration, and affects reliance on and effectiveness of informal or formal mechanisms of social control (Angell 1974). Minnesota is almost totally white; all other racial groups account for only 3.4% of the total population. In 1980, blacks (1.3%), Spanish/Hispanics (0.6%), and Native Americans (0.9%) accounted for most of the racial diversity. Significantly, minority racial groups are concentrated almost exclusively in the two urban counties. Black households account for more than ten times the proportion of urban households (3.2%) as they do of suburban (0.3%) or rural (0.1%) households. All nonwhites are nearly four times more likely to reside in urban counties (6.7%) than in either suburban (1.8%) or rural (1.7%) settings. If racial heterogeneity decreases the effectiveness of informal social controls, then urban counties may need more formal mechanisms of control.

## INCOME DISTRIBUTION

Affluence or poverty may affect both crime rates and community responses. On the one hand, poverty may increase the likelihood of offending. On the other hand, poverty and a low tax base may reduce expenditures on formal social controls. Moreover, the relationship between crime and poverty is complex and may result from relative deprivation and not simply low income (Bailey 1984; Messner 1982). Table 6-1 includes several indicators of geographic variations in income distribution. By all measures—number of households with income of less than $10,000, proportion of households below the poverty level, and proportion of children living in poverty—a similar pattern emerges. Larger proportions of households, people, and children are poor in rural counties, followed by urban counties, with the least poverty in the suburban and small urban settings. Paradoxically, however, the greater prevalence of rural poverty may decrease relative deprivation and result in less crime (Messner 1982). Moreover, the rural poor may be more fully integrated into community institutions, such as churches and schools, than in urban settings, where economic stratification carries over into other social institutions as well.

## POPULATION STABILITY

An inverse relationship exists between crime rates and residential stability and supports the stereotype that transient populations contribute dispro-portionally to crime (Harries 1976). An integrated social system fosters consensus in norms and values, cohesiveness and social solidarity, and a sense of belonging among members of a community; in contrast, mobil-ity weakens social integration. For example, Crutchfield, Geerken, and Gove (1982) reported that population mobility weakens social integra-tion and results in higher crime rates. Schuerman and Kobrin (1986) ob-served a relationship between a shift from single-family to multifamily dwellings and rising residential mobility, and neighborhood deterioration and rising crime rates. Johnson (1977) analyzed juvenile delinquency re-ferral rates and found that stable communities develop shared community standards and interpersonal linkages that provide mechanisms to control juvenile misbehavior, while rapid growth, in-migration, and population diversity may disrupt informal control strategies. Table 6-1 includes in-dicators of population and residential stability—the proportions of owner-occupied homes and of persons born in the state. The greatest res-idential stability occurs in the rural counties, followed closely by the sub-urban counties. In the urban counties, about 7% fewer residents were born in the state and nearly 15% fewer owned the houses in which they lived.

Quite clearly, the urban, suburban, and rural counties differ consis-tently on social structural dimensions that affect both rates of offending and the effectiveness of informal controls. As contrasted with the urban counties' diversity, rural counties' greater stability and homogeneity sug-gest they would rely less heavily on formal means of social control. Racial diversity is almost exclusively an urban phenomenon, and a larger pro-portion of households are headed by a single, female parent. While more people in rural counties are poor, they are also more homogeneous and residentially stable. The suburban-small urban counties are nearly as sta-ble and homogeneous as the rural counties and more affluent than either the urban or rural counties.

## URBAN, SUBURBAN, AND RURAL VARIATIONS IN CRIME AND LAW ENFORCEMENT RESOURCES

### Crime

Crime, especially serious crime, is primarily an urban phenomenon. Reliance on official crime statistics is criticized frequently because of concern about underreporting of crime by victims to the police as well as by police departments to the FBI, and selection bias by police in detecting, recording, and reporting crime (Sampson 1986b). Despite those concerns, official data are used here for the limited purpose of highlighting geographic variation. Table 6-2 summarizes the urban, suburban, and rural distribution of serious crimes and the deployment of law enforcement resources.

More than half of the FBI Part I offenses in 1980 in Minnesota were committed in the two urban counties. Even after crime rates are standardized for differences in population bases, the greater prevalence of crime in the urban counties remains. There were 703.1 serious offenses per 10,000 people in the urban settings as contrasted with only 308.5 per 10,000 in the rural counties. The urban rate of serious crime is 157% higher than in the suburbs and 228% higher than in the rural counties. Although the Minnesota Bureau of Criminal Apprehension (BCA) defines urban-rural differently than does this study, it provided another indicator of geographic differences in the distribution of offenses when it reported that the urban-rural ratio of serious crime was about seven to one in 1986 (Minnesota Bureau 1987). Indeed, such urban-rural disparities in crime are observed regularly; Laub (1983), for example, contends that if urban crime rates were similar to rural rates, then violent crime would be less than half and property crime would be reduced by one-third of the present level.

### Juvenile Crime

A similar pattern is evident with respect to juvenile crime. Table 6-2 reports juveniles arrested in 1986 for FBI Part I and Part II offenses and the arrest rates per 10,000 juveniles. Almost one-half of all juveniles arrested for serious and less serious offenses (45.6% and 44.5%) reside in the two urban counties. The pattern remains even after controlling for population differences. In the whole state, 297.2 juveniles per 10,000 aged ten to seventeen were arrested for serious felony offenses. However, when this rate is disaggregated geographically, 441.7 urban juveniles per 10,000 were arrested for serious crimes, as compared to 299.4 suburban and only 187.9 rural juveniles. Similarly, urban juveniles were arrested for less serious offenses 146% more often than suburban youths and 217% more

**Table 6-2   Urban, Suburban, and Rural County Crime Characteristics (1980) and Law Enforcement Resources**

|  | State | Urban | Suburban | Rural |
|---|---|---|---|---|
| | | **Crime** | | |
| Number of Reported Serious Crimes in 1980 (FBI Pt. I)[a] | 194,598 | 98,155 | 45,792 | 50,630 |
| Serious Crime Rate Per 10,000[b] People | 479.6 | 703.1 | 448.9 | 308.5 |
| | | **Juvenile Crime** | | |
| Juvenile Arrests in 1986 (FBI Pt. I)[c] | 16,886 | 7,696 | 4,797 | 4,393 |
| Juvenile Arrest Pt. I Rate Per 10,000[d] | 297.2 | 441.7 | 299.4 | 187.9 |
| Juvenile Arrests in 1986 (FBI Pt. II)[e] | 16,470 | 7,324 | 4,614 | 4,532 |
| Juvenile Arrest Pt. II Rate Per 10,000 | 289.8 | 420.3 | 288.0 | 193.8 |
| | | **Deployment of Law Enforcement Resources** | | |
| Police Officers (1982) | 5,468 | 2,212 | 1,379 | 1,877 |
| Police Officers Per 10,000 People | 13.42 | 15.79 | 13.41 | 11.40 |
| Local Government Police Protection Expenditures Per 10,000 People | $551.57 | $716.88 | $535.31 | $421.01 |
| Serious Crimes Per Police Officer | 35.59 | 44.37 | 33.21 | 26.97 |

a. FBI Part I offenses reflect information on eight "serious" crime categories: murder, rape, aggravated assault, robbery, burglary, larceny, motor vehicle theft, and arson.

b. The FBI 1980 population basis differs slightly from that used by the Census. The FBI population totals for the entire state and for urban, suburban, and rural counties are respectively: 4,057,503, 1,396,023, 1,020,143, and 1,641,337.

c. Data for 1986 juvenile arrests and rates were obtained from the Minnesota Bureau of Criminal Apprehension (BCA), which is the agency responsible for collecting activity information from law enforcement agencies throughout Minnesota.

d. The juvenile population base used to calculate rates of offending in 1986 differs slightly from the population reported in the 1980 census in Table 6-1 for juveniles aged 10–17. The 1986 juvenile population estimates, obtained from the NCJJ, for the entire state and for urban, suburban, and rural counties are respectively: 568,264; 174,249; 160,212; and 233,803.

e. FBI Part II offenses include a miscellany of "less serious offenses" including simple assaults, forgery, stolen property, vandalism, weapons possession, prostitution, drugs, driving while intoxicated, disorderly conduct, vagrancy, and other non-Part I offenses.

often than rural youths. Thus, it is readily apparent that urban youngsters are both quantitatively and qualitatively more criminally active than their suburban or rural counterparts.

### Law Enforcement Resources

Table 6-2 indicates that the deployment of law enforcement resources follows the distribution of crime in the state. The largest numbers of police officers are located in the urban counties. For every 10,000 inhabitants, there are 15.79 police officers in urban counties, 13.41 in the suburban counties, and only 11.4 in rural counties. Moreover, the urban counties spend more money per capita, about 170% more, to provide law enforcement services than do the suburban or rural counties. As indicated by allocations of law enforcement resources, the urban settings appear to place greater reliance on formal, rather than informal, social control.

By another measure, however, urban counties may be *underpoliced* relative to suburban or rural settings. Calculating the number of serious crimes per police officer indicates that there are 35.59 serious crimes for each police officer in the state (194,598/5,468). However, the ratio of serious crimes per officer varies with geography; there are 44.37 serious crimes per officer in urban settings, 33.21 in suburban counties, and only 26.97 in the rural counties. Even with the greater geographic dispersion of rural police, it may be argued that urban settings have available fewer law enforcement resources with which to respond to their crime problems than do the other locales and this in turn may affect the types of cases they process formally.

## URBAN, SUBURBAN, AND RURAL VARIATIONS IN JUVENILE JUSTICE ADMINISTRATION

Tables 6-3 and 6-4 introduce Minnesota's juvenile justice system in its geographic context. Because of geographic differences in social structure, population density, and volume of cases, juvenile courts are organized differently throughout the state. In the two urban counties, a full-time district court judge presides who is assisted by other judges on a part-time basis, referees, and a large probation staff. Urban judges serve exclusively in juvenile court for several years and provide stability and predictability to the courtroom work groups. Due to lower volume, district court judges in nonurban counties are less specialized and hear juvenile cases as part of their general dockets. In many nonurban counties, several judges in a district may preside over delinquency matters on a rotating basis with correspondingly less functional specialization. Thus, the urban courts are the most formally organized, highly bureaucratized and specialized.

## SCREENING CASES—URBAN, SUBURBAN, AND RURAL JUVENILE COURT OFFENSES AND PETITIONS

Table 6-3 reports the total number of juveniles against whom petitions were filed and the types of offenses with which they were charged in the state and in the various geographic locales. The largest number and proportion of juveniles against whom petitions were filed were located in the rural counties, which reflects both the larger number of rural counties and the distribution of the juvenile-court-aged population in the state (Table 6-1). Slightly more than one-third (36.5%) of the state's delinquents are in urban settings, slightly more than one-fifth (21.4%) are in suburban locales, with the remainder (42.1%) in the rural counties. The suburban juvenile courts "underpetition" youths relative to their proportion of the youth population (21.4% vs. 28.2%) while the urban courts "overpetition" juveniles (36.5% vs. 30.6%) relative to their percentage of the youth population.

Throughout the state, 18.4% of juveniles were charged with offenses that would be felonies if committed by adults, 54.4% were charged with minor offenses such as misdemeanors and gross misdemeanors, and 27.2% were charged with status offenses, juvenile misconduct that would not be criminal if committed by an adult, such as truancy, running away, alcohol consumption and the like (Minn. Stat. § 260.015, subd. 19–24 [West 1986]). Within the felony category, offenses against property, primarily burglary, predominated. Similarly, within the minor offense category, property offenses such as shoplifting and theft predominated. Less than 10% of delinquency cases involved felony or minor offenses against the person, and more than one-quarter involved noncriminal status offenses.

Different patterns of petitioned offenses emerge when they are examined separately for the urban, suburban, and rural counties. Despite the greater prevalence of reported serious crime in the urban counties (Table 6-2), the largest proportion of felony petitions are filed in the suburban, rather than urban, counties. The suburban county courts charge the largest proportion of juveniles with felonies against the person as well as against property. The smallest proportion of felony petitions are filed in the rural settings. This is consistent with the lower rates of rural juvenile felony arrests (Table 6-2), as well as other research on the prevalence of urban and rural juvenile crime (Laub and Hindelang 1981). Propor-

**Table 6-3  Petitioned Offenses and Prior Records**

| | Statewide | Urban | Suburban | Rural |
|---|---|---|---|---|
| **Juvenile Population Aged 10–17** | | | | |
| % | 100.0 | 30.6 | 28.2 | 41.1 |
| N | (571,648) | (175,152) | (161,345) | (235,151) |
| **Delinquent & Status Offenders** | | | | |
| % | 100.0 | 36.5 | 21.4 | 42.1 |
| N | (17,195a) | (6,273) | (3,681) | (7,241) |
| **Felony** | | | | |
| % | 18.4 | 17.5 | 23.0 | 16.9 |
| N | (3,153) | (1,095) | (842) | (1,216) |
| Felony Offense Against Person | | | | |
| % | 4.0 | 4.5 | 5.0 | 2.9 |
| N | (680) | (282) | (185) | (213) |
| Felony Offense Against Property | | | | |
| % | 14.4 | 13.0 | 17.8 | 13.9 |
| N | (2,473) | (813) | (657) | (1,003) |
| **Misdemeanor** | | | | |
| % | 54.4 | 55.3 | 55.8 | 52.9 |
| N | (9,298) | (3,457) | (2,040) | (3,801) |
| Minor Offense Against Person | | | | |
| % | 5.2 | 6.0 | 6.2 | 3.9 |
| N | (889) | (376) | (230) | (283) |
| Minor Offense Against Property | | | | |
| % | 32.3 | 27.3 | 34.9 | 35.3 |
| N | (5,554) | (1,714) | (1,284) | (2,556) |
| Other Delinquency | | | | |
| % | 16.6 | 21.8 | 14.3 | 13.3 |
| N | (2,855) | (1,367) | (526) | (962) |
| **Status** | | | | |
| % | 27.2 | 27.2 | 21.2 | 30.0 |
| N | (4,649) | (1,704) | (776) | (2,169) |
| **Prior Referrals Overall** | | | | |
| 0 | | | | |
| % | 71.9 | 64.7 | 71.8 | 78.1 |
| N | (12,359) | (4,060) | (2,642) | (5,657) |
| 1–2 | | | | |
| % | 23.0 | 27.1 | 23.9 | 19.1 |
| N | (3,962) | (1,700) | (881) | (1,381) |
| 3–4 | | | | |
| % | 3.9 | 6.1 | 3.5 | 2.1 |
| N | (669) | (385) | (129) | (155) |
| 5+ | | | | |
| % | 1.2 | 2.0 | 0.8 | 0.7 |
| N | (205) | (128) | (29) | (48) |

a. Of the 17,195 total juvenile offenders 95 are missing data on their present offenses. Those missing offense data include: 17 urban, 23 suburban, and 55 rural youths.

tionally more rural juveniles charged with felonies are accused of property offenses than are their urban or suburban counterparts. Rural counties handle the largest proportion of status offenders in the state (30.0%) while the suburban counties handle the smallest proportion (21.2%).

Table 6-3 also reports the prior record of court referrals. For the entire state, 71.9% of juvenile offenders made their first appearance in juvenile courts; only 1.2% were chronic recidivists with five or more prior appearances. When geographic locale is examined, a different pattern emerges. In the urban settings, only 64.7% of youths made their first appearance as contrasted with 71.8% and 78.1% of juveniles in the suburban and rural counties, respectively. Thus, substantially more delinquency petitions had been filed previously against urban juveniles than had been filed against their nonurban counterparts. Not only did urban juveniles have more prior referrals, but their predominance increased with the number of priors. Almost twice as many urban juveniles had three or four priors as contrasted with suburban and rural youths (6.1% versus 3.5% and 2.1%), and more than twice as many had five or more prior referrals (2.0% versus 0.8% and 0.7%). As gauged by their prior records, urban delinquents constitute a more delinquent population than their nonurban counterparts.

There is a seeming anomaly between distribution of juvenile offenses and juvenile court petitioning practices. Serious crime and juvenile arrests are concentrated in the urban locales (Table 6-2), while the largest proportion of felony charges are filed against suburban juveniles. Table 6-2 describes all *reported* offenses, while Table 6-3 includes only juveniles actually *charged* with delinquency or status offenses. While adult and juvenile differences in patterns of offending, apprehending, and justice administration likely account for some of the disparity between reported and charged offenses, the primary difference probably lies in geographic differences in prepetition screening of cases.

Typically, juvenile delinquency cases begin with a referral either to the county attorney, a county juvenile court, or its juvenile probation or intake department (Feld 1984). Many referrals are dismissed or disposed of informally by counseling, warning, referral to another agency, or informal probation. Unfortunately, the SJIS data do not include court referrals resolved informally but only reports formally petitioned cases. In some unknown proportion of cases, a petition—the formal initiation of the juvenile process—is filed by the county attorney. As noted in Chapters Three and Four, while about half of all juvenile court referrals result in formal petitions, the ratio of petitions to referrals is highly variable both among states, within states, and from year to year (Nimick et al. 1985). The relationship between the screening functions of a juvenile court's intake staff and the charging functions in the county attorney's office may also vary from county to county. Undoubtedly, court personnel and county attorneys in different counties use different criteria to decide whether or not to file a formal delinquency petition, and the selection of delinquent populations will vary accordingly. Despite differences in prepetition screening, the common denominator of these cases is that each was formally charged in its respective county.

Without direct information about juvenile court referrals that do not result in petitions, some differences in screening practices may be inferred from rates of referral per 10,000 juveniles aged ten to seventeen years, and from ratios of felony arrests to felony petitions. As Table 6-4 reveals, for the entire state, 293.2 juveniles per 10,000 age-eligible youths had petitions filed against them. In the urban counties, 341.2 juveniles per 10,000 were charged as compared with 297.2 in rural counties and only 242.4 in the suburban counties. Thus, in relation to their eligible youth populations, urban courts cast the broadest net of social control, whereas suburban counties are more selective and refer a smaller proportion of juveniles. This confirms the earlier observation (Table 6-3) that the urban courts "overpetition" in relation to the eligible youth population whereas the suburban courts "underpetition."

Because of these differences in prepetition screening practices, a larger proportion of age-eligible urban youths are charged than are their suburban counterparts. These higher overall rates of urban referrals for all offenses mask the more serious offenses with which urban youths also are charged. Suburban counties, by contrast, file proportionally fewer petitions in relation to population, appear to screen their cases for seriousness, and charge more juveniles with felony and misdemeanor offenses than with status offenses. This is consistent with other research that

**Table 6-4   Urban, Suburban, and Rural County Juvenile Court Characteristics**

|  | State | Urban | Suburban | Rural |
|---|---|---|---|---|
| Rate of Referral Per 10,000 Youths Age 10–17 | 293.2 | 341.2 | 242.4 | 297.2 |
| Felony Petitions Per 10,000 Youths Aged 10–17 | 55.16 | 62.52 | 52.19 | 51.71 |
| Felony Petitions as a Proportion of Juvenile Felony Arrests Per 10,000 Youths (%) | 18.6 | 14.2 | 17.4 | 27.5 |
| Proportion of Youths Tried in Same Type County as in Which They Reside (%) | — | 98.9 | 97.4 | 99.3 |

found that urban counties had higher rates of referral than did more stable, relatively poorer rural counties (Johnson 1977).

Some of the differences in juveniles' prior records (Table 6-3) probably reflect these differences in prepetition screening as well. Since larger numbers of eligible urban juveniles are petitioned to juvenile courts (341.2 per 10,000) than are their suburban (242.4) or rural (297.2) counterparts, they have a substantially greater opportunity to accumulate more extensive prior records over time. Since previous juvenile court dispositions affect later ones, some component of urban juveniles' more extensive prior records likely reflect these cumulative differences in precharge screening practices (Thornberry and Christenson 1984; Henretta, Frazier, and Bishop 1986; Feld 1989).

Some research indicates that courts may sentence "local" offenders differently than "outsiders" with the latter receiving more severe sentences (Austin 1981, 1985). Austin (1985) argues that in communities characterized by normative consensus, crimes committed by outsiders will be deemed more threatening to local stability than crimes committed by insiders and will result in harsher sanctions. Table 6-4 reports the proportion of juveniles tried in the same type of county as that in which they reside. Virtually all juveniles are tried in the same type, if not the same, county as the one in which they reside. Since rural youths are more geographically isolated and have to travel greater distances in order to offend in a different type of county, 99.3% of them are tried in rural juvenile courts. Because of the geographic propinquity of the two urban counties, almost all urban juveniles (98.9%) are tried in urban courts. Even the suburban or small-urban youths who can migrate more readily into either urban or rural counties, are most likely to be tried in suburban counties (97.4%).

Table 6-4 also reports the number of felony petitions filed per 10,000 youths aged ten to seventeen. Despite differences in prepetition screening practices and rates of referral, once the population is standardized, the urban preeminence in serious crime reappears with 62.52 felony petitions filed per 10,000 urban youths at risk as compared with 52.19 in the suburban and 51.71 in the rural counties. Even though the suburban counties charge a larger proportion of juveniles with serious offenses, relative to other types of delinquency, larger numbers of urban youths commit serious crimes (1,095 vs. 842); however, the overall larger volume of urban delinquency petitions masks this reality.

A second indicator of geographic differences in precharge screening practices may be obtained by comparing the juvenile felony arrest rates (Table 6-2) with the juvenile felony petition rates in Table 6-4. For the entire state, 297.2 juveniles per 10,000 aged ten to seventeen were arrested for FBI Part I felony offenses. However, petitions alleging felonies were only filed against 55.16 youths per 10,000, or 18.6% of all those arrested (Table 6-4). Comparing the proportion of felony arrests that result in felony petitions in different locales reveals that the urban courts charged the lowest proportion of arrested juveniles with felonies (14.2%), while the rural counties charged the highest (27.5%). Although proportionally more than twice as many urban juveniles as rural juveniles are arrested for felonies (Table 6-2), almost twice as many rural juveniles who were arrested for felonies were actually charged with them. This suggests that geographic differences in police apprehension practices as well as prosecutorial charging practices may affect the eventual population of "official" delinquents.

Although urban courts file more petitions overall, suburban and rural courts may screen their cases more rigorously. While formal petitions were filed in all of the cases analyzed herein, the informal threshold for referring to court and charging youths may differ by geography. This introduces some important potential sample-selection biases into the data. Compared to suburban courts, a smaller proportion of serious offenses and larger proportions of other delinquency and status offenses are charged in urban courts. Since a petty petition alleging minor ordinance violations or status offenses may be filed directly with the court by peace officers or attendance officers, some differences in urban petitioning rates also may be attributed to petty petitions that were not screened by prosecutors or court intake (Minn. R. Juv. Pro. R. 19.02(2) [West 1991]).

In addition, the criminal behavior required to qualify for official attention in urban settings may be qualitatively more serious than in rural or suburban areas. As noted in the analysis of Table 6-2, compared with suburban and rural settings, urban areas may be *underpoliced* relative to their volume of serious crime, that is, the ratio of serious crimes per police officer may be greater. If this is so, then the qualitative "seriousness" of crimes falling in the same official offense categories may actually be greater in urban settings. If each urban police officer has a significantly higher number of serious crimes to deal with, individual officers and the system as a whole may be more selective in screening the kinds of delinquency events that they formally refer to court. With substantially higher felony arrest rates, police or other referral sources in cities may view shoplifting, underaged drinking, or vandalism as simply less important, relative to more serious violent and property crimes, than similar behaviors may appear to police and other referral sources in suburban and rural areas. With greater urban anonymity and more bureaucratized social control, minor juvenile deviance may represent less of a tear in the social fabric than it constitutes in more socially cohesive areas. Heavier caseloads and a higher volume of more serious crimes may lead urban officials to overlook some juvenile deviance that other areas do not ignore. In short, even though all of the youths in this study were formally charged in their respective counties, geographic differences in rates of apprehension and prepetition selection of cases for prosecution suggest that not all "delinquents" are necessarily equal.

## SOURCE OF PETITIONS

Chapter Four revealed that the source of a referral to juvenile court—police, probation officers, parents, or schools—strongly influences courts' actions. As Tables 6-5a and 6-5b indicate, while police are the primary source of referrals for all offenses (89.2%), probation officers and schools (designated as "other" in Tables 6-5a,b), refer many juveniles, especially in the other delinquency and status offense categories. Other delinquency is a mixed category that includes minor drug offenses such as possession of marijuana, disorderly conduct and public order offenses, and, most importantly, contempt of court and probation violations. These latter charges account for the presence of probation officers as a significant referral source.

While police referrals predominate throughout the state, the proportion of nonpolice referrals differs in urban, suburban, and rural counties. Although schools are the next largest source of referrals, urban courts

**Table 6-5a   Offense and Petitioner**

| | Statewide | | | | Urban | | | |
|---|---|---|---|---|---|---|---|---|
| Petitioner | Police | Probation Officer | Parent | Other | Police | Probation Officer | Parent | Other |
| **Overall (%)** | 89.2 | 2.3 | 1.5 | 7.0 | 83.5 | 5.3 | 2.1 | 9.1 |
| **Felony (%)** | 95.8 | 0.2 | 0.1 | 4.0 | 93.8 | 0.3 | 0.1 | 5.8 |
| Felony Offense Against Person (%) | 94.6 | 0.1 | 0.3 | 5.0 | 90.1 | — | 0.4 | 9.6 |
| Felony Offense Against Property (%) | 96.1 | 0.2 | — | 3.7 | 95.1 | 0.4 | — | 4.6 |
| **Misdemeanor (%)** | 91.8 | 3.2 | 0.1 | 4.6 | 85.9 | 6.8 | 0.6 | 6.7 |
| Minor Offense Against Person (%) | 95.7 | 0.3 | 0.2 | 3.7 | 94.7 | 0.5 | 0.3 | 4.5 |
| Minor Offense Against Property (%) | 95.8 | 0.3 | 0.4 | 3.6 | 95.2 | 0.6 | 0.1 | 4.1 |
| Other Delinquency (%) | 82.8 | 9.7 | 0.8 | 6.8 | 71.9 | 16.2 | 1.5 | 10.5 |
| **Status (%)** | 79.8 | 2.2 | 4.4 | 13.7 | 72.4 | 5.6 | 6.5 | 15.6 |

**Table 6-5b   Offense and Petitioner**

|  | Suburban | | | | Rural | | | |
| --- | --- | --- | --- | --- | --- | --- | --- | --- |
| Petitioner | Police | Probation Officer | Parent | Other | Police | Probation Officer | Parent | Other |
| **Overall (%)** | 91.2 | 1.6 | 1.3 | 5.9 | 93.0 | 0.1 | 1.1 | 5.8 |
| **Felony (%)** | 97.7 | 0.1 | — | 2.1 | 96.2 | 0.1 | 0.2 | 3.5 |
| Felony Offense Against Person (%) | 98.9 | 0.5 | — | 0.5 | 96.7 | — | 0.5 | 2.8 |
| Felony Offense Against Property (%) | 97.4 | — | — | 2.6 | 96.1 | 0.1 | 0.1 | 3.7 |
| **Misdemeanor (%)** | 93.6 | 2.6 | 0.4 | 3.4 | 96.1 | 0.2 | 0.5 | 3.3 |
| Minor Offense Against Person (%) | 95.2 | 0.4 | 0.4 | 3.9 | 97.5 | — | — | 2.5 |
| Minor Offense Against Property (%) | 96.5 | — | 0.4 | 3.1 | 95.8 | 0.1 | 0.7 | 3.4 |
| Other Delinquency (%) | 85.7 | 9.9 | 0.4 | 4.0 | 96.6 | 0.3 | — | 3.1 |
| **Status (%)** | 78.4 | 0.3 | 4.9 | 16.5 | 86.2 | 0.1 | 2.5 | 11.2 |

receive almost twice as many petitions originating from schools as do courts in other areas (9.1% vs. 5.9%, 5.8%), including more for criminal offenses. While schools refer 1,187 truancy-status offense cases for 6.9% of all juvenile court petitions, there is relative geographic parity for truancy (15.6% vs. 16.5%, 11.2%). By contrast, schools in urban counties refer about twice as many cases of criminal activity as they do in the suburban or rural counties (felony, 5.8% vs. 2.1%, 3.5%; misdemeanor, 6.7% vs. 3.4%, 3.3%).

The counties also differ in the proportion of probation and parental referrals. Probation officers in the urban counties refer more than three times as many juveniles (5.3%) as they do in the suburban (1.6%) or rural (0.1%) counties. Again, this disproportionality appears primarily in the categories of other delinquency and status offenses. Since somewhat more urban juveniles have prior records (Table 6-3), their ongoing relationships with probation officers increase their opportunity for probation violation referrals. The urban probation referral rate also provides one indicator of those courts' greater formality and bureaucratization. Urban courts also receive more parental referrals (2.1% vs. 1.3%, 1.1%), primarily for status offenses. With greater urban family disruptions, more urban parents may resort to the juvenile court for reenforcement of their parental authority than in the other settings.

The higher urban court rates of referral (Table 6-4) and the more extensive nonpolice referrals suggest that the urban courts pursue a different strategy of social control than do their suburban or rural counterparts. The greater proportion of probation, parental, and school referrals indicate that urban courts throw a wider and more inclusive net and place greater reliance on all community resources to maximize formal social control. Even if urban police have a higher "seriousness" threshold before referring a routine criminal case to juvenile court, when youths lack family or community supports, formal bureaucratized social control may result in the filing of more petitions against them. By contrast, in suburban and rural counties, police and schools are the primary agents of formal control.

## AGE AND OFFENSE

Juveniles aged fifteen to seventeen constitute more than two-thirds (69.5%) of Minnesota's juvenile court clients. The length of a youth's prior record increases with age; recidivism peaks at fifteen.[1] Tables 6-6a, 6-6b, 6-6c, and 6-6d summarize the relationships between age, delinquency, and prior referrals. Minnesota's juvenile court jurisdiction includes any person under the age of eighteen as well as any person who is alleged to have committed their offense prior to age eighteen (Minn. Stat. Ann. § 260.015(2) [West 1986]). In some instances, a person who committed an offense at age seventeen might be eighteen by the time he or she is charged as a delinquent.

In the state, 27.7% of all delinquents are fourteen or younger, as are 28.8% of those charged with felony offenses, 27.9% of those charged with misdemeanors, and 26.3% of those charged with status offenses. The seriousness of the present offense appears to influence the decision to charge younger juveniles. Comparing juveniles' age makeup with their contribution to the various offense categories indicates that the younger juveniles are charged somewhat more often with felony offenses than their overall percentage of the court population would dictate and somewhat less frequently with status offenses. For example, twelve-year-olds constitute 6.1% of all delinquents but 7.0% of all those charged with felony offenses; thirteen-year-old youths constitute 7.8% of the court population and 8.1% of the felony petitions. Conversely, these youngest juveniles are charged with a smaller proportion of status offenses, 4.3% and 7.5%. While younger juveniles may be charged with serious offenses about as often as their older colleagues, because of their age, they have not had as long an opportunity to accumulate prior referrals. In the state, about 10% fewer juveniles aged twelve and under have prior referrals

**Table 6-6a    Age, Offense, and Prior Referral (Statewide)**

| Age | 12 and Under | 13 | 14 | 15 | 16 | 17 | 18 |
|---|---|---|---|---|---|---|---|
| % Delinquents | 6.1 | 7.8 | 13.8 | 21.1 | 22.6 | 25.8 | 2.8 |
| | **Present Offense** | | | | | | |
| **Felony (%)** | 7.0 | 8.1 | 13.7 | 21.5 | 24.1 | 23.1 | 2.6 |
| Felony Offense Against Person (%) | 8.8 | 10.7 | 13.5 | 21.2 | 20.1 | 23.2 | 2.4 |
| Felony Offense Against Property (%) | 6.6 | 7.3 | 13.7 | 21.6 | 25.2 | 23.0 | 2.6 |
| **Misdemeanor (%)** | 6.5 | 7.9 | 13.5 | 19.9 | 22.7 | 26.3 | 3.2 |
| Minor Offense Against Person (%) | 5.8 | 12.0 | 13.9 | 19.0 | 21.9 | 25.1 | 2.1 |
| Minor Offense Against Property (%) | 8.7 | 8.3 | 14.4 | 20.0 | 22.1 | 23.8 | 2.8 |
| Other Delinquency (%) | 2.6 | 5.7 | 11.6 | 19.9 | 24.1 | 31.7 | 4.3 |
| **Status (%)** | 4.3 | 7.5 | 14.5 | 23.5 | 21.5 | 26.5 | 2.1 |
| | **Prior Referrals** | | | | | | |
| 0 | 79.6 | 72.7 | 69.0 | 68.9 | 72.5 | 73.4 | 70.2 |
| 1–2 | 16.5 | 22.5 | 24.6 | 24.5 | 22.8 | 22.7 | 25.0 |
| 3–4 | 2.9 | 4.1 | 4.9 | 4.8 | 3.6 | 3.0 | 4.2 |
| 5+ | 1.1 | 0.7 | 1.5 | 1.7 | 1.1 | 0.9 | 0.6 |

when compared with fifteen-year-olds, the youths with the most extensive prior records.

The relationship between age and petitioned offenses varies with geographic locale. The urban courts charge a higher percentage of younger juveniles than the suburban and rural courts, which tend to charge a higher percentage of older delinquents. In the urban counties, 31.3% of the delinquents are fourteen or younger, as compared to 24.6% in the suburban counties and 26.0% in the rural counties. Conversely, while 51.4% of the delinquents in the state are sixteen or older, sixteen and seventeen-year-olds account for 42.7% of all delinquents in the urban courts, 49.7% in the suburban courts, and 52.7% in the rural courts.

The age disparities occur because urban courts charge proportionately more young offenders with status offenses and proportionately fewer with felony offenses than the suburban or rural courts. By contrast, the rural courts charge proportionately more younger juveniles with serious offenses and older youths with status offenses. For example, while 27.7% of all youths in the state are fourteen or under, only 26.3% of

**Table 6-6b   Age, Offense, and Prior Referral (Urban)**

| Age | 12 and Under | 13 | 14 | 15 | 16 | 17 | 18 |
|---|---|---|---|---|---|---|---|
| % Delinquents | 6.3 | 9.5 | 15.5 | 23.6 | 20.4 | 22.3 | 2.4 |
| | **Present Offense** | | | | | | |
| **Felony (%)** | 6.8 | 8.3 | 13.6 | 21.3 | 24.0 | 23.9 | 2.0 |
| Felony Offense Against Person (%) | 9.6 | 12.1 | 10.6 | 20.2 | 22.3 | 23.8 | 1.4 |
| Felony Offense Against Property (%) | 5.9 | 7.0 | 14.6 | 21.6 | 24.6 | 24.0 | 2.2 |
| **Misdemeanor (%)** | 5.9 | 7.6 | 12.7 | 21.7 | 22.2 | 26.9 | 3.0 |
| Minor Offense Against Person (%) | 8.5 | 16.2 | 13.0 | 20.2 | 17.0 | 24.5 | 0.5 |
| Minor Offense Against Property (%) | 7.8 | 7.4 | 13.3 | 20.7 | 22.5 | 26.0 | 2.5 |
| Other Delinquency (%) | 2.9 | 5.6 | 11.9 | 23.3 | 23.3 | 28.6 | 4.3 |
| **Status (%)** | 6.7 | 13.8 | 22.5 | 29.0 | 14.5 | 12.0 | 1.3 |
| | **Prior Referrals** | | | | | | |
| 0 | 68.6 | 64.2 | 60.1 | 61.8 | 65.9 | 68.9 | 66.9 |
| 1–2 | 23.9 | 28.5 | 29.6 | 28.1 | 26.9 | 24.9 | 25.7 |
| 3–4 | 5.8 | 6.2 | 7.7 | 7.5 | 5.0 | 4.7 | 6.1 |
| 5+ | 1.8 | 1.0 | 2.7 | 2.6 | 2.2 | 1.5 | 1.4 |

those charged with status offenses are. However, in the urban courts 43.0% of those charged with status offenses are youths fourteen or younger, as contrasted with 19.9% in suburban courts and 15.7% in rural courts. Conversely, suburban and rural counties charge proportionately more than twice as many sixteen or seventeen-year-old juveniles with status offenses as do the urban courts (54.1% and 62.7% vs. 26.5%).

Since the status offense data are aggregated, one can only speculate from the sources of referral that younger urban juveniles may be charged with truancy or incorrigibility while older rural and suburban youths may be charged with alcohol or curfew violations that bring them into contact with police. Coupling the geographic distribution of offenses (Table 6-3) with the sources of petitions (Tables 6-5a and 6-5b) and the age distribution of charges (Tables 6-6a through 6-6d) suggests that the urban courts intervene more readily in the lives of younger "problematic" or "nuisance" juveniles, while suburban and rural courts allow these youths to exhaust informal community controls before intervening formally. By

Table 6-6c    Age, Offense, and Prior Referral (Suburban)

| Age | 12 and Under | 13 | 14 | 15 | 16 | 17 | 18 |
|---|---|---|---|---|---|---|---|
| % Delinquents | 4.5 | 7.0 | 13.1 | 22.7 | 23.8 | 25.9 | 3.0 |
| **Present Offense** | | | | | | | |
| **Felony (%)** | 4.5 | 8.6 | 12.6 | 25.3 | 23.2 | 22.8 | 3.1 |
| Felony Offense Against Person (%) | 3.8 | 12.4 | 14.1 | 27.6 | 16.2 | 22.7 | 3.2 |
| Felony Offense Against Property (%) | 4.7 | 7.5 | 12.2 | 24.7 | 25.1 | 22.8 | 3.0 |
| **Misdemeanor (%)** | 4.9 | 7.3 | 13.9 | 21.3 | 23.7 | 26.0 | 3.1 |
| Minor Offense Against Person (%) | 3.0 | 7.4 | 16.5 | 18.7 | 30.0 | 22.2 | 2.2 |
| Minor Offense Against Property (%) | 6.6 | 7.6 | 13.8 | 21.9 | 23.4 | 23.7 | 3.0 |
| Other Delinquency (%) | 1.3 | 6.5 | 12.9 | 20.9 | 21.5 | 33.3 | 3.6 |
| **Status (%)** | 3.4 | 4.8 | 11.7 | 23.6 | 25.0 | 29.1 | 2.4 |
| **Prior Referrals** | | | | | | | |
| 0 | 86.1 | 71.0 | 72.2 | 70.7 | 70.9 | 70.9 | 73.1 |
| 1–2 | 12.1 | 24.7 | 22.2 | 24.5 | 24.8 | 25.7 | 21.3 |
| 3–4 | 0.6 | 3.9 | 4.8 | 3.6 | 3.8 | 2.7 | 5.6 |
| 5+ | 1.2 | 0.4 | 0.8 | 1.2 | 0.6 | 0.7 | — |

contrast, rural courts respond more readily to crimes by younger juveniles and intervene earlier than do the urban courts. Finding that urban courts charge more of the younger status-offenders provides additional support for the view that these courts rely more extensively on formal controls, especially for problem youths who lack alternative resources.

## URBAN, SUBURBAN, AND RURAL VARIATIONS IN RATES OF REPRESENTATION— PROCEDURAL FORMALITY IN JUVENILE COURT

The presence of defense counsel is central to a procedurally formal model of juvenile courts. The Supreme Court in *Gault* held that juvenile offenders were constitutionally entitled to the assistance of counsel in delinquency proceedings because "a proceeding where the issue is whether the child will be found to be 'delinquent' and subjected to the loss of his liberty for years is comparable in seriousness to a felony prosecution" (*Gault*, 387 U.S. 1 at 36 [1967]). Chapter Three revealed that despite the

**Table 6-6d   Age, Offense, and Prior Referral (Rural)**

| Age | 12 and Under | 13 | 14 | 15 | 16 | 17 | 18 |
|---|---|---|---|---|---|---|---|
| % Delinquents | 6.6 | 6.8 | 12.7 | 18.2 | 23.9 | 28.7 | 3.0 |
| **Present Offense** | | | | | | | |
| **Felony (%)** | 9.0 | 7.5 | 14.6 | 19.1 | 24.8 | 22.5 | 2.7 |
| Felony Offense Against Person (%) | 12.2 | 7.5 | 16.9 | 16.9 | 20.7 | 23.0 | 2.8 |
| Felony Offense Against Property (%) | 8.3 | 7.5 | 14.1 | 19.5 | 25.6 | 22.3 | 2.7 |
| **Misdemeanor (%)** | 8.0 | 8.4 | 14.0 | 17.5 | 22.7 | 26.0 | 3.4 |
| Minor Offense Against Person (%) | 4.6 | 10.2 | 13.1 | 17.7 | 21.9 | 28.3 | 4.2 |
| Minor Offense Against Property (%) | 10.3 | 9.3 | 15.4 | 18.6 | 21.2 | 22.3 | 2.8 |
| Other Delinquency (%) | 2.9 | 5.4 | 10.5 | 14.4 | 26.8 | 35.1 | 4.8 |
| **Status (%)** | 2.8 | 3.6 | 9.3 | 19.0 | 25.7 | 37.0 | 2.6 |
| **Prior Referrals** | | | | | | | |
| 0 | 86.4 | 83.6 | 76.9 | 75.8 | 78.3 | 77.6 | 70.9 |
| 1–2 | 11.9 | 14.2 | 20.5 | 20.4 | 18.7 | 19.9 | 26.4 |
| 3–4 | 1.3 | 1.6 | 2.1 | 2.6 | 2.4 | 1.9 | 2.3 |
| 5+ | 0.4 | 0.6 | 0.5 | 1.1 | 0.6 | 0.6 | 0.5 |

Court's ruling in *Gault*, the promise of counsel often remains unrealized. In Minnesota, less than half of juveniles adjudicated delinquent consistently receive the assistance of counsel to which they are constitutionally and statutorily entitled. In 1984, only 46.8% of juveniles charged with delinquency and status offenses were represented; in 1986, only 45.3% youths had lawyers; in 1988, only 47.8% had attorneys at their adjudication (Juvenile Representation Study 1990).

The routine presence of defense counsel, the primary indicator of a procedurally formal, adversarial juvenile court, has significant implications for many aspects of juvenile justice administration. Table 6-7 reports rates of representation by type of offense in the various settings. Overall, only 45.3% of juveniles in Minnesota were represented. For the state as a whole, about two-thirds (66.1%) of juveniles charged with felonies, less than half (46.4%) of those charged with misdemeanors, and about one-quarter (28.9%) of those charged with status offenses had counsel.

As expected, these rates differ by geography and offense. In the urban

**Table 6-7    Rate of Representation and Offense**

| Counsel | Statewide | | Urban | | Suburban | | Rural | |
|---|---|---|---|---|---|---|---|---|
| | Yes | No | Yes | No | Yes | No | Yes | No |
| **Overall** | | | | | | | | |
| % Counsel at Adjudication | 45.3 | 54.7 | 62.6 | 37.4 | 55.2 | 44.8 | 25.1 | 74.9 |
| **Felony (%)** | 66.1 | 33.9 | 82.9 | 17.1 | 67.9 | 32.1 | 49.6 | 50.4 |
| Felony Offense Against Person (%) | 77.3 | 22.7 | 88.8 | 11.2 | 74.9 | 25.1 | 63.7 | 36.3 |
| Felony Offense Against Property (%) | 63.0 | 37.0 | 80.8 | 19.2 | 65.8 | 34.2 | 46.7 | 53.3 |
| **Misdemeanor (%)** | 46.4 | 53.6 | 64.3 | 35.7 | 57.9 | 42.1 | 23.5 | 76.5 |
| Minor Offense Against Person (%) | 62.4 | 37.6 | 80.7 | 19.3 | 57.3 | 42.7 | 40.7 | 59.3 |
| Minor Offense Against Property (%) | 44.6 | 55.4 | 70.8 | 29.2 | 56.7 | 43.3 | 20.6 | 79.4 |
| Other Delinquency (%) | 44.9 | 55.1 | 51.3 | 48.7 | 61.0 | 39.0 | 26.6 | 73.4 |
| **Status (%)** | 28.9 | 71.1 | 45.6 | 54.4 | 33.9 | 66.1 | 14.3 | 85.7 |
| **Overall** | | | | | | | | |
| % Counsel at Disposition | 38.9 | 61.1 | 43.9 | 56.1 | 53.5 | 46.5 | 26.5 | 73.5 |

courts, 62.6% of all juveniles are represented, as are 55.2% of suburban youths. By contrast, only one-quarter (25.1%) of rural youths have counsel. The geographic variations in rates of representation appear through all offense categories. Of those charged with felonies, in the urban settings 82.9% had counsel, in the suburban counties 67.9% did, while in the rural counties less than half (49.6%) had lawyers. There was an even sharper drop-off in rates of representation in rural counties for juveniles charged with misdemeanors (23.5%) and status offenses (14.3%). A higher percentage of urban and suburban youths charged with misdemeanors had counsel (64.3%, 57.9%) than rural juveniles charged with felonies (49.6%). Proportionately more urban and suburban youths charged with status offenses had counsel (45.6%, 33.9%) than did rural youths charged with misdemeanors (23.5%). These findings are similar to those reported by Kempf, Decker, and Bing (1990:51) in Missouri, where for youths charged with violent offenses, 41.5% of urban black youths and 39.0% of urban white youths had counsel as contrasted with only 1.1% of rural black youths and 11.5% of rural white youths.

Using counsel as an indicator of procedural formality and a due-process orientation, the urban courts are the most formal and legalistic while the rural courts adhere most closely to the traditional, informal model. Moreover, justice agencies are loosely connected; the structural features that determine a court's orientations are likely to be reflected in decisions by other law enforcement agencies as well (Smith 1984; Wilson 1968). This is consistent with the hypothesis that urban courts rely more heavily on formal social control than do courts in other locations (Table 6-4).

The last row of Table 6-7 provides another indicator of differences in courts' orientation. Comparing the rates of representation at adjudication (arraignment, plea, or trial) with those at disposition reveals that 6.4% fewer juveniles have counsel at sentencing than at earlier proceedings. Virtually all of the decrease in representation at dispositions occurs in the urban counties (62.6% vs. 43.9%). If prosecutors in more bureaucratized courts prescreen cases using formal legal criteria, then there may be a correspondingly greater legal role for defense counsel at adjudication. Using the "courtroom work group" model (Eisenstein and Jacob 1977), defense counsel are as effective as the juvenile justice system will allow them to be. Functioning in a procedurally formal adjudicative context is a more familiar and comfortable role for defense lawyers than is participating in a "messy" social-services-dominated dispositional proceeding. Perhaps, urban defense attorneys appreciate that their participation at disposition may be an exercise in futility or may even adversely affect the eventual disposition. In any event, once the proceeding shifts from formal legality to substantive rationality (i.e., social services disposition), urban defense lawyers apparently exit in droves.

Chapters Three and Four reported that representation in juvenile courts is almost exclusively a public sector activity. Privately retained counsel appear in only 5.1% of all delinquency cases. If juveniles have lawyers at all, then they are most likely to be public defenders (28.5%). As Table 6-8 indicates, there are some geographic patterns in the type of representation: urban counties deliver legal services almost exclusively through public defenders; suburban and small urban counties rely about equally on public defenders and court appointed counsel; rural counties rely primarily on court appointed attorneys. Chapter Five suggested that these different strategies of delivering legal services may also result in qualitative differences in the performance of counsel (Table 5-4).

Just as offense seriousness increases the likelihood of representation (Table 6-7), it also increases the proportion of private attorneys who appear. For example, charging a juvenile with a felony against the person doubles the presence of private attorneys compared with their overall rate of appearance (11.2% vs. 5.1%). The presence of private counsel also differs by geographic locale. Overall, a substantially larger proportion of

**Table 6-8  Attorney Type and Offense**

| | Statewide | | | | Urban | | | | Suburban | | | | Rural | | | |
|---|---|---|---|---|---|---|---|---|---|---|---|---|---|---|---|---|
| | Private | PD[a] | CA[b] | None | Private | PD | CA | None | Private | PD | CA | None | Private | PD | CA | None |
| **Overall (%)** | 5.1 | 28.5 | 11.7 | 54.7 | 8.0 | 54.5 | 0.1 | 37.4 | 2.5 | 29.7 | 23.0 | 44.8 | 3.8 | 5.1 | 16.2 | 74.9 |
| **Felony (%)** | 8.1 | 36.0 | 21.9 | 33.9 | 13.2 | 69.6 | — | 17.1 | 3.8 | 33.3 | 30.7 | 32.1 | 6.3 | 7.6 | 35.6 | 50.4 |
| Felony Offense Against Person (%) | 11.2 | 43.5 | 22.7 | 22.7 | 15.7 | 72.7 | 0.4 | 11.2 | 6.9 | 34.9 | 33.1 | 25.1 | 8.8 | 10.9 | 44.0 | 36.3 |
| Felony Offense Against Property (%) | 7.2 | 34.0 | 21.7 | 37.0 | 12.4 | 68.5 | — | 19.2 | 3.0 | 32.8 | 30.0 | 34.2 | 5.8 | 6.9 | 33.9 | 53.3 |
| **Misdemeanor** | 5.5 | 29.4 | 11.5 | 53.6 | 9.1 | 55.2 | — | 35.7 | 2.2 | 30.9 | 24.8 | 42.1 | 3.9 | 4.6 | 15.0 | 76.5 |
| Minor Offense Against Person (%) | 6.4 | 40.5 | 15.5 | 37.6 | 10.1 | 70.7 | — | 19.3 | 2.3 | 30.0 | 25.0 | 42.7 | 4.7 | 6.6 | 29.5 | 59.3 |
| Minor Offense Against Property (%) | 4.9 | 27.5 | 12.2 | 55.4 | 10.4 | 60.4 | 0.1 | 29.2 | 1.7 | 27.8 | 27.2 | 43.3 | 2.6 | 4.7 | 13.2 | 79.4 |
| Other Delinquency (%) | 6.5 | 29.7 | 8.7 | 55.1 | 7.1 | 44.1 | 0.1 | 48.7 | 3.2 | 38.8 | 19.0 | 39.0 | 7.3 | 3.6 | 15.8 | 73.4 |
| **Status (%)** | 2.1 | 21.6 | 5.1 | 71.1 | 2.3 | 43.2 | — | 54.4 | 2.0 | 22.0 | 9.9 | 66.1 | 2.0 | 4.8 | 7.4 | 85.7 |

a. Public Defender.
b. Court Appointed.

private attorneys appear in urban courts (8.0%) than in suburban (2.5%) or rural (3.8%) courts. When the effects of the seriousness of the offense are combined with the geographic disparities in retaining private counsel, 13.2% of urban juveniles charged with felonies appear with private counsel as contrasted with 3.8% in suburban and 6.3% in rural courts. Similarly, 9.1% of urban juveniles charged with misdemeanors retain private counsel as contrasted with 2.2% and 3.9% respectively in the suburban and rural counties.

This geographic pattern may reflect the concentration of Minnesota's lawyers in the urban counties. It also suggests a more procedurally formal, legalistic court in the urban counties. Private attorneys who do not appear regularly in juvenile court are less likely to need to maintain personal relationships with court personnel at the expense of their clients and are more likely to bring a "criminal" court style of representation than may be true of public attorney regulars (Blumberg 1967; Clarke and Koch 1980; Lefstein, Stapleton, and Teitelbaum 1969). The continual presence of private, "outside" attorneys in the urban juvenile courts subjects the courts to ongoing scrutiny, providing a mechanism to independently monitor the performance of the juvenile justice system and to insist that it adhere to legal processes. By contrast, the lower rates of appearance by "nonregulars" in suburban settings, and the virtual absence of any attorneys except those appointed by the judges themselves in the rural counties assures that a more traditional, informal juvenile justice system will continue to operate there free of any outside criticism.

Chapter Four examined the determinates and impact of attorneys in counties in which they often, sometimes, and seldom appeared. As Tables 6-7 and 6-8 indicate, locale is one important factor that influences rates of representation and procedural formality in juvenile courts. The next three tables summarize the regression equations for the initial decision to appoint an attorney in the urban, suburban, and rural settings. The variables, their coding, and the regression analyses are identical to those reported in Chapter Four (Tables 4-19 through 4-22), except that these aggregate the counties by geography in order to examine the influence of social structure.

Chapter Four reported that for the entire state, the most important variables influencing the appointment of counsel were the seriousness of the present offense, a prior record, a subsequent home removal sentence, detention, and a prior sentence removing a juvenile from home (Table 4-19). Table 6-9 reveals that in the urban counties, most of the same variables enter the regression equation, albeit in a somewhat different order, and account for about the same amount of variance in the appointment decision (13.2% vs. 13.0% for the whole state). In the urban counties, the seriousness of the present offense is the most important factor affecting representation (beta = .270 vs. .123 for home removal). Whether a juvenile is eventually removed from his or her home accounts for an additional 3% of the variance in appointing counsel. Unlike the regression equations for the entire state (Table 4-19), and for the suburban (Table 6-10) and rural counties (Table 6-11), an urban juvenile's pretrial detention status is not associated with the decision to appoint counsel. Even though the urban counties have the highest rates of detention (Table 6-14), the relationships between the present offense, prior record, previous sentences, and eventual sentence apparently account for any association between representation and detention.

**Table 6-9   Regression Model of Factors Influencing the Appointment of Counsel (Urban Counties)**

| Independent Variables | Zero-Order r | Standardized Beta Coefficient | Multiple R | $R^2$ |
|---|---|---|---|---|
| Offense Severity | .291* | .270* | .291 | .085 |
| Home Removal | .219* | .123* | .339 | .115 |
| Prior Record | −.162* | −.085* | .358 | .128 |
| Prior Home Removal Disposition | .175* | .062* | .361 | .130 |
| Age | .021*** | .028*** | .362 | .132 |

*$p < .001$
**$p < .01$
***$p < .05$

**Table 6-10   Regression Model of Factors Influencing the Appointment of Counsel (Suburban Counties)**

| Independent Variables | Zero-Order r | Standardized Beta Coefficient | Multiple R | $R^2$ |
|---|---|---|---|---|
| Offense Severity | .195* | .178* | .195 | .038 |
| Prior Record | −.181* | −.108* | .264 | .070 |
| Institutional Confinement | .165* | .086* | .283 | .080 |
| Detention | −.100* | −.071*** | .293 | .086 |
| Prior Home Removal Disposition | .182* | .072*** | .298 | .089 |

*$p < .001$
**$p < .01$
***$p < .05$

In the suburban counties, the seriousness of the present offense and the prior record account for most of the variance (7%) in the decision to appoint counsel. Unlike the urban or rural settings, it is the subsequent decision to institutionalize a youth, rather than simply to remove a youth from home, that significantly determines the presence of counsel. Again, this raises the question of how judges can anticipate at the initial stages of the process, cases in which they will impose the most severe sentence. As was seen in Chapter Four, a juvenile's pretrial detention status is also associated with the appointment of counsel because of the need for representation at the detention hearing. Finally, while somewhat more than half of all suburban youths are represented, the regression equation can explain only 8.9% of the variance in the appointment decision, the least of any locale.

In the rural counties, the seriousness of the present offense and an eventual home removal sentence account for most of the variance in the appointment of counsel. In addition, a juvenile's pretrial detention status and prior record make similar contributions to the appointment decision. Altogether, those variables account for 12% of the variance in the appointment of counsel.

The regression equations for appointment of counsel in urban, suburban, and rural settings are consistent with those observed in Chapter Four as well as the bivariate geographic analyses (Table 6-7). Juveniles charged with more serious offenses, those with prior records, those who are held in pretrial detention, and those who eventually receive home removal or secure confinement sentences are most likely to be represented. Again, as in Chapter Four, the surprising finding is how little of the variance in the decision to appoint counsel the relevant legal variables explain.

**Table 6-11   Regression Model of Factors Influencing the Appointment of Counsel (Rural Counties)**

| Independent Variables | Zero-Order r | Standardized Beta Coefficient | Multiple R | R² |
|---|---|---|---|---|
| Offense Severity | .254* | .212* | .254 | .064 |
| Home Removal | .227* | .132* | .312 | .097 |
| Detention | −.177* | −.111* | .330 | .109 |
| Prior Record | −.164* | −.103* | .345 | .119 |
| Age | .014 | .024*** | .346 | .120 |

*p < .001
**p < .01
***p < .05

The remainder of this chapter will examine the impact of social context on juvenile justice administration. Obviously, one way in which juvenile courts differ considerably is in their degree of procedural formality and that, in turn, has implications for other aspects of their operations.

## URBAN, SUBURBAN, AND RURAL JUVENILE COURT SENTENCING AND DETENTION PRACTICES

The preceding analyses described some of the characteristics of the courts and of the juveniles referred to them in different counties. The next analyses explore the consequences for juveniles of being tried in courts in different locations.

### Present Offense and Disposition

Chapter Four summarized the prior research on juvenile court sentencing and reported that sentencing practices in Minnesota's juvenile courts varied in counties with different rates of representation. It also indicated that despite juvenile courts' theoretical commitment to rehabilitation and individualized dispositions, the seriousness of the present offense and the prior record or previous sentences influenced judicial decision making. At the same time, juvenile court personnel enjoy greater discretion than their adult-process counterparts, and most of the variation in sentencing practices could not be explained simply by the legal variables.

While the SJIS data do not include information on several social variables—family structure, socioeconomic status, school achievement, or the like—that would be useful to a fuller understanding of juvenile court dispositions, the data do lend themselves to an exploration of the relationship between social structure and sentencing practices. In addition, Chapter Seven will examine the influences of race and gender on dispositional decision making in the different geographic contexts. Table 6-12 uses two measures of juvenile court dispositions: 1) out-of-home placement and 2) secure confinement. Both types of sentences provide clear lines that lend themselves to cross-county comparisons. It reports the dispositions in the state and geographic locales by categories of offenses.

For the whole state, 18.5% of all petitioned juveniles are removed from their homes, and 11.1% of all juveniles are incarcerated in state or local institutions. However, the urban, suburban, and rural counties differ markedly in their sentencing practices. In urban counties, about one of four (24.0%) juveniles is removed from home. In suburban counties, about one of six (17.5%) is removed. In rural counties, only about one

**Table 6-12   Offense and Disposition: Out-of-Home Placement/Secure Confinement**

|  | Statewide | Urban | Suburban | Rural |
|---|---|---|---|---|
| **Overall** | | | | |
| % Home | 18.5 | 24.0 | 17.5 | 14.2 |
| % Secure | 11.1 | 15.1 | 9.1 | 8.7 |
| **Felony** | | | | |
| % Home | 34.3 | 42.3 | 23.7 | 29.5 |
| % Secure | 24.4 | 33.3 | 13.6 | 20.4 |
| Felony Offense Against Person | | | | |
| % Home | 42.2 | 51.0 | 33.1 | 38.3 |
| % Secure | 27.5 | 40.2 | 11.4 | 24.6 |
| Felony Offense Against Property | | | | |
| % Home | 32.1 | 43.4 | 21.1 | 29.9 |
| % Secure | 23.6 | 34.3 | 14.1 | 20.8 |
| **Misdemeanor** | | | | |
| % Home | 17.6 | 21.5 | 16.3 | 12.7 |
| % Secure | 11.3 | 14.1 | 9.5 | 8.3 |
| Minor Offense Against Person | | | | |
| % Home | 24.0 | 28.8 | 19.5 | 21.3 |
| % Secure | 14.5 | 16.8 | 10.7 | 14.5 |
| Minor Offense Against Property | | | | |
| % Home | 16.0 | 22.4 | 14.6 | 12.4 |
| % Secure | 10.8 | 16.6 | 8.0 | 8.4 |
| Other Delinquency | | | | |
| % Home | 18.9 | 20.9 | 22.2 | 14.4 |
| % Secure | 11.3 | 12.0 | 13.8 | 8.8 |
| **Status** | | | | |
| % Home | 12.4 | 17.4 | 13.2 | 8.1 |
| % Secure | 3.5 | 5.0 | 3.0 | 2.5 |

out of seven (14.2%) is removed. Similarly, urban youths (15.1%) receive secure confinement dispositions almost twice as often as suburban (9.1%) or rural (8.7%) juveniles.

The seriousness of the present offense substantially alters a youth's risk of removal or confinement. Despite the courts' statutory emphases on individualized dispositions, actual sentencing practice evidence an element of proportionality. Juveniles charged with felony offenses against person or property and minor offenses against the person have the highest rates of out-of-home placement and secure confinement. For the state as a whole, more than one third (34.3%) of all juveniles charged with a felony offense are removed from their homes, and about one quarter (24.4%) are incarcerated. Conversely, about half as many juveniles charged with misdemeanors—minor property offenses such as theft and shoplifting, or other delinquency—are removed from home (17.6%) or confined (11.3%). As a result of legal restrictions on the placement of status offenders, they have the lowest proportion of removal from the home or secure confinement (Minn. Stat. Ann. § 260.194 [West 1982]; *L.E.A. v. Hammergren*, 294 N.W.2d 705 [Minn. 1980]). Even though legislation prohibits secure confinement of status offenders, 3.5% of those charged with noncriminal offenses are in county or state institutions (Minn. Stat. Ann. § 260.185, subd. 1(c)(5)(d)[1986]).

While there is a direct relationship between the seriousness of the present offense and the severity of disposition, there are also marked differences between the sentences imposed in the urban, suburban, and rural counties. For nearly every offense category, the more formal, urban judges sentence more severely than do either the suburban or rural judges. For example, of delinquents adjudicated for felonies, urban judges incarcerate one-third (33.3%) as contrasted with only about one-seventh (13.6%) in the suburban counties and one-fifth (20.4%) in the rural counties. Urban judges are nearly as likely to remove juveniles charged with misdemeanors from their homes (21.5%) as suburban judges are likely to remove juveniles charged with felony offenses (23.7%). Urban judges institutionalize more youths charged with misdemeanors (14.1%) than suburban judges do youths charged with felonies (13.6%).

The greater volume of crime, including serious crime, in urban settings may encourage judges to intervene more formally and sentence more severely. Even though suburban courts apparently prescreen their cases (Table 6-4) to produce court dockets that contain more serious offenses and fewer trivial ones (Table 6-3), urban courts still sentence similarly situated offenders more severely. Only juveniles charged with "other delinquency" receive more severe sentences in suburban courts than they do in urban or rural settings. Otherwise, suburban and rural sentencing practices are more like each other than either is like the urban courts. Rural judges sentence youths charged with felony offenses somewhat more severely than do the suburban judges, but more leniently than do the urban judges. Rural judges sentence juveniles charged with misdemeanor or status offenses comparably or even more leniently than do the suburban judges. Since the largest proportion of rural juveniles are minor and status offenders (Table 6-3), overall rural youths receive the least intrusive interventions.

Perhaps, there are qualitative differences in offenses that account for the geographical differences in sentencing practices. For example, within comparable offense categories, urban juveniles' crimes may be more serious than rural youths' crimes in ways that statistical controls cannot capture (e.g., amount of injury to victim or value of property stolen) but that may affect sentencing severity. As speculated earlier, because there is a greater volume of urban delinquency, there may be a higher threshold of seriousness before a case is referred to a juvenile court. As a result, categorically similar cases may be qualitatively different. However, the scant research on geographic variations in the "quality" of crime reports that "rural and urban victimizations are similar with respect to their consequences to victims (e.g., injury) and characteristics (e.g., the nature and extent of weapon use)" (Laub and Hindelang 1981:70). Laub (1983:138) compared urban and rural patterns of offending and concluded that

> more interesting and perhaps more important were the findings of *similarities* in urban and rural victimizations. For example, the extent of weapon use did not vary across the urban-rural dimension. Similarly, the types of weapons used—guns, knives, or other weapons— did not differ in victimizations across urban, suburban, and rural areas. Moreover, urban and rural victimizations had very similar consequences. For instance, success in theft, rates of victim injury, and financial loss did not differ across urban, suburban, and rural areas. Thus, although rates of victimization were much higher in urban areas, when victimizations did occur, the outcomes were not very different across the urban-rural dimension.

Moreover, the most common juvenile offense is a misdemeanor property crime (Table 6-3). It is difficult to hypothesize aggregate qualitative differences, for example, in shoplifting that could account for the sentencing disparities in which proportionally almost twice as many urban as rural youths are removed from their homes (22.4% vs. 12.4%) or confined (16.6% vs. 8.4%) (Table 6-12).

### Prior Referrals and Dispositions

In addition to the seriousness of the present offense, a history of delinquency referrals and previous sentences affects a juvenile's eventual disposition (Clarke and Koch 1980; Henretta, Frazier, and Bishop 1986). Recall that a juvenile's prior record in 1986 was constructed by merging 1984, 1985, and 1986 annual data tapes and matching a youth's identification number across years. The prior record only includes cases that resulted in formal petitions; it does not include previous referrals to court in which formal charges were not filed. The record of prior referrals are coded as 0, 1–2, 3–4, and 5 or more.

Tables 6-13a and 6-13b report the percentages of juveniles with prior records and the relationship between the present offense, prior referrals, and out-of-home placement and secure confinement dispositions. For the entire state, 71.9% of the youths against whom petitions were filed appeared in juvenile court for the first time. As noted earlier (Table 6-3), the rate of prior referrals varied by geographic locale. Compared to the urban juveniles, 7.1% more of the suburban juveniles and 13.4% of rural youths made their first appearance with correspondingly fewer recidivists. This reinforces the observation (Table 6-3) that rural juveniles were less sophisticated delinquents than their urban cousins.

Table 6-13a and 6-13b also report the relationship between the present offense, prior record, and out-of-home placement and secure confinement dispositions. Quite clearly, both overall and within categories of offenses, a prior record substantially alters a youth's likelihood of receiving a more severe disposition. In the aggregate, each additional one or two prior referrals increases the proportion of juveniles' receiving out-of-home placements and secure confinements; the largest increase occurs between those juveniles with one or two prior referrals and those with three or four. Regardless of the nature of the present offense, by the time juveniles appear in court for the third or fourth time, more than half (52.9%) will be removed from home and more than one-third (39.9%) will be confined.

Within each offense level, there is a nearly perfect linear relationship between additional prior referrals and more severe dispositions. For example, of those juveniles who commit a felony offense against the person, 35.7% who have no prior referrals, 51.9% who have one or two, 84.8% with three or four, and 100% with five or more priors receive out-of-home placements. Similar patterns prevail for all offense and prior referrals.

Even though the direct relationship between prior referrals and sentencing severity is similar in all types of counties, urban judges remove and confine larger proportions of juveniles than do their suburban and rural counterparts. Comparing forty-eight possible sentences (six categories of present offense times four prior record groups times two types of disposition) reveals only ten instances in which suburban courts sentenced more severely than did urban judges and only four cells in which rural judges did. Four of the suburban deviations were for "other delinquency."

The rural judges' dispositional leniency may reflect budgetary constraints, since the costs of placements are borne by county welfare funds (Minn. Stat. Ann. § 260.251 [West 1986]). In rural counties, with smaller populations and tax bases, and greater poverty (Table 6-1), extensive, and therefore expensive, intervention may simply be fiscally prohibitive for all but the most serious or troubled delinquents. There is no financial expla-

**Table 6-13a   Present Offense, Prior Record, and Rate of Disposition (Home/Secure)**

| Priors | Statewide | | | | Urban | | | |
|---|---|---|---|---|---|---|---|---|
| | 0 | 1–2 | 3–4 | 5+ | 0 | 1–2 | 3–4 | 5+ |
| **Priors Overall** | | | | | | | | |
| % | 71.9 | 23.0 | 3.9 | 1.2 | 64.7 | 27.1 | 6.1 | 2.0 |
| N | (12,359) | (3,962) | (669) | (205) | (4,060) | (1,700) | (385) | (128) |
| **Disposition Overall** | | | | | | | | |
| % Home | 12.4 | 29.5 | 52.9 | 61.6 | 15.9 | 32.4 | 57.6 | 70.1 |
| % Secure | 6.8 | 17.7 | 39.9 | 48.8 | 9.5 | 19.0 | 44.2 | 54.3 |
| **Felony** | | | | | | | | |
| % Home | 23.8 | 47.4 | 78.4 | 73.1 | 32.0 | 49.0 | 86.9 | 89.7 |
| % Secure | 17.5 | 32.1 | 65.5 | 55.8 | 25.4 | 36.8 | 71.4 | 72.4 |
| Felony Offense Against Person | | | | | | | | |
| % Home | 35.7 | 51.9 | 84.8 | 100.0 | 40.9 | 47.9 | 90.9 | 100.0 |
| % Secure | 22.9 | 33.3 | 60.6 | 100.0 | 31.7 | 42.3 | 59.1 | 100.0 |
| Felony Offense Against Property | | | | | | | | |
| % Home | 21.7 | 46.4 | 76.5 | 72.0 | 28.7 | 49.3 | 85.5 | 88.9 |
| % Secure | 16.0 | 31.9 | 67.0 | 54.0 | 23.0 | 35.1 | 75.8 | 70.4 |
| **Misdemeanor** | | | | | | | | |
| % Home | 11.4 | 29.9 | 49.7 | 62.4 | 13.6 | 30.7 | 51.5 | 67.7 |
| % Secure | 6.7 | 19.3 | 37.1 | 53.5 | 8.4 | 19.2 | 41.1 | 55.4 |
| Minor Offense Against Person | | | | | | | | |
| % Home | 14.2 | 38.5 | 62.2 | 73.3 | 15.1 | 36.0 | 62.5 | 100.0 |
| % Secure | 8.0 | 22.6 | 40.5 | 66.7 | 8.2 | 19.0 | 45.8 | 85.7 |
| Minor Offense Against Property | | | | | | | | |
| % Home | 10.4 | 27.3 | 49.0 | 65.2 | 14.5 | 28.2 | 52.3 | 67.7 |
| % Secure | 6.6 | 18.8 | 39.5 | 52.2 | 10.5 | 20.4 | 43.2 | 51.6 |
| Other Delinquency | | | | | | | | |
| % Home | 12.4 | 31.5 | 46.9 | 55.0 | 11.9 | 32.2 | 46.3 | 59.3 |
| % Secure | 6.7 | 19.2 | 31.9 | 50.0 | 5.8 | 17.9 | 35.8 | 51.9 |
| **Status** | | | | | | | | |
| % Home | 8.7 | 19.3 | 38.9 | 48.8 | 10.6 | 25.2 | 44.0 | 57.6 |
| % Secure | 1.6 | 5.8 | 23.5 | 30.2 | 1.9 | 6.9 | 25.3 | 36.4 |

nation for the suburban judges' leniency, however, since these are the most affluent counties.

Tables 6-13a and 6-13b provide strong evidence that the juvenile courts judges have reintroduced de facto the principle of offense as a dispositional guideline (Matza 1964:122). The present offense and prior record, the two principal components in Minnesota's adult sentencing

**Table 6-13b    Present Offense, Prior Record, and Rate of Disposition (Home/Secure)**

| | Suburban | | | | Rural | | | |
|---|---|---|---|---|---|---|---|---|
| Priors | 0 | 1–2 | 3–4 | 5+ | 0 | 1–2 | 3–4 | 5+ |
| **Priors Overall** | | | | | | | | |
| % | 71.8 | 23.9 | 3.5 | 0.8 | 78.1 | 19.1 | 2.1 | 0.7 |
| N | (2,642) | (881) | (129) | (29) | (5,657) | (1,381) | (155) | (48) |
| **Disposition Overall** | | | | | | | | |
| % Home | 11.9 | 28.0 | 50.0 | 60.7 | 10.1 | 26.8 | 43.5 | 39.6 |
| % Secure | 4.8 | 16.5 | 37.5 | 50.0 | 5.8 | 17.0 | 31.2 | 33.3 |
| **Felony** | | | | | | | | |
| % Home | 15.5 | 38.9 | 64.0 | 72.7 | 21.7 | 46.5 | 67.4 | 38.9 |
| % Secure | 7.8 | 22.2 | 56.0 | 54.5 | 14.9 | 32.0 | 50.0 | 27.8 |
| Felony Offense Against Person | | | | | | | | |
| % Home | 30.3 | 39.5 | 100.0 | — | 28.1 | 57.1 | 75.0 | — |
| % Secure | 14.1 | 7.9 | 100.0 | — | 18.1 | 38.1 | 50.0 | — |
| Felony Offense Against Property | | | | | | | | |
| % Home | 10.8 | 38.8 | 57.1 | 80.0 | 20.3 | 44.6 | 65.8 | 38.9 |
| % Secure | 5.8 | 25.3 | 47.6 | 60.0 | 14.1 | 31.0 | 50.0 | 27.8 |
| **Misdemeanor** | | | | | | | | |
| % Home | 10.1 | 28.1 | 52.6 | 64.3 | 8.8 | 25.4 | 34.7 | 42.9 |
| % Secure | 4.7 | 18.0 | 38.2 | 57.1 | 5.7 | 16.6 | 25.0 | 42.9 |
| Minor Offense Against Person | | | | | | | | |
| % Home | 15.2 | 25.9 | 70.0 | 50.0 | 13.6 | 36.5 | 20.0 | 50.0 |
| % Secure | 8.2 | 15.5 | 40.0 | 50.0 | 10.1 | 23.0 | 20.0 | 50.0 |
| Minor Offense Against Property | | | | | | | | |
| % Home | 9.0 | 25.6 | 47.6 | 83.3 | 8.4 | 25.0 | 34.0 | 30.0 |
| % Secure | 3.8 | 15.9 | 35.7 | 66.7 | 5.4 | 16.6 | 30.0 | 30.0 |
| Other Delinquency | | | | | | | | |
| % Home | 10.8 | 34.3 | 54.2 | 50.0 | 8.7 | 21.6 | 41.2 | 57.1 |
| % Secure | 5.6 | 23.4 | 41.7 | 50.0 | 5.3 | 13.6 | 11.8 | 57.1 |
| **Status** | | | | | | | | |
| % Home | 12.8 | 13.1 | 29.6 | — | 6.8 | 14.3 | 29.4 | 14.3 |
| % Secure | 2.1 | 3.6 | 18.5 | — | 1.7 | 6.1 | 17.6 | — |

guidelines (Minnesota Sentencing 1980), both exert substantial influences on a youth's eventual disposition, albeit to different degrees in different geographic settings.

## Pretrial Detention

Chapters Three and Four noted that there is a relationship between a youth's pretrial detention status and subsequent disposition. These findings confirm those of other studies that report that while similar variables affect both initial detention and later dispositions, after statistical controls, detention per se exhibits an independent effect on dispositions (Krisberg and Schwartz 1983; Frazier and Bishop 1985; Clarke and Koch 1980; McCarthy 1987). The next analyses examine the relationships between detention, offenses, and dispositions in the different locales.

## Detention by Offense

Table 6-14 shows the overall numbers and percentages of juveniles in pretrial detention by present offense and prior referrals. Detention, as used here, refers to a juvenile's custody status following arrest or referral but prior to formal court action—adjudication or disposition. Detention, as distinguished from shelter care, connotes a physically restrictive facility, such as a detention center, state institution, or adult jail (Minn. Stat. Ann. § 260.015, subd. 16 and 17 [1986]; Schwartz, Harris, and Levi 1988). Minnesota detention statutes and court rules authorize pretrial preventive detention if the child constitutes a danger to self or others or will not make court appearances (Minn. Stat. Ann. §§ 260.171, subd. 1; 260.172, subd. 1 (1986); Minn. R.P.Juv.Ct. 18.02(2)(A)(i); 18.06(5)(b)(i); 18.09(2)(D)(i); Feld 1984). The offense that a juvenile allegedly committed is not an explicit statutory criterion for detention except insofar as a juvenile court judge may view it as evidence of "endangering" self or others.

Chapters Three and Four also noted that Minnesota's apparent low rate of pretrial detention (Tables 3-5, 4-15), results, in part, from its restrictive definition of "detention." Juveniles are only counted as detained if a detention hearing is held after a juvenile was taken into custody, usually within about two court days. Many juveniles who are detained pending the arrival of parents or even held for one or two days but released prior to a detention hearing are not counted as detained in Minnesota as they are in other jurisdictions such as California (Table 3-5).

The use of pretrial detention follows a similar pattern in the state as a whole as well as in the different geographic locales. While only a small proportion (7.6%) of all juveniles in the state receive a detention hearing, the seriousness of the present offense and the length of the prior record both appear to alter substantially a youth's likelihood of being detained (Bailey 1981; Cohen and Kluegel 1979; McCarthy 1987). For the entire state, about twice as many juveniles charged with a felony offense are detained (14.9% vs. 7.6%) as the overall rate. A direct relationship exists between prior referrals and rates of detention. However, even when youths are charged with the most serious offenses or have extensive prior

**Table 6-14  Offense, Prior Referral, and Rate of Detention**

|  | Statewide | Urban | Suburban | Rural |
|---|---|---|---|---|
| **Overall** | | | | |
| % Detention | 7.6 | 12.9 | 4.8 | 4.4 |
| N | 1,309 | 812 | 176 | 321 |
| **Felony Offense** | | | | |
| % | 14.9 | 25.9 | 7.4 | 10.2 |
| N | 470 | 284 | 62 | 124 |
| Felony Offense Against Person | | | | |
| % | 24.3 | 37.6 | 11.4 | 17.8 |
| N | 165 | 106 | 21 | 38 |
| Felony Offense Against Property | | | | |
| % | 12.3 | 21.9 | 6.2 | 8.6 |
| N | 305 | 178 | 41 | 86 |
| **Misdemeanor** | | | | |
| % | 6.5 | 11.5 | 3.9 | 3.4 |
| N | 606 | 397 | 80 | 129 |
| Minor Offense Against Person | | | | |
| % | 11.4 | 17.0 | 7.4 | 7.1 |
| N | 101 | 64 | 17 | 20 |
| Minor Offense Against Property | | | | |
| % | 6.0 | 12.4 | 3.5 | 2.9 |
| N | 332 | 212 | 45 | 75 |
| Other Delinquency | | | | |
| % | 6.1 | 8.9 | 3.4 | 3.5 |
| N | 173 | 121 | 18 | 34 |
| **Status** | | | | |
| % | 4.8 | 7.6 | 3.9 | 2.9 |
| N | 221 | 129 | 30 | 62 |
| | **Prior Referrals % Detention** | | | |
| 0 | 5.5 | 9.3 | 4.1 | 3.5 |
| 1–2 | 11.3 | 17.2 | 6.2 | 7.3 |
| 3–4 | 19.9 | 28.1 | 6.2 | 11.0 |
| 5+ | 20.5 | 27.3 | 13.8 | 6.3 |

records, the vast majorities are not detained. Because most delinquents are not serious offenders (Table 6-3), in purely numerical terms, more minor offenders are detained than are felons. Indeed, for the entire state, slightly more than one-third of detainees are charged with felonies (35.9%), and most are charged with misdemeanors (46.3%) or even some status offenses (16.9%). For example, more shoplifters (332) are detained than are burglars (305). These inconsistencies explain why Chapter Four found very little formal legal rationale for detention practices and could explain only 9.0% of the variance (Table 4-23).

When the urban, suburban, and rural county detention practices are examined, similar patterns emerge. Youths charged with felony offenses, offenses against the person, and those with longer prior records are detained more frequently than their less delinquent counterparts. However, most juveniles even with these adverse characteristics are not detained and the largest numbers and proportion of detainees are charged with minor offenses.

While the offense pattern of detention is similar, its geographical use differs substantially. Detention is used most heavily in the urban counties, which detain proportionally two or three times as many youths as do suburban or rural counties. For youths charged with felony offenses, urban courts detain about one of four (25.9%) as contrasted with about one of ten in the rural counties (10.2%) and one of thirteen in the suburban counties (7.4%). Urban counties use detention disproportionately for juveniles charged with misdemeanors (11.5% vs. 3.9% and 3.4%) and status offenses (7.6% vs. 3.9% and 2.9%), as well as for those with prior records (e.g., 1–2 priors = 17.2% vs. 6.2% and 7.3%).

Tables 6-15, 6-16, and 6-17 summarize the regression equations for the detention decision in the urban, suburban, and rural counties. Again, the coding and analytic strategy are similar to those reported in Chapter Four (Tables 4-23 through 4-26), but now examine the social structural influences. Recall that for the whole state, the variables of a home removal sentence, the presence of an attorney, the seriousness of the present offense, prior record, gender, and age could explain only 9% of the variance in the detention decision (Table 4-23). Most of those same variables operate in the different geographic locales, albeit in different orders and with different influences.

In the urban counties, which detain the largest numbers and proportion of juveniles, Table 6-14 indicates and Table 6-15 confirms that the eventual sentence, the present offense, prior record, and prior sentences explain most of the variance. While a subsequent sentence of home removal has the largest beta weight ($-.195$), all of the variables can account for only 9.7% of the detention decision. After controlling for the influence of the other variables, juveniles who are female and those who are older are somewhat more likely to be detained than similarly situated youths without those characteristics. As was noted in Chapter Four, because the eventual sentence occurs weeks or months after the initial detention decision, the most benign interpretation is that both decisions share certain underlying common elements, albeit those that cannot be identified by the legal variables. A less charitable interpretation is that there is little rationale for the initial decision to detain (Frazier and Bishop 1985), even though a youth's detention status significantly affects later dispositions.

In the suburban counties, the regression equation can account for only 5.9% of the variance in detention, and most of that is attributable

**Table 6-15   Regression Model of Factors Influencing the Detention Decision (Urban Counties)**

| Independent Variables | Zero-Order r | Standardized Beta Coefficient | Multiple R | R² |
|---|---|---|---|---|
| Home Removal | −.262* | −.195* | .262 | .068 |
| Offense Severity | −.166* | −.142* | .290 | .084 |
| Prior Record | .159* | .064* | .304 | .093 |
| Prior Home Removal | −.185* | −.063* | .308 | .095 |
| Gender | −.017 | .039* | .310 | .096 |
| Age | −.031** | .028*** | .311 | .097 |

$*p < .001$
$**p < .01$
$***p < .05$

**Table 6-16   Regression Model of Factors Influencing the Detention Decision (Suburban Counties)**

| Independent Variables | Zero-Order r | Standardized Beta Coefficient | Multiple R | R² |
|---|---|---|---|---|
| Home Removal | −.203* | −.267* | .203 | .041 |
| Secure Confinement | −.077* | .117* | .219 | .048 |
| Attorney | −.100* | −.071* | .232 | .054 |
| Age | −.055* | .037*** | .236 | .056 |
| Gender | −.042** | .048** | .239 | .057 |
| Offense Severity | −.060* | −.042*** | .243 | .059 |

$*p < .001$
$**p < .01$
$***p < .05$

to the eventual sentences imposed, home removal (beta = $-.267$) and secure confinement (beta = $.117$). The suburban regression equation for appointment of counsel also noted the relationship between representation and detention (Table 6-10). All other things being equal, female and older juveniles are at somewhat greater risk to be detained than are male or younger juveniles. While being female explains only .1% of the variance in detention, the beta weight indicates that that is a more significant determinant of the detention decision than the seriousness of a youth's offense.

In the rural counties, in which comparatively few juveniles are detained (Table 6-14), four variables explain 9.4% of the variance in the detention decision. As in the other settings, an eventual sentence of home removal is by far the most important (beta = $-.247$) followed by the fact that a juvenile is represented ($R^2 = .091$). In settings in which most juveniles appear without counsel (Table 6-7), detention provides a significant impetus to appoint a lawyer for those few youths who are detained. Like their urban and suburban counterparts, female delinquents are at greater risk of being detained than are their male counterparts.

The heavier reliance on detention in urban settings probably stems from the greater availability of detention facilities. A primary determinant of a state or county's detention rate is the availability of detention bedspace (Krisberg and Schwartz 1983; Kramer and Steffensmeier 1978; Lerman 1977; Pawlak 1977; Bookin-Weiner 1984; Frazier and Bishop 1985). Since each of the urban counties has its own detention facility, their availability provides an inducement for their use. The greater availability and use of detention in urban settings reflects the presence of a critical mass of eligible juveniles, greater reliance on formal mechanisms of control, and a more punitive orientation. Urban courts operate in a milieu that provides fewer mechanisms for informal social control, such as stable families to whom youths can return pending court appearances.

Table 6-17   Regression Model of Factors Influencing the Detention Decision (Rural Counties)

| Independent Variables | Zero-Order r | Standardized Beta Coefficient | Multiple R | $R^2$ |
|---|---|---|---|---|
| Home Removal | $-.279*$ | $-.247*$ | .279 | .078 |
| Attorney | $-.177*$ | $-.115*$ | .302 | .091 |
| Gender | $-.029**$ | $.041*$ | .304 | .093 |
| Offense Severity | $-.099*$ | $-.030***$ | .306 | .094 |

$*p < .001$

$**p < .01$

$***p < .05$

With fewer urban counties whose practices can vary, greater overall use of detention, and a heavier emphasis on the present offense and prior record, there is a seemingly greater rationality to the detention decision ($R^2$ = .097) than there is in the suburban settings ($R^2$ = .059). At the same time, however, these data and the regression equations are unable to identify many significant variables that can logically explain much of the decisions to detain. Indeed, in suburban and rural settings, being female has more bearing on detention than does the offense committed. As already noted in Chapter Four, apart from the negative experiences of detention per se, it may also impair a juvenile's ability to prepare legal defenses and increase the probability of conviction and the likelihood of home removal following adjudication.

## CONCLUSION

There is a relationship between social structure, youthful criminality, and juvenile justice administration. Urban, suburban, and rural counties differ in homogeneity, stability, and social cohesion. This, in turn, is related to differences in rates of youthful criminality. Urban counties, with fewer informal social controls, rely more heavily on formal mechanisms of control as evidenced by process formality and detention and sentencing practices. Juvenile courts in rural counties, by contrast, do not confront as serious a youth crime problem and do not intervene as early or as severely as their urban counterparts.

Different types of justice obtain in different parts of the state. The urban courts emphasize a more procedurally formal, due-process model of justice in which juvenile courts function in a fashion similar to adult criminal courts. The rural courts, on the other hand, appear to adhere to a more informal, traditional pre-*Gault* model of juvenile justice. At least on first impression, the relationship between informality and leniency provides some support for the traditional juvenile court. Chapter Seven provides an additional test of whether adherence to informal, discretionary decision making is warranted, by examining the relationships between race, gender, and juvenile justice administration in different structural contexts.

## NOTE

1. Intuitively, one expects a stepwise progression downward by age in the percentage with no prior referrals and upward in each prior referral category, such that more sixteen and seventeen-year-old juveniles than fourteen and fifteen-year-old youths would have prior records. Recall that the prior record was constructed

by merging 1984, 1985, and 1986 data tapes and matching identifying numbers across annual files. Thus, the prior record of a juvenile charged in January, 1986, could be only two years long (1984, 1985), while that of a youth charged in December, 1986, could be nearly three years long. Despite the inability to integrate prior records more than two years earlier or to control for the length of time within which the prior record was obtained, there are no obvious reasons why recidivism peaks at fifteen, rather than at sixteen or seventeen.

**chapter seven** ───────────────────────────

# THE INFLUENCE OF RACE, GENDER, AND SOCIAL STRUCTURE ON JUVENILE JUSTICE ADMINISTRATION

Chapter Six focused on the relationships between legal variables — present offense, prior record, and pretrial detention — social structure, and dispositions. A number of studies indicate that demographic characteristics, such as race (McCarthy and Smith 1986; Fagan, Slaughter, and Hartstone 1987; Pope and Feyerherm 1990a, 1990b) or gender (Chesney-Lind 1977) also influence juvenile justice administration. Chapter Seven examines the effects of race and gender on juvenile justice administration in different types of settings.

## RACE AND JUVENILE JUSTICE ADMINISTRATION

The wide frame of relevance associated with individualized justice raises concerns about the impact of discretionary decision making on lower-class and nonwhite youths who are frequently overrepresented in the juvenile justice system (Fagan, Slaughter, and Hartstone 1987; Krisberg et al. 1987; McCarthy and Smith 1986; Dannefer and Schutt 1982; Pope and Feyerherm 1990a, 1990b). When practitioners of "individualized justice" base discretionary judgments on social characteristics that indirectly mirror race, rather than on legal variables, their decisions frequently result in differential processing and more severe sentencing of minority youths relative to whites and raise issues of fairness and equality.

A basic issue of equal justice in juvenile courts is whether individualized, discretionary sentences based, at least in part, on social characteristics result in more severe sentencing of similarly situated minority youths (Krisberg et al. 1987; Fagan, Slaughter, and Hartstone 1987; McCarthy and Smith 1986); or whether, despite a nominal commitment to individualized justice, sentences are based on offenses, and the racial disproportionality results from real differences in rates of offending by race (Wolfgang, Figlio, and Sellin 1972; Hindelang 1978; Huizinga and Elliott 1987); or whether the structure of juvenile justice decision making itself acts to the detriment of minority juveniles (Pope and Feyerherm 1990a, 1990b). In short, to what extent do legal offense factors, social variables, or justice system processing variables influence juvenile court judges' sentencing decisions?

One possible nondiscriminatory explanation for the disproportionate overrepresentation of minority youths in the juvenile justice process is that dispositional decisions are based on the principle of offense (i.e., legal variables) rather than on an assessment of individual needs, and that minority and lower-class youths commit more and serious crimes. Thus, their overrepresentation in the juvenile system may result from real differences in their rates of delinquent activity rather than discrimination by decision makers. Wolfgang, Figlio, and Sellin (1972) observed that "official delinquents," youths whose contacts with law enforcement personnel resulted in official records, were disproportionately concentrated in poor and minority communities, and that in every socioeconomic category, black youths engaged in delinquency to a greater extent than their white counterparts. Similarly, Hindelang (1978) concluded that racial differentials in the criminal justice system probably reflect real differences in rates of behavior rather than the effects of discriminatory decision making. On the other hand, Huizinga and Elliot (1987:212) contended that

> it does not appear that differences in incarceration rates between racial groups can be explained by differences in the proportions of persons of each racial group that engage in delinquent behavior. Even if the slightly higher rates for more serious offenses among minorities were given more importance than is statistically indicated, the relative proportions of Whites and minorities involved in delinquent behavior could not account for the observed differences in incarceration rates.

Similarly, Krisberg et al. (1987:196) also argued that "differences in incarceration rates by race cannot be explained by the proportions of each racial group that engage in delinquent behavior."

Recent research notes that some of the racial differences in the sentencing of juveniles cannot be accounted for by the legal variables (Krisberg et al. 1987; Fagan, Slaughter, and Hartstone 1987; McCarthy and

Smith 1986). While evaluations of juvenile court sentencing practices are sometimes contradictory (Fagan, Slaughter, and Hartstone 1987; McCarthy and Smith 1986), two general findings emerge. First, the present offense and prior record account for most of the variance in sentencing that can be explained (Horowitz and Wasserman 1980; McCarthy and Smith 1986; Clarke and Koch 1980; Barton 1976; Phillips and Dinitz 1982). In those multivariate studies, as in this one (Table 4-27), legal variables typically account for about 25% of the variance in sentencing.

A second finding was that after controlling for legal offense variables, individualized discretion was often synonymous with racial disparities in sentencing juveniles (Pope and Feyerherm 1990a, 1990b; Krisberg et al. 1987; Fagan, Slaughter, and Hartstone 1987; McCarthy and Smith 1986; National Council of Juvenile and Family Court Judges 1990). Many of these studies reported that minority or lower-class youths received more severe dispositions than did white youths after controlling for legally relevant variables (Arnold 1971; Thomas and Cage 1977; Thomas and Fitch 1975; Thornberry 1979; Dannefer and Schutt 1982; Carter and Clelland 1979; Carter 1979). Thomas and Cage (1977:250) concluded that when legal variables were held constant, the juvenile court's individualized justice "typically applies harsh sanctions to blacks, those who have dropped out of school, those in single parent or broken homes, [and] those from lower socioeconomic backgrounds."

Other research reports that juveniles' race only affects the dispositions of minor offenders, while for serious or repeat offenders, sentencing disparities between the races decline (Cohen and Kluegel 1978; Carter 1979; Clarke and Koch 1980). Of course, the bulk of most juvenile courts' caseloads are minor offenders (Tables 3-1, 4-1, and 6-3). Contrary to expectations, a few earlier studies reported that white youths received more severe dispositions than blacks (Scarpitti and Stephenson 1971; Ferster and Courtless 1972). Some studies suggest that substantive factors such as family and school problems, along with legal criteria, explain some of the racial variations in sentencing (Horwitz and Wasserman 1980; Thomas and Fitch 1975).

Examining the effects of race or social class only at the time of sentencing may mask the more significant effect that these personal characteristics may have had in the initial screening stages of juvenile justice administration. Frazier and Cochran (1986) and Bortner and Reed (1985) reported that race influenced initial detention decisions, with black youths more likely to be detained than white youths, and that detained youths were more likely to receive more severe sentences. Bishop and Frazier (1988) reported that race, as well as legal factors, influenced detention and dispositional decisions and that black youths were more disadvantaged than white youths as they proceeded further into the system. McCarthy and Smith (1986) reported that while screening, detention, charging, and adjudication decisions were strongly influenced by the principle of offense, as cases penetrated further into the process, race and class directly affected dispositions, with minority youths receiving more severe sentences. Fagan, Slaughter, and Hartstone (1987:252) reported that initial screening decisions were not overtly discriminatory but that decisions made at six points in the juvenile process amplified racial effects as minority youths moved through the system and as a result, "minority youth receive consistently harsher sentences." They concluded that

> [t]he evidence for racial discrimination in this study is compelling. Its sources may lie in the individual attitudes of decision makers in the system's independent agencies, but it is unlikely that these seemingly isolated decision makers of substantially different backgrounds would produce such consistent, systemic behaviors. Rather than a chance convergence of independent behaviors, they seem to reflect a sociological process, if not a generalized perspective, shared across decision makers of disparate backgrounds. Like other societal institutions, the justice system is not blind to ethnic and racial differences. (Fagan, Slaughter, and Hartstone 1987:253)

Almost a decade earlier, Liska and Tausig (1979:205) reanalyzed juvenile sentencing studies and reported "clear and consistent evidence of a racial differential operating at each decision level. Moreover, the differentials operate continuously over various decision levels to produce a substantial accumulative racial differential which transforms a more or less heterogeneous racial arrest population into a homogeneous institutionalized black population."

The most comprehensive recent review of the influence of race on juvenile sentencing concluded that "race effects may occur at various decision points, they may be direct or indirect, and they may accumulate as youths are processed through the system" (Pope and Feyerherm 1990a:331). To summarize, prior research indicates that the principle of offense is the most significant factor influencing juvenile court dispositions of juveniles. However, an additional amount of the variance in sentencing appears to be related to a juvenile's race, either because race correlates with other disadvantageous social characteristics, such as family structure, socioeconomic status, or school performance, which affect individualized sentencing, or as a result of conscious or unconscious racial discrimination.

The present study provides a limited opportunity to analyze the relationships between a juvenile's race, juvenile justice decision making, and sentences. Although the Minnesota SJIS code forms include the variable "race," racial information is the only variable omitted by court personnel in most counties in the state. In part, this reflects the Minnesota reality that racial diversity is almost exclusively an urban phenomenon (Table 6-1). Fortunately, one of the urban counties, Hennepin County (Minneapolis), which has the largest proportion of minority youths in Minnesota (U.S. Department of Commerce 1982:25–198), records a juvenile's race more routinely.[1] The following analyses report the effects of race on juvenile justice administration only in Hennepin County, an urban setting.

Based on the 1980 census, there were approximately 116,000 youths aged ten to seventeen living in Hennepin County of whom slightly more than 105,000 were white and about 5,400 were black (U.S. Department of Commerce 1982:25–198). The next largest urban racial grouping was Native American youths (almost 2,300), with a smaller smattering of Hispanic and Asian youngsters (U.S. Department of Commerce 1982:25–246).

While blacks and other racial minorities make up about 8.7% of Hennepin County's youth population, they constitute about one-third (34.0%) of the clientele of the Hennepin County juvenile court. As indicated in Table 7-1, almost one of four (23.6%) youths against whom petitions were filed were black and about one in ten (10.4%) were Native American or other minorities. Thus, the characteristic disproportionate overrepresentation of minorities reported in other studies appears in Hennepin County as well.

An examination of juveniles' race, present offense, and prior record suggests that at least part of the overrepresentation of minority youths may be attributed to differences in their offense patterns. As a group, a larger proportion of blacks and other minorities are charged with felony offenses and offenses against the person than are whites. Compared with whites, 3.6% more black youths are charged with felony offenses and 3.0% more other minority youths are. Much of the disparity may be attributed to offenses against the person, with proportionally twice as many black youths as whites charged with felony (7.8% vs. 3.1%) and misdemeanor (10.1% vs. 4.0%) crimes against the person. Black and other minority youths are significantly underrepresented relative to whites only in the category of other delinquency, the public order offenses, drug possession, and probation violations. Significantly, a much larger proportion of urban Native American youths appear in juvenile courts for status offenses (40.8%) than for any other type of offense or than either of the other racial groups.

Black and other minority youths also had more extensive records of prior delinquency involvement than did their white counterparts. Ap-

**Table 7-1   Race, Present Offense, and Prior Record (Hennepin County)**

|  | White | Black | Other |
|---|---|---|---|
| **% Delinquents** | 65.9 | 23.6 | 10.4 |
| **N** | (2,232) | (800) | (353) |
| **Felony** | | | |
| % | 16.5 | 20.1 | 19.5 |
| N | (369) | (161) | (69) |
| Felony Offense Against Person | | | |
| % | 3.1 | 7.8 | 4.5 |
| N | (70) | (62) | (16) |
| Felony Offense Against Property | | | |
| % | 13.4 | 12.4 | 15.0 |
| N | (299) | (99) | (53) |
| **Misdemeanor** | | | |
| % | 55.9 | 55.8 | 39.7 |
| N | (1,248) | (446) | (140) |
| Minor Offense Against Person | | | |
| % | 4.0 | 10.1 | 4.8 |
| N | (89) | (81) | (17) |
| Minor Offense Against Property | | | |
| % | 27.5 | 31.1 | 24.9 |
| N | (613) | (249) | (88) |
| Other Delinquency | | | |
| % | 24.5 | 14.5 | 9.9 |
| N | (546) | (116) | (35) |
| **Status** | | | |
| % | 27.5 | 24.0 | 40.8 |
| N | (613) | (192) | (144) |
| | **Prior Referrals** | | |
| 0 | 70.6 | 58.1 | 59.8 |
| 1–2 | 23.6 | 31.3 | 29.5 |
| 3–4 | 4.5 | 8.0 | 8.8 |
| 5+ | 1.3 | 2.6 | 2.0 |

proximately 10% more whites than blacks and others appeared in juvenile court for the first time. Conversely, blacks and other minorities were
nearly twice as likely as whites to have records of chronic recidivism.
Recall, too, that urban juveniles in general had the highest rates of recidivism (Tables 6-3, 6-13) and that the urban courts threw a wider net of
formal social control than did courts in other settings. Thus, the more
extensive prior records reflect both the fact these youths were charged in
an urban county as well as every previous discretionary decision made by
every juvenile justice operative. While the more extensive record of prior
referrals may reflect real differences in rates of behavior by race similar
to those reported for the present offenses, it may also indicate cumulative
differential selection of juveniles by race over time (Fagan, Slaughter, and
Hartstone 1987; McCarthy and Smith 1986).

## RACE AND REPRESENTATION BY COUNSEL

The rates of representation for the Hennepin County sample containing
information on juveniles' race were: private attorneys, 10.3%; public defenders, 37.5%; and unrepresented, 52.1%.[2] Thus, even in the most populous county in Minnesota with a well-established public defender system, the majority of juveniles still appeared without the assistance of
counsel.

Table 7-2 reports the relationship between race, offense, and rates of
representation and reveals that larger proportions of blacks and other
minorities than white juveniles were represented. Compared with white
juveniles, overall 15.4% more black youths and 10% more youths of
other racial minorities had counsel. As seen in previous chapters, a serious
present offense and prior record increased the likelihood of representation (Tables 3-2, 4-3, 4-13, 6-7). The greater presence of counsel is consistent with black and other minority youths' somewhat more extensive
and serious delinquency involvements. Because Table 7-2 controls for the
seriousness of the present offense, however, the differences in rates of
representation by race remain.

Table 6-8 reported that private counsel represented only 5.1% of all
Minnesota's delinquents and 8.0% of those appearing in urban courts.
In Hennepin County, 10.4% of all juveniles retained private counsel.
Larger proportions of white youths retained private counsel while public
defenders were more likely to represent black and other minority youths.
Chapter Four reported that youths charged with serious crimes were more
likely to retain private counsel (Table 4-4). Comparing the uses of private
counsel by race reveals that when charged with felony against the person,
white youths are almost three times more likely than blacks to have pri-

**Table 7-2    Race and Representation by Counsel (Hennepin County)**

|  | White | | | Black | | | Other | | |
|---|---|---|---|---|---|---|---|---|---|
|  | Private | PD[a] | None | Private | PD | None | Private | PD | None |
| **Overall** | | | | | | | | | |
| % Counsel | 11.5 | 31.7 | 56.7 | 7.9 | 50.7 | 41.3 | 8.1 | 45.2 | 46.7 |
| N | 245 | 674 | 1,205 | 59 | 378 | 308 | 26 | 145 | 150 |
| **Felony (%)** | 22.7 | 51.0 | 26.3 | 10.4 | 68.8 | 20.8 | 13.8 | 65.5 | 20.7 |
| Felony Offense Against Person (%) | 30.3 | 51.5 | 18.2 | 10.2 | 72.9 | 16.9 | 28.6 | 71.4 | — |
| Felony Offense Against Property (%) | 20.9 | 50.9 | 28.2 | 10.6 | 65.9 | 23.5 | 9.1 | 63.6 | 27.3 |
| **Misdemeanor (%)** | 12.5 | 29.9 | 57.6 | 9.1 | 55.0 | 35.7 | 10.9 | 55.8 | 33.3 |
| Minor Offense Against Person (%) | 12.5 | 51.1 | 36.4 | 12.8 | 64.1 | 23.1 | 5.9 | 58.8 | 35.3 |
| Minor Offense Against Property (%) | 15.1 | 35.6 | 49.3 | 7.4 | 56.6 | 36.0 | 10.5 | 58.1 | 31.4 |
| Other Delinquency (%) | 9.5 | 19.8 | 70.7 | 10.1 | 45.9 | 44.0 | 14.3 | 48.6 | 37.1 |
| **Status (%)** | 2.4 | 23.4 | 74.2 | 2.9 | 24.6 | 72.5 | 2.4 | 24.0 | 73.6 |

a. Public Defender.

vate counsel (30.3% vs. 10.2%) and, when charged with a felony involving property, twice as likely to have private counsel (20.9% vs. 10.6%). Conversely, blacks are most likely to be represented by the public defender. The few Native American and other minority juveniles charged with a felony offense against the person are nearly as likely as white youths to retain private counsel, but less likely than blacks to retain private counsel when charged with a felony involving property.

Unfortunately, the SJIS data tapes do not include information on juveniles' family status or socioeconomic status. However, black and other minority delinquents' greater use of public defenders rather than private attorneys may be an indirect indicator of their comparatively lower socioeconomic status than white delinquents. The only other study to examine the relationship between race and type of representation reported that "Anglo youth are more likely to have private counsel . . . whereas minority youth are more likely to have public defenders or court-appointed attorneys. . . . Public defenders are more likely to represent minority youth, an artifact of the race/social class interaction" (Fagan, Slaughter, and Hartstone 1987:242). Earlier chapters suggested that private attorneys were marginally more successful than public attorneys in avoiding the most severe sentences for their clients (Tables 4-11, 5-4). Similarly,

Fagan, Slaughter, and Hartstone (1987) reported a relationship between counsel and rates of dismissal—25% for white youths versus 19% for black youths—which resulted in more minority offenders being adjudicated.

Chapter Four reported that juveniles with counsel consistently received more severe dispositions than did those without representation (Table 4-9). Similarly, Table 4-11 suggested that youths represented by private counsel perhaps received marginally more lenient sentences than did those who were represented by public defenders or court appointed attorneys. A larger proportion of minority youths were represented by public defenders than white juveniles (Table 7-2). Table 7-3 compares the disposition rates of represented and unrepresented youths of different races. The pattern observed in Chapter Four (Tables 4-9 and 4-14) of larger proportions of represented juveniles than unrepresented ones receiving more severe sentences prevails within each racial group. Thus, it is highly unlikely that the small variations in the type of representation

**Table 7-3  Race, Representation, and Rate of Disposition (Hennepin County)**

| Counsel | White | | Black | | Other | |
|---|---|---|---|---|---|---|
| | Yes | No | Yes | No | Yes | No |
| **Felony Offense Against Person** | | | | | | |
| % Home | 49.1 | 22.2 | 57.4 | 50.0 | 25.0 | — |
| % Secure | 39.6 | 11.1 | 48.9 | 37.5 | 16.7 | — |
| **Felony Offense Against Property** | | | | | | |
| % Home | 47.7 | 25.8 | 50.0 | 31.3 | 58.8 | 16.7 |
| % Secure | 39.0 | 25.8 | 46.9 | 25.0 | 44.1 | 16.7 |
| **Minor Offense Against Person** | | | | | | |
| % Home | 30.8 | 16.7 | 34.5 | 17.6 | 36.4 | 20.0 |
| % Secure | 15.4 | 8.3 | 16.4 | — | 18.2 | 20.0 |
| **Minor Offense Against Property** | | | | | | |
| % Home | 31.7 | 20.3 | 23.2 | 14.9 | 25.0 | 35.0 |
| % Secure | 24.8 | 14.8 | 16.6 | 13.4 | 17.9 | 20.0 |
| **Other Delinquency** | | | | | | |
| % Home | 21.2 | 10.7 | 27.1 | 15.2 | 21.1 | 8.3 |
| % Secure | 11.6 | 6.7 | 22.0 | 4.3 | 15.8 | 8.3 |
| **Status** | | | | | | |
| % Home | 27.5 | 12.4 | 26.7 | 6.5 | 14.7 | 9.2 |
| % Secure | 5.1 | 1.4 | 11.1 | — | 2.9 | 1.1 |

account for differences in the ways that white and minority youths' cases are processed.

## RACE, OFFENSE, PRIOR RECORD, DETENTION, AND DISPOSITION

Table 7-4 examines the dispositions received by juveniles of different races on the basis of their present offense. In the aggregate, about 5% more black youths and 2% to 3% more youths of other minorities received out-of-home placement and secure confinement dispositions than whites.

The racial differences in sentencing are most conspicuous for black juveniles charged with felony offenses and offenses against the person, the offense categories in which black youths predominate relative to whites (Table 7-1). For those charged with felony offenses, 10.3% more blacks than whites were removed from their homes and 12.2% more were institutionalized. For juveniles of other races, the pattern is more complicated, with less severe sentencing than whites for those charged with felony offenses against the person, but higher rates for those charged with felony offenses against property, such as burglary. While "other delinquency" was the only offense category in which minority youths were underrepresented compared to whites (Table 7-1), proportionally more minority youths in this category received out-of-home and secure confinement dispositions as well. It was only in the sentencing of status offenders that white youths consistently received more severe sentences than minority youths. While the largest proportion of youths charged with status offenses were Native American and other minority youths, 40.8% (Table 7-1), they also experienced the least juvenile court intervention.

The apparent racial differences in sentencing may be the result of differences in the white and minority juveniles' prior records. Tables 4-12 and 6-13 summarized the nearly linear relationship between additional priors and increased sanctions; judges' de facto sentencing practices conformed to informal sentencing guidelines. The more extensive prior records of delinquency of black and other minority juveniles than their white counterparts (Table 7-1) may account for some of the apparent differences in their dispositions.

Table 7-5 summarizes juveniles' dispositions—out-of-home and secure confinement—while controlling for the seriousness of the present offense and the prior record simultaneously. Even with controls, larger proportions of black juveniles charged with felony offenses against the person and property and other delinquency received out-of-home placement and secure confinement dispositions than did similarly situated white offenders. These differences are most conspicuous for black juve-

**Table 7-4  Race, Offense, and Rate of Disposition
(Home/Secure) (Hennepin County)**

|  | White | Black | Other |
|---|---|---|---|
| **Overall** | | | |
| % Home | 21.0 | 25.8 | 23.5 |
| % Secure | 13.3 | 18.5 | 15.0 |
| **Felony** | | | |
| % Home | 42.5 | 52.8 | 52.9 |
| % Secure | 34.3 | 46.5 | 39.7 |
| Felony Offense Against Person | | | |
| % Home | 45.7 | 57.4 | 33.3 |
| % Secure | 34.3 | 49.2 | 26.7 |
| Felony Offense Against Property | | | |
| % Home | 41.8 | 50.0 | 58.5 |
| % Secure | 34.3 | 44.9 | 43.4 |
| **Misdemeanor** | | | |
| % Home | 18.5 | 23.1 | 24.6 |
| % Secure | 12.8 | 15.6 | 17.4 |
| Minor Offense Against Person | | | |
| % Home | 22.5 | 30.8 | 29.4 |
| % Secure | 11.2 | 14.1 | 17.6 |
| Minor Offense Against Property | | | |
| % Home | 23.4 | 20.2 | 27.9 |
| % Secure | 17.8 | 15.8 | 19.8 |
| Other Delinquency | | | |
| % Home | 12.3 | 23.9 | 14.3 |
| % Secure | 7.5 | 16.2 | 11.4 |
| **Status** | | | |
| % Home | 13.8 | 10.4 | 9.1 |
| % Secure | 2.1 | 2.6 | 1.4 |

niles charged with felony offenses who receive sentences of secure confinement. Of the juveniles charged with a felony offense against the person, 12% more black juveniles than white youths with no prior record, 26.2% with one or two priors, and 11.4% more of those with three or more prior petitions were incarcerated. Similarly, 4.8%, 7.2%, and 15.1% more blacks than whites charged with felony offenses against property received secure confinement sentences. For youths charged with "other delinquency," 1.6%, 8.7%, and 12.9% more blacks than whites were incarcerated. There were no consistent patterns in the sentencing of youths of other races or in other categories of offenses.

**Table 7-5   Race, Offense, Priors, and Rate of Disposition (Home/Secure) (Hennepin County)**

| Priors | White | | | Black | | | Other | | |
|---|---|---|---|---|---|---|---|---|---|
| | 0 | 1–2 | 3+ | 0 | 1–2 | 3+ | 0 | 1–2 | 3+ |
| **Felony Offense Against Person** | | | | | | | | | |
| % Home | 44.4 | 27.3 | 100.0 | 55.6 | 50.0 | 85.7 | 20.0 | 16.7 | 75.0 |
| % Secure | 35.2 | 18.2 | 60.0 | 47.2 | 44.4 | 71.4 | 20.0 | 16.7 | 50.0 |
| **Felony Offense Against Property** | | | | | | | | | |
| % Home | 32.1 | 48.0 | 89.7 | 41.2 | 45.2 | 87.5 | 42.9 | 72.2 | 85.7 |
| % Secure | 28.5 | 34.7 | 72.4 | 33.3 | 41.9 | 87.5 | 32.1 | 44.4 | 85.7 |
| **Minor Offense Against Person** | | | | | | | | | |
| % Home | 16.7 | 29.4 | 66.7 | 13.3 | 48.0 | 75.0 | 10.0 | 50.0 | 100.0 |
| % Secure | 6.1 | 17.6 | 50.0 | 6.7 | 16.0 | 50.0 | — | 33.3 | 100.0 |
| **Minor Offense Against Property** | | | | | | | | | |
| % Home | 19.9 | 31.5 | 36.8 | 8.1 | 27.1 | 61.5 | 23.4 | 28.6 | 45.5 |
| % Secure | 15.3 | 24.4 | 23.7 | 5.9 | 23.5 | 42.3 | 14.9 | 17.9 | 45.5 |
| **Other Delinquency** | | | | | | | | | |
| % Home | 9.4 | 19.5 | 33.3 | 12.5 | 35.0 | 46.2 | 13.6 | 12.5 | 20.0 |
| % Secure | 4.7 | 13.8 | 33.3 | 6.3 | 22.5 | 46.2 | 13.6 | — | 20.0 |
| **Status** | | | | | | | | | |
| % Home | 9.7 | 20.2 | 29.7 | 7.0 | 14.3 | 28.6 | 6.2 | 16.7 | 10.0 |
| % Secure | 1.0 | 3.6 | 8.1 | 0.8 | 4.1 | 14.3 | 1.0 | 2.8 | — |

## RACE AND DETENTION

The previous analyses of the effects of detention on dispositions (Tables 3-7, 4-15, 4-17, 4-23) indicated that pretrial detention exerted a significant independent influence on a juvenile's ultimate disposition. It may be that the racial disparities in the sentencing of black juveniles reported above are the function of differences in rates of pretrial detention (Krisberg et al. 1986; Krisberg et al. 1987).

Table 7-6 reports the overall rates of detention for Hennepin County as well as separately for white youths, black youths, and other minority youths. Recall, that 7.6% of all Minnesota youths were detained as were 12.9% of all urban juveniles (Table 6-14). In Hennepin County, 14.1% of the juveniles referred to the juvenile court received one or more detention hearings. This rate of detention is nearly double the state average and reflects a higher rate of detention for every offense category except status offenses.

**Table 7-6    Race, Offense, Priors, and Rate of Detention (Hennepin County)**

| Priors | | White | | | Black | | | Other | | |
|---|---|---|---|---|---|---|---|---|---|---|
| | | 0 | 1–2 | 3+ | 0 | 1–2 | 3+ | 0 | 1–2 | 3+ |
| | | | | | **County Total %** | | | | | |
| **Overall % Detention** | 14.1 | | 10.6 | | | 22.6 | | | 17.3 | |
| Felony Offense Against Person (%) | 42.6 | 24.1 | 27.3 | 60.0 | 52.8 | 72.2 | 71.4 | 40.0 | 33.3 | 50.0 |
| Felony Offense Against Property (%) | 27.9 | 15.0 | 30.1 | 54.7 | 33.3 | 42.0 | 75.0 | 25.0 | 33.3 | 100.0 |
| Minor Offense Against Person (%) | 23.2 | 9.1 | 35.2 | 66.7 | 17.8 | 28.0 | 50.0 | 10.0 | 50.0 | — |
| Minor Offense Against Property (%) | 15.8 | 7.1 | 20.4 | 23.7 | 18.4 | 24.7 | 38.4 | 19.1 | 14.3 | 45.5 |
| Other Delinquency (%) | 7.9 | 5.2 | 9.3 | 20.0 | 9.4 | 22.5 | 15.4 | 4.5 | 25.0 | — |
| Status (%) | 5.4 | 3.9 | 5.4 | 18.9 | 2.4 | 10.2 | 14.3 | 5.1 | 8.4 | 20.0 |

Although 14.1% of all referrals are detained, the rates of detention differ substantially by race: only 10.6% of white juveniles are detained as compared with 22.6% of blacks and 17.3% of other minority youths. More than twice as many black and half again as many other minority youths as white juveniles are detained. The earlier analyses reported higher rates of detention for youths charged with more serious present offenses and for those with records of prior referrals (Table 6-14). Somewhat larger proportions of minority youths were charged with serious offenses and had more extensive prior records than did their white counterparts (Table 7-1). Thus, it is necessary to control for the effects of the present offense and prior record on the decision to detain before attributing the racial disparities in sentencing to differential rates of detention.

Table 7-6 reports the rates of detention separately for juveniles of different races while controlling simultaneously for the seriousness of the present offense and prior record. Thus, 42.6% of all Hennepin County juveniles charged with a felony offense against the person are detained. While a larger proportion of black youths than white youths commit felony offenses against the person (Table 7-1), it is readily apparent that proportionately more black and minority youths than white youths are detained for the same category of offense. For juveniles appearing in juvenile court for the first time who are charged with a felony offense against the person, more than twice as many blacks as whites are detained—52.8% versus 24.1%. For juveniles with one or two prior referrals who are charged with a felony offense against the person, again more than twice as many black youths as white youths are detained—72.2% versus 27.3%. Even for youths with three or more prior referrals charged presently with a felony offense against the person, 11.4% more black youths than white youths are detained. Comparisons of rates of detention across races while controlling for the present offense and prior record suggest that at least some of the differences in the sentencing of minority youths charged with felony offenses against person and property probably result from the variations in rates of pretrial detention. This finding is consistent with other evaluations of the effects of race on pretrial detention and disposition (Fagan, Slaughter, and Hartstone 1987; McCarthy and Smith 1986; Frazier and Bishop 1985). Perhaps most directly on point, Kempf, Decker, and Bing (1990:81–82) analyzed the interaction of race and geography on detention and concluded that "within nearly every category, black youths were detained more often than white youths, overall. This outcome was accentuated in urban courts [where 31% of black youths and 21% of white youths were detained]."

**Table 7-7   Race, Detention, and Rate of Disposition (Home/Secure) (Hennepin County)**

|  | White | | Black | | Other | |
|---|---|---|---|---|---|---|
| Detention | Yes | No | Yes | No | Yes | No |
| Felony Offense Against Person |  |  |  |  |  |  |
| % Home | 70.0 | 38.3 | 63.9 | 50.0 | 50.0 | 12.5 |
| % Secure | 50.0 | 31.9 | 55.6 | 40.9 | 50.0 | — |
| Felony Offense Against Property |  |  |  |  |  |  |
| % Home | 73.8 | 35.0 | 70.7 | 36.5 | 85.0 | 46.7 |
| % Secure | 55.7 | 30.6 | 63.4 | 32.7 | 75.0 | 26.7 |
| Minor Offense Against Person |  |  |  |  |  |  |
| % Home | 56.3 | 18.0 | 52.6 | 25.0 | 50.0 | 23.1 |
| % Secure | 31.3 | 8.2 | 36.8 | 7.1 | 25.0 | 15.4 |
| Minor Offense Against Property |  |  |  |  |  |  |
| % Home | 56.9 | 22.0 | 38.9 | 16.5 | 47.1 | 23.3 |
| % Secure | 33.8 | 17.8 | 25.9 | 14.1 | 35.3 | 15.0 |
| Other Delinquency |  |  |  |  |  |  |
| % Home | 61.1 | 11.5 | 50.0 | 18.9 | 66.7 | 10.7 |
| % Secure | 38.9 | 6.8 | 31.3 | 12.6 | 33.3 | 10.7 |
| Status |  |  |  |  |  |  |
| % Home | 53.1 | 12.8 | 40.0 | 8.9 | 40.0 | 7.0 |
| % Secure | 12.5 | 1.7 | 10.0 | 2.2 | — | 1.6 |

Table 7-7 summarizes the disposition rates of white and minority youths who were detained. The relationship between pretrial detention and more severe sentences prevails for both white and minority juveniles. Although about 5% more detained black juveniles than detained white youths charged with felony offenses against person and property and minor offenses against the person received secure confinement dispositions, it is unlikely that these differences account for the more substantial disparities observed in Tables 7-4 and 7-5.

Black and other minority youths likely share certain characteristics that increase their likelihood of receiving more severe sentences than white juveniles. Their more serious present offenses and prior records (Table 7-1) generally are associated with more severe dispositions (Table 6-13). These offense patterns are also associated with higher rates of representation by counsel (Table 7-2) which, in turn, is associated with more severe sentences (Tables 4-14 and 6-14). Black and other minority juveniles are held in detention at higher rates than are white youths, even after controlling for the present offense and prior record (Table 7-6); detention of any juvenile, regardless of race, is associated with more severe sentences (Tables 4-17 and 7-7). Finally, after controlling for the seriousness of the present offense (Table 7-4) and the length of the prior record (Table 7-5), it appears that black and other minority youths are still somewhat more likely to receive severe sentences than their white counterparts. As later analyses suggest, however, these modest differences in sentencing by race are not necessarily evidence of racial discrimination.

## REGRESSING APPOINTMENT OF COUNSEL, PRETRIAL DETENSION, AND DISPOSITIONS FOR INDEPENDENT VARIABLES INCLUDING A JUVENILE'S RACE

Tables 7-1 through 7-7 reported the bivariate analyses of race. The following regression equations follow the format in Chapter Four, were computed for Hennepin County only, and include a juvenile's race—white, black, and other—as an additional independent variable. Race was "dummy" coded separately for black and Native American juveniles (1 = not black, 2 = black; 1 = not Native American; 2 = Native American). Creating separate variables to reflect a youth's minority status permits an assessment of the impact of race on juvenile justice decision making.

Table 7-8 reports the regression factors influencing the appointment of counsel. As in other analyses (Tables 4-19 through 4-22), the serious-

**Table 7-8  Regression Model of Factors Influencing the Appointment of Counsel Including Juvenile's Race (Hennepin County)**

| Independent Variables | Zero-Order r | Standardized Beta Coefficient | Multiple R | $R^2$ |
|---|---|---|---|---|
| Offense Severity | .370* | .336* | .370 | .137 |
| Prior Home Removal Disposition | .171* | .051* | .395 | .156 |
| Home Removal | .217* | .102* | .406 | .165 |
| Prior Record | −.144* | −.082* | .412 | .170 |
| Black | −.097* | −.065* | .415 | .173 |
| Native American | −.031*** | −.051** | .418 | .175 |

*$p < .001$
**$p < .01$
***$p < .05$

ness of the present offense is the principal determinate of the decision to appoint counsel (beta = .336). Comparing the regression variables for both urban counties (Table 6-9) with those for only Hennepin County reveals that the seriousness of the present offense carries substantially more weight in Hennepin County relative to other variables (beta = .336 vs. .270). In addition, the regression equation confirms the observation that being a black or Native American juvenile increases the likelihood of representation relative to their white counterparts (Table 7-2). The regression equation controls for the fact that minority youths are involved somewhat more often in serious offenses and have more extensive prior records which, in turn, increase their likelihood of representation. The beta weights for race (black beta = −.065, Native American beta = −.051) are comparable to those for a prior record and a prior home removal disposition, suggesting a small but significant residual relationship between minority racial status and the appointment of counsel. Interestingly, the regression equation for Hennepin County, which includes juveniles' race, explains 17.5% of the variance, with most attributable to legal variables. This suggests a greater degree of formal legal rationality in the appointment decision in the most urban county than in any of the other settings examined (Tables 4-19 through 4-22, 6-9 through 6-11).

Table 7-9 reports the regression factors influencing the detention decision in Hennepin County. A comparison of the detention regression variables with those for both of the urban counties (Table 6-15) reveals many common features. An eventual home removal disposition, the seriousness of the present offense, and the presence of a prior record dominate both decisions. However, in Hennepin County, the fourth variable

**Table 7-9   Regression Model of Factors Influencing the Detention Decision Including Juvenile's Race (Hennepin County)**

| Independent Variables | Zero-Order r | Standardized Beta Coefficient | Multiple R | R² |
|---|---|---|---|---|
| Home Removal | −.297* | −.266* | .297 | .088 |
| Offense Severity | −.235* | −.176* | .341 | .117 |
| Prior Record | .168* | .081* | .361 | .131 |
| Black | .113* | .090* | .371 | .138 |
| Prior Secure Confinement Disposition | −.195* | −.069* | .375 | .141 |
| Native American | .029 | .046** | .378 | .143 |
| Secure Confinement Disposition | −.235* | .063*** | .380 | .144 |

*p < .001
**p < .01
***p < .05

to enter the regression equation is a juvenile's race (black beta = .090). This confirms the observation that, after controlling for the present offense and prior record, black juveniles in Hennepin County were being detained at higher rates than their white counterparts (Table 7-6). Indeed, comparing the betas indicates that a youth's race has a greater impact on the detention decision than does having a prior record of offenses or a prior training school commitment. The influence of being a Native American juvenile on the detention decision is about half of that for a black youth (beta = .046) but is still significant. Moreover, any residual influence of a juvenile's race on the detention decision after controlling for the present offense and prior record raises further troubling questions about the administration of this practice.

The final set of regression equations examine the impact of a juvenile's race on the dispositional decisions—out-of-home placement and secure confinement. A comparison of the regression equations for Hennepin County with those for the urban counties (Table 7-15) reveals that the same variables have comparable weights and account for about the same amount of variance. However, in the regression equations in Table 7-10, a juvenile's race is also associated with the decision to remove him or her from home. Although the effects of race are small compared with the other variables, they are still statistically significant. Moreover, while a juvenile's race is associated with more serious offenses (Table 7-1) and influences somewhat the initial decision to detain (Tables 7-6 and 7-9), even after controlling for differences in offenses and detention status,

**Table 7-10   Regression Model of Factors Influencing Out-of-Home Placement and Secure Confinement Dispositions Including Juvenile's Race (Hennepin County)**

| Independent Variables | Zero-Order r | Standardized Beta Coefficient | Multiple R | R² |
|---|---|---|---|---|
| | | **Out-of-Home Placement** | | |
| Prior Home Removal Disposition | .347* | .287* | .347 | .120 |
| Detention | −.297* | −.200* | .417 | .174 |
| Offense Severity | .239* | .125* | .448 | .200 |
| Representation | .217* | .094* | .455 | .207 |
| Number of Offenses at Disposition | −.103* | −.051** | .458 | .210 |
| Black | −.016 | .056** | .461 | .212 |
| Native American | −.006 | .037*** | .462 | .214 |
| | | **Secure Confinement** | | |
| Prior Secure Confinement Disposition | .354* | .284* | .354 | .126 |
| Offense Severity | .312* | .186* | .446 | .199 |
| Detention | −.235* | −.118* | .460 | .212 |
| Gender | .191* | .085* | .478 | .219 |
| Representation | .213* | .066* | .472 | .223 |
| Number of Offenses at Disposition | −.118* | −.057* | .475 | .226 |
| Age | −.099* | .053** | .478 | .229 |

*$p < .001$
**$p < .01$
***$p < .05$

minority youths remain at somewhat greater risk for removal from their homes. Somewhat surprisingly, there are no independent racial disparities in the decision to commit juveniles to secure institutions, although indirect racial differences in sentencing may be subsumed by the other variables with a racial component such as offenses, detention, and representation.

While these data provide some evidence of disparities in the detention and sentencing of minority youths, there are other possible explanations besides racial discrimination for which this study cannot account. Historically, juvenile court judges base their decisions on a host of individual characteristics of the offender. Because the SJIS data only include legal

variables, this study cannot control for many of the factors that the principle of individualized justice deems relevant—family status, socioeconomic status, clinical evaluations, "treatment needs," school progress,
employment status, and the like. Indeed, the differential access of white
and minority youth to private counsel provides an indirect indicator that
black offenders may be somewhat poorer (Table 7-2). While individualized social variables that correlate with race may account for some of the
racial differences in detention and out-of-home placement, it simply
raises under a different guise the propriety of individualizing sentences
on the basis of factors other than present offense and prior record when
doing so produces a disparate impact (Feld 1978, 1988b; Coffee 1978).

## GENDER AND JUVENILE JUSTICE
## ADMINISTRATION

The next analyses examine the relationships between youths' gender and
juvenile justice administration as another test of the contextual effects of
achieved versus ascribed characteristics. Table 7-11 reports the distribution of offenses by sex in the state and in urban, suburban, and rural
counties. For the state as a whole, approximately three-quarters (74.5%)
of delinquents were male and one-quarter (25.5%) were female. The urban counties petitioned a larger proportion of females (30.7%) than did
either the suburban (21.2%) or rural (23.2%) courts.

When the relationships between a juvenile's sex, offense, and locale
are analyzed two patterns emerge. First, in the state and in the urban,
suburban, and rural counties, delinquency is predominantly a male activity. In the felony offense categories, male offenders outnumber female
offenders by a 9 to 1 ratio; in the misdemeanor offense categories, males
predominate by about a 3 to 1 ratio. It is only in the status offense category that the sexes approach parity with about a 3 to 2 ratio of males to
females. Female offenders also have less extensive prior records than do
males. About 5% more girls than boys made their first appearances in
juvenile court with conversely fewer female recidivists. Based on present
offenses and prior records, females are far less delinquent than males.

Second, urban females are substantially more delinquent than their
suburban or rural counterparts. Compared with the girls in other parts of
the state, they are charged with larger proportions of criminal offenses,
including violence against the person as well as status offenses. A larger
proportion of urban girls also have prior records of delinquency; only
69.4% of urban girls made their first appearance as compared with
78.1% of suburban girls and 82.9% of rural ones. Earlier analyses reported relationships between present offense, prior record, rates of rep-

**Table 7-11  Offenses and Prior Referrals by Sex**

|  | Statewide | | Urban | | Suburban | | Rural | |
|---|---|---|---|---|---|---|---|---|
|  | Male | Female | Male | Female | Male | Female | Male | Female |
| **Overall (%)** | 74.5 | 25.5 | 69.3 | 30.7 | 78.8 | 21.2 | 76.8 | 23.2 |
| **N** | (12,806) | (4,385) | (4,348) | (1,925) | (2,898) | (780) | (5,560) | (1,680) |
| **Felony (%)** | 91.1 | 8.9 | 89.5 | 10.5 | 92.5 | 7.5 | 91.5 | 8.5 |
| Felony Offense Against Person (%) | 90.6 | 9.4 | 88.7 | 11.3 | 90.8 | 9.2 | 93.0 | 7.0 |
| Felony Offense Against Property (%) | 91.2 | 8.8 | 90.5 | 9.5 | 92.5 | 7.5 | 90.8 | 9.2 |
| **Misdemeanor (%)** | 76.2 | 23.8 | 71.8 | 28.2 | 78.9 | 21.1 | 78.6 | 21.4 |
| Minor Offense Against Person (%) | 72.7 | 27.3 | 68.6 | 31.4 | 76.1 | 23.9 | 75.3 | 24.7 |
| Minor Offense Against Property (%) | 76.3 | 23.7 | 73.2 | 26.8 | 79.3 | 20.7 | 77.0 | 23.0 |
| Other Delinquency (%) | 77.2 | 22.8 | 71.2 | 28.8 | 80.2 | 19.8 | 84.1 | 15.9 |
| **Status (%)** | 59.9 | 40.1 | 50.8 | 49.2 | 63.4 | 36.6 | 65.9 | 34.1 |
| **Prior Referrals** | | | | | | | | |
| 0 | 70.4 | 76.1 | 62.7 | 69.4 | 70.1 | 78.1 | 76.7 | 82.9 |
| 1–2 | 24.0 | 20.2 | 28.0 | 25.1 | 25.3 | 19.0 | 20.3 | 15.2 |
| 3–4 | 4.3 | 2.8 | 6.9 | 4.4 | 3.7 | 2.7 | 2.4 | 1.1 |
| 5+ | 1.3 | 0.9 | 2.4 | 1.2 | 0.9 | 0.3 | 0.6 | 0.8 |

resentation, detention, and dispositions (Tables 6-7 through 6-17). The differences in the distribution of offenses and prior records by gender suggest that boys and girls should differ in rates of representation, detention, and sentencing as well.

## Representation by Counsel and Sex of Juvenile

Table 7-12 reports the overall rates of representation for male and female delinquents by type of offense. While 45.3% of all juveniles in Minnesota were represented (Table 6-7), there was 46.7% representation for males and 41.1% representation for females. Because of the relationship between the seriousness of the offense and representation (Tables 6-7 through 6-11) and the distribution of offenses by sex (Table 7-11), the 5.6% disparity in representation does not necessarily indicate gender discrimination in the appointment of counsel.

Examining the relationships between offense, sex, and rates of representation reveals that a somewhat larger proportion of males than females charged with similar offenses are represented in most offense cat-

**Table 7-12    Rate of Representation by Counsel and Sex of Juvenile**

|  | Statewide | | Urban | | Suburban | | Rural | |
|---|---|---|---|---|---|---|---|---|
|  | Male | Female | Male | Female | Male | Female | Male | Female |
| **Overall (%)** | | | | | | | | |
| **Counsel** | 46.7 | 41.1 | 65.8 | 55.0 | 56.9 | 49.1 | 26.3 | 21.3 |
| **Felony (%)** | 66.4 | 62.4 | 83.2 | 80.4 | 68.1 | 65.0 | 50.4 | 40.6 |
| Felony Offense Against Person (%) | 78.1 | 69.5 | 89.4 | 84.4 | 76.9 | 53.3 | 64.6 | 50.0 |
| Felony Offense Against Property (%) | 63.2 | 60.3 | 81.0 | 78.7 | 65.6 | 68.9 | 47.4 | 39.3 |
| **Misdemeanor (%)** | 46.2 | 46.9 | 65.1 | 62.2 | 58.1 | 56.9 | 23.8 | 22.7 |
| Minor Offense Against Person (%) | 62.0 | 63.6 | 81.5 | 78.9 | 57.8 | 55.6 | 40.8 | 40.4 |
| Minor Offense Against Property (%) | 45.1 | 43.2 | 72.5 | 66.2 | 57.7 | 52.5 | 20.6 | 20.5 |
| Other Delinquency (%) | 43.8 | 48.4 | 50.9 | 52.4 | 59.1 | 68.8 | 27.1 | 23.9 |
| **Status (%)** | 27.8 | 30.5 | 48.5 | 42.4 | 34.8 | 32.3 | 13.0 | 16.9 |

egories. The interesting exceptions to this pattern occur in the categories of other delinquency, where more urban and suburban girls have counsel, and status offenses, where more rural girls are represented. As will be seen, these are the offenses for which larger proportions of girls are detained and eventually receive more severe sentences than do similarly situated boys. However, the urban, suburban, and rural regression equations for the appointment of counsel (Tables 6-9 through 6-11), control for the effect of these other variables and do not indicate any disparities in the appointment of counsel by gender.

## Pretrial Detention, Disposition, and Sex of Juvenile

Combining the relationship between offenses and detention (Table 6-14) with the offense patterns of male and female juveniles (Table 7-11) suggests that proportionately fewer girls than boys should be detained. And yet the regression equations for the detention decision (Tables 6-15 through 6-17) indicated that in all geographic locales, female juveniles were at greater risk of detention than their male counterparts. Table 7-13 reports on rates of detention for male and female overall and controls for offense in order to identify where the apparent gender disparity occurs.

In the state as a whole, even though females are involved in less serious delinquency and have less extensive prior records than male offenders (Table 7-11), larger proportions are detained (8.3% vs. 7.4%). The disproportional detention and sentencing of females charged with minor

**Table 7-13    Rate of Detention by Sex of Juvenile**

|  | Statewide | | Urban | | Suburban | | Rural | |
|---|---|---|---|---|---|---|---|---|
|  | Male | Female | Male | Female | Male | Female | Male | Female |
| **Overall (%)** **Detention** | 7.4 | 8.3 | 13.5 | 11.7 | 4.4 | 6.3 | 4.2 | 5.4 |
| **Felony (%)** | 14.6 | 18.1 | 25.9 | 26.6 | 7.2 | 9.1 | 9.7 | 15.0 |
| Felony Offense Against Person (%) | 24.2 | 25.0 | 38.0 | 34.4 | 11.3 | 11.8 | 17.7 | 20.0 |
| Felony Offense Against Property (%) | 12.0 | 16.1 | 21.7 | 23.4 | 6.1 | 8.2 | 8.0 | 14.1 |
| **Misdemeanor (%)** | 6.0 | 8.1 | 11.1 | 12.4 | 3.8 | 4.2 | 3.0 | 4.8 |
| Minor Offense Against Person (%) | 11.6 | 10.7 | 17.8 | 15.3 | 7.4 | 7.3 | 7.5 | 5.7 |
| Minor Offense Against Property (%) | 5.7 | 6.9 | 12.4 | 12.4 | 3.5 | 3.4 | 2.5 | 4.2 |
| Other Delinquency (%) | 5.1 | 9.4 | 7.7 | 11.7 | 3.1 | 4.8 | 3.0 | 6.5 |
| **Status (%)** | 3.2 | 7.1 | 6.5 | 8.7 | 1.2 | 8.5 | 1.9 | 4.7 |

and status offenses has been reported in several studies (Pawlak 1977; Sarri 1974; Chesney-Lind 1977, 1988a, 1988b). Comparing the rates of detention by sex (Table 7-13) with the overall rates of detention (Table 6-14) indicates that the disparities in detention occur for females in all offense categories *except* minor offenses against the person. The differences in rates of detention are most conspicuous for the girls charged with the least serious misdeeds like other delinquency and status offenses. Even though suburban and rural counties detain smaller proportions of all juveniles overall (Table 6-14), they also detain disproportionately more female juveniles.

Chapter Four confirmed a detrimental relationship between pretrial detention and dispositions (Tables 4-27 through 4-30). It also reported that smaller proportions of juveniles charged with less serious, albeit far more numerous, offenses were detained (Table 4-15), and that when those juveniles were detained, they experienced considerably higher rates of home removal and secure confinement than did youths charged with minor offenses who were not detained (compare Table 4-6 with 4-17). Chapter Seven reveals that girls are detained at greater rates than boys, especially for minor offenses.

Table 7-14 examines whether the gender disparities in detention affect subsequent sentencing practices as well. For the state overall, as well as in the urban, suburban, and rural counties separately, proportionately fewer females than males are removed from their homes or incarcerated.

The disparities are most striking for the use of secure confinement where, proportionately, nearly twice as many males (12.6%) as females (6.7%) are incarcerated. Of course, the male bias in incarceration simply reflects the male predominance in felony offenses, which have the highest rates of secure confinement (Table 6-12). In addition, the availability of fewer bedspaces for female offenders in Minnesota's juvenile institutions constrains judges' dispositional options.

While the overall rate of home removal sentences for females is lower than that of males (16.5% vs. 19.2%), the rates of out-of-home place-

**Table 7-14    Disposition (Home/Secure) by Sex**

|  | Statewide | | Urban | | Suburban | | Rural | |
|---|---|---|---|---|---|---|---|---|
|  | Male | Female | Male | Female | Male | Female | Male | Female |
| **Overall** | | | | | | | | |
| % Home | 19.2 | 16.5 | 26.3 | 18.7 | 17.7 | 16.6 | 14.3 | 13.7 |
| % Secure | 12.6 | 6.7 | 18.6 | 7.1 | 9.8 | 6.2 | 9.4 | 6.2 |
| **Felony** | | | | | | | | |
| % Home | 33.0 | 26.2 | 43.7 | 29.6 | 24.8 | 10.8 | 29.3 | 32.1 |
| % Secure | 24.1 | 12.9 | 35.2 | 15.7 | 14.5 | 3.1 | 20.9 | 16.0 |
| Felony Offense Against Person | | | | | | | | |
| % Home | 40.8 | 30.2 | 48.0 | 38.7 | 35.1 | 17.6 | 36.4 | 26.7 |
| % Secure | 27.2 | 20.6 | 38.0 | 29.0 | 15.5 | 5.9 | 23.6 | 20.0 |
| Felony Offense Against Property | | | | | | | | |
| % Home | 30.9 | 25.0 | 42.3 | 26.0 | 21.9 | 8.3 | 27.8 | 33.0 |
| % Secure | 23.2 | 10.6 | 34.2 | 10.4 | 14.2 | 2.1 | 20.3 | 15.4 |
| **Misdemeanor** | | | | | | | | |
| % Home | 16.9 | 16.2 | 22.4 | 18.9 | 16.4 | 16.3 | 12.6 | 12.7 |
| % Secure | 11.4 | 8.5 | 16.0 | 9.2 | 9.6 | 9.0 | 8.6 | 7.4 |
| Minor Offense Against Person | | | | | | | | |
| % Home | 24.1 | 18.5 | 27.5 | 20.3 | 21.1 | 20.0 | 22.3 | 14.3 |
| % Secure | 15.2 | 10.7 | 16.7 | 11.0 | 12.0 | 12.7 | 16.1 | 8.6 |
| Minor Offense Against Property | | | | | | | | |
| % Home | 16.0 | 13.9 | 23.1 | 16.7 | 14.8 | 12.5 | 12.1 | 12.3 |
| % Secure | 11.3 | 7.7 | 18.3 | 9.3 | 8.4 | 6.0 | 8.4 | 7.2 |
| Other Delinquency | | | | | | | | |
| % Home | 16.5 | 19.8 | 20.1 | 21.1 | 18.1 | 24.0 | 11.4 | 13.7 |
| % Secure | 10.5 | 9.3 | 13.0 | 8.5 | 11.6 | 14.4 | 7.1 | 7.8 |
| **Status** | | | | | | | | |
| % Home | 10.6 | 15.3 | 17.6 | 17.0 | 10.6 | 18.4 | 6.5 | 12.2 |
| % Secure | 3.8 | 3.4 | 6.8 | 3.6 | 3.1 | 2.8 | 2.2 | 3.5 |

ment of female offenders consistently exceed those of males statewide for the least serious offenses, other delinquency (19.8% vs. 16.5%) and status offenses (15.3% vs. 10.6%). These were also the offense categories for which proportionately more female offenders than males were detained (Table 7-13). The disproportionate detention and home removal of female offenders charged with other delinquency and status offenses may reflect "double standards" and "paternalistic" attitudes for which scholars have criticized juvenile courts extensively (Chesney-Lind 1973, 1977; Anderson 1976; Armstrong 1977; Datesman and Scarpitti 1980).

## REGRESSING OUT-OF-HOME PLACEMENT AND SECURE CONFINEMENT DISPOSITIONS ON INDEPENDENT VARIABLES

The preceding analyses focused primarily on bivariate relationships between selected variables while controlling for the effects of one or more other variables. The final analyses reported in Tables 7-15 through 7-18 use multiple regression procedures to analyze the relative contributions of the independent variables to the eventual sentences juveniles receive in various geographic locales. The regression analytic strategy and the coding of the variables is the same as in Chapters Four and Six.

The tables report the zero-order correlation coefficient (r) between each independent variable and the dependent variable, the standardized beta coefficient (beta), which expresses the strength of the relationship between each independent variable and the dependent variable once the effects of the other variables are taken into account, the multiple regression correlation coefficient (R), and $R^2$. In addition to the other independent variables used in the earlier regression analyses, the statewide regression equation (Table 7-18) includes an urban "dummy" variable (0 = urban; 1 = nonurban).

Table 7-15 reports the regression equations for home removal and secure confinement in urban counties. A previous home removal or institutional commitment explains most of the variance in the current home removal or secure placement sentences. Pretrial detention, a prior record, and the seriousness of the present offense also influence both decisions. Chapter Five reported that the number of offenses at dispositions indicated a more serious case (Table 5-1), which affects urban sentencing practices as well. Even though the urban counties have the highest rates of representation, 62.6%, the presence of an attorney is an aggravating factor at sentencing, accounting for 1.7% of the variance in home removal and .4% of the variance in institutional confinement. Finally, being older and male are associated with the decision to institutionalize.

**Table 7-15   Regression Model of Factors Influencing Out-of-Home Placement and Secure Confinement Dispositions (Urban Counties)**

| Independent Variables | Zero-Order r | Standardized Beta Coefficient | Multiple R | R² |
|---|---|---|---|---|
| | | **Out-of-Home Placement** | | |
| Prior Home Removal Disposition | .415* | .334* | .415 | .172 |
| Detention | −.262* | −.162* | .456 | .208 |
| Representation | .219* | .106* | .474 | .225 |
| Offense Severity | .166* | .086* | .483 | .233 |
| Number of Offenses at Disposition | −.105* | −.077* | .489 | .239 |
| Prior Record | −.296* | −.047 | .490 | .240 |
| | | **Secure Confinement** | | |
| Prior Secure Confinement Disposition | .394* | .314* | .394 | .155 |
| Offense Severity | .239* | .155* | .448 | .200 |
| Detention | −.197* | −.104* | .461 | .212 |
| Number of Offenses at Disposition | −.108* | −.066* | .465 | .217 |
| Representation | .187* | .065* | .470 | .221 |
| Gender | .146* | .055* | .474 | .224 |
| Prior Record | −.268* | −.066* | .477 | .227 |
| Age | −.055* | −.040* | .478 | .229 |

*$p < .001$
**$p < .01$
***$p < .05$

Table 7-16 presents the regression statistics for out-of-home placement and secure confinement of juveniles in suburban counties. A prior home removal disposition and pretrial detention status are the most influential determinants of a current home removal. Prior secure confinement, an attorney, the present offense, and pretrial detention are the most significant determinants of the decision to commit a youth to an institution. Pretrial detention exerts a stronger influence on out-of-home placement than on secure confinement (out-of-home beta = −.163, institutional beta = −.036).

In the rural counties, Table 7-17, a previous sentence removing or confining a juvenile, pretrial detention, the seriousness of the offense, and

**Table 7-16   Regression Model of Factors Influencing Out-of-Home Placement and Secure Confinement Dispositions (Suburban Counties)**

| Independent Variables | Zero-Order r | Standardized Beta Coefficient | Multiple R | R² |
|---|---|---|---|---|
| | | **Out-of-Home Placement** | | |
| Prior Home Removal Disposition | .443* | .418* | .443 | .196 |
| Detention | −.203* | −.163* | .474 | .225 |
| Counsel | .157* | .056* | .478 | .229 |
| Offense Severity | .083* | .045** | .480 | .231 |
| | | **Secure Confinement** | | |
| Prior Secure Confinement Disposition | .468* | .432* | .468 | .219 |
| Counsel | .165* | .066* | .476 | .226 |
| Offense Severity | .090* | .060* | .480 | .230 |
| Detention | −.077* | −.036*** | .481 | .231 |
| Prior Record | −.269* | −.040*** | .482 | .232 |

*p < .001
**p < .01
***p < .05

the presence of an attorney explain most of the variance in dispositions. Again, the previous sentence is clearly the dominant influence (out-of-home beta = .346; institutional beta = .359) followed by pretrial detention. Despite the differences in rates of representation in urban, suburban, and rural counties, a comparison of the beta weights for the effects of attorney on dispositions indicates that their presence exerts about the same deleterious effect in all types of counties.

In the rural counties, there is a weak but significant relationship between gender and the home removal decision; rural female juveniles are more at risk for out-of-home placement than are their male counterparts. Although female offenders commit less serious offenses and have less extensive prior records than the males (Table 7-11), larger proportions are detained (Table 7-13). Moreover, there is a clear and consistent gender bias in the detention decisions in all geographic locales (Tables 6-15 through 6-17). Table 7-17 indicates that even after controlling for the effects of gender bias at detention, rural girls are still somewhat more likely to be removed from their homes than are boys.

This research corroborates other studies that report gender biases in detaining and sentencing minor female offenders. The association between gender and geography suggests that ascriptive characteristics may be more influential in traditional, informal juvenile courts than in the more formal, urban ones. Or, it may be that the greater rates of detention and home removal of female compared to male juveniles charged with minor offenses may reflect a "family sponsorship" effect (Matza 1964). For some reason, parents of rural female juveniles charged with minor delinquencies may be less willing than those of male juveniles similarly charged to have the child at home, either prior to trial or following adjudication. What initially appears as judicial gender discrimination at detention and disposition may actually reflect judicial responsiveness to parental preferences. However, this explanation is tempered somewhat by recalling that rural parents refer proportionally the fewest juveniles for other delinquency and status offenses of any parents (Table 6-5).

The most striking feature of these regression equations is their substantial similarity despite the major differences in sentencing practices in different geographic locales. Recall that urban courts removed substantially larger proportions of juveniles from their homes and institutionalized them than did the suburban or rural courts (Table 6-12). Controlling for the present offense and prior record simultaneously, urban courts sentenced similarly situated juveniles more severely than did suburban or rural judges (Table 6-13). Despite these pronounced differences in overall severity of sentencing, the same variables enter the urban, suburban, and rural regression equations in approximately the same order, with about the same beta weights, and account for virtually the same amount of variance in all types of counties. In urban counties, the regression equations account for 24.0% of the variance in home removal and 22.9% of the variance in institutionalization. In suburban counties, they explain 23.1% of the home removal variance and 23.2% of the variance in institutionalization. And, in rural counties, they account for 24.8% of the home removal variance and 23.0% of the variance in institutionalization.

Table 7-18 reports the regression variables for juvenile court sentencing decisions for the entire state. The data and analyses in Table 7-18 are virtually identical to those in Table 4-27, except that Table 7-18 also includes an urban "dummy" variable to account for geographic variations in sentencing. The independent variables, including the urban dummy, account for 24.5% of the variance in home removal and 22.6% of the variance in institutionalization. A previous sentence removing a juvenile from the home is the most powerful determinant of the present decision to remove from home (beta = .367). Similarly, a previous secure confinement sentence is the most powerful determinant of the present decision to incarcerate (beta = .354). In addition, the urban dummy variable en-

**Table 7-17   Regression Model of Factors Influencing Out-of-Home Placement and Secure Confinement Dispositions (Rural Counties)**

| Independent Variables | Zero-Order r | Standardized Beta Coefficient | Multiple R | R² |
|---|---|---|---|---|
| | | **Out-of-Home Placement** | | |
| Prior Home Removal Disposition | .401* | .346* | .401 | .161 |
| Detention | −.279* | −.201* | .463 | .214 |
| Offense Severity | .192* | .098* | .481 | .232 |
| Representation | .227* | .105* | .492 | .242 |
| Number of Offenses at Disposition | −.138* | −.073* | .497 | .247 |
| Gender | .003 | −.029** | .498 | .248 |
| | | **Secure Confinement** | | |
| Prior Secure Confinement Disposition | .400* | .359* | .400 | .160 |
| Detention | −.223* | −.158* | .442 | .195 |
| Offense Severity | .203* | .126* | .467 | .218 |
| Representation | .194* | .081* | .474 | .225 |
| Number of Offenses at Disposition | −.137* | −.063* | .478 | .229 |
| Age | −.017 | −.033** | .479 | .230 |

*$p < .001$
**$p < .01$
***$p < .05$

ters the regression equations for both the home removal and secure confinement dispositions. Recall that more urban juveniles committed serious offenses and had lengthier prior records (Table 6-5), a larger proportion were held in pretrial detention (Table 6-14), and they had higher rates of representation (Table 6-7). After controlling for these other urban-related variables that aggravate sentencing, simply being tried in an urban court exerts an additional, independent effect on the severity of sentences. There is "justice by geography."

The overall findings in this study are consistent with other research on juvenile court sentencing practices. Marshall and Thomas (1983:57) report that careful measurement of legal and extralegal variables "account for only a little more than a quarter of the variance in the judicial dispositions"; Thomas and Fitch (1975:75) report that "the levels of as-

**Table 7-18   Regression Model of Factors Influencing Out-of-Home Placement and Secure Confinement Dispositions (Statewide)**

| Independent Variables | Zero-Order r | Standardized Beta Coefficient | Multiple R | $R^2$ |
|---|---|---|---|---|
| | | **Out-of-Home Placement** | | |
| Prior Home Removal Disposition | .422* | .367* | .422 | .178 |
| Detention | −.265* | −.174* | .467 | .218 |
| Counsel | .229* | .103* | .483 | .233 |
| Offense Severity | .157* | .076* | .490 | .240 |
| Number of Offenses at Disposition | −.084* | −.061* | .494 | .244 |
| Urban | | .023* | .494 | .244 |
| Age | .039* | .018** | .495 | .245 |
| | | **Secure Confinement** | | |
| Prior Secure Confinement Disposition | .414* | .354* | .414 | .171 |
| Offense Severity | .191* | .122* | .445 | .198 |
| Detention | .194* | −.111* | .462 | .214 |
| Counsel | .197* | .073* | .469 | .220 |
| Number of Offenses at Disposition | −.086* | −.053* | .471 | .222 |
| Prior Record | −.260* | −.037* | .473 | .223 |
| Age | −.023** | −.033* | .474 | .224 |
| Urban | | .032* | .475 | .225 |
| Gender | .080* | .023** | .475 | .226 |

*$p < .001$
**$p < .01$
***$p < .05$

sociation between both objective and personal variables and case dispositions are of weak to moderate magnitude, suggesting that no single factor exerts a major independent influence on judicial decisionmaking"; and Horowitz and Wasserman (1980:411) conclude that even inclusion of social background variables with offense variables only accounts for one-quarter of the variance. While legal variables exhibit a stronger statistical relationship with dispositions than do social variables, a very substantial amount of the variation in sentencing juveniles cannot be explained. Generally, the present offense and prior record—for which a prior disposition often serves as a surrogate in this study—are the best predictors of dispositions. However, they, too, only account for about one-quarter of the variance in sentencing (Table 7-18, out-of-home $R^2$ = .245; institutional $R^2$ = .226). Commentators have observed, with respect to the large amount of unexplained variation, that "the juvenile justice process is so ungoverned by procedural rules and so haphazard in the attribution of relevancy to any particular variables or set of variables that judicial dispositions are very commonly the product of an arbitrary and capricious decision-making process" (Marshall and Thomas 1983:57). Moreover, while this study could not explain the determinants of pretrial detention, its pronounced negative effect on subsequent sentences introduces another "arbitrary and capricious" factor into the dispositional process. Finally, the cumulative, adverse effects of representation and urban locale on subsequent sentences raises further questions about the justice of the dispositional process.

The absence of any powerful, explanatory relationship between the legal variables and dispositions may be interpreted as true "individualized justice"; that is, every child is the recipient of a unique disposition tailored to his or her individual needs and social circumstances without regard to the present offense or prior record. "Given the philosophy of the juvenile court system, this finding might be interpreted as quite positive in the sense that it could imply that judges consider a broad spectrum of both legal and social variables in their attempt to individualize decisions" (Thomas and Cage 1977:244).

An equally plausible interpretation, however, is that there is no rationale to dispositional decision making; it consists of little more than hunch, guesswork, and hopes, constrained marginally by the youth's present offense, prior record, and previous dispositions. In such a case, individualization is simply a euphemism for subjectivity, arbitrariness, and discrimination:

> [T]hese findings also suggest the possibility that those who share various social characteristics will be treated in a significantly different fashion from those drawn from other categories in the population; those against whom complaints are filed by one type of complainant will be treated differently than those who have engaged in comparable behavior, but whose offense has been brought to the attention of social control agencies by a different complainant; and those who come before one judge will be disposed of differently than those who appear before another judge, regardless of who they are or what their present and past offense record might be. (Thomas and Cage 1977:244)

A system of justice in which the most powerful explanatory legal variables—present offense and prior record—typically account for only about 25% of the variance in sentencing remains a highly discretionary and, perhaps, discriminatory one. To the extent that the data permit inferences of bias, female juveniles in all settings are at greater risk of pretrial detention, which prejudices later dispositions, and urban black youths and rural female youths are at greater risk of home removal than are other similarly situated juveniles. At the same time, the large amount of unexplained variance means that there is substantial attenuation between a youth's criminal behavior and the severity of the disposition; minor offenders can receive much more severe dispositions than serious offenders. Similarly situated offenders—defined in terms of their present offense or prior record—can receive markedly dissimilar dispositions depending upon the county in which they are tried, the judge before whom they appear, the manner in which their guilt is determined, or their race or gender. The desirability of perpetuating such subjective and idiosyncratic detention and sentencing of similarly situated offenders goes to the heart of the juvenile court as an institution. The next chapter examines the implications of these findings for juvenile justice administration.

## NOTES

1. In Hennepin County, a juvenile's race is reported in 79.8% of all petitions, or 3,385 cases. Thus, the data reported here constitute a very large subset of the total cases in the county. Comparing this "race" subsample with the county totals suggests that it is representative; that is, the cases missing information on race do not appear to introduce any systematic bias. For example, for the entire Hennepin County juvenile court population (4,243) and the "race sample," the proportion of offenses are respectively: felony against person, 4.1% and 4.4%; felony against property, 12.9% and 13.3%; minor offense against person, 5.2% and 5.5%; minor offense against property, 26.8% and 28.1%; other delinquency, 21.8% and 20.6%; and status, 29.0% and 28.0%. Similarly, for Hennepin County as a whole and for the "race sample," the proportions of juveniles with priors are: 0 = 66.7% and 66.5%; 1–2 = 26.1% and 26.0%; 3–4 = 5.6% and 5.8%; and 5+ = 1.6% and 1.7%.

2. These proportions are nearly identical with the entire Hennepin County juvenile court population in which only 47.7% of youths had attorneys, 10.4% had private attorneys, and 37.3% had public defenders.

————————————————————

# chapter eight

# VARIETIES OF JUVENILE JUSTICE

Lawyers, Procedural Formality,
and Juvenile Justice Administration

The idealized portrayal of the traditional juvenile court is one of procedural informality in the quest of the goals of treatment and rehabilitation
(Mack 1909). Historically, the predominant focus on characteristics of
the young offender fostered judicial discretion and organizational diversity rather than uniformity.

> Since the court intended to rehabilitate the individual delinquent, and
> not primarily to exact the just measure of the law, the judge's hands
> could not be tied with procedural requirements. But translated into
> practice, this grant of authority meant that juvenile courts would be
> as different from each other as judges were different from each
> other. . . . Without set rules of evidence, without fixed guidelines,
> and, in many cases, without the prospect of appeal, the court quite
> literally had the delinquent at its mercy. The person of the judge him-
> self assumed an altogether novel significance. . . . [A]ny attempt to
> analyze the workings of a given court demanded a lengthy evaluation
> of its judge (Rothman 1980:238)

Evaluations of contemporary juvenile courts continue to emphasize the
diversity of judges and the broad legal framework that allows for "very
individualistic interpretation and clearly different application" of laws
(Rubin 1985:7; Kfoury 1987).

Notwithstanding its original rehabilitative and informal design, however, the juvenile court is an institution in transition (Feld 1991). Recent

changes in juvenile court jurisdiction, sentencing practices, and procedures reflect ambivalence about the role of juvenile courts and the control
of children. Increasingly, juvenile courts converge procedurally and substantively with adult criminal courts.

There is a strong, nationwide movement, both in theory and in practice, repudiating therapeutic individualized dispositions in favor of punitive sentences (Feld 1987, 1988b, 1991). In the decades since the Supreme
Court's *McKeiver* decision denied juveniles the right to a jury trial, many
states have adopted "designated felony" and "serious offender" sentencing statutes, determinate sentencing guidelines, mandatory minimum
sentencing laws, or correctional release guidelines (Feld 1988b). These
formal legislative and administrative changes and actual judicial dispositional practices eliminate many of the differences between juvenile and
adult sentencing policies. Juvenile codes' purpose clauses have been
amended to emphasize accountability and responsibility rather than therapy (Feld 1988b). Court decisions affirming the legitimacy of punishment
in juvenile courts eliminate even rhetorical support for rehabilitation (*In
re D.F.B.*, 430 N.W.2d 476 [Minn. Ct. App. 1988]; *State ex rel. D.D.H.
v. Dostert*, 269 S.E.2d 401 [W.Va. 1980]; *In re Seven Minors*, 664 P.2d
947 [Nev. 1983]). As a result, "the purposes of the juvenile process have
become more punitive, its procedures formalistic, adversarial and public,
and the consequences of conviction much more harsh" (*In re Javier A.*,
159 Cal. App. 3d 913, 963 [1984]). All these changes contradict *Mc-
Keiver*'s premise that therapeutic juvenile courts operate in a child's "best
interests," that youths should be treated differently than adults and, especially, that they require fewer procedural safeguards.

This research provides a comprehensive empirical description and
analysis of juvenile justice administration. It raises a number of disturbing
and troubling questions about the quality of "justice" in juvenile courts
in Minnesota and, by implication, in many other states. The sociolegal
analyses and empirical findings bear on a number of important juvenile
justice policy issues. What degree of county and judicial diversity in pretrial detention and sentencing is tolerable or desirable within a nominally
statewide juvenile justice system? How should issues of racial or gender
disparity in detention and sentencing be addressed? Should explicit and
objective offense criteria be adopted to limit the initial use and subsequent
impact of pretrial detention? Should "in/out" — commitment and release — and "durational" sentencing guidelines be used in juvenile courts
to reduce idiosyncratic and geographical sentencing disparities? What
can be done to improve the mechanisms for delivering legal services to
juveniles, especially in rural counties? What legal standards should be
used to assess the validity of waivers of counsel, especially those by

younger juveniles? What can be done to eliminate the impact of prior, uncounseled convictions on subsequent sentencing of youths both as juveniles and as adults? Finally, as juvenile courts pursue goals of formal legal rationality and social control, and converge procedurally and substantively with adult criminal courts, is there any reason to retain a separate juvenile court whose only distinguishing characteristics are procedures under which no adult would consent to be tried (Feld 1984, 1988b, 1991).

## VARIETIES OF JUVENILE JUSTICE

Although the same juvenile code and court rules of procedure apply, Chapter Four identified procedural variations and Chapter Six revealed substantial geographic diversity—"justice by geography"—in the operation of juvenile courts in Minnesota. Kempf, Decker, and Bing's (1990:118) recent examination of juvenile justice administration in Missouri made very similar findings.

> The results of this study show differential processing within two distinct court systems operating in Missouri juvenile justice. One court type is rural and the other is primarily urban. . . . Rural courts typically are guided by one judge who holds the position for several years where the majority of decisions are made by one chief juvenile officer. Rural courts rarely have separate detention facilities, and have less access to local treatment facilities. Decisions are made individually, that is, on a case by case basis, in rural courts. In urban courts the judges rotate to other types of courts frequently. Different staff are responsible at different stages in the process. Decision making is guided more often by written standards, but policies still enable discretionary choices. Urban courts operate their own facilities, and have greater access to both home and residential placement services. These two types of courts function by different standards as well. Rural courts seem to adhere to traditional, pre-Gault, juvenile court *parens patriae* criteria in their handling of youths. Urban courts appear more legalistic in orientation and process cases more according to offense criteria.

These recurring findings of extensive intrastate variations in rates of representation, and detention and sentencing practices raise important issues for juvenile courts.

The substantive and procedural differences in juvenile courts relate consistently to urban, suburban, and rural social structural variations (Table 6-1). Urban courts operate in milieus that provide fewer mechanisms for informal social control. While there are proportionally fewer children and families with children in the urban counties than in the suburban or rural ones, there are more disrupted urban families. The urban counties have more racial heterogeneity and less population stability than the suburban or rural counties. As contrasted with the suburban or rural counties, the urban counties are more diverse and less well integrated and cohesive communities that place greater emphasis on formal, rather than informal, mechanisms of social control.

The geographic and social structural influences on formal versus informal means of control results in extensive variation in juvenile justice administration. The urban courts received a larger proportion of juveniles in all offense categories in relation to their youth population (Tables 6-3 and 6-4). They threw a broader net of social control that encompassed more troublesome youths in the community. Compared with suburban or rural courts, urban courts received a larger proportion of referrals from nonpolice sources, particularly probation officers and schools (Table 6-5). The diversity of urban referral sources reflects a greater reliance on a more inclusive network of formal social control compared with the suburban or rural courts. By contrast, the suburban courts, with the lowest overall rate of juvenile court referrals, screened cases more selectively and focused more on serious offenders and less on status offenders. Perhaps parental affluence and stability, relative to the urban or rural counties, enabled parents and court intake personnel to develop informal, alternative dispositions in lieu of formal court intervention for less serious suburban offenders. Finally, the rural courts dealt with the smallest proportions of juveniles charged with serious crimes and the largest proportion charged with status offenses.

As a result of geographic differences in youthful criminality, referral sources, and prepetition screening, the responses of the respective courts differed. Urban courts intervened more extensively in the lives of younger juveniles, especially status offenders (43.0%), as contrasted with the suburban (19.9%) or rural (15.7%) courts (Table 6-6). Conversely, suburban and rural courts processed more young serious offenders and older status offenders. The differential age and offense distribution suggests that in nonurban settings serious crime, especially by younger juveniles, requires an immediate response whereas for less serious offenses rural juveniles must exhaust informal community alternatives before the invocation of formal court processes.

Representation by counsel provides an indicator of a court's formality or due-process orientation. While the majority of youths in Minnesota appeared in juvenile courts without counsel (45.3%), there was geographic diversity in representation. The highest rates of representation occurred in the urban courts (62.6%), followed closely by the suburban courts (55.2%), while the rural courts provided only about one-quarter (25.1%) of delinquents with lawyers.

The differential presence of counsel suggests basic differences in court orientation — a due process or "formal rationality" model of justice as opposed to a traditional "substantive rationality" approach to juvenile justice. Quite apart from geographic or social structural variation, Chapter Four confirmed that justice was administered very differently in juvenile courts in which lawyers appeared regularly (94.5% representation rate), occasionally (46.8%), or seldom (19.3%). Chapter Four categorized juvenile courts based on the availability of attorneys, and found that the courts in high representation counties and low representation counties differed significantly in their "status offender orientation" (Stapleton, Aday, and Ito 1982:553). The high representation counties handled about 10% more juveniles charged with criminal offenses and correspondingly fewer status offenders than did the low representation counties (20.9% versus 30.5% status offenses, Table 4-1). As with urban formality, the formal procedures associated with higher levels of representation apparently are also associated with greater severity in sentencing practices. After controlling for differences in offense patterns, the judges in the procedurally formal, high representation counties imposed more severe sentences than did their counterparts in low representation counties, removing from their homes or confining almost twice as many youths (Tables 4-6 and 4-12). The judges in the high representation counties also appear to rely upon and reinforce the authority of their professional staff to a greater extent than do those in the low representation counties. For example, probation officers in the high representation counties refer substantially more cases than do their counterparts in low representation counties (Table 4-2), and those referrals result in more serious dispositions than might otherwise be expected (Table 4-6). The juvenile courts in the high representation counties detain proportionally more youths than do those in the low representation counties, and these disparities in detention increase in significance as the seriousness of the offenses declines (Table 4-15).

A relationship between procedural formality and the severity of sanctions prevailed whether the higher rates of representation were associated with urbanism, as in Chapter Six, or the presence of lawyers per se, as in Chapter Four. The more formal courts, where lawyers appeared routinely, sentenced juveniles more severely than did the informal courts where the presence of lawyers was the exception, although lawyers were an aggravating factor in sentencing in all settings. Chapter Six provided additional support for the relationship between procedural formality and dispositional severity. The urban courts sentenced youths charged with the same types of present offense more severely than did the suburban or rural courts (Table 6-12). Controlling simultaneously for the present offense and prior record (Table 6-13), the pattern of urban severity remained. The reliance on formal control and more severe intervention was also reflected in urban courts' greater use of pretrial detention (Table 6-14). Finally, the regression equations for sentencing decisions indicated that the urban (Table 7-15), suburban (Table 7-16), and rural courts (Table 7-17) employed similar "frames of relevance" and regarded the same substantive legal variables in much the same way. Despite this substantive similarity, however, simply being tried in an urban court resulted in more severe consequences (Table 7-18). And, despite the general presence of counsel in urban settings, attorneys were still an aggravating factor at sentencing (Table 7-15). Other research also reports that urbanism exerts an independent contextual influence on the severity of sentencing adults (Meyers and Talarico 1986, 1987) and juveniles (Kempf, Decker, and Bing 1990).

Finding "justice by geography" as well as substantial judicial diversity vastly complicates the tasks of criminologists. As this research demonstrates, there is both a theoretical and empirical relationship between variations in social structure and juvenile justice administration. Studies that analyze and interpret aggregated data without accounting for procedural, contextual, and structural characteristics, or intrastate variations, may systematically mislead and obscure rather than clarify. Both theoretically and operationally, further research is necessary to refine the relationships between social structure and justice administration. What structural features influence a juvenile court's procedural and substantive orientation? How does the local culture foster a traditional or due-process orientation? How do the roles of counsel operating in these different types of sociolegal settings differ?

Finding that juvenile courts are highly variable, rather than uniform, also has important implications for juvenile justice policy. Recent trends in juvenile justice which emphasize "punishment" over rehabilitation are associated with a corresponding increase in procedural formality (Feld 1984, 1987, 1988b). What is the relationship between procedural formality and sentencing severity? Does greater urban crime engender more punitive responses, which then require more formal procedural safeguards as a prerequisite? Or, does greater urban bureaucratization lead to more formal procedural safeguards, which then enable judges to exact a greater toll than they otherwise might? Increases or perceived increases in urban crime may foster a "war-on-crime" mentality that places immense pressures on the justice system to "get tough." As evidenced by the data on racial disparities in detention and sentencing practices (Tables 7-9 and 7-10), urban racial diversity may foster a more repressive response to crimes by "those people" than in more homogeneous rural settings. While Minnesota traditionally favored a progressive, rehabilitative approach to many social ills, urban formality and punitiveness may reflect a more recent trend in which the ethic of care and treatment is subordinated to securing social order.

What are the comparative costs and benefits of formal versus informal dispute resolution in juvenile courts? While the formal urban courts imposed the most severe sentences, the suburban courts were nearly as formal yet sentenced almost as leniently as did the rural courts. Although the relationship between formality and severity is troubling, an uncritical embrace of the traditional, informal juvenile court does not necessarily follow. In the rural juvenile courts, female juveniles are processed differently and more severely than are either rural males or female offenders in other settings. Despite the rural girls' less serious present offenses or prior records, larger proportions of them were detained (Table 7-13) and removed from their homes (Tables 7-14 and 7-17) than other youths in other contexts. Does rural "substantive justice" necessarily connote gender bias and the application of a paternalistic double standard for which informal juvenile courts are often criticized?

The policy choices between more or less formal juvenile justice are neither simple nor straightforward. Moreover, if a court's practices are rooted in its social structure, then simply amending laws may not produce the desired changes. While diversity rather than uniformity historically characterized juvenile courts, whether such extensive local variation should continue or be encouraged is questionable (Kempf, Decker, and Bing 1990). Should a system of laws and court rules of procedure be applied generally and uniformly throughout the state? Or should local norms and values influence the imposition of sanctions such that youths convicted of similar offenses receive widely disparate consequences depending upon the locale in which their case is heard? If formal legal guidelines are adopted to structure discretionary decisions, will they reduce the severity of urban courts' intervention or increase the severity of rural courts? Finally, since these decisions currently are being made de facto by the cumulative decisions of individual judges on an idiosyncratic basis behind closed doors without public and political debate or scrutiny, shouldn't the choices between greater or lesser formality and justice be made publicly and explicitly by the legislature via statutes or by the state supreme court through its rules of procedure?

Chapter Three documents substantial variation among states in the delivery of legal services and juvenile justice administration. Chapters Four and Six demonstrate that within a single state's juvenile justice system, there are substantial differences in offense screening, detention and sentencing practices, and in the role of counsel in justice administration. While diversity rather than uniformity traditionally characterized juvenile justice, the continued justifiability of such extensive local variation is highly questionable. Answering this question, however, depends upon additional research on the determinants and impact of diversity. This, in turn, requires much more information than is currently required or collected by most states' automated data systems. A few states' juvenile court information systems routinely collect information on a host of important legal and sociodemographic variables such as family status, school performance, use of weapons, injury to victims, and the like (NJCDA 1984, 1986b). Since this type of information is already collected and included in a juvenile's social services record, expanding the SJIS code forms to report such data would entail minor additional administrative burdens and would greatly enrich policy analysis.

## THE RIGHT TO COUNSEL AND THE WAIVER OF COUNSEL IN JUVENILE COURT — SHEDDING LIGHT ON THE DARK SECRET

Empirical evaluations of the impact of Supreme Court decisions on police and courtroom practices indicate that their influence often is limited and their policy goals frequently thwarted by the organizational requirements of the affected agencies (Oaks 1970; Sudnow 1965; Ingraham 1974). Several contemporaneous observers reported on the limited initial impact of *Gault* on the delivery and effectiveness of legal representation, and predicted continued judicial evasion of the Supreme Court's mandate (Lefstein, Stapleton, and Teitelbaum 1969; Duffee and Siegel 1971). Nearly twenty years after *Gault* held that juveniles are constitutionally entitled to the assistance of counsel and legislation was adopted to secure conformity, nearly half or more of all delinquents and status offenders in those states for which data is available are unrepresented (Table 3-5). Most petitioned youths in Minnesota are still unrepresented (Tables 4-3 and 4-4). Indeed, in only six of Minnesota's eighty-seven counties are even a majority of juveniles involved in delinquency proceedings represented, and in sixty-eight counties, a total of only 19.3% of such juveniles have counsel.

### Incarceration without Representation

Many juveniles who receive out-of-home placement and even secure confinement dispositions were adjudicated delinquent and sentenced without the assistance of counsel (Tables 3-4, 4-9, and 4-10). Nearly one-third of all juveniles in Minnesota who are removed from their homes and more than one-quarter of those who are incarcerated in secure institutions *were not represented* (Table 4-10). In the sixty-eight counties in the state with low rates of representation, *more than half* of the juveniles who were removed from their homes and who were incarcerated *were not represented* (Table 4-10). These findings are not aberrant; similar high rates of incarceration without representation prevail in other jurisdictions as well (Kempf, Decker, and Bing 1990). In Minnesota, these very high rates of home removal and incarceration without representation constitute an indictment of all the participants in the juvenile justice process—the juvenile court bench, the county attorneys, the organized bar, the legislature, and especially the Minnesota Supreme Court which has supervisory and administrative responsibility for the state's juvenile courts.

The United States Supreme Court held in *Scott v. Illinois* (440 U.S. 367 [1979]) and the Minnesota Supreme Court in *State v. Borst* (154 N.W.2d 888 [1967]) that it was improper to incarcerate an adult offender, even one charged with a minor offense, without either the appointment of counsel or a valid waiver of counsel. Moreover, both the United States and the Minnesota Supreme Courts have described the type of penetrating inquiry that must precede a "knowing, intelligent, and voluntary" waiver of the right to counsel.

Whether the typical *Miranda* advisory which is then followed by a waiver of rights under the "totality of the circumstances" is sufficient to assure a valid waiver of counsel by juveniles is highly questionable. Shortly after *Gault*, Lefstein, Stapleton, and Teitelbaum (1969:537–38) warned that simply importing adult waiver doctrines into delinquency proceedings threatened the entire fabric of rights that the *Gault* decision granted.

> [T]he concept of waiver of rights in juvenile delinquency proceedings is unrealistic. The Supreme Court in *Gault* assumed without discussion that the waiver doctrine could be imported to juvenile court hearings. . . . We submit that these special problems are extremely serious, and that a review of the appropriateness of this doctrine for juvenile courts is necessary.

The ease with which juvenile court judges often find waivers of rights by minors calls into question the legitimacy of the endeavor. Feld (1984:174–75) contends that

> considerable doubt remains as to whether a typical juvenile's waiver is, or even can be, "knowing, intelligent, and voluntary." Empirical

studies evaluating juveniles' understanding of their *Miranda* [and *Gault*] rights indicate that most juveniles who receive the *Miranda* warning may not understand it well enough to waive their constitutional rights in a "knowing and intelligent" manner. Such lack of comprehension by minors raises questions about the adequacy of *Miranda* warnings [or *Gault*'s advisory of the right to counsel] as a safeguard. The *Miranda* warning was designed to inform and educate a defendant to assure that subsequent waivers would indeed be "knowing and intelligent." If most juveniles lack the capacity to understand the warning, however, its ritual recitation hardly accomplishes that purpose.

No doubt, many juvenile court judges in Minnesota concluded that the majority of unrepresented juveniles who "waived" their right to counsel in delinquency proceedings did so in a "knowing and intelligent" fashion. And yet, an empirical study of waivers of counsel by adult defendants in Minnesota shortly after *Gideon v. Wainwright* (372 U.S. 335 [1963]) ordered appointment of counsel for indigent felons reported that

> the attempted waiver is the exceptional case. Although one prosecutor estimated that almost 10 percent of the accused attempted to decline counsel—especially if they expected to be granted probation—this figure was atypical. Most estimates ran under three percent, and even this minute figure is greatly fractionalized when the judge fully explains the important role a defense lawyer may play. On the basis of these findings, any appellate court would seem justified in begrudgingly treating a state's claim that counsel has been intelligently waived. (Kamisar and Choper 1963:36–37)

Can the majority of young juveniles in Minnesota whom judges found to have waived their rights to counsel really be that much more competent and legally sophisticated than the eighteen-year-old adult, tenth grade dropout in *State v. Burt* (256 N.W.2d 633 [1977]), whose attempt to waive counsel the Court rejected?

Continued judicial and legislative reliance on the "totality of the circumstances" test clearly is unwarranted and inappropriate in light of the multitude of factors implicated by the "totality" approach, the lack of guidelines as to how the various factors should be weighted, and the myriad combinations of factual situations that make every case unique. These factors result in virtually unlimited and unreviewable judicial discretion to deprive juveniles of their most fundamental procedural safeguard—the right to counsel.

Only the cynical or myopic can contend that immature, inexperienced, and impressionable young juveniles can waive their right to counsel alone and unaided. Flicker (1983:ii) noted that waivers of counsel by juveniles posed special problems because "[a] juvenile's youth, limited experience, and undeveloped cognitive skills create confusion and fear in an unfamiliar and threatening situation and a greater need for assistance in decisionmaking, case preparation, and dealing with law enforcement, social service, and court officials." How, then, explain the fact that in the sixty-eight counties with low rates of representation, only 18.6% of twelve-year-old juveniles involved in delinquency proceedings, have counsel, that only 19.9% of thirteen-year-old juveniles do, and that, in the entire state of Minnesota, less than half of the fourteen and fifteen-year-old juveniles do (Table 4-5)? Can that many juveniles be so mature as to make "knowing, intelligent, and voluntary" waivers of their constitutional rights alone and unaided in a frightening and alien courtroom environment? Or is it that the youngest juveniles do not need representation because the consequences of juvenile court adjudication and disposition are so benign? How, then, account for the fact that more than 20% of petitioned juveniles aged *thirteen* are removed from home—the highest rate for any age group—and nearly 10% of those thirteen-year-old youths are incarcerated (Table 4-8)?

## Delivering Legal Services in Juvenile Court

These findings have direct legislative and judicial policy implications. Legislation or judicial rules of procedure mandating the automatic and non-waivable appointment of counsel at the earliest stage in a delinquency proceeding is necessary (e.g., Iowa Code Ann. § 232.11 [West Supp. 1984–85]). Since *Gault*, many commentators have concluded that mandatory representation is essential at all stages of the juvenile process (Rubin 1977; Lefstein, Stapleton, and Teitelbaum 1969).

> In view of the inability of most juveniles to protect themselves from the consequences of the waiver of rights, or from the forces impelling them to effect a waiver, and because of the difficulties in placing substantial reliance on parental assistance, it may be argued that a minor should not, except in the most unusual circumstances [such as prior consultation with counsel], be held to a waiver of the right to counsel, nor an uncounselled minor to a waiver of the rights to silence, confrontation, and cross examination. (Lefstein, Stapleton and Teitelbaum 1969:553)

As long as it is possible for a juvenile to waive the right to counsel at all, juvenile court judges will continue to find such waivers on a discretionary basis under the "totality of the circumstances." The very fact that it is legally possible for a juvenile to waive counsel itself may discourage some youths from exercising their right if asserting it may be construed as an affront to the presiding judge. Handler (1965:33) argues that

> if the program of rights is to be effective, it must deal with the prob-
> lem of waiver—waiver by those who do not understand and waiver
> by those who, rightly or wrongly, think, or have been coerced into
> thinking that they have more to gain by playing ball or by manipula-
> tion. Waiver under either circumstance should not be allowed. . . .
> [T]he community's interest here is greater than that which the adoles-
> cent or the parent thinks his best interests are. Furthermore, if these
> rights are to serve the important function of testing and questioning
> the juvenile process, allowing waiver should increase coercive tactics
> by the officials who are going to be questioned. Paradoxically, then,
> for "rights" to be effective, they must be made mandatory.

Indeed, the finding that represented juveniles consistently receive more severe sentences than do unrepresented juveniles in different states and under different circumstances may provide some confirmation of Hand-ler's thesis of judicial coercion.

Policy groups, as well as commentators, have advocated the routine, nonwaivable appointment of counsel for juveniles. For example, the American Bar Association's *Juvenile Justice Standards* (1980b:89) rec-ommend that "[t]he right to counsel should attach as soon as the juvenile is taken into custody, . . . when a petition is filed, . . . or when the juvenile appears personally at an intake conference, whichever occurs first." In addition, "[the juvenile] should have 'the effective assistance of counsel at all stages of the proceeding' " and this right to counsel is mandatory and nonwaivable (American Bar Association 1980b:93).[1]

Some may question the utility of mandatory, nonwaivable counsel if, as this research suggests, so many of the consequences of representation are negative. Obviously, full representation of all juveniles would elimi-nate any variations in sentencing or processing associated with the pres-ence of attorneys. Full representation would "wash out" the apparently negative effects of representation. Clearly, a full representation model is quite compatible with contemporary juvenile justice administration. At least three large states—California, New York, and Pennsylvania (Table 3-2)—and five counties in Minnesota—urban, suburban, and rural which process 21% of all of the delinquents—already employ a full representa-tion system. The comparisons between the states and counties with high rates of representation and those with medium and low rates of represen-

246 JUSTICE FOR CHILDREN

tation do not indicate that juvenile justice grinds to a halt if juveniles are routinely represented.

The systematic introduction of defense counsel would provide the mechanism to create trial records that could be used on appeal to provide an additional safeguard to assure that juvenile court judges adhere more closely to the formal procedures and laws that are already required and to develop a comprehensive body of juvenile court law. Several courts have noted that juvenile cases exhibit far more procedural errors than do comparable adult cases and suggested that closed, confidential proceedings without the assistance of counsel foster a judicial casualness toward the law that visibility and appellate accountability might constrain (*R.L.R. v. State*, 487 P.2d 27 [Alaska 1971]; *In re Dino*, 359 So. 2d 586 [La. 1978]). Commentators have been even more critical of closed proceedings and the lack of appeals taken from juvenile courts.

> [A]ccess to juvenile delinquency hearings would function as a check on the abuse of power by judges, probation officers, and other public officials. The nature of the juvenile justice system, even more than the criminal system, suggests a compelling need to check the exercise of government power. Juvenile court judges, for example, exercise more discretion than their criminal trial counterparts. . . . Such a system relies heavily on subjective judgments, making the "compliant, biased, or eccentric judge" a particular hazard. Juvenile court judges, moreover, are often less qualified and less competent than other judges. As a result, juvenile courts often commit "much more extensive and fundamental error than is generally found in adult criminal cases." Because juvenile cases are only rarely appealed, public scrutiny of the juvenile justice system takes on added importance as a check against official misconduct. (Note 1983:1550–51)

Moreover, prohibiting waivers of counsel would increase the numbers of public attorneys appearing in juvenile courts. An enlarged cadre of juvenile public defenders would derive education, support, and encouragement from statewide association with one another similar to the post-*Gideon* revolution in criminal justice that resulted from the creation of statewide criminal defender systems. Grisso (1980:1164) concludes that

> [t]he beneficial effects of a per se requirement of counsel in juvenile waiver proceedings should be enhanced as the juvenile justice system increases its own support of a strong advocacy role for these attorneys. At a minimum, the requirement provides a reasonable level of protection for younger juveniles; without this protection, they would

be subjected to the very circumstances that *Miranda* [and *Gault*] sought to eliminate.

Most fundamentally, since the *Gault* decision, the juvenile court is first and foremost a legal entity engaged in formal social control and not simply a social welfare agency. As a legal institution exercising substantial coercive powers over young people and their families, ensuring the accuracy and reliability of the process and providing mechanisms to implement safeguards against unsolicited state intervention are essential. Indeed, even prior to *Gault*, Handler (1965:29) argued that adversary procedures were necessary to assure accurate fact-finding in delinquency proceedings and that "the nonadversary, solicitous procedure seriously underestimates the extraordinary task placed on the fact-finder adjudicator." While the Supreme Court in *McKeiver v. Pennsylvania* (403 U.S. 528 [1970]), asserted that judges were as capable as juries of accurate fact-finding, it did not disturb *Gault*'s fundamental premise that delinquency hearings were adversary proceedings. The *Gault* Court was unwilling to rely solely upon the benevolence of juvenile court judges or social workers to safeguard the interests of young people. Instead, it recognized the likely conflicts between the interests of the juvenile and those of the state and imposed the adversarial model of proof when it incorporated the privilege against self-incrimination. With *Gault*'s application of the Fifth Amendment, juvenile adjudications no longer could be characterized as either "noncriminal" or as "nonadversarial," because the privilege against self-incrimination, more than any other provision of the Bill of Rights, is the fundamental guarantor of an adversarial process and the primary mechanism for maintaining a balance between the state and the individual (*Murphy v. Waterfront Comm'n*, 378 U.S. 52 [1964]). In an adversarial process, only lawyers can invoke effectively the procedural safeguards that are the right of every citizen, including children, as a condition precedent to unsolicited state intervention. "[I]t is belaboring the obvious to assert that within the confines of the adversary system, the accuracy of a finding that a particular defendant is guilty or not guilty—especially the former—is greatly improved by providing him with a lawyer" (Kaplan 1986:229).

A rule mandating nonwaivable assistance of counsel for juveniles appearing in juvenile court might impose substantial burdens on the delivery of legal services in rural areas, such as the seventy-seven rural counties in Minnesota in which only 25.1% of juveniles are currently represented. Presumably, however, those rural counties already provide adult defendants with representation and standby counsel in criminal proceedings, so the organizational mechanisms already exist. Moreover, despite any possible fiscal or administrative concerns, every juvenile is already entitled by *Gault* and statute to the assistance of counsel at every critical stage in the process, and only an attorney can redress the imbalance between a vulnerable youth and the state. As the Supreme Court said in *Gault*, "the condition of being a boy does not justify a kangaroo court" (387 U.S. at 280), especially if the justification preferred for such a proceeding is simply the state's fiscal convenience. The issue is not one of entitlement, since all are entitled to representation, but rather the ease or difficulty with which waivers of counsel are found, which in turn has enormous implications for the entire administration of juvenile justice.

Short of mandatory and nonwaivable counsel, a prohibition on waivers of counsel without prior consultation with and the concurrence of counsel on the record would provide greater assurance than does the current, standardless practice that any eventual waiver was truly "knowing, intelligent, and voluntary." The National Advisory Committee on Juvenile Justice (1976:550) recommended that a juvenile should be represented throughout the juvenile process and that "if a juvenile who has not consulted a lawyer indicates intent to waive assistance of counsel, a lawyer should be provided to consult with the juvenile and his or her parents on the wisdom of such a waiver. The court should not accept a waiver of counsel unless it determines after thorough inquiry that the juvenile has conferred at least once with a lawyer, and is waiving the right competently." These recommendations are bolstered by an empirical study of juveniles' understanding of their right to counsel, which concluded that

> the appointment of legal counsel at an earlier point in the juvenile justice process is recommended as a means of enhancing juveniles' understanding of the law and the legal process, and ensuring that any waiver of their legal rights is an informed waiver with a full understanding of the possible consequences of the waiver. Earlier appointment of legal counsel would also reduce the wide variation in the quality of legal counsel and the amount of time attorneys are able to spend in case preparation. (Lawrence 1983:57)

Because waivers of rights, especially the right to counsel, involve legal and strategic considerations as well as knowledge and understanding of rights and an appreciation of consequences, it is difficult to see how any less stringent alternative could be as effective. A per se requirement of consultation with counsel prior to a waiver takes account of the immaturity of youths and their lack of experience in law enforcement situations. In addition, it recognizes that only attorneys possess the skills and training necessary to assist the child in the adversarial process. Most importantly, a requirement of consultation with counsel prior to waiver would assure the development of legal services delivery systems that would then facilitate the more routine representation of juveniles.

At the very least, court rules or legislation should prohibit the removal from home or incarceration of any juvenile who was neither represented by counsel nor provided with standby counsel following any purported waiver. Such a limitation on dispositions is already the law for adult criminal defendants (e.g., *Scott v. Illinois*, 440 U.S. 367 [1979]), for juveniles in some jurisdictions (Wis. Stat. Ann. § 48.23 [West 1983]), and the operational practice in jurisdictions such as New York and Pennsylvania, where virtually no unrepresented juveniles are removed or confined (Table 3-4).

Apart from simply documenting variations in rates of representation, this research also examined the determinants of representation. It examined the relationship between legal variables—seriousness of offense, detention status, prior referrals—and the appointment of counsel. In each analysis, it showed the relationship between the legal variables and dispositions, the legal variables and the appointment of counsel, and the effects of representation on dispositions, while controlling for those legal variables. The regression equations summarized the interrelationship between those variables and their effects on the appointment of counsel and the influence of counsel on dispositions.

There are complex relationships between the factors producing more severe dispositions and the factors influencing the appointment of counsel. Each legal variable that is associated with a more severe disposition is also associated with higher rates of representation. Yet, within the limitations of this research, it appears that representation by counsel is an additional aggravating factor in a juvenile's disposition. When controlling for the seriousness of the present offense, unrepresented juveniles seem to fare better than do those with lawyers (Tables 3-4 and 4-10). When controlling for the seriousness of the present offense and prior referrals, the presence of counsel produces more severe dispositions (Tables 3-11 and 4-14). When controlling for offense and detention status, unrepresented juveniles again fare better than do those with representation (Tables 3-8 and 4-18). When multiple regression controls for the effects of all of the independent variables simultaneously, the relationship between the presence of an attorney and severity of disposition persists (Tables 4-27 through 4-30, 7-15 through 7-18). In short, while the legal variables enhance the probabilities of representation, the fact of representation appears to exert an independent effect on the severity of dispositions.

Although other studies have alluded to the negative effects of representation (Bortner 1982; Clarke and Koch 1980), this study provides strong and consistent evidence that the presence of counsel redounds to the disadvantage of a juvenile. Why? One possible explanation is that the lawyers who appear in juvenile courts are incompetent and prejudice their clients' cases (Fox 1970a; Platt 1977; Knitzer and Sobie 1984). While systematic qualitative evaluations of the actual performance of counsel in juvenile courts are lacking, the available evidence suggests that even in jurisdictions where counsel are routinely appointed, there are grounds for concern about their effectiveness. In New York, for example, which had the highest rate of representation (Table 3-2), a study of the performance of counsel concluded that despite their routine presence, there are grounds for concern about the quality of their performance. Knitzer and Sobie (1984:8–9) reported a number of very disturbing findings.

> Using the most basic criteria of effectiveness—that the law guardian meet the client, be minimally prepared, have some knowledge of the law and of possible dispositions, and be active on behalf of his or her client—serious and widespread problems are evident.
>
> —Overall, 45% of the courtroom observations reflected either seriously inadequate or marginally adequate representation; 27% reflected acceptable representation, and 4% effective representation . . .
>
> Specific problems center around lack of preparation and lack of contact with the children.
>
> —In 47% of the observations it appeared that the law guardian had done no or minimal preparation. In 5% it was clear that the law guardian had not met with the client at all. . . . Further, in 35% of the cases, the law guardians did not talk to, or made only minimal contact with their clients during the court proceedings. . . . In addition, ineffective representation is characterized by violations of statutory or due process rights; almost 50% of the transcripts included appealable errors made either by law guardians or made by judges and left unchallenged by the law guardians.

Another observer of lawyers' performances in juvenile trials has characterized them as " 'only marginally contested,' and marked by 'lackadaisical defense efforts.' Defense counsel generally make few objections, and seldom move to exclude evidence on constitutional grounds. Defense witnesses rarely are called, and the cross-examination of prosecution witnesses is 'frequently perfunctory and reveals no design or rationale on the part of the defense attorney.' Closing arguments are sketchy when they are made at all" (Ainsworth 1991:1127–28).

There are a variety of organizational and institutional reasons why defense representation and the overall quality of procedural justice may be less than adequate. Because juvenile cases are tried informally, behind closed doors and without a jury, the low visibility of the proceedings allows lawyers working under the pressure of crushing caseloads to cut corners. This tendency is "often tacitly encouraged by judges anxious to process cases as expeditiously as possible" (Ainsworth 1991:1128).

The undistinguished performance of many defense attorneys is exacerbated by the combination of inexperience and overwork. Public defender offices in many jurisdictions often assign their least capable lawyers or newest staff attorneys to juvenile courts to get trial experience and these neophytes may receive less adequate supervision than their prosecutorial counterparts. Flicker (1983:2) notes that

> [i]n some defender offices, assignment to "kiddie court" is the bottom rung of the ladder, to be passed as quickly as possible on the way up to more visible and prestigious criminal court assignments. Little attention may be paid by superiors to performance in juvenile court, providing few incentives for hard work. Finally, the problem of co-optation is prevalent in juvenile court and many public defenders choose to join with the other child-savers in the court, sacrificing their clients' rights to zealous representation to the treatment goals of probation officers, judges, and other officials.

Similarly, court appointed counsel may be beholden to the judges who select them and more concerned with maintaining an ongoing relationship with court personnel than vigorously protecting the interests of their frequently changing clients. Again, Flicker (1983:4) contends that the problem of preserving the independence of attorneys from the influence of judges and other court personnel

> is acute in juvenile courts because of its relative informality and smaller size. The continued reliance by probation officers, judges, and other officials on the concepts of rehabilitation and best interests of the child create a tension between the adversarial role of defense counsel and the interventionist objectives of those who see themselves as providers of social services. The court officials' hostility to counsel's efforts has resulted in negative performance evaluations, slashed fees, and even pressure from the court to remove the offending attorneys from the panel.

The reluctance of many lawyers to appear in juvenile courts is often matched by judges who avoid or resist assignment to juvenile court for similar reasons. "[T]he juvenile court is considered to be the lowest rung on the judicial ladder. Rarely does the court attract men [or women] of maturity or ability. The work is not regarded as desirable or appropriate for higher judgeships" (Handler 1965:17).

The unfortunate, negative aspects of representation at adjudication may simply reflect the quality of legal and judicial personnel associated with a justice system in which the rule of law is subordinated to personalities. Regardless of the legal services delivery system, the conditions of employment in juvenile courts are not conducive to quality representation and are unlikely to attract and retain the most competent attorneys. Long hours, low pay, inadequate support and social service resources, a depressing sense of futility compounded by crushing caseloads and difficult clients are likely to discourage all but the most dedicated lawyers from devoting their professional careers to advocacy on behalf of children.

Measuring defense attorney performance by dispositional outcomes also raises questions about the meaning of effective assistance of counsel in a court system in which many of the participants—juvenile court judges, probation officers, and county attorneys—do not regard a juvenile's acquittal as a "victory." What does it take to be an effective attorney in juvenile court? In *State ex rel. D.D.H. v. Dostert* (269 S.E.2d 401 at 412–13 [W. Va. 1980]), the West Virginia Supreme Court discussed thoughtfully and extensively the role of defense counsel at a dispositional hearing.

> [C]ounsel has a duty to investigate all resources available to find the least restrictive alternative. . . . Court appointed counsel must make an independent investigation of the child's background. . . . Armed with adequate information counsel can then present the court with all reasonable alternative dispositions to incarceration and should have taken the initial steps to secure the tentative acceptance of the child into those facilities.

Perhaps it is this type of demanding, time-consuming, social services investigation that explains why fewer defense attorneys appear at the time of juveniles' sentencing even than do at adjudications (Tables 4-3 and 6-7). This judicial expectation may also explain why the performance of so many lawyers at dispositions is inadequate. Knitzer and Sobie (1984:10), for example, report that "substantial numbers of law guardians assume virtually no role at dispositional proceedings. Instead, they rely almost totally upon others." Since virtually all petitioned juveniles are convicted of some offense (Table 5-1) whereby the court obtains jurisdiction to intervene, how might attorneys for juveniles become more familiar with dispositional alternatives and more effective advocates for the substantive interests of their clients?

There are other possible explanations for the association between representation and severity of sentences. One is that the negative relationship between the presence of counsel and the increased severity of disposition may be spurious. The fact of an association does not necessarily demonstrate causal ordering. For example, the eventual sentence may cause the initial judicial decision to appoint counsel, rather than the presence of an attorney affecting the ultimate sentence. It may be that early in a proceeding, a juvenile court judge's familiarity with a case alerts him or her to the likely disposition that will be imposed if the child is convicted, and the judge may appoint counsel if he or she anticipates more severe consequences (Aday 1986). In many states and counties, the same judge who presides at a youth's arraignment and detention hearing will later decide the case on the merits and then impose a sentence. The single judge's domination of the entire juvenile justice process is fraught with prejudicial possibilities. For example, Feld (1984:240–41) notes that

> at a detention hearing, a judge may be exposed to a youth's "social history" file and the youth's prior record of police contacts and delinquency adjudications, all of which bear on the issue of the appropriate pretrial placement of the youth. When that same judge is subsequently called on to determine the admissibility of evidence in a suppression hearing and the guilt of the juvenile in the same proceeding, the risks of prejudice become almost insuperable. To whatever degree a judge is unable to compartmentalize, a juvenile is denied the basic right to a fair trial by an impartial tribunal with a determination of guilt based on admissible evidence.

Thus, the formality-severity relationship may appear because the initial decision to appoint counsel is based upon the evidence developed at those earlier stages, which also influences later dispositions. In short, perhaps judges attempt to conform to the dictates of *Scott*, try to predict, albeit imperfectly, when more severe dispositions will be imposed, and then appoint counsel in such cases. Even if this explains somewhat the greater severity of sentences of represented juveniles than unrepresented ones, it remains the case that the requirements of *Scott* and *Borst* are not consistently fulfilled since a substantial proportion of unrepresented juveniles also are removed from their homes and incarcerated (Table 4-10). A fundamental dilemma posed by *Scott* is how to obtain the information necessary to determine before the trial whether, upon conviction, the eventual sentence will result in incarceration and thus will require the appointment of counsel without simultaneously prejudging the case and prejudicing the interests of the defendant.

A third possible explanation is that there is a direct and causal relationship between process formality and sentencing severity. The relationship may occur because juvenile court judges may treat more formally and sentence more severely juveniles who appear with counsel than those without. Within statutory limits, if a youth is represented, then a judge may feel less constrained at sentencing, since adherence to the form of due process insulates any sentence from appellate reversal. Duffee and Siegel (1971:548–49) contended that "juveniles who are represented by counsel should be subjected to controls more often than those who waive their rights. When the appearance of due process has been maintained, the juvenile court should feel secure about future challenges and safer in prescribing even stricter controls over its wards."

Is severity the price of formal procedures? The most charitable interpretation is that judges do not necessarily punish juveniles who are represented because they are accompanied by counsel, but rather that the judges may be more lenient toward those youths who appear unaided and "throw themselves on the mercy of the court." While such an interpretation is consistent with this data, it raises in a different guise the question of judicial hostility toward adversarial litigants. Why should the fact that a youth avails himself of an elementary, constitutional procedural safeguard result in an aggravated sentence compared to that of an unrepresented juvenile? Does the presence of counsel produce a sentencing differential equivalent to that experienced by adult criminal defendants who plead guilty rather than having their guilt determined by a jury trial? At the very least, further research, including qualitative studies of the processes of initial appointment and performance of counsel in several jurisdictions will be required to untangle this complex web.

Qualitative studies are also necessary to determine what attorneys actually do in juvenile court proceedings. In light of this research, the right to counsel and the role of counsel in juvenile court entails a two-step process. The first is simply assuring the presence of counsel at all. In many jurisdictions, simply getting an attorney into juvenile court remains problematic. Once an attorney is present, however, the role he or she adopts is also fraught with difficulties. A number of commentators have questioned whether attorneys can function as adversaries in juvenile courts and, yet, whether there is any utility to their presence in any other role (Ferster, Courtless, and Snethen 1972; Platt and Friedman 1968; Lefstein, Stapleton and Teitelbaum 1969; Kay and Segal 1973; McMillian and McMurtry 1970; Guggenheim 1984). A juvenile court judge in a closed, discretionary proceeding can bring a variety of pressures to bear on a defense attorney in order to assure his or her cooperation in expediting the court's calendar.

> The defense lawyer who is seen as obstreperous in her advocacy will
> be reminded subtly, or overtly if necessary, that excessive zeal in rep-
> resenting her juvenile clients is inappropriate and counter-produc-
> tive. If she ignores these signals to temper her advocacy, the appointed
> defense lawyer is vulnerable to direct attacks, such as having her fees
> slashed or being excluded from the panel of lawyers from which the
> court makes indigent appointments. . . . For most defense lawyers,
> withstanding the psychological debilitation attendant upon being the
> sustained focus of judicial and prosecutorial disapproval is hopeless.
> (Ainsworth 1991:1129)

Apart from the institutional pressures to cooperate, some defenders
are reluctant simply to transplant the role of counsel established in adult
criminal courts into juvenile proceedings because of the perceived differences between adult and child defendants as well as differences in sentencing policies occasioned by the more "therapeutic" orientation of juvenile courts. The ideology of treatment and the legacy of parens patriae
paternalism encourages lawyers to sacrifice their clients' legal rights to
their perceived long term best interests. Thus, commentators prescribe
different roles for counsel during the fact-finding adjudicative stage than
for the dispositional process. Whether there are sufficient differences between punishment in criminal courts and treatment in juvenile courts to
sustain any differences in the role of counsel is certainly open to question
(Feld 1988b). But the greater discretion exercised by juvenile court judges,
compared with their adult counterparts, places defense attorneys at a considerable strategic disadvantage. At the very least, however, many more
observational and qualitative studies of attorneys' actual performance
must precede efforts to prescribe appropriate roles.

## ENHANCEMENT WITHOUT REPRESENTATION: THE USE OF PRIOR UNCOUNSELED CONVICTIONS TO ENHANCE SENTENCES AS JUVENILES AND AS ADULTS

The United States, Minnesota, and other jurisdictions include some juvenile delinquency convictions in their adult sentencing guidelines' criminal
history score (e.g., Minnesota Sentencing, 1980:22–24; Pennsylvania
Sentencing, 42 Pa. Cons. Stat. § 9721(b) [Purdon 1982]; 204 Pa. Code
§ 303.7(b) (1) (ii)).[2] The inclusion of previous delinquency or even status
convictions for sentencing youths who are convicted as adults, and the
influence of prior dispositions on present juvenile court sentences raises
the issue of enhancement of sentences based on prior, uncounseled con-

victions. Judges who sentence adult offenders, whether by guidelines or on a discretionary basis, consider juveniles' prior records of delinquency. The nature of any previously imposed sentences as well as a juvenile's prior record influences juvenile court judges' present sentencing decisions (Tables 4-27 through 4-30, 7-15 through 7-18).

A number of Federal and Minnesota state cases—*Baldasar v. Illinois* (446 U.S. 222 [1980]), *United States v. Tucker* (404 U.S. 443 [1972]), *Burgett v. Texas* (398 U.S. 109 [1967]), *State v. Nordstrom* (331 N.W.2d 901 [Minn. 1983]), and *State v. Edmison* (379 N.W.2d 85 [Minn. 1985])—have condemned the enhancement of a defendant's current sentence on the basis of a prior conviction at which the defendant was unrepresented. Such enhancement may occur either formally by statute or guideline or informally as an exercise of judicial sentencing discretion.

This research demonstrates that many unrepresented juveniles are routinely adjudicated delinquent and removed from their homes or incarcerated (Tables 4-9 and 4-10). In addition, within each offense category, first offenders have the lowest rate of representation (Table 4-13), thereby increasing the probability that any subsequent sentences they receive will be based upon those prior, uncounseled convictions. Status offenders have the lowest initial rate of representation (Table 4-3). If they return to juvenile court for violating a condition of probation or a court order, then they may be adjudicated delinquent and sentenced to an institution like any other delinquent despite the absence of counsel at their original hearing for the status offense (*L.E.A. v. Hammergren*, 294 N.W.2d 705 [Minn. 1980]). Moreover, earlier dispositions are consistently the most important variable explaining later ones. Finally, it is undoubtedly the case that many of these unrepresented juveniles will later be tried as adults and have their prior, uncounseled convictions included in their adult criminal history scores.

As a matter of sentencing policy, the Federal and Minnesota Sentencing Guidelines Commissions' decisions to include juveniles' prior records in the adult criminal history score is probably correct.

> The Sentencing Guidelines Commission's decision to include juvenile felony convictions in an adult criminal history score was predicated on several substantial policy considerations. The commission initially found that including such information was consistent with existing adult sentencing practices, especially in the urban counties of the state. . . . The commission chose to include in the sentencing framework features of incapacitation, which focus on persistence of criminal activity, as well as features of "just deserts," which focus on the seriousness of criminal activity. A pattern of criminal violations is

reliable evidence of persistence, regardless of whether it occurs while
the offender is a juvenile or an adult. (Feld 1981:234–35)

In *State v. Little* (423 N.W.2d 722 [Minn. Ct. App. 1988]), the Minnesota Court of Appeals upheld the use of juvenile convictions to enhance
the sentence of an adult defendant. The court noted that the protections
afforded by the Juvenile Court Act were consistent with the inclusion of
juvenile adjudications in the sentencing guidelines.

> The legislature has drawn a line between the mistakes of youth that
> are not repeated and those which continue into young adulthood.
> The system punishes only those offenders who have abused the juve-
> nile court's leniency and then does so only within the confines and
> safeguards supplied by the Minnesota Sentencing Guidelines. . . . The
> one point limit was deemed consistent with the purpose of including
> a juvenile record in the criminal history—to distinguish the young
> adult felon with no juvenile record of felony-type behavior from the
> young adult offender who has a prior juvenile record of repeated fel-
> ony-type behavior. The one point limit also was deemed advisable to
> limit the impact of findings obtained under a juvenile court procedure
> that does not afford the full procedural rights available in adult courts
> (423 N.W.2d at 724–25).

While the last quoted sentence reflects the court's recognition that juvenile
and criminal proceedings are not procedurally equivalent, the court emphasized that Little was represented by counsel in his juvenile proceedings.

Having decided to use prior juvenile convictions for sentencing purposes, both juvenile and adult sentencing authorities must now confront
the reality of the quality of adjudication in juvenile courts. Both the
United States Supreme Court and the Minnesota Supreme Court have
denied juveniles the right to jury trials, contending that a juvenile court
judge's factual determinations are as reliable as a jury's (*McKeiver v.
Pennsylvania*, 403 U.S. 528, 543 [1970]; *In re K.A.A.*, 410 N.W.2d 836
[Minn. 1987]). While this equation is doubtful, it is even more questionable in view of the routine absence of counsel in delinquency proceedings.

If juvenile adjudications are to be used to enhance sentences for juveniles or adults, then a mechanism must be developed to assure that only
constitutionally obtained prior convictions are considered. Again, automatic and mandatory appointment of counsel in all cases is the obvious
device to assure the validity of the criminal history score. Anything less
will subject a juvenile or young adult's sentence to direct or collateral
attack, produce additional appeals, and impose a wasteful and time-con-

suming burden on the prosecution to establish the validity of prior convictions.

Until provisions for the mandatory appointment of counsel are implemented, jurisdictions like Minnesota, in which the majority of youths are unrepresented should amend their guidelines or sentencing provisions to create a presumption that all prior juvenile convictions included in the adult criminal history score were obtained *without* the assistance of counsel and place the burden of proving the validity of the prior convictions on the prosecution. Such a presumption recognizes that more than one-third (33.9%) of all juvenile felony adjudications and, in many parts of the state, over half of all felony convictions (58.9%, Table 4-3; 50.4%, Table 6-7) were obtained without counsel. The United States Sentencing Guidelines criminal history includes state juvenile misdemeanor and petty offense convictions that result in probation, and for which even larger proportions of youths are typically unrepresented (53.6% statewide, 76.5% rural, Table 6-7). A presumption that all prior juvenile adjudications are *invalid* for purposes of enhancement would increase the prosecutor's institutional interest in juvenile justice administration and provide a nonjudicial mechanism to assure that juveniles charged with crimes are represented and that any waivers of counsel were adequately documented on the record.

## REGULATING PRETRIAL DETENTION

One recurring theme of juvenile justice administration is the overuse and abuse of pretrial detention. The United States Supreme Court in *Schall v. Martin* (467 U.S. 283 [1984]) upheld the constitutionality of preventive detention of juveniles. As a practical matter, however, the types of statutes approved in *Schall* and used in Minnesota and other jurisdictions are deficient and lack any objective administrative criteria. Feld (1984:203–4) contends that

> [t]he lack of statutory standards or criteria about ultimately speculative future behavior remits the detention decision to the individual discretion of each judge. As the [*Schall*] dissent noted, unstructured discretion both creates the danger that many juveniles will be detained "erroneously" and fosters arbitrariness, inequality and discrimination in a process that impinges on fundamental liberty interests.

The virtual absence of meaningful substantive standards in detention statutes and the minimal procedural safeguards used to implement them invariably result in the excessive detention of many juveniles who pose no threat to themselves or others. The majority of all juveniles detained are charged either with misdemeanor property offenses or status offenses, rather than with serious offenses (Tables 3-5, 4-15, and 6-14).

Empirical studies in several jurisdictions report that because detention statutes lack any objective criteria, there is no apparent rationale for detention decisions (Clarke and Koch 1980; Frazier and Bishop 1985; McCarthy 1987). The present study confirms that there are minimal discernible legal or substantive rationales for detention in Minnesota either. The regression equations (Tables 4-23 through 4-26, 6-15 through 6-17) only explain about 9% of the variance in detention decisions, and the sentence later imposed is the most important factor. Moreover, the analyses suggest both gender and racial bias in the administration of detention (Tables 6-15 through 6-17, 7-9). Like other studies, this one also confirms the substantial deleterious impact of detention on later dispositions (Tables 4-27 through 4-30, 7-15 through 7-18). The analyses of sentencing decisions indicate that pretrial detention status is generally the second or third most important factor in the decisions to remove youths from homes or to commit them to institutions.

Detention constitutes a highly arbitrary and capricious process of pretrial, short-term confinement with no tenable or objective rationale. Once it occurs, however, it then increases the likelihood of additional postadjudication sanctions as well. In operation, detention almost randomly seems to impose punishment on some juveniles for no obvious reason and then punishes them again for having been punished before. Apart from the legal variables, among the most salient factors in the detention decision are a youth's gender, race, or residence.

The legislatures and supreme courts in Minnesota and other jurisdictions that use discretionary, effectively standardless detention statutes are responsible for perpetuating an unjust process of punishment before trial. The present research provides additional evidence of the deficiencies of the current detention statute, the prejudicial and cumulative impact of detention decisions, and the need for substantive revisions.

There are a number of recommended standards for detention that courts and legislatures might consider to limit the scope of detention. The American Bar Association's Juvenile Justice Standards project, for example, recommended that a juvenile not be detained unless the youth is charged with a serious crime of violence which, if proven, would likely result in commitment to a secure facility; the youth is an escapee from an institution to which he has been previously committed as an adjudicated delinquent; or the juvenile will not appear at subsequent proceedings based on a demonstrated history of prior failures to appear (American Bar Association 1980c:6.6.). Similarly, the National Juvenile Justice Advisory Committee (1976:390) recommends detention only "[t]o prevent the juvenile from inflicting bodily harm on others" and cautions against detaining "a youth simply to prevent the predicted commission of property offenses." Commentators have recommended that "[c]riteria for detention should be explicit and limited solely to acts that would be felonies requiring detention if committed by adults" (Sarri 1974:68). In Minnesota (Tables 4-15 and 6-14), the adoption of such restrictive offense criteria would dramatically reduce the numbers of juveniles detained initially and, perhaps, subsequently removed from their homes.

In addition to objective, offense-based detention criteria, court rules or law should create a presumption against the detention of any non-felony offenders with a heavy burden on the proponent to establish both the need for detention and the exhaustion of all nonsecure alternative placements. When adult defendants are chargeable with misdemeanor offenses, for example, the Minnesota rules of criminal procedure create a presumption for citation in lieu of custodial arrest or detention (Minn. R. Crim. Proc. 6.01, subd. 1 (1) (a), (b)). Such a presumption would reduce by half the numbers of youths incarcerated prior to trial (Table 6-14). To the extent that female offenders charged with minor delinquencies and status offenses are disproportionately at risk for pretrial detention and subsequent home removal (Tables 7-13, 7-14), shelter care alternatives to secure detention are necessary.

The emphasis on enhancing the delivery of legal services, improving the quality of lawyers' performance, and regularizing the administration of pretrial detention are specific examples of policies to formalize juvenile justice administration and bring the rule of law to bear on a traditionally discretionary institution. As this research demonstrates, procedural formality is not without its costs in sentencing severity. And yet, as *Gault* recognized, the contemporary juvenile court is not so benign that there is any alternative to increased procedural formality. The final chapter considers the implications of process formality and punishment for the future of the juvenile court.

## NOTES

1. The commentary to the pretrial standards does qualify the absolute, nonwaivable nature of the right to counsel. "[I]n recommending that the respondent's right to counsel in delinquency proceedings should be nonwaivable, this standard is not intended to foreclose absolutely the possibility of *pro se* representation by a juvenile" (American Bar Association 1980b:93). While the Supreme Court held

in *Faretta v. California* (422 U.S. 806 [1976]) that an adult defendant in a state criminal trial has a constitutional right to proceed without counsel when he or she voluntarily and intelligently elects to do so, whether a juvenile defendant can meet the requirements of a *Faretta* waiver is questionable. Moreover, while the *Faretta* right to proceed *pro se* was based on the Sixth Amendment right to counsel, *Gault* based its holding on the Fourteenth Amendment. A court or legislature could conclude that the "special circumstances" of youth, immaturity, and inexperience imposed a significantly higher, effectively unattainable standard for competence before allowing the waiver of counsel by a young juvenile. Flicker's (1983:i) analysis of the A.B.A.'s juvenile justice standards concluded that "providing accused juveniles with a non-waivable right-to-counsel is probably the most fundamental of the hundreds of standards in juvenile justice."

2. The following excerpt from the Minnesota Sentencing Guidelines Report (1980:29) explicitly includes the felony convictions of juveniles aged sixteen or older in the adult criminal history score:

4. The offender is assigned one point for every two juvenile adjudications for offenses that would have been felonies if committed by an adult, provided that:

   a. The juvenile adjudications were pursuant to offenses occurring after the offender's sixteenth birthday;

   b. The offender had not attained the age of twenty-one at the time the felony was committed for which he or she is being currently sentenced; and

   c. No offender may receive more than one point for prior juvenile adjudications.

   The United States Sentencing Guidelines (U.S.S.G. § 4A1.2(C)) include in the adult defendant's criminal history score any juvenile prior conviction that resulted in either thirty days of "imprisonment" or a term of probation of at least one year. Because of "real crime" sentencing, that is, a judicial assessment of the real criminal conduct underlying a conviction, even juvenile status offenses may be used to enhance the adult defendant's criminal history score (*United States v. Unger*, 915 F.2d 759 [1st Cir. 1990]).

# chapter nine ─────────────────────────────

## FROM THE "BEST INTERESTS" OF THE OFFENDER TO THE SERIOUSNESS OF THE OFFENSE

### Punishment and the Future of the Juvenile Court

Historically, juvenile courts based their dispositional decisions on an individualized assessment of a youth's "best interests." Increasingly, however, the seriousness of the offense, rather than characteristics of the offender, dominates juvenile court sentencing decisions. The changes in sentencing philosophy from treatment to punishment are reflected in juvenile court legislation, sentencing statutes, and correctional dispositional guidelines that emphasize proportional and determinate sentences based on the present offense and prior record and that dictate the length, location, and intensity of intervention (Feld 1988b, 1991).

The fundamental justification for denying juveniles the right to a jury trial and, more basically, for maintaining a juvenile justice system separate from the adult one is based on the differences between punishment and treatment (Gardner 1982; Feld 1988b). Punishment involves the imposition by the state, for purposes of retribution or deterrence, of burdens on an individual who has violated legal prohibitions (Hart 1968; Packer 1968). Punishment assumes that responsible, volitional moral actors who make blameworthy choices deserve to suffer the prescribed consequences of their acts, and imposes unpleasant consequences because of an offender's *past offenses* (Hart 1968; Von Hirsch 1976). Treatment, by contrast, focuses on the mental health, status, and welfare of the individual rather than on the commission of prohibited acts (Packer 1968; Allen 1964, 1981). Most forms of rehabilitative treatment assume a degree of determinism, that antecedent factors caused the undesirable behavior, and that intervention strategies can be applied that will improve the offender's *future welfare* (Matza 1964).

When analyzing juvenile court sentencing practices, it is useful to examine whether the decision is based upon the past offense or the future welfare of the offender. Sentences based on characteristics of the offense are typically determinate and proportional. Just deserts sentencing, with its strong retributive foundation, punishes offenders according to their past behavior rather than on the basis of who they are or may become. Similarly situated offenders are defined and sanctioned on the basis of relatively objective and legally relevant factors such as seriousness of offense, culpability, or criminal history (Von Hirsch 1976, 1986). By contrast, sentences based upon characteristics of the offender are typically open-ended, nonproportional and indeterminate. Individualized justice deems all personal and social characteristics as relevant and does not assign controlling significance to any one factor (Matza 1964).

The influence of just deserts principles for sentencing adults has spilled over into the routine sentencing of juveniles as well (Feld 1987, 1988b; Gardner 1987). Whether juvenile courts are punishing youths for past offenses or treating them for their future welfare may be determined by examining (1) legislative purpose clauses and court opinions, (2) juvenile court sentencing statutes and actual sentencing practices, and (3) conditions of institutional confinement (Feld 1988b). All of these indicators consistently reveal that, despite persisting rehabilitative rhetoric, treating juveniles closely resembles punishing adult criminals. But punishing juveniles has constitutional consequences, since the *McKeiver* Court justified the procedural differences of juvenile court by positing a therapeutic, rather than punitive, purpose. Moreover, juveniles currently may serve longer sentences than their adult counterparts convicted of the same offense because they purportedly receive treatment rather than punishment.[1]

## THE LEGISLATIVE PURPOSE OF THE JUVENILE COURT

Among the factors upon which the Supreme Court relies to determine whether seemingly punitive and coercive governmental intervention constitutes punishment or treatment is the stated legislative purpose (*Allen v. Illinois*, 478 U.S. 364 [1986]; Gardner 1982). Most states' juvenile court statutes contain a "purpose clause" or preamble that states the underlying rationale of the legislation as an aid to courts in interpreting the statute. These statutory statements of legislative intent provide one indicator of the purpose of juvenile court intervention.

Forty-two of the states' juvenile codes contain a legislative purpose clause (Feld 1988b). Within the past decade, about one-quarter of the states have redefined their juvenile codes' statements of legislative purpose (Feld 1988b:842 n. 84). These amendments de-emphasize rehabilitation and the child's "best interest" and assert the importance of "provid[ing] for the protection and safety of the public" (Cal. Welf. & Inst. Code § 202 [West Supp. 1988]); "protect[ing] society . . . [while] recognizing that the application of sanctions which are consistent with the seriousness of the offense is appropriate in all cases" (Fla. Stat. Ann. § 39.001(2)(a) [West Supp. 1988]); "render[ing] appropriate punishment to offenders" (Haw. Rev. Stat. § 571-1 [1985]); "protect[ing] the public by enforcing the legal obligations children have to society" (Ind. Code Ann. § 31–6–1–1 [Burns 1980]) and the like (Feld 1981a, 1988b; Walkover 1984).

Many courts recognize that these changes in purpose clauses signal a basic philosophical reorientation in juvenile justice (*State ex rel. D.D.H. v. Dostert*, 269 S.E.2d 401 [W. Va. 1980]). The Washington Supreme Court reasoned that "sometimes punishment is treatment" and upheld the legislature's conclusion that "accountability for criminal behavior, the prior criminal activity and punishment commensurate with age, crime and criminal history does as much to rehabilitate, correct and direct an errant youth as does the prior philosophy of focusing on the particular characteristics of the individual juveniles" (*State v. Lawley*, 91 Wash. 2d 654, 656, 591 P.2d 772, 773 [1979]). The Nevada Supreme Court endorsed punishment and held that "by formally recognizing the legitimacy of punitive and deterrent sanctions for criminal offenses juvenile courts will be properly and somewhat belatedly expressing society's firm disapproval of juvenile crime and will be clearly issuing a threat of punishment for criminal acts to the juvenile population" (*In re Seven Minors*, 99 Nev. 427, 433, 664 P.2d 947, 950 [1983]). Although a legislature certainly may conclude that punishment is an appropriate goal and a legitimate strategy for controlling young offenders, when it opts to shape behavior by punishment, it must provide the procedural safeguards of the criminal law, such as juries and lawyers (Feld 1988b).

## JUST DESERTS DISPOSITIONS—JUVENILE COURTS' SENTENCING LEGISLATION AND OPERATIONAL PRACTICES

Sentencing statutes and actual sentencing practices provide another indicator of whether a juvenile court is punishing or treating delinquents. Originally, juvenile court sentences were indeterminate and nonproportional to achieve the child's "best interests" (Rothman 1980; Mack

1909). While the majority of jurisdictions' juvenile sentencing statutes continue to mirror their Progressive origins, several states that use indeterminate sentences instruct judges to consider the seriousness of the offense, the child's culpability, age, and prior record when imposing a sentence (Feld 1988b).

## Determinate Sentences in Juvenile Court

Despite the courts' history of indeterminate sentencing, about one-third of the states now use the present offense and prior record to regulate at least some sentencing decisions through determinate or mandatory minimum sentencing statutes or correctional administrative guidelines (Feld 1988b). The clearest departure from traditional juvenile court sentencing practices occurred in 1977 when Washington State enacted just deserts legislation that based presumptive sentences on a youth's age, present offense, and prior record (Wash. Rev. Code §§ 13.40.01 *et seq.* [Supp. 1988]; Fisher, Fraser, and Forst 1985; Schneider and Schram 1983). The Washington Code creates three categories of offenders—serious, middle, and minor—with presumptive sentences and standard ranges for each. A sentencing guidelines commission developed dispositional and presumptive length-of-stay guidelines in the form of standard ranges that are proportionate to the seriousness of the present offense, age, and prior record (Feld 1988b). In other states as well, juvenile court judges consider present offense, criminal history, and statutory "aggravating and mitigating" factors when imposing determinate sentences on juveniles (N.J. Stat. Ann. §§ 2A:4A-43(a), 44(a),(d) [West 1987]); Tex. Fam. Code Ann. §§ 53.045, 54.04(d)(3) [Vernon Supp. 1988]).

## Mandatory Minimum Terms of Confinement
## Based on Offense

A number of states impose mandatory minimum sentences for certain "designated felonies" (N.Y. Fam. Ct. Act § 352.2 [1987 and Supp. 1988]; Ohio Rev. Code Ann. § 2151.355 [Anderson Supp. 1987]; Feld 1988b). While some mandatory minimum sentencing statutes are discretionary, others require the court to commit youths for the mandatory minimum period (Del. Code Ann. tit. 10, § 937(c)(1) [Supp. 1986]; Feld 1988b). These "therapeutic" sentencing laws are addressed to "violent and repeat offenders," "aggravated juvenile offenders," "serious juvenile offenders," or "designated felons" (Colo. Rev. Stat. § 19–3–113.1 [1986]; Conn. Gen. Stat. § 46B-141(a) [1986]; Ga. Code Ann. § 15–11–37(a)(2) [1985 and Supp. 1988]). The minimum terms of mandatory confinement range from twelve to eighteen months, to age twenty-one, or to the adult limit for the same offense (Feld 1988b). Basing mandatory min-

266 JUSTICE FOR CHILDREN

imum sentences on the offense precludes any individualized consideration of the offender's "real needs."

### Administrative Sentencing and Parole Release Guidelines

Several states' departments of corrections have adopted administrative
guidelines that use offense criteria to specify proportional mandatory
minimum terms and these provide another form of just deserts sentencing
(Ariz. Dept. Corr. 1986; Ga. D.Y.S. 1985; Forst, Friedman, and Coates
1985; Feld 1988b). While adult prison and parole authorities have used
guidelines for decades, their use for juveniles is more recent. In California,
juveniles committed to the Youth Authority are released by the Youthful
Offender Parole Board (Forst and Blomquist 1991). The Board uses offense-based categories to establish the parole consideration date that reflect its assessment of the "seriousness of the specific [offense] and the
degree of danger those committed to the Youth Authority pose to the
public" (Cal. Admin. Code tit. 15, § 4945 (1987); Private Sector 1987).

## CONDITIONS OF JUVENILE CONFINEMENT

Another way to determine whether juvenile courts punish or treat young
offenders is to examine the correctional facilities to which they are sent.
The Court in *Gault* belatedly recognized the longstanding contradictions
between rehabilitative rhetoric and punitive reality; conditions of confinement motivated the Court to insist upon minimal procedural safeguards
for juveniles. Historical studies of early Progressive training schools provide a dismal account of institutions that not only failed to rehabilitate
but that were scarcely distinguishable from their adult penal counterparts
(Rothman 1980; Schlossman 1977). Indeed, the juvenile court's lineage
of punitive confinement in the name of rehabilitation can be traced to its
institutional precursor, the House of Refuge (Hawes 1971; Mennel 1973;
Rothman 1971; Sutton 1988).

Contemporary evaluations of juvenile institutions reveal a continuing
gap between rehabilitative rhetoric and punitive reality (Bartollas, Miller,
and Dinitz 1976; Feld 1977, 1981b; Lerner 1986). Research in Massa-
chusetts described violent and punitive institutions in which staff physically abused inmates and were frequently powerless to prevent inmate
violence and predation (Feld 1977, 1981b). A study in Ohio described a
similarly violent and oppressive institutional environment for the "rehabilitation" of young delinquents (Bartollas, Miller, and Dinitz 1976).
Studies in other jurisdictions report staff and inmate violence, physical
abuse, and degrading make-work (Guggenheim 1978; Lerner 1986). The
California Youth Authority (CYA) conducted extensive reviews of its in-

stitutions and concluded that "a young man convicted of a crime cannot pay his debt to society safely. The hard truth is that the CYA staff cannot protect its inmates from being beaten or intimidated by other prisoners" (Lerner 1986:12). The daily reality for juveniles confined in many "treatment" facilities is one of violence, predatory behavior, and punitive incarceration.

Coinciding with these post-*Gault* evaluations, lawsuits challenged conditions of confinement, alleged that they violated inmates' "right to treatment," inflicted "cruel and unusual punishment," and provided another outside view of juvenile corrections (Feld 1978, 1984).[2] In *Nelson v. Heyne* (355 F. Supp. 451 [N.D. Ind. 1972], aff'd, 491 F.2d 352 [7th Cir. 1974]), the court found that inmates were beaten with a "fraternity paddle," injected with psychotropic drugs for social control purposes, and deprived of minimally adequate care and individualized treatment. In *Inmates of Boys' Training School v. Affleck* (346 F. Supp. 1354 [D.R.I. 1972]), the court found inmates confined in dark and cold dungeon-like cells in their underwear, routinely locked in solitary confinement, and subjected to a variety of antirehabilitative practices. In *Morales v. Turman* (383 F. Supp. 53 [E.D. Tex. 1974], *rev'd on other grounds*, 535 F.2d 864 [5th Cir. 1976]), the court found numerous instances of physical brutality and abuse, including physical hazing by staff and inmates, staff-administered beatings and tear-gassings, homosexual assaults, extensive use of solitary confinement, repetitive and degrading make-work, and minimal clinical services. In *Morgan v. Sproat* (432 F. Supp. 1130 [S.D. Miss. 1977]), the court found youths confined in padded cells with no windows or furnishings and only flush holes for toilets, who were denied access to all services or programs except a Bible. In *State v. Werner* (242 S.E.2d 907 [W. Va. 1978]), the court found inmates locked in solitary confinement, beaten, slapped, kicked, and sprayed with mace by staff, required to scrub floors with a toothbrush, and subjected to punitive practices such as standing and sitting for prolonged periods without changing position. Unfortunately, these cases are not atypical, as the many decisions documenting inhumane conditions in juvenile institutions and even adult jails where juveniles are also held demonstrate (Krisberg et al. 1986). Rehabilitative euphemisms such as "providing a structured environment" cannot disguise the punitive reality of juvenile confinement. Although the institutional experience of confined juveniles is not as unmitigatedly bad as that of adult prison inmates (Forst, Fagan, and Vivona 1989), juvenile correctional facilities certainly are not so benign and therapeutic as to justify depriving those who face commitment to them with adequate procedural safeguards.

## Effectiveness of Treatment

Evaluations of the effectiveness of juvenile rehabilitation programs provide scant encouragement (Lab and Whitehead 1988; Whitehead and Lab 1989). The Progressives' optimistic assumptions about human malleability are challenged by empirical evaluations that question both the efficacy of treatment programs and the "scientific" underpinnings of those who administer the enterprise. Martinson's (1974:25) conclusion that "with few and isolated exceptions, the rehabilitative efforts that have been reported so far have had no appreciable effect on recidivism," challenged the fundamental premise of the juvenile court. In another survey of correctional evaluations, Greenberg (1977:140) concluded that

> many correctional dispositions are failing to reduce recidivism, and it thus confirms the general thrust of [Martinson]. Much of what is now done in the name of "corrections" may serve other functions, but the prevention of return to crime is not one of them. Here and there a few modest results alleviate the monotony, but most of these results are modest and obtained through evaluations seriously lacking in rigor. The blanket assertion that "nothing works" is an exaggeration, but not by very much.

More recent evaluations counsel skepticism about the availability of programs that consistently or systematically rehabilitate adult or serious juvenile offenders (Sechrest, White, and Brown 1979; Whitehead and Lab 1989). A meta-analysis of the impact of juvenile treatment on recidivism concluded that "the results are far from encouraging for rehabilitation proponents" (Lab and Whitehead 1988:77).

While the general conclusion that "nothing works" in juvenile or adult corrections has not been persuasively refuted (Melton 1989), it has been strenuously resisted. Gendreau and Ross (1979, 1987), Greenwood and Zimring (1985), Garrett (1985), Izzo and Ross (1990), Roberts and Camasso (1991), and Palmer (1991), for example, stress that some types of programs may have positive effects on selected clients under certain conditions. However, even Palmer's (1991:340) optimistic assessment of the rehabilitation of "rehabilitation" concludes only that "several methods seem promising, but none have been shown to usually produce major reductions [in recidivism] when applied broadly to typical composite samples of offenders."

The critique of the juvenile court does not rest on the premise that "nothing works" or ever can work. Indeed, some demonstration model programs may produce positive changes in some offenders under some conditions. However, after a century of unfulfilled promises, a continuing societal unwillingness to commit scarce resources to the rehabilitative endeavor, and intervention strategies of dubious efficacy, the possibility of an effective treatment program is too fragile a reed upon which to construct an entire, separate adjudicative apparatus. Rather, the inability to treat consistently or effectively coupled with the individious consequences of discretionary decision making suggests the need for restraint in delegating coercive powers to penal therapists to use on a subjective, nonscientific basis. Characterizing coercion as therapy is especially problematic, since rehabilitation is an expansive concept that widens nets of social control and promotes abuse through self-delusion (Cohen 1978; Allen 1964, 1981).

## PUNISHMENT IN JUVENILE COURT AND THE RIGHT TO A JURY TRIAL

There is a strong nationwide movement, both in theory and in practice, away from therapeutic, individualized dispositions toward punitive, offense-based sentences (Feld 1988b; Forst and Blomquist 1991; Gardner 1987). In 1970, when the *McKeiver* Court denied juveniles the right to a jury trial, no states used determinate or mandatory minimum sentencing statutes or administrative guidelines. In the mid- to late seventies, several states adopted "designated felony" and serious offender sentencing legislation, and determinate sentencing guidelines (Feld 1988b). Since 1980, eleven more states have adopted mandatory minimum, determinate sentences, or administrative guidelines, so that now about one-third of the states use explicitly punitive juvenile sentencing strategies (Feld 1988b). During this same period, a similar shift occurred in the use of offense criteria to transfer some juvenile offenders into criminal courts (Feld 1987).

These formal changes, as well as the empirical evaluations of actual sentencing practices, eliminate most of the differences between juvenile and adult criminal sentencing. Basing sentences on the offense and prior record contradicts any therapeutic purpose for juvenile dispositions. Imposing mandatory minimum sentences based on the seriousness of the offense avoids any reference to a youth's "real needs" or "best interests." The revised juvenile court purpose clauses and court decisions endorsing punishment eliminate even rhetorical support for rehabilitation.

The substantive convergence between juvenile and criminal courts serves to underline the remaining procedural differences between the two systems, notably access to juries and to counsel. Based on depictions of courtroom dramas and publicized criminal trials, young people have a cultural expectation of what a "real" trial should be. The contrast be-

tween the ideal-typical jury trial and the "actualized caricature" of a juvenile bench trial fosters a sense of injustice that may delegitimate the
legal process (Ainsworth 1991:1119). Litigants' sense that a legal process
is a just one is affected not only by the outcome of the case, but also by
its procedural aspects which foster a belief that the process itself is fair
(Melton 1989; Ainsworth 1991).

> [T]he key factors contributing to a sense of procedural justice are
> consistency in the process, control of the process by the litigant, re-
> spectful treatment of the litigant, and ethicality of the fact-finder.
> Consistency in the process means both that the system always follows
> prescribed rules and that everyone is treated equally within the sys-
> tem. Process control is the litigant's ability to determine which issues
> will be contested and upon what basis the contest will proceed. Re-
> spectful treatment of the litigant connotes more than just courteous
> interchange; it also includes investing the litigant with the full com-
> plement of rights possessed by other actors in the system. Ethicality
> of the fact-finder entails a sense that the judge is honest, non-biased,
> forthright and non-arbitrary in adjudication. (Ainsworth 1991:1120)

Judged by these criteria, the practices of juvenile courts undermine any
juvenile's sense that he or she has received procedural justice. Denying
juveniles jury trials erodes the consistency norm by treating young people
differently from adults in a quasi-criminal proceeding. The routine absence of defense counsel and the paternalism of juvenile court officials
and even defense lawyers undermines the litigant's control of the process
(Guggenheim 1984; Melton 1989). "Confidence in the ethicality of the
fact-finder is undercut by the dual roles of the juvenile court judge as
finder of fact and sentencing authority . . . [which] creates the unseemly
appearance that guilt has been pre-judged" (Ainsworth 1991:1120). The
perceived and actual procedural deficiencies of the juvenile court undermine its ability to achieve its goals of rehabilitation and legal socialization
(Matza 1964; Melton 1989; Tapp and Kohlberg 1977).

The most striking instance of procedural inequality occurred when
the Supreme Court in *McKeiver* denied to juveniles a right to a jury trial.
In so doing, the Court invoked the traditional treatment rationale, emphasized factual accuracy at trials, and posited parity between the quality
of juvenile and adult adjudications (403 U.S. 528 at 543–48). In light of
the increased punitiveness of juvenile courts, however, equating the roles
of judges with juries as a justification for lesser procedural rights for
young people is questionable.

Judges and juries apply *Winship*'s "proof beyond a reasonable
doubt" standard and decide cases differently (Feld 1984:245).

Juries serve special protective functions in assuring the accuracy of factual determinations, and studies show that juries are more likely to acquit than are judges. Substantive criminal guilt is not just "factual guilt" but a complex assessment of moral culpability. The power of jury nullification provides a nexus between the legislature's original criminalization decision and the community's felt sense of justice in the application of laws to a particular case. These tendencies are attributable to various factors, including jury-judge evaluations of evidence, jury sentiments about the "law" (jury equity), and jury sympathy for the defendant [of which youthfulness garnered the greatest support]. (Feld, 1984:245)

As a result of the *McKeiver* Court's decision to deny juries, a youth tried by a judge in juvenile court is more likely to be convicted, based on the same evidence, than if tried by a jury of detached citizens in a criminal proceeding (Kalven and Zeisel 1966). Greenwood et al. (1983:30–31) compared the conviction rates of similar types of cases in juvenile and adult courts in California and concluded that "it is easier to win a conviction in the juvenile court than in the criminal court, with comparable types of cases."

Ainsworth (1991:1124) offers a variety of reasons why juvenile court judges would convict more readily than do juries. Fact-finding by judges is intrinsically different from fact-finding by juries, since the former try hundreds of cases every year while the latter hear only a few. As a result of hearing many cases routinely, judges may become less meticulous in considering evidence, may evaluate facts more casually than jurors, and may apply less stringently the concepts of reasonable doubt and presumption of innocence. Not only do the personal characteristics of judges differ from those of the members of a jury pool, but it is also more difficult for a defendant to determine how those personal characteristics will affect the decision in a case. While litigants may examine jurors about their attitudes, beliefs, and experiences that may bear upon the way they will decide the case, there is no comparable opportunity to explore a judge's background to determine the presence of judicial biases. In addition to the novelty of deciding cases, juries and judges evaluate testimony differently. Juvenile court judges hear testimony from the same police and probation officers on a recurring basis and develop a settled opinion about their credibility. Similarly, as a result of hearing earlier charges against a juvenile, or presiding over a detention hearing or pretrial motion to suppress evidence, a judge already may have a predetermined view of a youth's credibility and character (Ainsworth 1991:1124). Moreover, fact-finding by a judge differs from that by a jury because an individual fact-finder does not have to discuss either the law or the evidence with a group before coming to a conclusion. In addition, a jury must be instructed explicitly about the law to be applied to a case. By contrast, because the judge in a bench trial is not required to articulate the law, it is more difficult to determine whether the judge understood and applied it correctly (Ainsworth 1991:1125).

While the *McKeiver* Court's facile equation of judges' and juries' fact-finding prowess was arguably wrong, that decision also ignored the additional function that procedural safeguards serve, namely to prevent governmental oppression. This function is especially important in a punitive juvenile court. In *Duncan v. Louisiana* (391 U.S. 145 [1968]), which granted adults the constitutional right to a jury trial in state criminal proceedings, the Court held that fundamental fairness in adult criminal proceedings requires both factual accuracy and protection against governmental oppression. The *Duncan* Court identified the manifold benefits of a jury trial: protection from a weak or biased judge; injection of the community's values into the decision making process; and providing visibility and accountability for the workings of the process. The Court in *Duncan* described the multiple safeguards a jury provides in a criminal proceeding:

> A right to jury trial is granted to criminal defendants in order to prevent oppression by the Government. Those who wrote our constitutions knew from history and experience that it was necessary to protect against unfounded criminal charges brought to eliminate enemies and against judges too responsive to the voice of higher authority. . . . Providing an accused with the right to be tried by a jury of his peers gave him an inestimable safeguard against the corrupt or overzealous prosecutor and against the compliant, biased, or eccentric judge. If the defendant preferred the common-sense judgment of a jury to the more tutored but perhaps less sympathetic reaction of the single judge, he was to have it. Beyond this, the jury trials provisions . . . reflect a fundamental decision about the exercise of official power—a reluctance to entrust plenary powers over the life and liberty of the citizen to one judge or to a group of judges. Fear of unchecked power . . . found expression in the criminal law in this insistence upon community participation in the determination of guilt or innocence. (391 U.S. at 155–56 [1968])

Despite *McKeiver*, at least some state supreme courts recognize that all of these concerns are equally applicable in juvenile proceedings (e. g., *R.L.R. v. State*, 487 P.2d 27 [Alaska 1971].

The increasingly punitive nature of juvenile justice raises a dilemma of constitutional dimensions:

> Is it fair, in the constitutional sense, to expose minors to adult sanctions for crimes, without granting them the same due process rights as adults? . . . The campaign to impose adult-type sanctions on children will collide with advocates who argue that children exposed to adult sanctions must have the same due process rights as adults. (Private Sector 1987:7)

Very few of the states that sentence juveniles on the basis of the "principle of offense" provide juveniles with jury trials. Several states that use offense-based sentencing schemes have explicitly rejected requests for jury trials (Feld 1988b). For juvenile justice operatives, the jury trial has symbolic implications out of proportion to its practical impact, since even in those jurisdictions in which the right to jury trial is available, it is seldom exercised (Burch and Knaup 1970; Note 1979; Ainsworth 1991). Symbolically, however, providing jury trials would acknowledge the punitive reality of juvenile justice as well as the need to provide safeguards against even benevolently motivated governmental coercion.

Providing jury trials in juvenile court requires candor and honesty about what actually transpires in the name of rehabilitation. While it is difficult to be critical of "doing good," it is also the case that benevolence, therapy, and rehabilitation are expansive concepts that may widen the net of social control. Allen (1964:18) has elaborated on this theme:

> It is important . . . to recognize that when, in an authoritative setting, we attempt to do something for a child "because of what he is and needs," we are also doing something to him. The semantics of "socialized justice" are a trap for the unwary. Whatever one's motivations, however elevated one's objectives, if the measures taken result in the compulsory loss of the child's liberty, the involuntary separation of a child from his family, or even the supervision of a child's activities by a probation worker, the impact on the affected individuals is essentially a punitive one. Good intentions and a flexible vocabulary do not alter this reality. This is particularly so when, as is so often the case, the institution to which the child is committed is, in fact, a peno-custodial establishment. We shall escape much confusion here if we are willing to give candid recognition to the fact that the business of the juvenile courts inevitably consists, to a considerable degree, in dispensing punishment. If this is true, we can no more avoid the problem of unjust punishment in the juvenile court than in the criminal court.

As opposed to treatment, punishment acknowledges the harmfulness of coercion and carries with it a greater sense of limits and proportionality. "[S]anctioning culpable conduct on a principle of proportionality, severely limiting the amounts and types of deprivations that are available, and honestly recognizing that the deprivation is a 'hurt' has less chance for perversion than the perpetuation of the system we now have" (Cohen 1978:5).

If one is skeptical of the juvenile justice system's claims of benevolence, then is there anything about juveniles or justice that justifies denying jury trials in delinquency proceedings? In light of the fundamental shift in underlying assumptions about juvenile justice administration, proponents of the traditional juvenile court should demonstrate why juvenile court procedures should not be structured like any other institution that administers punishment. Is there anything about a criminal justice system for youth that justifies or requires different procedures than for similarly situated adults? If there is, does the difference lie in characteristics of juveniles or the nature of the punishments imposed? In light of the punitiveness of contemporary juvenile justice, the burden of proof must rest with proponents of the traditional juvenile court to justify with evidence, not just rhetoric, differences between juvenile and criminal proceedings.

## PUNISHMENT AND JUVENILE JUSTICE IN MINNESOTA

Reflecting the national shift from treatment to punishment in juvenile justice, Minnesota has changed the underlying philosophical premises and sentencing policies of its juvenile courts as well. In 1980, the Minnesota legislature redefined the purpose of juvenile courts.

> The purpose of the laws relating to children alleged or adjudicated to be delinquent is to promote public safety and reduce juvenile delinquency by maintaining the integrity of the substantive law prohibiting certain behavior and by developing individual responsibility for lawful behavior. (Minn. Stat. § 260.011(2) [1982])

Amending purpose clauses reflects more than legislative rhetorical flourishes. Courts base their decisions on those changes. For example, the Minnesota Court of Appeals decided, as a matter of law on the basis of the amended purpose clause, that a juvenile charged with murder should be tried as an adult (*In re D.F.B.*, 430 N.W.2d 475 [Minn. Ct. App. 1988]; Feld 1990). The court noted that "the 1980 amendments also reflect a shift in legislative attitude regarding punishment as a goal of juvenile courts. Prior to the amendments, the stated purpose of those courts was to secure care and guidance. . . . Subsequent to the 1980 amendment . . .

[f]or [those] youths charged with the commission of a crime, a more punitive approach is emphasized" (430 N.W.2d at 478 [1988]). Minnesota's new statement of purpose is adopted from the A.B.A.'s Juvenile Justice Standards, which also recommended determinate and proportional sentences, mandatory counsel, and jury trials (American Bar Association 1980a:5.2).

While the explicit endorsement of punishment in juvenile courts marks a fundamental philosophical departure from its previous rehabilitative orientation, the legislature did not provide for either a jury trial (Feld 1981) or mandatory representation. Moreover, in *In re K.A.A.* (410 N.W.2d 836 [Minn. 1987]), the Minnesota Supreme Court held that a juvenile could not voluntarily waive juvenile court jurisdiction in order to obtain a jury trial and other procedural safeguards in an adult criminal proceeding. "The legislature could, and apparently did, conclude that allowing a juvenile to waive juvenile court jurisdiction for some perceived short-term benefit ignores the best interests of the State in addressing juvenile problems as well as the overall interests of the juvenile" (410 N.W.2d at 840). As a result of *K.A.A.*, juveniles are trapped in a procedurally deficient, Kafkaesque justice system from which there is no possibility of escape.

In theory, juvenile court sentences in Minnesota are "indeterminate"; every sanction is individualized and there is no necessary relationship between the seriousness of the offense and the nature of the disposition. In actual practice, as the dispositional regression analyses indicate (Tables 4-27 through 4-30, 7-15 through 7-18), the legal variables—the present offense, prior record, and previous sentences—account for virtually all of the variance in sentencing that can be explained.

Moreover, the theory of indeterminacy is being eroded in law as well. Minnesota's juvenile sentencing statute, after providing the customary range of dispositional options, requires the judge to set forth in writing "(a) why the best interests of the child are served by the disposition ordered; and (b) what alternative dispositions were considered by the court and why such dispositions were not appropriate in the instant case" (Minn. Stat. Ann. § 260.185 [1986]). In *In re welfare of L.K.W.* (372 N.W.2d 392 [Minn. Ct. App. 1985]), the Minnesota Court of Appeals interpreted this language to require consideration of "less restrictive alternatives" and proportionality of sanctions.

> To measure what is necessary, a trial court must assess two factors, the severity of the child's delinquency, and the severity of the proposed remedy. When the severity of intervention is disproportionate to the severity of the problem, the intervention is not necessary and

cannot lawfully occur. The court must take the least drastic necessary step. (372 N.W.2d at 398)

Reintroducing proportionality and reestablishing the connection between the seriousness of the offense and the severity of the sanction represents a further erosion of the court's rehabilitative premise.

Within the statutory indeterminate framework, the initial decision to commit a youth to a state or private facility remains solely within the discretion of each juvenile court judge who has authority to determine the nature and location of dispositions. For those juveniles who are committed to the state department of corrections, a youth's length of stay is within the discretion of the commissioner of corrections. In 1980, the Minnesota Department of Corrections administratively rejected the theory of indeterminacy and implemented a determinate sentencing plan for youths committed to the state's juvenile institutions. Based on the juvenile's present offense and prior record, the plan "provide[s] a more definite and distinct relationship between the offense and the amount of time required to bring about positive behavior change" (Minnesota Department 1980:2–3). Under the Minnesota Department of Corrections sentencing guidelines, a juvenile's length of stay is based on the seriousness of the offense committed and the weight of "risk of failure" factors that are "predictive to some degree of future delinquent behavior" (Minnesota Department 1980:7). The recidivism "risk factors" included in the juvenile release guidelines are prior felony adjudications and probation and parole failures. Minnesota's sentencing guidelines for adult offenders, which are explicitly punitive and expressly designed to achieve just deserts, rely on severity of the offense and past criminal history as the controlling factors in its determinate sentencing regime (Minnesota Sentencing 1980).

The Minnesota Department of Corrections' decision to implement a determinate sentencing system administratively reflected its concern with the adequacy and equity of individualized treatment dispositions. Prior to the adoption of the guidelines, an evaluation of commitment and release decision making in Minnesota's juvenile correctional institutions concluded that there were no consistent or systematic criteria used in making decisions about when to institutionalize or parole juveniles. Chein (1976:33–37) found that commitment and release decisions were so "individualized" that no personal factors could explain staffs' handling of different youths, that there was no relationship between the seriousness of juveniles' offenses and their dispositions, and that the only significant variable affecting youths' length of confinement was the institution to which they were committed.

The inconsistent and contradictory sentencing patterns in Minnesota's correctional facilities are apparently general characteristics of juvenile correctional "treatment." For example, Wheeler reports that within a nominally "indeterminate" juvenile sentencing system, incarcerated youths serve "fixed sentences" based on the institutions to which they are committed. "The particular institution to which the male offender was assigned appears to be more important in determining length of stay than the offender's social characteristics or offense" (Wheeler 1978:40). As a result, a pattern of uniformity in sentences, rather than individualized differentiation, prevails and "institutional assignment emerges as more important in terms of predicting length of incarceration than the offender's social characteristics or offense" (Wheeler 1978:41).

Apparently, some of Minnesota's juvenile court judges also have informally adopted determinate sentencing guidelines. In *In re D.S.F.* (416 N.W.2d 772 [Minn. Ct. App. 1987]), Judge Crippen observed that "it is evident that a determinate sentence of incarceration imposed by the trial court was prompted by unpublished sentencing guidelines, based singularly on the offense committed, and not by the spontaneous exercise of discretion by the presiding judge" (416 N.W.2d at 779). Judge Crippen further noted that where the sentence is based on type of offense, "we are dealing . . . with a criminal justice sentence, not a juvenile court disposition aimed at doing what is best for the individual. The juvenile has been ordered incarcerated for a definite term as part of a predetermined sentencing practice" (416 N.W.2d at 780). The juvenile in *D.S.F.* received a ninety-day sentence of incarceration for a serious assault. In rejecting a less restrictive alternative disposition, the trial court asserted that confinement was required because "a specific consequence was necessary to impress upon D.S.F. the seriousness of his behavior" (416 N.W.2d at 774).

Determinate and proportional sentencing strikes at the very heart of the traditional juvenile court. While the majority in *D.S.F.* concluded that the disposition was within the broad sentencing discretion that juvenile courts enjoy, the dissent characterized it as "a purely offense-based determinate sentence of incarceration as a largely predetermined consequence for a serious assault. . . . [T]he sentence was chosen based solely on the occurrence of a serious offense . . . and acceptance by the trial court of a settled local court sentencing practice" (416 N.W.2d at 775). Judge Crippen noted that

> [d]eliberate acceptance of offense-based determinate sentencing categorically belies the promises which are the foundation for the 1971 due process analysis of the United States Supreme Court [in *McKeiver*]. Appellate affirmation of criminal justice sentencing in the

> juvenile court unravels the rationale underlying the equal protection
> analysis of the Minnesota Supreme Court [in *In re K.A.A.*]. A system
> already on the brink of its demise is pushed still closer to a long
> postponed day of reckoning. (416 N.W.2d at 777)

If a youth's present offense and prior record already strongly influence juvenile court judges' sentencing decisions both in law and in fact and determine juveniles' institutional length of stay, then shouldn't the dispositional process be formalized through the adoption of statewide sentencing guidelines to regularize commitment, release, and durational decisions? The rationale for the Minnesota Sentencing Guidelines Report (1980:13) is "to reduce sentencing disparity by providing recommendations" governing both the decision to incarcerate and the length of confinement. The legislature's decision to adopt sentencing guidelines was based, in part, on the commission's research, which found some evidence of both racial disparities and regional disparities in the sentencing of offenders (Minnesota Sentencing 1980). Quite clearly, as Chapters Six and Seven indicate, similar racial, gender, and geographic disparities occur in the administration of juvenile justice as well.

## THE FUTURE OF THE JUVENILE COURT: THREE SCENARIOS

For more than two decades, juvenile courts have deflected, co-opted, ignored, or accommodated constitutional and legislative reforms with minimal institutional change. Despite its transformation from a welfare agency into a criminal court, the juvenile court remains essentially unreformed. Public and political concerns about drugs and youth crime encourage the repression rather than rehabilitation of young offenders. With fiscal constraints, budget deficits, and competition from other interest groups, there is little likelihood that treatment services for delinquents will expand. Coupling the emergence of punitive policies with society's unwillingness to provide for the welfare of children in general (National Commission on Children 1991), much less to those who commit crimes, there is scant reason to believe that the juvenile court, as originally conceived, can be rehabilitated.

The recent changes in jurisdiction (Feld 1987), sentencing (Feld 1988b), and procedures (Feld 1984) reflect ambivalence about the role and purpose of juvenile courts and the social control of children. As juvenile courts converge procedurally and substantively with criminal courts, is there any reason to maintain a separate court whose only remaining distinctions are procedures under which no adult would agree to be tried (Dawson 1990a; Federle 1990; Wolfgang 1982; Wizner and Keller 1977; McCarthy 1977b; Guggenheim 1978)? While most commentators acknowledge the emergence of a punitive juvenile court, they recoil at the prospect of its outright abolition, emphasize that children are different from people, and that distinctions between "delinquents" and "criminals" should be maintained (Gardner 1987; Melton 1989; Dawson 1990a; Rubin 1979). Most conclude, however, that the juvenile court sorely needs a new rationale, perhaps one that melds punishment with reduced culpability and with procedural justice (Walkover 1984; Melton 1989; Gardner 1989; American Bar Association 1980a; Rubin 1979).

There are three plausible responses to a juvenile court that imposes punishment in the name of treatment and simultaneously denies young offenders elementary procedural justice: (1) juvenile courts could be "restructured to fit their original [therapeutic] purpose," (*McKeiver v. Pennsylvania*, 403 U.S. at 557 [1970]); (2) punishment could be embraced as an acceptable and appropriate part of delinquency proceedings but coupled with all criminal due-process safeguards (Melton 1989; Forst and Blomquist 1991; American Bar Association 1980a); or (3) juvenile court jurisdiction over criminal conduct could be abolished and young offenders tried in criminal courts with certain modifications in substantive and procedural criminal law (Feld 1984, 1988b; Ainsworth 1991).

### Return to an Informal, "Rehabilitative" Juvenile Court

Some proponents of an informal, therapeutic juvenile court contend that the "experiment" cannot be declared a failure since it has never been implemented fully or effectively (Ferdinand 1991). From their inception, juvenile courts and correctional facilities have had more in common with penal facilities than with welfare agencies, hospitals, or clinics (Rothman 1980; Schlossman 1977). By the 1960s and the *Gault* decision, the failures of implementation were readily apparent (President's Commission 1967a, 1967b). Therefore, any proponent of reinvigorating the juvenile court as an informal, therapeutic welfare agency must first demonstrate why resources and personnel that have not been available previously will now become available.

Even if a coterie of clinicians suddenly descended on a juvenile court, it would be a dubious social and legal policy to recreate the juvenile court as originally conceived. Interwoven throughout this critique of "individualized justice" is the premise that juvenile courts are substantively and procedurally lawless (American Friends 1971). Despite the existence of statutes and procedural rules, juvenile courts operate effectively unconstrained by the rule of law.

To the extent that judges make dispositions based on individualized assessments of an offender's "best interests" or "real needs," judicial discretion is formally unrestricted. If there are neither practical scientific or clinical bases by which judges can classify for treatment (Sechrest 1987), then the exercise of "sound discretion" is simply a euphemism for idiosyncratic judicial subjectivity and arbitrariness. If intervention were consistently benign and effective, perhaps differential processing would be tolerable. But juveniles committed to penal institutions or whose liberty is restrained regard the experience as a sanction rather than as beneficial (Wizner and Keller 1977). At the least, similarly situated offenders will be handled differently based on extraneous personal characteristics such as race or gender, or on social structural vagaries for which they are not responsible. At the worst, if juvenile courts effectively punish, then discretionary sentences based on individualized assessments permit unequal and discriminatory sanctions on invidious bases.

Procedural informality is the concomitant of substantive discretion. The traditional juvenile court's informal procedures are predicated on the assumption of benevolence (*Gault*, 387 U.S. 1 [1967]). If clinical decision making is not constrained substantively, then it cannot be limited procedurally either, since every case is unique (Matza 1964). A primary role of lawyers is to manipulate legal rules for their clients' advantage; a discretionary court without objective laws or formal procedures is unfavorable terrain. The limited presence and role of counsel in many juvenile courts may reflect judicial adherence to a treatment model that no longer exists, if it ever did. But the absence of lawyers reduces the ability of the legal process to invoke existing laws to make courts conform to their legal mandates. The closed, informal, and confidential nature of delinquency proceedings reduces visibility and accountability, and precludes external checks on coercive intervention.

The fundamental shortcoming of the traditional juvenile court is not simply a failure of implementation, but a failure of conception. The original juvenile court was conceived of as a social service agency in a judicial setting, a fusion of social welfare and social control. But providing for child welfare is ultimately a societal responsibility rather than a judicial one (National Commission on Children 1991). It is unrealistic to expect juvenile courts, or any other legal institution, to resolve all of the social ills afflicting young people. Young people, especially the clients of the juvenile court, are the poorest and most disadvantaged segment of the population. Despite claims of being a child-centered nation, we care less about other people's children than we do our own, especially when they are children of other colors or cultures (National Commission on Children 1991; Edelman 1987). Without a societal commitment to social service systems that meet the minimum medical, housing, education, nutrition and nurturing needs of all young people on a voluntary basis, the juvenile court functions primarily as a coercive mechanism for involuntary control, however ineffective it may be in delivering services or rehabilitating offenders. Historical analyses of juvenile justice suggest that when social services and social control are combined in one setting, social welfare considerations are quickly subordinated to custodial ones (Rothman 1980; Ferdinand 1989, 1991; Sutton 1988; Platt 1977).

In part, the juvenile court's inevitable subordination of social welfare to custody and social control stems from its fundamentally penal focus. Rather than focusing on the characteristics of children for which they are not responsible and which could improve their life circumstances—their lack of decent education, their lack of adequate housing, their unmet health needs, their deteriorated family and social circumstances (National Commission on Children 1991)—juvenile court law focuses on a violation of criminal law that is their fault and for which they are responsible (Fox 1970b). As long as juvenile courts emphasize the characteristics of children least likely to elicit sympathy and ignore the social conditions most likely to engender a desire to nurture and help all young people, the law reinforces retributive rather than rehabilitative impulses. So long as juvenile courts operate in a societal context that does not provide adequate social services for children in general, intervention in the lives of those who commit crimes inevitably will be for purposes of social control rather than social welfare.

## PROCEDURAL DUE PROCESS AND PUNISHMENT IN JUVENILE COURT

Articulating new purposes for juvenile courts requires more than invoking treatment versus punishment formulae. The contemporary reality is that there are no practical or operational differences between the two. Acknowledging that juvenile courts punish imposes an obligation to provide all criminal procedural safeguards, since "the condition of being a boy does not justify a kangaroo court" (*In re Gault*, 387 U.S. at 28). While procedural parity with adults may realize the *McKeiver* Court's fear of ending the juvenile court experiment, to fail to do so perpetuates injustice. Treating similarly situated juveniles dissimilarly, punishing them in the name of treatment, and denying them basic safeguards fosters a sense of injustice that thwarts any reform efforts (Melton 1989).

Articulating alternative rationales for handling young offenders requires reconciling the two contradictory impulses provoked by recognizing that the child is a criminal and the criminal is a child. If the traditional juvenile court provides neither therapy nor justice and cannot be rehabilitated, then the policy alternatives for responding to young offenders are either (1) to make juvenile courts more like criminal courts, or (2) to make criminal courts more like juvenile courts. In reconsidering basic premises, issues of substance and procedure must be addressed whether young offenders ultimately are tried in a separate juvenile court or in a criminal court (Feld 1988b). Issues of substantive justice include developing and implementing a doctrinal rationale—diminished responsibility or reduced capacity—for sentencing young offenders differently, and more leniently, than older defendants (Feld 1988b; Melton 1989; Gardner 1989; Twentieth Century Fund 1978). Issues of procedural justice include providing youths with *all* of the procedural safeguards adult receive *and* additional protections that recognize their immaturity (Rosenberg 1980; Feld 1984; Melton 1989).

Many recent commentators acknowledge that "the assumptions underlying the juvenile court show it to be a bankrupt legal institution" that is increasingly penal in character (Melton 1989:166). Rather than proposing to abolish the juvenile court, they propose to transform it into an explicitly penal court, albeit one which limits punishment based on reduced culpability and provides enhanced procedural justice (Walkover 1984; Melton 1989; Gardner 1989; American Bar Association 1980a; Forst and Blomquist 1991; Rubin 1979).

The paradigm of the "new juvenile court" is that propounded by the American Bar Association's Juvenile Justice Standards project. The twenty-six volumes of Juvenile Justice Standards recommend the repeal of jurisdiction over status offenders, the use of proportional and determinate sentences to sanction delinquent offenders, the use of restrictive offense criteria to regularize pretrial detention and judicial transfer decisions, and the provision of all criminal procedural safeguards, including nonwaivable counsel and jury trials (Flicker 1983; McCarthy 1977; Wizner and Keller 1977). Under the Juvenile Justice Standards, "the rehabilitative model of juvenile justice is rejected and the principles of criminal law and procedure become the cornerstones of a new relationship between the child and the state" (McCarthy 1977:1094).

While proponents of the "criminal juvenile court" model advocate a fusion of reduced culpability sentencing with greater procedural justice (Melton 1989; Gardner 1989; ABA 1980a; Rubin 1979), they often fail to explain why these principles must be implemented within a separate juvenile court rather than in a criminal court. The Juvenile Justice Standards assert that "removal of the treatment rationale does not destroy the rationale for a separate system or for utilization of an ameliorative approach; it does, however, require a different rationale" (American Bar Association 1980d:19 n. 5). Unfortunately, even though the standards propose a virtual replication of adult criminal procedure, they do not provide any rationale for doing so in a separate juvenile system.

Other commentators have suggested some possible rationales. Gardner (1987) suggests that maintaining a separate punishment system for juveniles may avoid some of the stigmatic effects of a "criminal" label. Rubin (1979) speculates that since there would need to be some specialized juvenile procedures and dispositional facilities, that it is more practical and less risky to retain specialized juvenile divisions of general trial courts rather than to abolish juvenile courts entirely. Given institutional and bureaucratic inertia, however, it may be that only a clean break with the personnel and practices of the past could permit the implementation of the procedures and policies they endorse.

Proponents of a criminal juvenile court point to the deficiencies of criminal courts—overcriminalization, ineffective defense representation and excessive caseloads, poor administration, insufficient sentencing alternatives (Rubin 1979)—to justify retaining a separate juvenile court. Unfortunately, these characteristics are equally applicable to juvenile courts (Dawson 1990a). While certain elements of the criminal justice system, such as bail, might pose additional problems if applied without modification to juveniles (Dawson 1990a), those are not compelling justifications for retaining a complete and separate judicial system. Rather, such arguments suggest a comparison of the relative quality of juvenile and criminal justice in each state to determine in which system young people are more likely to be treated justly and fairly.

The only real substantive difference between the "criminal juvenile court" that the Juvenile Justice Standards recommend and adult criminal courts is that the former would impose shorter sentences on youths than do criminal courts (Wizner and Keller 1977). Particularly for serious young offenders, the quality and quantity of punishment imposed in juvenile court is less than that in criminal courts (Melton 1989). Maintaining a separate court may be the only way to achieve uniformly shorter sentences and insulate youths from criminal courts' "get tough" sentencing policies (Gardner 1987).

If, as this research indicates, there is a relationship between procedural formality and substantive severity, could a separate "criminal juvenile court" continue to afford leniency? As juvenile courts become more formal—lawyers insisting on adherence to the rule of law; openness, visibility, and accountability; proportional and determinate sentencing guidelines—would the convergence between juvenile and criminal courts increase juvenile courts' repressiveness and erode sentencing differences? Comparing the sentencing practices in the more formal urban juvenile courts with those of the more informal rural courts provides some indication of the formality-severity connections. Can juvenile courts only be lenient because their substantive and procedural discretion is exercised behind closed doors? Would the imposition of the rule of law prevent them from affording leniency to most youths? These issues are not even recognized, much less answered, by the Juvenile Justice Standards.

## YOUNG OFFENDERS IN CRIMINAL COURT

If the child is a criminal and the primary purpose of intervention is social control, then all young offenders could be tried in criminal courts alongside their adult counterparts. Before returning young offenders to criminal courts, however, there are preliminary issues of substance and procedure that courts and legislatures must address. Issues of substantive justice include developing a rationale for sentencing young offenders differently, and more leniently, than older defendants. Issues of procedural justice include affording youths alternative safeguards *in addition* to full procedural parity with adult defendants. Taken in combination, legislation can avoid the "worst of both worlds" (*Kent v. United States*, 383 U.S. at 556) by providing both more procedural protections than those afforded to adults and more justice in sentencing.

## SUBSTANTIVE JUSTICE—JUVENILES' CRIMINAL RESPONSIBILITY

The primary virtue of the contemporary juvenile court is that serious young offenders typically receive shorter sentences than do adult offenders convicted of comparable crimes. As a policy goal, young offenders should survive the mistakes of adolescence with their life chances intact (Twentieth Century Fund 1978; Zimring 1982). This goal is threatened if youths sentenced in criminal courts received the same draconian sentences inflicted on eighteen-year-old "adults." But, of course, the contemporary juvenile court's seeming virtue of shorter sentences for serious offenders is offset by the far more numerous minor offenders who receive longer sentences as juveniles than they would as adults (Ainsworth 1991).

To provide shorter sentences for young people does not require that they be tried in separate juvenile courts. Both juvenile and adult courts are supposed to separate the determination of guilt or innocence from sentencing and confine discretion largely to the sentencing phase (Dawson 1990a). Adult courts are capable of dispensing lenient sentences to youthful offenders when appropriate (Wizner and Keller 1977). Several commentators have developed a variety of doctrinal and policy justifications for sentencing young people less severely than their adult counterparts (Feld 1988b; Gardner 1987, 1989; Melton 1989; Twentieth Century Fund 1978).

The premise of the original juvenile court was that children were immature and irresponsible. These assumptions about lack of criminal capacity built upon the common law's infancy mens rea defense (Fox 1970b; McCarthy 1977; Walkover 1984; Weissman 1983). At common law, children less than seven years old were conclusively presumed to lack criminal capacity, while those fourteen years of age and older were treated as fully responsible. Between the ages of seven and fourteen years, there was a rebuttable presumption of criminal incapacity (Fox 1970b; McCarthy 1977; Weisman 1983). The common-law infancy gradations reflect developmental differences that render youths less culpable or criminally responsible than their adult counterparts. Juvenile court legislation simply extended upward by a few years the general presumption of youthful criminal incapacity.

The common-law infancy defense and other "diminished responsibility" doctrines provide a conceptual basis for shorter sentences for juveniles. When sentencing within a framework of deserved punishment, it would be fundamentally unjust to impose the same penalty upon a juvenile as upon an adult. Deserved punishment emphasizes censure, condemnation, and blame (Von Hirsch 1976, 1986). Penalties proportionate to the seriousness of the crime reflect the connection between the nature of the conduct and its blameworthiness.

Because the principle of commensurate punishment proportions sanctions to the seriousness of the offense, it shifts the analytical focus to the meaning of seriousness. The seriousness of an offense is the product of two components—harm and culpability (Von Hirsch 1976). Evaluations of harm focus on the degree of injury inflicted, risk created, or value taken. The perpetrator's age is of little consequence when assessing the harmfulness of a criminal act.

Assessments of seriousness, however, also include the quality of the actor's choice to engage in the conduct that produced the harm. It is with respect to the culpability of choices—the blameworthiness of acting in a particular harm-producing way—that the issue of youthfulness becomes especially relevant.

Psychological research indicates that young people move through developmental stages of cognitive functioning with respect to legal reasoning, internalization of social and legal expectations, and ethical decision making (Kohlberg 1969; Piaget 1932; Tapp and Kohlberg 1977). This developmental sequence and the changes in cognitive processes are strikingly parallel to the imputations of responsibility associated with the common-law infancy defense. Developmental psychology research indicates that individuals acquire most of the legal and moral values and reasoning capacity that will guide their behavior through later life by mid-adolescence (Kohlberg 1964; Tapp 1976).

While a youth fourteen years of age or older may know "right from wrong," that is, possess the requisite criminal capacity, he or she is still not as blameworthy and deserving of comparable punishment as an adult offender. While juveniles are as capable as older offenders of inflicting harms and of being aware abstractly of "right from wrong," they are less able to make sound judgments or moral distinctions and thus are not as culpable (Kohlberg 1964). Relative to adults, juveniles are less able to form moral judgments, less capable of controlling their impulses, and less aware of the consequences of their acts.

> [A]dolescents, particularly in the early and middle teen years, are more vulnerable, more impulsive, and less self-disciplined than adults. Crimes committed by youths may be just as harmful to victims as those committed by older persons, but they deserve less punishment because adolescents have less capacity to control their conduct and to think in long-range terms than adults. (Twentieth Century Fund 1978:7)

Because juveniles are less blameworthy than adults, their diminished responsibility means that they "deserve" less punishment than adults for the same crime.

The crimes of children are seldom their fault alone. Families, schools, and communities are responsible for socializing young people, and society shares at least some of the blame for their offenses. Moreover, to the extent that the ability to make responsible choices is learned behavior, the dependent status of youth systematically deprives them of opportunities to learn to be responsible (Zimring 1982). Finally, children live their lives, as they commit their crimes, in groups. Young people are more susceptible to peer group influences than their older counterparts, which lessens, but does not excuse, their criminal liability (Zimring 1981).

The Supreme Court in *Thompson v. Oklahoma* (108 S. Ct. 2687 [1988]) analyzed the criminal responsibility of young offenders and provided additional support for shorter sentences for reduced culpability even for youths older than the common-law infancy threshold of age fourteen. In vacating Thompson's capital sentence for a murder committed at fifteen years of age, the plurality concluded that "a young person is not capable of acting with the degree of culpability that can justify the ultimate penalty" (*Thompson*, 108 S. Ct. at 2692). Although a plurality of the Supreme Court subsequently upheld the death penalty for youths who were sixteen or seventeen at the time of their offenses (*Stanford v. Kentucky*, 109 S. Ct. 2969 [1989]), it did so on the narrow grounds that there was no clear national consensus that such executions violated "evolving standards of decency" in the Eighth Amendment's prohibition against "cruel and unusual" punishment.

In *Thompson*, the Court concluded that juveniles are less blameworthy for their crimes than are their adult counterparts. Earlier decisions also noted that youthfulness was a mitigating factor at sentencing (*Lockett v. Ohio*, 438 U.S. 584 [1978]; *Eddings v. Oklahoma*, 455 U.S. 104 [1982]). In *Eddings* (455 U.S. at 116), the Supreme Court observed that "the chronological age of a minor is itself a relevant mitigating factor of great weight, [as is] the background and mental and emotional development of a youthful defendant [at] sentencing." The Court in *Thompson* (108 S. Ct. at 2698) emphasized that deserved punishment must reflect individual culpability and concluded that "[t]here is also broad agreement on the proposition that adolescents as a class are less mature and responsible than adults." Significantly, even though Thompson was responsible for his crime, he could not be punished as severely as an adult, simply because of his age.

> [Y]outh is more than a chronological fact. It is a time and condition of life when a person may be most susceptible to influence and to psychological damage. Our history is replete with laws and judicial recognition that minors, especially in their earlier years, generally are less mature and responsible than adults. Particularly "during the formative years of childhood and adolescence, minors often lack the experience, perspective, and judgement" expected of adults. . . . [T]he Court has already endorsed the proposition that less culpability should attach to a crime committed by a juvenile than to a comparable crime committed by an adult. (*Thompson v. Oklahoma*, 108 S. Ct. at 2698)

The Court emphasized that even though a youth may be capable of inflicting blameworthy harm, the culpability of the choice may be less than that of an adult.

> Inexperience, less education, and less intelligence make the teenager less able to evaluate the consequences of his or her conduct while at the same time he or she is much more apt to be motivated by mere emotion or peer pressure than is an adult. The reasons why juveniles are not trusted with the privileges and responsibilities of an adult also explain why their irresponsible conduct is not as morally reprehensible as that of an adult. (*Thompson*, 108 S. Ct. at 2699)

The Court cited numerous other instances—serving on a jury, voting, marrying, driving, and drinking—in which juveniles' lack of experience and judgment resulted in their being treated differently from adults (*Thompson*, 108 S. Ct. at 2693). In all of those cases, states act paternalistically and impose disabilities because of youths' presumptive incapacity to "exercise choice freely and rationally" (*Thompson*, 108 S. Ct. at 2693 n. 23). The Court emphasized that it would be both inconsistent and a cruel irony to suddenly find juveniles as culpable as adult defendants for purposes of capital punishment. "[T]he very assumptions we make about our children when we legislate on their behalf tells us that it is likely cruel, and certainly unusual, to impose on a child a punishment that takes as its predicate the existence of a fully rational, choosing agent" (*Thompson*, 108 S. Ct. at 2693 n. 23).

Quite apart from differences in culpability, there are other reasons why juveniles deserve less severe punishment than adults for comparable crimes. The ways offenders subjectively experience a penalty differ with age. Penalties—whether adult punishment or juvenile "treatment"—are measured in days, months, or years. However, youths and adults conceive of and experience similar lengths of time differently. Youths and adults differ in their subjective and objective assessments of time both with respect to "future time perspective" and "present duration" (Cottle 1976; Friedman 1982; Piaget 1969). The progression from children to adults in thinking about and experiencing time follows a developmental sequence similar to the development of responsibility for making blameworthy choices. Without a mature appreciation of future time, juveniles are less able to understand the consequences of their acts and are correspondingly less culpable. Because juveniles do not have an "objective" sense of the duration of time comparable to an adult, objectively equivalent sentences are experienced subjectively as unequal. While a three-month sentence may be lenient for an adult offender, it is the equivalent of an entire summer vacation for a youth, a very long period of time. Because juveniles are more dependent on their parents, removal from home is a more severe punishment than it would be for adults. Thus, sentencing adults and juveniles to similar terms for similar offenses would be unjust.

Shorter sentences for reduced responsibility is a more modest rationale for treating young people differently than adults than the rehabilitative justifications advanced by the Progressive child savers. Shorter sentences for reduced culpability can be achieved in adult courts by providing youths with fractional reductions of adult sentences. This could take the form of an explicit "youth discount" at the time of sentencing. For example, a fourteen-year-old might receive 25% or 33% of the adult penalty, a sixteen-year-old 50% or 66%, and an eighteen-year-old the full adult penalty as is presently the case. Of course, a proposal for explicit fractional reductions in youth sentences can only be made against the backdrop of realistic, humane, and determinate adult sentencing practices. Several of the "serious" juvenile offender or designated felony sentencing statutes provide terms for young offenders that are considerably shorter than sentences for their adult counterparts. For youths below the age of fourteen, the common-law mens rea infancy defense would acquire new vitality for proportionally shorter sentences or even noncriminal dispositions.

A graduated age/culpability sentencing scheme could avoid some of the inconsistency and injustice associated with the binary either/or juvenile versus adult sentencing played out in judicial waiver proceedings (Feld 1987, 1990). Depending upon whether transfer is ordered, the sentences that youths receive can differ by an order of magnitude or more (Fagan and Deschenes 1990). Because of the differences in consequences, transfer hearings consume a disproportionate amount of juvenile court time and energy (Dawson 1990a). Abolishing the juvenile court would eliminate the need for transfer hearings, save considerable resources that are ultimately expended to no purpose, eliminate the punishment gap that occurs when youths cross from one system to the other, and assure similar consequences to similar offenders.

Trying young people in criminal courts with full procedural safeguards would not especially diminish judges' expertise about appropriate dispositions for young people. The Progressives envisioned a specialized juvenile court judge who would possess the wisdom of a "kadi" (Matza 1964). Increasingly, however, district court judges handle juvenile matters as part of their general docket or rotate through juvenile court on short-term assignments without acquiring any special juvenile dispositional expertise. Even in specialized juvenile courts, the information necessary for just dispositions resides with the court services personnel who advise the judge on sentences, rather than with the court itself. For a youth who is criminally convicted, court services personnel can still advise the judge as to the appropriate sentence, and young offenders could be transferred to family court if a welfare disposition is appropriate.

Even a punitive sentence does not require incarcerating juveniles in adult jails and prisons. The existing detention facilities, training schools and institutions provide the option of age-segregated dispositional facilities. Moreover, insisting explicitly on humane conditions of confinement could do at least as much to improve the lives of incarcerated youths as has the "right to treatment" or the "rehabilitative ideal" (Feld 1977, 1981b). A recognition that most young offenders will return to society imposes an obligation to provide the resources for self-improvement on a voluntary basis.

## PROCEDURAL JUSTICE—PROVIDING SAFEGUARDS FOR YOUTHS

The decades since *Gault* have witnessed a procedural convergence between juvenile courts and adult criminal courts. At least in theory, many of the formal procedural attributes of criminal courts are routine aspects of juvenile justice administration as well. The same laws and rules apply to arresting adults and taking juveniles into custody, to searches, and to pretrial identification procedures (Dawson 1990a). Juveniles charged with felony offenses are subjected to the same types of fingerprinting, photographing, and booking processes as adult criminal defendants.

The greater procedural formality and adversary nature of the juvenile court reflects the attenuation between the court's therapeutic mission and its social control functions. The many instances in which states choose to treat juvenile offenders procedurally like adult criminal defendants is one aspect of this process (Feld 1984). Despite the criminalizing of juvenile justice, it remains nearly as true today as two decades ago that "the child receives the worst of both worlds . . . receiving neither the protections accorded to adults nor the solicitous care and regenerative treatment postulated for children" (*Kent v. United States*, 383 U.S. at 556). Most states' juvenile codes provide neither special procedural safeguards to protect juveniles from the consequences of their own immaturity nor the full panoply of adult criminal procedural safeguards to protect them from punitive state intervention. Instead, juvenile offenders are treated like adult criminal defendants when formal equality redounds to their disadvantage and are subjected to less effective juvenile court procedures when those procedural deficiencies redound to the advantage of the state (Feld 1984). Commentators have identified numerous instances in which the procedural protections for juveniles are not comparable either formally or functionally to those provided to adult criminal defendants (Feld 1984; McCarthy 1977; Melton 1989; Rosenberg 1980; Ainsworth 1991).

Differences in age and competence suggest that youths should receive more protections than adults rather than less (Melton 1989). The rationales to sentence juveniles differently from adults also justify providing them with *all* of the procedural safeguards adult defendants receive *and* additional protections that recognize their immaturity. This dual-maximal strategy would provide enhanced protection for children explicitly because of their vulnerability and immaturity (Rosenberg 1980; Melton 1989).

One example where this dual-maximal procedural strategy would produce different results is the waiver of Fifth and Sixth Amendment constitutional rights. The Supreme Court in *Gault* noted that the appointment of counsel for juveniles is the prerequisite to procedural justice (387 U.S. at 38). In the decades since *Gault*, the promise of counsel remains unrealized and many youths in many states do not receive the assistance of counsel to which they are constitutionally entitled. The principal reason that so many youths are unrepresented is because judges determined that they waived their right to counsel in a "knowing, intelligent, and voluntary" manner under the "totality of the circumstances." In so doing, juvenile courts use the adult waiver standard to gauge juveniles' exercises of rights despite compelling evidence that youths are simply not as competent to make such decisions (Grisso 1980, 1981). A system of justice that recognizes the disabilities of youths would provide that there could be no waivers of the right to counsel or the privilege against self-incrimination without prior consultation with counsel (American Bar Association 1980b). The right to counsel would attach as soon as a juvenile is taken into custody and would be self-invoking (American Bar Association 1980b). It would not require a juvenile to affirmatively request counsel as is the case for adults (*Moran v. Burbine*, 475 U.S. 412 [1986]). The presence and availability of counsel throughout the process would assure that juveniles' rights are respected and implemented. The Juvenile Justice Standards proposed this policy, albeit in a juvenile court setting.

Full procedural parity in criminal courts, coupled with alternative substantive and procedural safeguards, can provide the same or greater protections than does the current juvenile court. Expunging criminal records and eliminating collateral civil disabilities following the successful completion of a sentence could avoid "criminal" labels and afford equivalent relief from an isolated youthful folly as does juvenile court confidentiality.

## THE JUVENILE COURT AND THE FUTURE OF CHILDHOOD

Ideological changes in strategies of social control and in the cultural conception of children a century ago produced the juvenile court. One of these ideas, strategies of social control, no longer distinguishes juvenile from criminal courts. The former are primarily inadequate replicas of the latter. Despite their inability to prevent or reduce youth crime, juvenile courts survive and even prosper. Despite statutory and judicial reforms, official discretion arguably has increased rather than decreased. Why, even without empirical support, does the ideology of therapeutic justice persist so tenaciously?

The answer is that the social control is directed at children. But the judicial and legal conception of children is changing as well. The concept of childhood is as much a social construction as a biological fact (Ainsworth 1991). The original juvenile court was premised on certain beliefs and assumptions about the irresponsible and dependent nature of children. More recently, however, the assumption that young people are inherently and essentially different from adults is being eroded (Ainsworth 1991). In *Fare v. Michael C.* (442 U.S. 707 [1979]), the Supreme Court rejected the suggestion that a juvenile's purported waiver of his or her rights should be judged by a standard other than that used for adults (Ainsworth 1991:1116). The shift from sentences based on characteristics of the offender to sentences based on the seriousness of the offense implies a degree of criminal responsibility by young people that Progressives would not have acknowledged (Feld 1988b). The imposition of substantial penalties in juvenile court, as well as the execution of juveniles waived to and convicted in criminal courts, provides a stark indicator of changes in attitudes about the criminal responsibility of adolescents (*Stanford v. Kentucky*, 109 S. Ct. 2969 [1989]).

Abolishing the juvenile court would force a long overdue and critical reassessment of the entire social construction of "childhood." As long as young people are regarded as fundamentally different from adults, it becomes too easy to rationalize and justify an inferior justice system. The gap between the quality of justice afforded juveniles and adults can be conveniently rationalized on the grounds that "after all, they are only children," and children are entitled only to custody, not liberty (*Schall v. Martin*, 467 U.S. 260 [1984]). So long as the mythology prevails that juvenile court intervention is "benign" coercion and that in any event children should not expect more, youths will continue to receive "the worst of both worlds."

Rothman (1980:288–89) concluded his analysis of the Progressive origins of the juvenile court with trenchant insights and questions:

> In sum, one searches in vain for any thorough reappraisal of the Progressive ideology or any coherent effort to review reform postulates in light of their marginal relationship to actual practice.
>
> It is difficult to trace this record without some impatience and disappointment. Our predecessors should have known better. But rather than second-guess them, it is appropriate to analyze why they remained so dedicated to their principles, so unwilling to entertain self-doubt. In part, it may be inevitable that reformers become partisans,

unable to examine the outcome of their efforts. In part, [they] . . . were frightened that the obvious alternatives to their design would generate even worse abuses. . . . The past was so bleak and so lacking in humanitarian spirit, that to undermine the Progressive program would be to return to barbarism. . . .

Reformers did have one last defense: how could anyone condemn their principles or search for alternatives when their recommendations had never been truly implemented? Failures reflected not faulty conceptualization but inadequate funding. Hence it was appropriate to call for more clinics, better probation officers, smaller cottages, and better trained house parents. . . .

All of these contentions had a point. Given the many flaws in implementation, there was no shortage of corrective measures that might be adopted, and then perhaps rehabilitation would occur. And Progressives were entitled to believe that only an ethic of rehabilitation could dampen the spirit of retribution. The points certainly were fair—but they did not reach to the heart of the problem, to the tension between punishment and treatment. How condemn a court's casual indifference to the child when it claimed to be helping him? How condemn the severity of an institution when it purported to be acting in the child's best interest? But these were issues that could not be raised on the Progressive agenda.

Any assessment of the contemporary juvenile court must answer the same questions and address the fundamental procedural and substantive tensions between the ideology of treatment and the reality of punishment. With the explicit emergence of retribution in juvenile courts coupled with a lack of public and political will to provide for the welfare of children, especially those who commit crimes, there is no reason to believe that the juvenile court system can be rehabilitated.

But issues of procedure and substance, while important, focus too narrowly on the legal domain. The ideology of therapeutic justice and its discretionary apparatus persist because the social control is directed at children. Current cultural and legal conceptions of children support institutional arrangements that deny the personhood of young people (Zimring 1982; Ainsworth 1991). A new purpose for the juvenile court, or its abolition, cannot be formulated successfully without critically reassessing the meaning of childhood and creating social institutions to assure the welfare of the next generation.

## NOTES

1. The California Supreme Court in *People v. Olivas*, 17 Cal. 3d 236, 551 P.2d 375, 131 Cal. Rptr. 55 (1976), limited the maximum sentence that could be im-

posed upon an adult misdemeanant committed to the California Youth Authority to the maximum length that could be imposed on an adult sentenced for the same offense. By contrast, in *People v. Eric J.*, 25 Cal. 3d 522, 601 P.2d 549, 159 Cal. Rptr. 317 (1979), the court refused to apply the *Olivas* adult sentence limitations when sentencing juveniles to the Youth Authority and upheld a longer term imposed on a juvenile than could be imposed on an adult sentenced for the same offense. In so doing, the court emphasized that unlike "punitive" sentences for adults, "[t]here has been no like revolution in society's attitude toward juvenile offenders. It is still true that '[j]uvenile commitment proceedings are designed for the purposes of rehabilitation and treatment, not punishment' " (601 P.2d at 554).

The *Eric J.* court's assessment that juvenile proceedings are for treatment rather than punishment is susceptible to dispute. Forst and Blomquist (1991), for example, conclude that California is one of the leading states "cracking down" on juveniles. Moreover, they report that "YA [youth authority] wards on average served *longer* terms of confinement than adults sentenced to prison for the same offense. In a comparison with inmates of the California Department of Corrections (CDC) for fourteen categories of serious felony offenses, YA Department officials found that YA wards served 28.5 months of confinement overall while CDC prisoners served only 23.6 months. Specifically, in eleven out of the fourteen offenses, YA wards served as much or more time as their adult inmate counterparts" (Forst and Blomquist 1991:355).

2. The right to treatment follows from the state's invocation of its parens patriae power to intervene for the benefit of the individual. In a variety of settings other than juvenile corrections, such as institutions for the mentally ill and retarded, states confine individuals without affording them the procedural safeguards associated with criminal incarceration for punishment. In all of these settings, it is the promise of benefit that justifies the less stringent procedural safeguards. Failure to deliver the promised treatment is a denial of due process. *Donaldson v. O'Connor*, 493 F.2d 507 (5th Cir. 1974), *vacated on other grounds*, 422 U.S. 563 (1975); *Rouse v. Cameron*, 373 F.2d 451 (D.C. Cir. 1966); *Wyatt v. Stickney*, 325 F. Supp. 781 (M.D. Ala. 1971), *aff'd in part, rev'd in part sub nom. Wyatt v. Aderholt*, 503 F.2d 1305 (5th Cir. 1974).

The constitutional rationale of the civil commitment cases has been invoked to secure treatment for juveniles incarcerated in state training schools. *Pena v. New York State Div. for Youth*, 419 F. Supp. 203 (S.D.N.Y. 1976); *Robinson v. Leahy*, 401 F. Supp. 1027 (N.D. Ill. 1975); *Morales v. Turman*, 383 F. Supp. 53 (E.D. Tex. 1974), *rev'd on other grounds*, 535 F.2d 864 (5th Cir. 1976); *Nelson v. Heyne*, 355 F. Supp. 451 (N.D. Ind. 1972), *aff'd*, 491 F.2d 352 (7th Cir. 1974); *Martarella v. Kelley*, 349 F. Supp. 575 (S.D.N.Y. 1972); *Inmates of Boys' Training School v. Affleck*, 346 F. Supp. 1354 (D.R.I. 1972); *Baker v. Hamilton*, 345 F. Supp. 345 (W.D. Ky. 1972); *Lollis v. New York State Dep't of Social Serv.*, 322 F. Supp. 473 (S.D.N.Y. 1970).

The right to treatment has been relied upon in juvenile institutions in cases in which rehabilitative services were not forthcoming and custodial warehousing or barbaric practices were shown. *In re Elmore*, 382 F.2d 125 (D.C. Cir. 1967); *Creek v. Stone*, 379 F.2d 106 (D.C. Cir. 1967). However, the First Circuit rejected any "right to treatment," holding that "there is no legally cognizable quo to trigger a compensatory quid. . . . [A]lthough rehabilitative training is no doubt desirable and sound as a matter of policy and, perhaps, of state law, plaintiffs have no constitutional right to that rehabilitative training" (*Santana v. Collazo*, 714 F.2d 1172, 1177 [1st Cir. 1983]).

# BIBLIOGRAPHY

Aday, David P., Jr. 1986. "Court Structure, Defense Attorney Use, and Juvenile Court Decisions." *Sociological Quarterly* 27:107–19.

Ainsworth, Janet E. 1991. "Re-Imagining Childhood and Reconstructing the Legal Order: The Case for Abolishing the Juvenile Court." *North Carolina Law Review* 69:1083–1133.

Allen, Francis A. 1964. "Legal Values and the Rehabilitative Ideal." In *The Borderland of the Criminal Law: Essays in Law and Criminology.* Chicago: University of Chicago Press.

———. 1975. "The Judicial Quest for Penal Justice: The Warren Court and the Criminal Cases." *University of Illinois Law Forum* 1975:518–42.

———. 1981. *The Decline of the Rehabilitative Ideal: Penal Policy and Social Purpose.* New Haven, Conn.: Yale University Press.

American Bar Association. Institute for Judicial Administration. 1980a. *Juvenile Justice Standards Relating to Juvenile Delinquency and Sanctions.* Cambridge, Mass.: Ballinger.

———. 1980b. *Juvenile Justice Standards Relating to Pretrial Court Proceedings.* Cambridge, Mass.: Ballinger.

———. 1980c. *Juvenile Justice Standards Relating to Interim Status.* Cambridge, Mass.: Ballinger.

———. 1980d. *Juvenile Justice Standards Relating to Dispositions.* Cambridge, Mass.: Ballinger.

American Friends Service Committee. 1971. *Struggle for Justice*. New York: Hill & Wang.

Anderson, Etta A. 1976. "The 'Chivalrous' Treatment of the Female Offender in the Arms of the Criminal Justice Systems: A Review of the Literature." *Social Problems* 23:350–57.

Angell, Robert Cooley. 1974. "The Moral Integration of American Cities: II." *American Journal of Sociology* 80:607–29.

Aries, Philippe. 1962. *Centuries of Childhood: A Social History of Family Life*. New York: Vintage Books.

Arizona Department of Corrections, 1986. *Length of Confinement Guidelines for Juveniles*. Phoenix, Az.

Armstrong, Gail. 1977. "Females under the Law—'Protected' but Unequal." *Crime and Delinquency* 23:109–20.

Arnold, William R. 1971. "Race and Ethnicity Relative to Other Factors in Juvenile Court Dispositions." *American Journal of Sociology* 77:211–27.

Austin, Thomas L. 1981. "The Influence of Court Location on Type of Criminal Sentence: The Rural-Urban Factor." *Journal of Criminal Justice* 9:305–16.

———. 1985. "Does Where You Live Determine What You Get? A Case Study of Misdemeanant Sentencing." *Journal of Criminal Law and Criminology* 76:490–511.

Bailey, William C. 1981. "Preadjudicatory Detention in a Large Metropolitan Juvenile Court." *Law and Human Behavior* 5:19–43.

———. 1984. "Poverty, Inequality, and City Homicide Rates." *Criminology* 22:531–50.

Bartollas, Clemens, Stuart J. Miller, and Simon Dinitz. 1976. *Juvenile Victimization*. New York: Wiley.

Barton, William H. 1976. "Discretionary Decision-Making in Juvenile Justice." *Crime and Delinquency* 22:470–80.

Bell, Duran, Jr., and Kevin Lang. 1985. "The Intake Dispositions of Juvenile Offenders." *Journal of Research in Crime and Delinquency* 22:309–28.

Bishop, Donna M., and Charles S. Frazier. 1988. "The Influence of Race in Juvenile Justice Processing." *Journal of Research in Crime and Delinquency* 25:242–63.

Bittner, Egon. 1976. "Policing Juveniles: The Social Context of Common Practice." In *Pursuing Justice for the Child*, edited by Margaret K. Rosenheim. Chicago: University of Chicago Press.

Black, Donald J., and Albert J. Reiss, Jr. 1970. "Police Control of Juveniles." *American Sociological Review* 35:63–77.

Blau, Judith R., and Peter M. Blau. 1982. "The Cost of Inequality: Metropolitan Structure and Violent Crime." *American Sociological Review* 47:114–29.

Bledstein, Burton J. 1976. *The Culture of Professionalism: The Middle Class and the Development of Higher Education in America*. New York: W. W. Norton.

Blumberg, Abraham S. 1967. "The Practice of Law as a Confidence Game: Organizational Cooptation of a Profession." *Law and Society Review* 1:15–39.

Bookin-Weiner, Hedy. 1984. "Assuming Responsibility: Legalizing Preadjudicatory Juvenile Detention." *Crime and Delinquency* 30:39–67.

Bortner, M. A. 1982. *Inside a Juvenile Court: The Tarnished Ideal of Individualized Justice*. New York: New York University Press.

Bortner, M. A., and W. L. Reed. 1985. "The Preeminence of Process: An Example of Refocused Justice Research." *Social Science Quarterly* 66:413–25.

Bringhurst, Bruce. 1979. *Antitrust and the Oil Monopoly*. Westport, Conn.: Greenwood Press.

Burch, Charles H., and Kathianne Knaup. 1970. "The Impact of Jury Trials upon the Administration of Juvenile Justice." *Clearinghouse Review* 4:345–353.

Byrne, James M., and Robert J. Sampson, eds. 1985. *The Social Ecology of Crime*. New York: Springer-Verlag.

Carrington, Peter J., and Sharon Moyer. 1988a. "Legal Representation and Workload in Canadian Juvenile Courts." Ottawa: Department of Justice, Canada.

———. 1988b. "Legal Representation and Dispositions in Canadian Juvenile Courts." Ottawa: Department of Justice, Canada.

Carter, Timothy J. 1979. "Juvenile Court Dispositions: A Comparison of Status and Nonstatus Offenders." *Criminology* 17:341–59.

Carter, Timothy J., and Donald Clelland. 1979. "A Neo-Marxian Critique, Formulation and Test of Juvenile Dispositions as a Function of Social Class." *Social Problems* 27:96–108.

Chein, David B. 1976. *Decision Making in Juvenile Corrections Institutions: Research Summary and Recommendations*. State of Minnesota Department of Corrections.

Chesney-Lind, Meda. 1973. "Judicial Enforcement of the Female Sex

Role: The Family Court and the Female Delinquent." *Issues in Criminology* 8, no. 2:51–69.

———. 1977. "Judicial Paternalism and the Female Status Offenders: Training Women to Know Their Place." *Crime and Delinquency* 23:121–30.

———. 1988a. "Girls and Status Offenses: Is Juvenile Justice Still Sexist?" *Criminal Justice Abstracts* 20:144–65.

———. 1988b. "Girls in Jail." *Crime and Delinquency* 34:150–168.

Chused, Richard H. 1973. "The Juvenile Court Process: A Study of Three New Jersey Counties." *Rutgers Law Review* 26:488–615.

Cicourel, Aaron V. 1968. *The Social Organization of Juvenile Justice.* New York: Wiley.

Clarke, Stevens H., and Gary G. Koch. 1980. "Juvenile Court: Therapy or Crime Control, and Do Lawyers Make a Difference?" *Law and Society Review* 14:263–308.

Clinard, Marshall Barron, and Daniel J. Abbott. 1973. *Crime in Developing Countries: A Comparative Perspective.* New York: Wiley.

Coates, Robert B., Martin Forst, and Bruce Fisher. 1985. *Institutional Commitment and Release Decision-making for Juvenile Delinquents: An Assessment of Determinate and Indeterminate Approaches—A Cross-State Analysis.* San Francisco: URSA Institute.

Coates, Robert B., Alden D. Miller, and Lloyd E. Ohlin. 1978. *Diversity in a Youth Correctional System.* Cambridge, Mass.: Ballinger.

Coffee, John C., Jr. 1978. "The Repressed Issues in Sentencing: Accountability, Predictability, and Equality in the Era of the Sentencing Commission." *Georgetown Law Journal* 66:975–1107.

Cogan, Neil H. 1970. "Juvenile Law, Before and After the Entrance of 'Parens Patriae.' " *South Carolina Law Review* 22:147–81.

Cohen, Fred. 1978. "Juvenile Offenders: Proportionality vs. Treatment." *Children's Rights Reporter* 8:1–16.

Cohen, Lawrence E., and James R. Kluegel. 1978. "Determinants of Juvenile Court Dispositions: Ascriptive and Achieved Factors in Two Metropolitan Courts." *American Sociological Review* 27:162–76.

———. 1979. "The Detention Decision: A Study of the Impact of Social Characteristics and Legal Factors in Two Metropolitan Juvenile Courts." *Social Forces* 58:146–61.

Comment. 1983. "The Supreme Court and Pretrial Detention of Juveniles: A Principled Solution of a Due Process Dilemma." *University of Pennsylvania Law Review* 132:95–119.

Cottle, Thomas. 1976. *Perceiving Time: A Psychological Investigation with Men and Women*. New York: Wiley-Interscience Publications.

Crank, John P. 1990. "The Influence of Environmental and Organizational Factors on Police Styles in Urban and Rural Environments." *Journal of Research in Crime and Delinquency* 27:166–89.

Cremin, Lawrence. 1961. *The Transformation of the School: Progressivism in American Education, 1876–1957*. New York: Vintage Books.

Crutchfield, Robert D., Michael R. Geerken, and Walter R. Gove. 1982. "Crime Rate and Social Integration: The Impact of Metropolitan Mobility." *Criminology* 20:467–78.

Curtis, George B. 1976. "The Checkered Career of Parens Patriae: The State as Parent or Tyrant?" *De Paul Law Review* 25:895–915.

Dannefer, Dale, and Russell Schutt. 1982. "Race and Juvenile Justice Processing in Court and Police Agencies." *American Journal of Sociology* 87:1113–32.

Datesman, Susan K., and Frank R. Scarpitti. 1980. "Unequal Protection in the Juvenile Court." In *Women, Crime and Justice*, edited by Susan K. Datesman and Frank R. Scarpitti. New York: Oxford University Press.

Dawson, Robert O. 1988. "The Third Justice System: The New Juvenile Criminal System of Determinate Sentencing for the Youthful Violent Offender in Texas." *St. Mary's Law Journal* 19:943–1016.

———. 1990a. "The Future of Juvenile Justice: Is It Time to Abolish the System?" *Journal of Criminal Law and Criminology* 81:136–55.

———. 1990b. "The Violent Juvenile Offender: An Empirical Study of Juvenile Determinate Sentencing Proceedings as an Alternative to Criminal Prosecution." *Texas Tech Law Review* 21:1897–1939.

Degler, Carl. 1980. *At Odds: Women and the Family in America from the Revolution to the Present*. New York: Oxford University Press.

DeMause, Lloyd. 1974. "The Evolution of Childhood." In *The History of Childhood*, edited by Lloyd DeMause. New York: Psychohistory Press.

Demos, John, and Sarane Spence Boocock. 1978. *Turning Points: Historical and Sociological Essays on the Family*. Chicago: University of Chicago Press.

Duffee, David, and Larry Siegel. 1971. "The Organization Man: Legal Counsel in the Juvenile Court." *Criminal Law Bulletin* 7:544–53.

Durkheim, Emile. 1964. *The Division of Labor in Society*. New York: Free Press.

Edelman, Marian Wright. 1987. *Families in Peril: An Agenda for Social Change*. Cambridge, Mass.: Harvard University Press.

Eisenstein, James, and Herbert Jacob. 1977. *Felony Justice: An Organizational Analysis of Criminal Courts*. Boston: Little, Brown.

Emerson, Robert M. 1969. *Judging Delinquents: Context and Process in Juvenile Court*. Chicago: Aldine.

————. 1974. "Role Determinants in Juvenile Court." In *Handbook of Criminology*, edited by Daniel Glaser. Chicago: Rand McNally.

Empey, LaMar T. 1979a. "The Social Construction of Childhood and Juvenile Justice." In *The Future of Childhood and Juvenile Justice*, edited by LaMar T. Empey. Charlottesville, Va.: University Press of Virginia.

————. 1979b. "The Progressive Legacy and the Concept of Childhood." In *Juvenile Justice: The Progressive Legacy and Contemporary Reforms*, edited by LaMar T. Empey. Charlottesville, Va.: University Press of Virginia.

Fagan, Jeffrey, and Elizabeth Piper Deschenes. 1990. "Determinants of Judicial Waiver Decisions for Violent Juvenile Offenders." *Journal of Criminal Law and Criminology* 81:314–47.

Fagan, Jeffrey, Martin Forst, and Scott Vivona. 1987. "Racial Determinants of the Judicial Transfer Decision: Prosecuting Violent Youth in Criminal Court." *Crime and Delinquency* 33:259–86.

Fagan, Jeffrey, Ellen Slaughter, and Eliot Hartstone. 1987. "Blind Justice? The Impact of Race on the Juvenile Justice Process." *Crime and Delinquency* 33:224–58.

Federle, Katherine H. 1990. "The Abolition of the Juvenile Court: A Proposal for the Preservation of Children's Legal Rights." *Journal of Contemporary Law* 16:23–51.

Feld, Barry C. 1977. *Neutralizing Inmate Violence: Juvenile Offenders in Institutions*. Cambridge, Mass.: Ballinger.

————. 1978. "Reference of Juvenile Offenders for Adult Prosecution: The Legislative Alternative to Asking Unanswerable Questions." *Minnesota Law Review* 62:515–618.

————. 1981a. "Juvenile Court Legislative Reform and the Serious Young Offender: Dismantling the 'Rehabilitative Ideal.' " *Minnesota Law Review* 69:141–242.

————. 1981b. "A Comparative Analysis of Organizational Structure and Inmate Subcultures in Institutions for Juvenile Offenders." *Crime and Delinquency* 27:336–63.

————. 1984. "Criminalizing Juvenile Justice: Rules of Procedure for Juvenile Court." *Minnesota Law Review* 69:141–276.

————. 1987. "Juvenile Court Meets Principle of Offense: Legislative Changes in Juvenile Waiver Statutes." *Journal of Criminal Law and Criminology* 78:471–533.

————. 1988a. "*In re Gault* Revisited: A Cross-State Comparison of the Right to Counsel in Juvenile Court." *Crime and Delinquency* 34:393–424.

————. 1988b. "Juvenile Court Meets Principle of Offense: Punishment, Treatment, and the Difference It Makes." *Boston University Law Review* 68:821–915.

————. 1989. "The Right to Counsel in Juvenile Court: An Empirical Study of When Lawyers Appear and the Difference They Make." *Journal of Criminal Law and Criminology* 79:1185–1346.

————. 1990. "Bad Law Makes Hard Cases: Reflections on Teen-Aged Axe-Murders, Judicial Activism, and Legislative Default." *Journal of Law and Inequality* 8:1–101.

————. 1991. "Justice by Geography: Urban, Suburban, and Rural Variations in Juvenile Justice Administration." *Journal of Criminal Law and Criminology* 82:156–210.

Ferdinand, Theodore N. 1989. "Juvenile Delinquency or Juvenile Justice: Which Came First?" *Criminology* 27:79–106.

————. 1991. "History Overtakes the Juvenile Justice System." *Crime and Delinquency* 37:204–24.

Ferster, Elyce Zenoff, and Thomas F. Courtless. 1972. "Pre-dispositional Data, Role of Counsel and Decisions in a Juvenile Court." *Law and Society Review* 7:195–222.

Ferster, Elyce Zenoff, Thomas F. Courtless, and Edith Nash Snethen. 1971. "The Juvenile Justice System: In Search of the Role of Counsel." *Fordham Law Review* 39:375–412.

Fine, Kerry. 1983. *Out of Home Placement of Children in Minnesota: A Research Report*. St. Paul, Minn.: Minnesota House of Representatives.

Finestone, Harold. 1976. *Victims of Change: Juvenile Delinquents in American Society*. Westport, Conn.: Greenwood Press.

Fisher, Bruce, Mark Fraser, and Martin Forst. 1985. *Institutional Commitment and Release Decision-Making for Juvenile Delinquents: An Assessment of Determinate and Indeterminate Approaches, Washington State — A Case Study*. San Francisco: URSA Institute.

Flicker, Barbara. 1983. *Providing Counsel for Accused Juveniles.* American Bar Association-Institute of Judicial Administration.

Forst, Martin, and Martha-Elin Blomquist. 1991. "Cracking Down on Juveniles: The Changing Ideology of Youth Corrections." *Notre Dame Journal of Law, Ethics, and Public Policy* 5:323–75.

Forst, Martin, Jeffrey Fagan, and T. Scott Vivona. 1989. "Youth in Prisons and Training Schools: Perceptions and Consequences of the Treatment-Custody Dichotomy." *Juvenile and Family Court Journal* 40:1–14.

Forst, Martin, Elizabeth Friedman, and Robert Coates. 1985. *Institutional Commitment and Release Decison-Making for Juvenile Delinquents: An Assessment of Determinate and Indeterminate Approaches. Georgia—A Case Study.* San Francisco: URSA Institute.

Fox, Sanford J. 1970a. "Juvenile Justice Reform: An Historical Perspective." *Stanford Law Review* 22:1187–1239.

———. 1970b. "Responsibility in the Juvenile Court." *William and Mary Law Review* 11:659–84.

Frazier, Charles, and Donna Bishop. 1985. "The Pretrial Detention of Juveniles and Its Impact on Case Dispositions." *Journal of Criminal Law and Criminology* 76:1132–52.

Frazier, Charles, and J. K. Cochran. 1986. "Detention of Juveniles: Its Effects on Subsequent Juvenile Court Processing Decisions." *Youth and Society* 17:286–305.

Friedman, William J. 1982. *The Developmental Psychology of Time.* New York: Academic Press.

Gardner, Martin. 1982. "Punishment and Juvenile Justice: A Conceptual Framework for Assessing Constitutional Rights of Youthful Offenders." *Vanderbilt Law Review* 35:791–847.

———. 1987. "Punitive Juvenile Justice: Some Observations on a Recent Trend." *International Journal of Law and Psychiatry* 10:129–51.

———. 1989. "The Right of Juvenile Offenders to Be Punished: Some Implications of Treating Kids as Persons." *Nebraska Law Review* 68:182–215.

Garlock, Peter D. 1979. " 'Wayward' Children and the Law, 1820–1900: The Genesis of the Status Offense Jurisdiction of the Juvenile Court." *Georgia Law Review* 13:341–447.

Garrett, Carol J. 1985. "Effects of Residential Treatment on Adjudicated Delinquents: A Meta-Analysis." *Journal of Research in Crime and Delinquency* 22:287–308.

Gendreau, Paul, and Bob Ross. 1979. "Effective Correctional Treatment: Bibliotherapy for Cynics." *Crime and Delinquency* 25:463–89.

———. 1987. "Revivification of Rehabilitation: Evidence from the 1980s." *Justice Quarterly* 4:349–407.

Georgia Department of Human Resources—Division of Youth Services. 1985. *Policy and Procedure Manual*. Atlanta, Ga.

Gillis, John R. 1974. *Youth and History: Tradition and Change in European Age Relations 1770–Present*. New York: Academic Press.

Goldfarb, Ronald L. 1975. *Jails: The Ultimate Ghetto*. Garden City, N.Y.: Anchor Press.

Greenberg, David, ed. 1977. *Corrections and Punishment*. Beverly Hills, Calif.: Sage.

Greenwood, Peter, A. Lipson, A. Abrahamse, and Frank Zimring. 1983. *Youth Crime and Juvenile Justice in California: A Report to the Legislature* (R-3016-CSA). Santa Monica, Calif.: RAND.

Greenwood, Peter, and Franklin Zimring. 1985. *One More Chance: The Pursuit of Promising Intervention Strategies for Chronic Juvenile Offenders* (R-3214-OJJDP). Santa Monica, Calif.: RAND.

Grisso, Thomas. 1980. "Juveniles' Capacities to Waive Miranda Rights: An Empirical Analysis." *California Law Review* 68:1134–66.

———. 1981. *Juveniles' Waiver of Rights*. New York: Plenum Press.

Guggenheim, Martin. 1977. "Paternalism, Prevention and Punishment: Pretrial Detention of Juveniles." *New York University Law Review* 52:1064–92.

———. 1978. "A Call to Abolish the Juvenile Justice System." *Children's Rights Reporter* 2:7–19.

———. 1984. "The Right to Be Represented but Not Heard: Reflections on Legal Representation for Children." *New York University Law Review* 59:76–134.

Hagan, John. 1974. "Extra-legal Attributes and Criminal Sentencing: An Assessment of the Sociological Viewpoint." *Law and Society Review* 8:357–83.

Hamparian, Donna, Linda Estep, Susan Muntean, Ramon Priestino, Robert Swisher, Paul Wallace, and Joseph White. 1982. *Youth in Adult Courts: Between Two Worlds*. Washington, D.C.: OJJDP.

Handler, Joel F. 1965. "The Juvenile Court and the Adversary System: Problems of Function and Form." *Wisconsin Law Review* 1965:7–51.

Harries, Keith D. 1976. "Cities and Crime: A Geographic Model." *Criminology* 14:369–86.

Hart, H. L. A. 1968. *Punishment and Responsibility*. New York: Oxford University Press.

Hasenfeld, Yeheskel, and Paul P. Cheung. 1985. "The Juvenile Court as a People-Processing Organization: A Political Economy Perspective." *American Journal of Sociology* 90:801–24.

Hawes, Joseph. 1971. *Children in Urban Society: Juvenile Delinquency in Nineteenth-Century America*. New York: Oxford University Press.

Hawes, Joseph, and N. Hiner, eds. 1985. *American Childhood: A Research Guide and Historical Handbook*. Westport, Conn.: Greenwood Press.

Hayeslip, David W., Jr. 1979. "The Impact of Defense Attorney Presence on Juvenile Court Dispositions." *Juvenile and Family Court Journal* 30, no. 1:9–15.

Hays, Samuel P. 1957. *The Response to Industrialism 1885–1914*. Chicago: University of Chicago Press.

Henretta, John C., Charles E. Frazier, and Donna M. Bishop. 1986. "The Effects of Prior Case Outcomes on Juvenile Justice Decision-Making," *Social Forces* 65:554–62.

Higham, John. 1988. *Strangers in the Land: Patterns of American Nativism 1860–1925*. 2d ed. New Brunswick, N.J.: Rutgers University Press.

Hindelang, Michael J. 1978. "Race and Involvement in Common Law Personal Crimes." *American Sociological Review* 43:93–109.

Hofstadter, Richard. 1955. *The Age of Reform: From Bryan to F.D.R.* New York: Knopf.

Horowitz, Allan, and Michael Wasserman. 1980. "Some Misleading Conceptions in Sentencing Research: An Example and Reformulation in the Juvenile Court." *Criminology* 18:411–24.

Horowitz, Donald L. 1977. *The Courts and Social Policy*. Washington, D.C.: Brookings Institution.

Huizinga, David, and Delbert S. Elliott. 1987. "Juvenile Offenders: Prevalence, Offender Incidence, and Arrest Rates by Race." *Crime and Delinquency* 33:206–23.

Ingraham, Barton L. 1974. "The Impact of Argersinger—One Year Later." *Law and Society Review* 8:615–44.

Izzo, Rhena L., and Robert R. Ross. 1990. "Meta-Analysis of Rehabilitation Programs for Juvenile Delinquents." *Criminal Justice and Behavior* 17:134–42.

Johnson, Doyle Paul. 1977. "Community Characteristics, Law Enforcement Practices, and Delinquency Referral Rates." *Journal of Juvenile Law* 2:29–50.

Juvenile Representation Study Committee. 1990. *Report of the Juvenile Representation Study Committee to the Minnesota Supreme Court.* St. Paul, Minn.

Kalven, Harry, and Hans Zeisel. 1966. *The American Jury.* Chicago: University of Chicago Press.

Kamisar, Yale, and Jesse H. Choper. 1963. "The Right to Counsel in Minnesota: Some Field Findings and Legal-Policy Observations." *Minnesota Law Review* 48:1–117.

Kaplan, John. 1986. "Defending Guilty People." *University of Bridgeport Law Review* 7:223–55.

Kay, Richard, and Daniel Segal. 1973. "The Role of the Attorney in Juvenile Court Proceedings: A Non-Polar Approach." *Georgetown Law Journal* 61:1401–24.

Kelly, Robert, and Sarah Ramsey. 1982. "Do Attorneys for Children in Protection Proceedings Make a Difference? — A Study of the Impact of Representation under Conditions of High Judicial Intervention." *Journal of Family Law* 21:405–55.

Kempf, Kimberly, Scott H. Decker, and Robert L. Bing. 1990. *An Analysis of Apparent Disparities in the Handling of Black Youth Within Missouri's Juvenile Justice Systems.* St. Louis: University of Missouri, Department of Administration of Justice.

Kerlinger, Fred N., and Elazar J. Pedhazur. 1973. *Multiple Regression in Behavioral Research.* New York: Henry Holt & Company, Inc.

Kett, Joseph F. 1977. *Rites of Passage: Adolescents in America 1790 to the Present.* New York: Basic Books.

Kfoury, Paul R. 1987. *Children before the Court: Reflections on Legal Issues Affecting Minors.* Boston: Butterworth.

Kleinbaum, David G., and Lawrence L. Kupper. 1978. *Applied Regression Analysis and Other Multivariable Methods.* North Scituate, Mass.: Duxbury Press.

Knitzer, Jane, and Merril Sobie. 1984. *Law Guardians in New York State: A Study of the Legal Representation of Children.* Albany, N.Y.: New York State Bar Association.

Kohlberg, Lawrence. 1964. "Development of Moral Character and Moral Ideology." In *Review of Child Development Research*, vol. 1, edited by Martin Hoffman and Lois Hoffman. New York: Russell Sage Foundation.

———. 1969. "Stage and Sequence: The Cognitive-Developmental Approach to Socialization." In *Handbook of Socialization Theory and Research*, edited by David Goslin. Chicago: Rand McNally.

Kolko, Gabriel. 1963. *The Triumph of Conservatism: A Reinterpretation of American History, 1900–1916*. Chicago: Quadrangle Books.

————. 1965. *Railroads and Regulation 1877–1916*. Princeton, N.J.: Princeton University Press.

Kowalski, Gregory S. and John P. Rickicki. 1982. "Determinants of Juvenile Postadjudication Dispositions." *Journal of Research in Crime and Delinquency* 19:66–83.

Kramer, John H., and Darrell J. Steffensmeier. 1978. "The Differential Detention/Jailing of Juveniles: A Comparison of Detention and Non-Detention Courts." *Pepperdine Law Review* 5:795–807.

Krisberg, Barry, and Ira Schwartz. 1983. "Rethinking Juvenile Justice." *Crime and Delinquency* 29:333–64.

Krisberg, Barry, Ira Schwartz, Gideon Fishman, Zvi Eisikovits, Edna Guttman, and Karen Joe. 1987. "The Incarceration of Minority Youth." *Crime and Delinquency* 33:173–205.

Krisberg, Barry, Ira Schwartz, Paul Litsky, and James Austin. 1986. "The Watershed of Juvenile Justice Reform." *Crime and Delinquency* 32:5–38.

Lab, Steven P., and John T. Whitehead. 1988. "An Analysis of Juvenile Correctional Treatment." *Crime and Delinquency* 34:60–83.

Lasch, Christopher. 1977. *Haven in a Heartless World: The Family Besieged*. New York: Basic Books.

Laub, John H. 1983. "Patterns of Offending in Urban and Rural Areas." *Journal of Criminal Justice* 11:129–42.

Laub, John H., and Michael J. Hindelang. 1981. *Juvenile Criminal Behavior in Urban, Suburban, and Rural Areas*. Washington, D.C.: Government Printing Office.

Lawrence, Richard A. 1983. "The Role of Legal Counsel in Juveniles' Understanding of Their Rights." *Juvenile and Family Court Journal* 34, no. 4:49–58.

Lefstein, Norman, Vaughan Stapleton, and Lee Teitelbaum. 1969. "In Search of Juvenile Justice: *Gault* and Its Implementation." *Law and Society Review* 3:491–562.

Lerman, Paul. 1977. "Discussion of Differential Selection of Juveniles for Detention." *Journal of Research in Crime and Delinquency* 14:166–72.

Lerner, Steven. 1986. *Bodily Harm*. Bolinas, Calif.: Common Knowledge Press.

Levin, Martin A. 1977. *Urban Politics and the Criminal Courts*. Chicago: University of Chicago Press.

Lewis-Beck, Michael S. 1980. *Applied Regression: An Introduction*. Beverly Hills, Calif.: Sage Publications.

Liska, Allen E., and Mark Tausig. 1979. "Theoretical Interpretations of Social Class and Racial Differentials in Legal Decision-Making for Juveniles." *Sociological Quarterly* 20:197–207.

Lubove, Roy. 1965. *The Professional Altruist: The Emergence of Social Work as a Career*. Cambridge, Mass.: Harvard University Press.

Mack, Julian W. 1909. "The Juvenile Court." *Harvard Law Review* 23:104–22.

Mahoney, Anne Rankin. 1987. *Juvenile Justice in Context*. Boston: Northeastern University Press.

Marks, Raymond F. 1975. "Detours on the Road to Maturity: A View of the Legal Conception of Growing Up and Letting Go." *Law and Contemporary Problems* 39, no. 3:78–92.

Marshall, Ineke H., and Charles W. Thomas. 1983. "Discretionary Decision-Making and the Juvenile Court." *Juvenile and Family Court Journal* 34, no. 3:47–59.

Martinson, Robert. 1974. "What Works? Questions and Answers About Prison Reform." *The Public Interest* 35:22–54.

Matza, David. 1964. *Delinquency and Drift*. New York: Wiley.

McCarthy, Belinda R. 1987. "Preventive Detention and Pretrial Custody in the Juvenile Court." *Journal of Criminal Justice* 15:185–200.

McCarthy, Belinda R., and Brent L. Smith. 1986. "The Conceptualization of Discrimination in the Juvenile Justice Process: The Impact of Administrative Factors and Screening Decisions on Juvenile Court Dispositions." *Criminology* 24:41–64.

McCarthy, Francis Barry. 1977a. "The Role of the Concept of Responsibility in Juvenile Delinquency Proceedings." *University of Michigan Journal of Law Reform* 10:181–219.

———. 1977b. "Should Juvenile Delinquency be Abolished?" *Crime and Delinquency* 23:196–203.

———. 1981. "Pre-Adjudicatory Rights in Juvenile Court: An Historical and Constitutional Analysis." *University of Pittsburgh Law Review* 42:457–514.

McMillian, Theodore, and Dorothy L. McMurtry. 1970. "The Role of the Defense Lawyer in the Juvenile Court—Advocate or Social Worker?" *St. Louis University Law Journal* 14:561–603.

Melton, Gary B. 1989. "Taking *Gault* Seriously: Toward a New Juvenile Court." *Nebraska Law Review* 68:146–81.

Mennel, Robert. 1973. *Thorns and Thistles: Juvenile Delinquents in the United States 1825–1940*. Hanover, N.H.: University Press of New England.

———. 1983. "Attitudes and Policies Toward Juvenile Delinquency in the United States: A Historiographical Review." In *Crime and Justice: A Review of Research*, vol. 4, edited by Michael Tonry and Norval Morris. Chicago: University of Chicago Press.

Messner, Steven F. 1982. "Poverty, Inequality, and the Urban Homicide Rate: Some Unexpected Findings." *Criminology* 20:103–14.

Meyers, Martha A. and Susette M. Talarico. 1986. "Urban Justice, Rural Injustice? Urbanization and Its Effect on Sentencing." *Criminology* 24:367–91.

———. 1987. *The Social Context of Criminal Sentencing*. New York: Springer-Verlag.

Minnesota Bureau of Criminal Apprehension. 1987. *1986 Minnesota Annual Report on Crime, Missing Children, and Bureau of Criminal Apprehension Activities*. St. Paul, Minn.: BCA.

Minnesota Department of Corrections. 1980. *Juvenile Release Guidelines*. St. Paul, Minn.

———. 1985. *Juvenile Release Guidelines*. St. Paul, Minn.

Minnesota Sentencing Guidelines Commission. 1980. *Report to the Legislature, January 1, 1980*. St. Paul, Minn.

Nardulli, Peter F. 1986. "Insider Justice: Defense Attorneys and the Handling of Felony Cases." *Journal of Criminal Law and Criminology* 77:379–417.

National Advisory Committee for Juvenile Justice and Delinquency Prevention. 1976. *Juvenile Justice and Delinquency Prevention*. Washington, D.C.: Government Printing Office.

National Commission on Children. 1991. *Beyond Rhetoric: A New American Agenda for Children and Families*. Washington, D.C.: Government Printing Office.

National Council of Juvenile and Family Court Judges. 1990. "Minority Youth in the Juvenile Justice System: A Judicial Response." *Juvenile and Family Court Journal* 41:1–60.

National Juvenile Court Data Archive. 1984. *Pennsylvania Juvenile Court*

*Judges' Commission Statistical Card Procedures.* Pittsburgh: National Juvenile Court Data Archive.

National Juvenile Court Data Archive. 1986a. *California Juvenile Court Case Records 1980–1985: User's Guide.* Pittsburgh: National Juvenile Court Data Archive.

————. 1986b. *Nebraska Juvenile Court Case Records 1975–1985: User's Guide.* Pittsburgh: National Juvenile Court Data Archive.

————. 1986c. *New York Juvenile Court Case Records 1977–1985: User's Guide.* Pittsburgh: National Juvenile Court Data Archive.

Nie, Norman, H., C. H. Hull, J. Jenkins, K. Steinbrenner, and D. H. Bent. 1975. *SPSS: Statistical Package for the Social Sciences.* 2d. ed. New York: McGraw-Hill.

Nimick, Ellen H., Howard N. Snyder, Dennis P. Sullivan, and Nancy J. Tierney. 1985a. *Juvenile Court Statistics 1982.* Washington, D.C.: Office of Juvenile Justice and Delinquency Prevention.

————. 1985b. *Juvenile Court Statistics 1983.* Washington, D.C.: Office of Juvenile Justice and Delinquency Prevention.

Note. 1966. "Juvenile Delinquents: The Police, State Courts, and Individualized Justice." *Harvard Law Review* 79:775–810.

Note. 1979. "The Right to a Jury under the Juvenile Justice Act of 1977." *Gonzaga Law Review* 14:420–458.

Note. 1983. "The Public Right of Access to Juvenile Delinquency Hearings." *Michigan Law Review* 81:1540–65.

Oaks, Dallin H. 1970. "Studying the Exclusionary Rule in Search and Seizure." *University of Chicago Law Review* 37:665–757.

Packer, Herbert L. 1968. *The Limits of the Criminal Sanction.* Stanford: Stanford University Press.

Palmer, Ted. 1991. "The Effectiveness of Intervention: Recent Trends and Current Issues." *Crime and Delinquency* 37:330–46.

Paternoster, Raymond. 1983. "Race of Victim and Location of Crime: The Decision to Seek the Death Penalty in South Carolina." *Journal of Criminal Law and Criminology* 74:754–85.

Paulsen, Monrad. 1966. "Kent v. United States: The Constitutional Context of Juvenile Cases." *Supreme Court Review* 1966: 167–201.

————. 1967. "The Constitutional Domestication of the Juvenile Court." *Supreme Court Review* 1967:233–66.

Pawlak, Edward J. 1977. "Differential Selection of Juveniles for Detention." *Journal of Research in Crime and Delinquency* 14:152–65.

Phillips, Charles D., and Simon Dinitz. 1982. "Labelling and Juvenile

Court Dispositions: Official Responses to a Cohort of Violent Juveniles." *Sociological Quarterly* 23:267–78.

Piaget, Jean. 1932. *The Moral Judgment of the Child.* London: K. Paul, Trench, Trubner & Co.

————. 1969. *The Child's Conception of Time,* translated by A. J. Pomerans. London: Routledge & Kegan Paul.

Pickett, Robert S. 1969. *House of Refuge: Origins of Juvenile Reform in New York State 1815–1857.* Syracuse, N.Y.: Syracuse University Press.

Pisciotta, Alexander W. 1982. "Saving the Children: The Promise and Practice of *Parens Patriae,* 1838–98." *Crime and Delinquency* 28:410–25.

Platt, Anthony. 1974. "The Triumph of Benevolence: The Origins of the Juvenile Justice System in the United States." In *Criminal Justice in America: A Critical Understanding,* edited by Richard Quinney. Boston: Little, Brown.

————. 1977. *The Child Savers.* 2d ed. Chicago: University of Chicago Press.

Platt, Anthony, and Ruth Friedman. 1968. "The Limits of Advocacy: Occupational Hazards in Juvenile Court." *University of Pennsylvania Law Review* 116:1156–84.

Platt, Anthony, Howard Schechter, and Phyllis Tiffany. 1968. "In Defense of Youth: A Case Study of the Public Defender in Juvenile Court." *Indiana Law Journal* 43:619–40.

Pope, Carl E. and William H. Feyerherm. 1990a. "Minority Status and Juvenile Justice Processing: An Assessment of the Research Literature (Part I)." *Criminal Justice Abstracts* 22:327–35.

————. 1990b. "Minority Status and Juvenile Justice Processing: An Assessment of the Research Literature (Part II)." *Criminal Justice Abstracts* 22:527–42.

President's Commission on Law Enforcement and Administration of Justice. 1967a. *The Challenge of Crime in a Free Society.* Washington, D.C.: Government Printing Office.

————. 1967b. *Task Force Report: Juvenile Delinquency and Youth Crime.* Washington, D.C.: Government Printing Office.

Private Sector Task Force on Juvenile Justice. 1987. *Final Report.* San Francisco: National Council on Crime and Delinquency.

Rendleman, Douglas R. 1971. "Parens Patriae: From Chancery to the Juvenile Court." *South Carolina Law Review* 23:205–59.

Roberts, Albert R. and Michael J. Camasso. 1991. "The Effects of Juvenile Offender Treatment Programs on Recidivism: A Meta-Analysis of 46 Studies." *Notre Dame Journal of Law, Ethics & Public Policy* 5:421–41.

Rosenberg, Irene M. 1980. "The Constitutional Rights of Children Charged with Crime: Proposal for a Return to the Not So Distant Past." *UCLA Law Review* 27:656–721.

Rosenberg, Irene M., and Yale L. Rosenberg. 1976. "The Legacy of the Stubborn and Rebellious Son." *Michigan Law Review* 74:1097–1165.

Rothman, David J. 1971. *The Discovery of the Asylum*. Boston: Little, Brown.

———. 1980. *Conscience and Convenience: The Asylum and Its Alternatives in Progressive America*. Boston: Little, Brown.

Rubin, H. Ted. 1977. "Juvenile Court's Search for Identity and Responsibility." *Crime and Delinquency* 23:1–13.

———. 1979. "Retain the Juvenile Court? Legislative Developments, Reform Directions and the Call for Abolition." *Crime and Delinquency* 25:281–98.

———. 1985. *Behind the Black Robes: Juvenile Court Judges and the Court*. Beverly Hills, Calif.: Sage Publications.

———. 1985. *Juvenile Justice: Policy, Practice, and Law*. 2d. ed. New York: Random House.

Rudstein, David S. 1982. "The Collateral Use of Uncounselled Misdemeanor Convictions After *Scott* and *Baldasar*." *University of Florida Law Review* 34:517–60.

Ryerson, Ellen. 1978. *The Best-laid Plans: America's Juvenile Court Experiment*. New York: Hill & Wang.

Sampson, Robert J. 1986a. "Effects of Socioeconomic Context on Official Reaction to Juvenile Delinquency." *American Sociological Review* 51:876–85.

———. 1986b. "Crime in Cities: The Effects of Formal and Informal Social Control." *Crime and Justice: An Annual Review* 8:271–311.

Sarri, Rosemary. 1974. *Under Lock and Key: Juveniles in Jails and Detention*. Ann Arbor: National Assessment of Juvenile Corrections, University of Michigan.

Sarri, Rosemary, and Yeheskel Hasenfeld. 1976. *Brought to Justice?: Juveniles, the Courts and the Law*. Ann Arbor: National Assessment of Juvenile Corrections, University of Michigan.

Scarpitti, Frank R., and Richard M. Stephenson. 1972. "Juvenile Court Dispositions: Factors in the Decision-Making Process." *Crime and Delinquency* 17:142–51.

Schlossman, Steven. 1977. *Love and the American Delinquent*. Chicago: University of Chicago Press.

Schlossman, Steven, and Stephanie Wallach. 1978. "The Crime of Precocious Sexuality: Female Juvenile Delinquency in the Progressive Era." *Harvard Educational Review* 48:65–94.

Schneider, Anne L., and Donna Schram. 1983. *A Justice Philosophy for the Juvenile Court*. Seattle: Urban Policy Research.

Schuerman, Leo, and Solomon Kobrin. 1986. "Community Careers and Crime." *Crime and Justice: An Annual Review* 9:67–100.

Schultz, J. Lawrence. 1973. "The Cycle of Juvenile Court History." *Crime and Delinquency* 19:457–76.

Schwartz, Ira M. 1989. *(In)Justice for Juveniles: Rethinking the Best Interests of the Child*. Lexington, Mass.: Lexington Books.

Schwartz, Ira M., Linda Harris, and Laurie Levi. 1988. "The Jailing of Juveniles in Minnesota: A Case Study." *Crime and Delinquency* 34:133–49.

Sechrest, Lee B. 1987. "Classification for Treatment." In *Prediction and Classification: Criminal Justice Decision-Making*, edited by Michael Tonry and Don M. Gottfredson. Vol. 9 of *Crime and Justice: A Review of Research*, edited by Michael Tonry and Norval Morris. Chicago: University of Chicago Press.

Sechrest, Lee B., Susan O. White, and Elizabeth D. Brown, eds. 1979. *The Rehabilitation of Criminal Offenders*. Washington, D.C.: National Academy of Sciences.

Shaw, Clifford R., and Henry D. McKay. 1942. *Juvenile Delinquency and Urban Areas: A Study of the Rates of Delinquency in Relation to Differential Characteristics of Local Communities in American Cities*. Rev. ed. Chicago: University of Chicago Press.

Shelley, Louise. 1981. *Crime and Modernization: The Impact of Industrialization and Urbanization on Crime*. Carbondale: Southern Illinois University Press.

Smith, Douglas A. 1984. "The Organizational Context of Legal Control." *Criminology* 22:19–38.

Snyder, Howard N., Terrence A. Finnegan, Ellen H. Nimick, Melissa H. Sickmund, Dennis P. Sullivan, Nancy J. Tierney. 1990. *Juvenile Court Statistics 1988*. Pittsburgh: National Center for Juvenile Justice.

Sonsteng, John O., and Robert Scott. 1985. *Minnesota Practice: Juvenile Law and Practice*. St. Paul, Minn.: West.

Stapleton, W. Vaughan, David P. Aday, Jr., and Jeanne A. Ito. 1982. "An

Empirical Typology of American Metropolitan Juvenile Courts." *American Journal of Sociology* 88:549–64.

Stapleton, W. Vaughan, and Lee Teitelbaum. 1972. *In Defense of Youth: A Study of the Role of Counsel in American Juvenile Courts.* New York: Russell Sage.

Sudnow, David. 1965. "Normal Crimes: Sociological Features of the Penal Code in a Public Defender's Office." *Social Problems* 12:255–76.

Sutton, John R. 1983. "Social Structure, Institutions, and the Legal Status of Children in the United States." *American Journal of Sociology* 88:915–47.

————. 1988. *Stubborn Children: Controlling Delinquency in the United States, 1640–1981.* Berkeley: University of California Press.

Tapp, June L. 1976. "Psychology and the Law: An Overture." *Annual Review of Psychology* 27:359–74.

Tapp, June L., and Lawrence Kohlberg. 1977. "Developing Senses of Law and Legal Justice." In *Law, Justice, and the Individual in Society,* edited by June L. Tapp and Felice Levine. New York: Holt, Rinehart and Winston.

Tepperman, Loren. 1973. "The Effects of Court Size on Organization and Procedure." *Canadian Review of Sociology and Anthropology* 10:346–368.

Thomas, Charles W., and Robin Cage. 1977. "The Effects of Social Characteristics on Juvenile Court Dispositions." *Sociological Quarterly* 18: 237–52.

Thomas, Charles W., and W. Anthony Fitch. 1975. "An Inquiry into the Association Between Respondents' Personal Characteristics and Juvenile Court Dispositions." *William and Mary Law Review* 17:61–83.

Thomas, Charles W., and Christopher M. Sieverdes. 1975. "Juvenile Court Intake: An Analysis of Discretionary Decision-Making." *Criminology* 12:413–33.

Thornberry, Terrence P. 1973. "Race, Socioeconomic Status and Sentencing in the Juvenile Justice System." *Journal of Criminal Law and Criminology* 64:90–98.

————. 1979. "Sentencing Disparities in the Juvenile Justice System." *Journal of Criminal Law and Criminology* 70:164–71.

Thornberry, Terrence P., and R. L. Christenson. 1984. "Juvenile Justice Decision- Making as Longitudinal Process." *Social Forces* 63:433–44.

Tiffin, Susan. 1982. *In Whose Best Interest? Child Welfare Reform in the Progressive Era.* Westport, Conn.: Greenwood Press.

Trattner, Walter I. 1965. *Crusade for the Children: A History of the Na-*

*tional Child Labor Committee and Child Labor Reform in New York State*. Chicago: Quadrangle Books.

————. 1984. *From Poor Law to Welfare State: A History of Social Welfare in America*. 3d ed. Westport, Conn.: Greenwood Press.

Twentieth Century Fund Task Force on Sentencing Policy Toward Young Offenders. 1978. *Confronting Youth Crime*. New York: Holmes & Meier.

United States Department of Commerce, Bureau of the Census. 1982. *1980 Census of Population: General Population Characteristics Minnesota*.

United States Sentencing Commission. 1991. *Guidelines Manual*. Washington, D.C.: Government Printing Office.

Von Hirsch, Andrew. 1976. *Doing Justice*. New York: Hill & Wang.

————. 1986. *Past vs. Future Crimes*. New Brunswick, N.J.: Rutgers University Press.

Wald, Patricia. 1976. "Pretrial Detention for Juveniles." In *Pursuing Justice for the Child*, edited by Margaret K. Rosenheim. Chicago: University of Chicago Press.

Walkover, Andrew. 1984. "The Infancy Defense in the New Juvenile Court." *UCLA Law Review* 31:503–62.

Walter, James D., and Susan A. Ostrander. 1982. "An Observational Study of a Juvenile Court." *Juvenile and Family Court Journal* 33:53–69.

Weber, Max. 1947. *The Theory of Social and Economic Organization*. New York: Oxford University Press.

————. 1954. *Max Weber on Law in Economy and Society*, edited by Max Rheinstein. Cambridge, Mass.: Harvard University Press.

Weissman, James C. 1983. "Toward an Integrated Theory of Delinquency Responsibility." *Denver Law Journal* 60:485–518.

Wells, Mary. 1979. "Women's Lives Transformed: Demographic and Family Patterns in America, 1600–1970." In *Women in America: A History*, edited by Ruth Berkin and Mary Beth Norton. Boston: Houghton Mifflin.

Wheeler, Gerald R. 1978. *Counter-Deterrence: A Report on Juvenile Sentencing and Effects of Prisonization*. Chicago: Nelson-Hall.

Wheeler, Gerald R., and Carol L. Wheeler. 1980. "Reflections on Legal Representation of the Economically Disadvantaged: Beyond Assembly Line Justice." *Crime and Delinquency* 26:319–32.

Whitehead, John T., and Steven P. Lab. 1989. "A Meta-Analysis of Juvenile Correctional Treatment." *Journal of Research in Crime and Delinquency* 26:276–95.

Wiebe, Robert H. 1962. *Businessmen and Reform: A Study of the Progressive Movement.* Cambridge, Mass.: Harvard University Press.

———. 1967. *The Search for Order 1877–1920.* New York: Hill & Wang.

Wilson, James Q. 1968. *Varieties of Police Behavior.* Cambridge, Mass.: Harvard University Press.

Wishy, Bernard W. 1968. *The Child and the Republic.* Philadelphia: University of Pennsylvania Press.

Wizner, Steven, and Mary F. Keller. 1977. "The Penal Model of Juvenile Justice: Is Juvenile Court Delinquency Jurisdiction Obsolete?" *New York University Law Review* 52:1120–35.

Wolfgang, Marvin. 1982. "Abolish the Juvenile Court System." *California Lawyer* 2, no. 10:12–13.

Wolfgang, Marvin, Robert Figlio, and Thorsten Sellin. 1972. *Delinquency in a Birth Cohort.* Chicago: University of Chicago Press.

Woods, John. 1980. "New York's Juvenile Offender Law: An Overview and Analysis." *Fordham Urban Law Journal* 9:1–50.

Zimring, Franklin. 1981. "Kids, Groups and Crime: Some Implications of a Well-Known Secret." *Journal of Criminal Law and Criminology* 72:867–902.

———. 1982. *The Changing Legal World of Adolescence.* New York: Free Press.

# INDEX

Rehabilitative ideal. *See also* Punishment vs. rehabilitation
disposition and, 88, 137
effectiveness of treatment and, 268–69
"new juvenile court" paradigm and, 282–83
Progressive era and, 11–12
Progressive juvenile court and, 12–14
return of juvenile court to, 279–81
social control and, 273–74
Rehnquist, Justice William H., 135
Representation, county level of
appointment of counsel and, 127–29
case-processing time and, 154, 155–56
classification of counties and, 77
detention by offense analysis and, 119
detention decision and, 131–34
disposition by prior referrals by representation analysis and, 112–13, 114–15
dispositions and, 91–93, 109, 138–41
impact of lawyers on charge reduction and, 147
multistate comparison methodology and, 46–47
rates of representation and, 82–83
sources of referral and, 79, 80
types of offenses and, 77–78
variations among juvenile courts and, 38–39, 156–57, 238–39
Representation, rates of, 4. *See also* Attorneys; Counsel, effectiveness of; Counsel, presence of; Counsel, right to; Counsel, waiver of; Nonrepresentation; Procedural formality; Representation, county level of
at adjudication vs. disposition, 82, 184, 255
appointment decision and, 100
classification of counties and, 77
detention by disposition analysis and, 122–24
detention decisions and, 119, 130–31

detention status and, 62–64, 66, 67, 120–21
disposition and, 58–60, 66, 67, 73, 91–93, 100, 101
disposition by offense analysis and, 103
disposition by prior referrals analysis and, 112–13, 114–15
gender and, 222–23
mandatory representation and, 244–54
prior referrals and, 68–71, 110–13
racial minorities and, 209–12
in state delinquency proceedings, 27–32
type of offense and, 54–56, 78, 79, 81–85
urban, suburban, and rural variation in, 181–89
variations among juvenile courts and, 37–38, 54–56, 58–60, 72–75
*Rizzo v. United States*, 33–34
Rothman, D. J., 292–93
*Rubin. See State v. Rubin*
Rubin, H. T., 283
Rule of law, and juvenile courts, 279–80
Rural areas
defined, 47, 162
gender bias in, 228–29, 240
legal variables in dispositions and, 227–28
mandatory representation and, 247–48

Sampson, R. J., 163
Sarri, R., 27, 28
*Schall v. Martin*, 135, 258
Schools, as source of referral, 176, 177
*Scott v. Illinois*, 26, 27, 102, 113, 242, 253
Screening cases
racial differences in, 205–6
urban, suburban, and rural variation in, 170–76
Secure confinement
defined, 46, 91
type of offense and, 57, 58, 64
Self-incrimination protection, 19–20, 247
Sellin, T., 204